Negotiating Paradise

The
University
of
North
Carolina
Press
*Chapel
Hill*

Negotiating Paradise

U.S. Tourism and Empire in
Twentieth-Century Latin America

DENNIS MERRILL

Designed by
Jacquline Johnson
Set in Minion
by Keystone
Typesetting, Inc.

Parts of this book have been reprinted with permission in revised form from "Negotiating Cold War Paradise: U.S. Tourism, Economic Planning, and Cultural Modernity in Twentieth Century Puerto Rico," *Diplomatic History* 25 (Spring 2001): 179–214.

The paper in this book meets the guidelines for permanence and durability of the Committee on Production Guidelines for Book Longevity of the Council on Library Resources.

The University of North Carolina Press has been a member of the Green Press Initiative since 2003.

Library of Congress Cataloging-in-Publication Data
Merrill, Dennis.
Negotiating paradise : U.S. tourism and empire in twentieth-century Latin America / Dennis Merrill. — 1st ed.
p. cm.
Includes bibliographical references and index.
ISBN 978-0-8078-3288-2 (cloth: alk. paper)
ISBN 978-0-8078-5904-9 (pbk.: alk. paper)
1. United States—Relations—Latin America. 2. Latin America—Relations—United States. 3. Americans—Latin America—History—20th century. 4. Tourists—Latin America—History—20th century. 5. Tourism—Latin America—History—20th century. 6. Tourism—Political aspects—Latin America—History—20th century.
7. Tourism—Social aspects—Latin America—History—20th century. 8. Latin America—Civilization—American influences. I. Title.
E1418.M453 2009
303.48'280730904—dc22 2009009380

cloth   13 12 11 10 09   5 4 3 2 1
paper   13 12 11 10 09   5 4 3 2 1

For my
daughters,
Nikki,
Iris,
& **Willa,**
and the
places
they'll go

Contents

Illustrations

Preface

I have enjoyed good-natured ribbing from friends. Brows furrowed, they ask, "The history of tourism? And where do you do your research?" I honestly can't say that I have endured hardship on my research trips, but it has been immensely challenging to mine multilingual archives, to probe the many points at which the history of international tourism intersects with the history of international relations, and to analyze and explain the findings.

What comes into focus when the history of twentieth-century U.S. relations with Latin America is viewed through the lens of leisure travel and tourism rather than the traditional prism of diplomacy? How has the history of holidaymaking paralleled and helped shape the history of U.S. military occupations and dollar diplomacy? What might interwar leisure travel to Mexico teach us about Franklin D. Roosevelt's Good Neighbor policy in the 1930s? What role did tourism play in the Cuban Revolution and its aftermath? What was the relationship between Yankee sun worshippers in Puerto Rico in the 1960s and John F. Kennedy's Alliance for Progress? How can the seemingly trivial pursuits of North American vacationers reflect on the history of dictatorships and dirty wars that consumed so much of Latin America during the 1970s and 1980s? These are just a few of the questions that drive this study.

After perhaps too many years of preparation, I have found the answers to be compelling enough to share with others. Readers familiar with current historiographical debates among foreign relations scholars will recognize how I have been influenced by the field's recent "cultural turn," with its emphasis on nonstate actors, transnational interest groups, identity formation, and popular constructions of race, class, and gender. On close examination, readers will also detect that I use cultural analysis to build on and complicate but not necessarily overturn conventional wisdom. In addition to Clifford Geertz, Edward Said, and Joan Robinson, the text reflects insights advanced by George F. Kennan, William Appleman Williams, and their many intellectual descendants. Alongside analysis of national identities, I discuss national interests.

I have long since concluded that the history of U.S. foreign relations cannot be told without an understanding of the nation's interior life. This examination of international travel has only reinforced that conviction. The social and cultural tensions associated with the "new era" of the 1920s, the Great Depression of the 1930s, the consumer culture of the postwar era, the African American struggle for civil rights and the women's movement, and the rise of evangelical religious thought have influenced how Americans—both travelers and diplomats—have viewed the world and the U.S. place in it. I seek not only to tell the history of mass tourism, an intriguing and significant topic in itself, but to use the narrative moment to address challenging issues in the history of U.S. foreign relations, to suggest ways to bridge the chasm that typically separates scholars of culture from those who study empire and international relations, and to stimulate debate in both fields.

I have conceived and written this book during an era when the discipline of history and the life of the planet have undergone major transformations. Since my years as an undergraduate, historical inquiry has been reshaped first by the rise of social history, or "history from the bottom up," and more recently by cultural history, feminist theory, subaltern studies, and postmodern paradigms. International affairs have similarly evolved from Cold War confrontation to détente to an ill-defined post–Cold War era, reconfigured by the rise of former colonial areas and the rush toward a not-yet-determined system of globalization. The world has shrunk temporally and linked peoples and societies as never before. Yet over the same period, nations have continued to wage wars, ethnic groups in various regions have committed unspeakable atrocities, famine remains a part of everyday life for millions, and the U.S. empire in Latin America still lives. My book has been influenced by all of these developments.

This history of international tourism illuminates the forces—cultural, economic, and political—that have helped create our globalized world and positioned the United States as its leader. It does so by examining international relations from the bottom up and at times from the outside in, frequently emphasizing the agency of the "other" within the U.S.-led empire. While the story cannot be told without reference to transnational elites, ambassadors, presidents, and members of Congress or to world wars, revolutions, and global markets, I hone in on ordinary tourists and the men and women who have played the role of host, arguing that these people have left their mark on the front lines of global change.

The book begins with an introduction that explains and analyzes the rise of modern mass tourism and conceptualizes the U.S. tourist presence abroad as a form of international soft power. In the Western Hemisphere, the consumer and cultural privileges enjoyed by visiting Yankees fused with U.S. financial and military power as a manifestation of empire. Tourist power, however, proved less cohesive, more imagined, and more susceptible to host society manipulation than the traditional tools of empire. Chapter 1 examines the hemisphere's first large-scale experiment in mass tourism, which took place in Mexico during the 1920s. The chapter follows the trails blazed by Prohibition-era Americans, many disaffected by the world's first modern global war and Wilsonian internationalism, who nonetheless sought to engage the outside world. Drunken cowboys, adventurers, would-be filibusters, poets, artists, social commentators, college students, and other more anonymous vacationers poured across the border. Some came as conquerors to impose their preconceived notions of Mexican identity on their hosts; others arrived in search of communion with the Mexican other. A corps of cooperative cross-border groups arose to build a tourist infrastructure, and visitors and hosts tested each other's power and helped bring the United States and postrevolutionary Mexico closer together politically as well as culturally.

Chapter 2 chronicles the growth of the Mexican tourist industry during the 1930s and probes its impact on the everyday life of the empire. The chapter examines how conflicting constructions of class, race, and gender produced culture clash between visiting consumers and hosts but also spurred negotiation. The struggle reached a turning point when populist president Lázaro Cárdenas (1934–40), best known for nationalizing Mexico's oil industry, intervened. The subsequent prohibition on casino gambling and allocation of state funds to Mexican-owned hotels and restaurants dramatically altered the tourist-host balance of power. That hardball tactics in both the oil and tourist industries did not disrupt the U.S.-Mexican diplomatic rapprochement reflected the shrinking significance of territorial borders in an age of mass transportation and intensifying cultural interaction.

Mexico's tourism industry continued to grow after the Second World War, but the foundational stones had been set in place by 1940. Chapter 3 moves forward chronologically from the interwar era to the Cold War, from the age of train travel to that of aviation, and shifts location from postrevolutionary Mexico to prerevolutionary Cuba. There, Fulgencio Batista's crony capitalism fed a tourist industry that catered primarily to the interests of U.S.-based corporations, North American mobsters, affluent Cold War consumers, and a repressive dictatorial regime. The U.S. government stood solidly behind the arrangement, gambling that despite the excesses, the island's capitalist development, including its robust travel industry, provided a hedge against communist expansion.

The Castro revolution that followed proved more uncompromising than Mexico's turn-of-the-century rebellion. Chapter 4 examines the process by which North America's Cold War paradise in Cuba slipped away, carrying the story through the final days of the Batista dictatorship, when partying U.S. tourists posed a surreal juxtaposition to guerrilla war. Fidel Castro's assumption of power did not immediately end the tourist trade. Castro's willingness to work with the North American travel industry to arrange a redistribution of power in tourist-host relations actually slowed the deterioration of U.S.-Cuban diplomatic ties. But over the next eighteen months, the negotiations succumbed to the weight of a half century of harsh U.S. hegemony and unexpectedly virulent Cuban nationalism.

Puerto Rico occupies a unique position in the history of inter-American tourism. Unlike Mexico and Cuba, Puerto Rico never underwent a full-fledged social revolution, and its political status as a U.S. commonwealth fell far short of nationhood. Yet in contrast to "independent" Cuba, Puerto Rico used tourism to gain at least a modicum of economic independence and display its Iberian, Taíno, and African heritages. Chapter 5 describes and analyzes Puerto Rico's strange odyssey from colony to commonwealth, its search for a suitable development strategy, and the origins of its planned postwar travel industry.

As the crowds thinned in Havana, Puerto Rico picked up the slack. Chapter 6 charts the commonwealth's rising stock as a reformist Cold War oasis. Starting in the late 1950s and continuing through the 1970s, Soviet-American tensions and the Cold War slowly eased, and global integration accelerated. At the same time, clashes between visitors and hosts in Puerto Rico's tourist zones intensified, although they never reached the breaking point. The Alliance for Progress trumpeted Puerto Rico's "modernization" as a model for U.S.-backed development in the region. But the commonwealth's unique blend of private and public enterprise, its political pluralism, and its methods of negotiating the shoals of identity in an increasingly interconnected world did not export well.

International tourism has grown exponentially since the end of the Cold War. North Americans still rank among the planet's most affluent and enthusiastic travelers, but they have been joined by growing numbers of citizens from other countries. In the early twenty-first century, U.S. citizens are as likely to play host to visitors from afar as they are to visit abroad. The global travel industry, moreover, has become increasingly dominated by multinational enterprises that may or may not reflect U.S. power. The book concludes with a brief survey of recent and contemporary trends in Latin American tourism, from Mexico's Cancún to Costa Rica's ecotourism to revolutionary Cuba's recent reembrace of tourists. I connect the dots between past and present and consider how the lessons learned from the Mexican, Cuban, and Puerto Rican stories inform and instruct.

Each and every chapter in this book has benefited from the assistance of fellow travelers at my university and in the larger scholarly community. First, I thank Matt Blankenship, Greta Kroeker Klassen, and Sarah Peterson, students at the University of Missouri–Kansas City who signed on as research assistants at various points in this project. I extend a special thank you to Dr. Joel Rhodes, my first assistant and my first doctoral student at UMKC, who has gone on to become an accomplished scholar in his own right. My conversations with campus Latin Americanists Viviana Grieco and Rebecca Lee have no doubt influenced this book for the better. I also thank the College of Arts and Sciences at UMKC and the University of Missouri Research Board for their financial support.

Numerous colleagues and friends have read portions of this book or related grant proposals or simply shared ideas and information. Frank Costigliola, Michael J. Hogan, Robert J. McMahon, Louis A. Pérez, Emily S. Rosenberg, and Francisco Scarano responded generously to requests for advice. Dina Berger shared her knowledge of Mexican travel posters and their artists. My longtime mentor and role model, Thomas G. Paterson, has supported and encouraged me for more than two decades and was especially helpful to this project's discussion of the tangled U.S.-Cuban relationship.

I am especially indebted to those who had the misfortune of closely reading earlier drafts of parts of this book or, more labor-intensive still, the entire manuscript at one phase or another. I am grateful for the collective wisdom of Laura Belmont, Chris Endy, Mark Gilderhus, and Glenn Penny, all of whom brought expertise to bear on this work. I owe much to these colleagues and friends, but I alone am responsible for any shortcomings that still plague the volume.

This work would never have taken shape without the professional assistance of many dedicated archivists and librarians. I will always keep a special place in my heart for those who led me by the hand to Spanish-language collections at the Archivo General in San Juan, Puerto Rico; the University of Puerto Rico's Centro de Investigaciones Históricas; the Luis Muñoz Marín Library in Trujillo Alto; and the Archivo General de la Nación in Mexico City. In the United States, the good people at Amherst College Archives and Special Collections, Columbia University Library Manuscripts Division, the Cuban Heritage Collection at the University of Miami, the Center for Puerto Rican Studies at Hunter College, the Conrad N. Hilton College Library and Archives at the University of Houston, and the Library of Congress Manuscript Division were all immensely helpful. The John F. Kennedy Presidential Library provided funding as well as access to important records. The De-Golyer Library at Southern Methodist University held a treasure trove of Mexican travel materials, and the Clements Center for Southwest Studies at SMU generously financed my research there. I also thank the individuals and institutions that assisted my search for the images that enliven the interior of this book.

This is the second time I have worked with the University of North Carolina Press and the first time I have had the pleasure of collaborating with Elaine Maisner. She and her editorial assistant, Tema Larter, have expertly guided my manuscript through the stages of review, acceptance, and production. It is an honor to have this monograph placed on the UNC Press list.

Finally, my family members have been my most devoted fellow travelers, sometimes accompanying me on research trips but more often cheering me on as I sat at the computer at home. My wife, Theresa Hannon, is my most generous supporter and trusted critic, subjecting my cultural deconstructions to the harsh realities of logic, her sharp wit, and her infectious laugh. Our daughters have brought me unimaginable joy, and I dedicate this book to them.

Introduction
Mass Tourism, Empire, and Soft Power

This book examines how tourists armed with suntan lotion, maps, golf shirts, straw hats, cameras, and swimsuits extended the U.S. presence in twentieth-century Latin America and helped internationalize U.S. culture.[1] The massive U.S. influence in Latin America is typically explained in terms of centralized power and systems of domination and dependence. According to traditional historiography, a small group of Washington policymakers, assisted or pressured by U.S. corporations and cooperative Latin American elites, have determined the key elements of inter-American relations. This study by no means dismisses the importance of political economy and the state, but it draws on postcolonial theory and poststructural concepts of "self" and "other" as well as on a growing literature on international cultural interaction to illuminate how tourists, hosts, and the transnational travel industry generated multistranded contacts across the Americas, actively shaped the social and cultural life of the empire, and influenced U.S. foreign relations.[2]

In contrast to many studies of empire, this one does not present tourism as a uniform system that Yankees imposed on Latin Americans, although in some circumstances tourism did mimic conquest. This volume instead explores tourism as an ongoing international negotiation and empire as a textured and fluid structure. Tourists, hosts, and the myriad of pressure groups that comprised the travel industry negotiated natural and built environments, the location of tourist attractions, the cultural meanings infused into those sites, the wages paid to labor, and the divvying up of profits. They struck deals on transportation routes, hotel ownership, and the legality and illegality of leisure activities. At the grassroots level, visitors and hosts negotiated etiquette, language, monetary tips, the boundaries of personal space, and meanings of race, class, gender, sexuality, and national and international identities.

Tourism is not a recent development. Ancient Romans sought rest, meditation, and pleasure along their empire's coastal reaches. Chaucer's medieval pilgrims journeyed to holy sites out of religious devotion, and early modern European elites had not come of age until they had completed the "Grand Tour" and gained exposure to the continent's physical wonders and high culture. Beginning in Europe's age of self-proclaimed enlightenment, the travel writings of botanists and ethnographers mapped the world's geographic contours, its social groupings, and its flora, fauna, and resources for purposes of political and commercial expansion.[3] But mass tourism—that of middle-class and working-class populations—did not arise until the late nineteenth and early twentieth centuries, largely a product of the Industrial Revolution and the globalization of markets and cultures.[4]

Rising incomes, increasingly available credit, expanded worker benefits, and modern systems of transportation and communication made possible a new mode of consumption based on the idea of leaving home and work in search of new experiences. Historian Kristin L. Hoganson has explained how a growing army of middle- and upper-class tourists embraced the "tourist mentality" in the decades following the U.S. Civil War, either by taking a physical sojourn abroad or through "imaginary travel" accomplished through attending public lectures on travel or reading the period's prolific travel literature.[5] International travel gained popularity with each decade, coming within the financial reach of increasing numbers of Americans. By the late 1920s, American travelers spent approximately $770 million outside the United States, an amount that ballooned to more than $3 billion annually by the early 1960s. The United Nations World Tourism Organization has estimated that by the end of the twentieth century, international travel had become a $3.4 trillion industry, second in size only to oil. With about 600 million departures and arrivals annually, the industry employed about 7 percent of the world's workforce, or some 230 million people. Analysts have estimated that in 2020, 1.6 billion of the world's 7.8 billion people will take a leisure trip abroad.[6]

International tourism can be analyzed through a variety of lenses. Tourism has generated a vast complex of business enterprises that produce and stage attractions, provide transportation and accommodations, peddle food and souvenirs, and of course, lure people to Eden through mass advertising, leading economists to ask whether tourism benefits local societies or primarily rewards international capital.[7] Modern travel has also piqued the interest of sociologists and anthropologists, who have theorized about why people travel and studied tourism's impact on host communities and cultures.[8] A growing number of historians have begun to contextualize tourism and explore the many ways it intersects with industrialization, nationalism, cultural identities, and consumerism.[9]

This study speaks to an interdisciplinary audience, including scholars of tourism, consumerism, and cultural studies. But it is positioned foremost as an analysis of U.S. empire, an inquiry into the inordinate North American influence on twentieth-century Latin America. I have chosen not to attempt a comprehensive history of U.S.-Latin American tourism relations. Such an undertaking would require a multivolume work, and important analytical points might easily get lost or muted in an expansive narrative. I have instead chosen three case studies, each a favorite U.S. vacation haunt at a key moment in international history: interwar Mexico, early Cold War Cuba, and Puerto Rico in transition from Cold War confrontation to Cold War détente. Collectively, they reveal how tourist relations have influenced and been influenced by demography and ethnicity, colonialism, decolonization, revolution, nation building, economic development, world wars, and the forty-year international conflict known as the Cold War, subjects that lie at the core of the history of U.S. foreign relations.

The story begins with 1920s Mexico, where a trickle of northern bohemians, men and women drawn for the most part from the U.S. middle and upper classes, discovered a postrevolutionary oasis for artistic experimentation, social reform, and rural tranquility. Prohibition and to some extent the U.S. women's movement sent hundreds of thousands of Yankees, mainly white males, to border-town watering holes and gambling dens to initiate the age of mass tourism. Disillusioned by war and antagonistic to modern social engineering, most of these visitors imagined Mexico as a remnant of North America's frontiers and sought refuge there from both the Eighteenth and Nineteenth Amendments. They often imagined the Mexican "other" as gendered female or perhaps as a childlike creature of color, awaiting manly Anglo-Saxon conquest, and favored local businesses that implemented Jim Crow–style racial segregation.[10]

The grassroots anti-imperialism that had fueled Mexico's recent revolution, along with postrevolutionary efforts to unite the country's diverse indigenous, mestizo, and European populations around a common national identity, generated clashes.[11] Presidential decree shut down the border-town casinos in the 1930s, and government subsidies flowed to Mexican hoteliers and restaurateurs in the nation's interior. State-sponsored archeological attractions constituted what Ricardo D. Salvatore has called "representational machines" that highlighted the grandeur of Mexico's precolonial societies.

The reorganization of the travel industry from border-town free-for-all to civilizational display complicated U.S. perceptions of its southern neighbor and softened harsh cultural stereotypes.[12]

The arrival of mass tourism in Cuba also coincided with Prohibition, but nowhere did tourist power go as unchecked as in 1950s Cuba. Dictator Fulgencio Batista structured the tourism industry to replicate the export-dependent sugar economy, and his regime leased out the hotel trade almost wholly to U.S. firms. The casino and illegal narcotics industries came under the domain of U.S. mobsters, including the notorious Meyer Lansky. Havana also played host to a huge commercial sex industry, staffed by an estimated 11,500 prostitutes, comparable to contemporary red-light districts at Thailand's Pattaya Beach, the Pat Bong district of Bangkok, or Manila's seediest slums.[13]

The international tensions and nuclear fears associated with the early Cold War, along with domestic unease over the assertiveness of racial minorities and women during the war years, provided the backdrop for Cuba's development as a postwar resort mecca. Ninety miles southeast of the Florida Keys, North Americans might enjoy momentary release from the burdens of international leadership and domestic social change. Batista imposed a facade of capitalist modernity over Havana by subsidizing the construction of highrise hotels, modern retail centers, and a highway system that facilitated suburban sprawl.[14] But Havana loomed first and foremost in the North American imagination as a tropical paradise where the moral and sexual codes associated with the postwar nuclear family—what Elaine Tyler May has called "domestic containment"—were relaxed.[15] The idea of Havana evoked fantasies of sensuous Latin and African Cuban women swaying to the rumba and inviting Yankee hedonism.[16] Modern tourism so misrepresented Cuban culture and diluted local identity that it helped destabilize the country's social order and contributed to the rise of Fidel Castro's communist regime.

As Cuba's travel industry collapsed, Puerto Rico rose to tourism stardom, drawing one million visitors annually by the late 1960s. Unlike interwar Mexico or Cold War Havana, Puerto Rico's main tourist attraction consisted of its beautiful oceanfront beaches. Often public, these sunny spaces became meeting grounds for differing standards of modesty, gender norms, language, and other cultural practices. In contrast to Cuba, the commonwealth government used its limited autonomy from the United States to regulate and contain the invasion. The government in San Juan dispensed tax breaks to U.S. and Puerto Rican investors, sprinkled in some government-owned hotels, regulated casinos, capped the industry's share of gross product at 5 to 10 percent, and promoted other industries to diversify the island's economy.

High-rise hotels soon dominated San Juan's oceanfront, but the island government also borrowed a page from the Mexican model, subsidizing the restoration of colonial Old San Juan and sponsoring archeological digs to recover the island's indigenous Taíno and African slave cultures.[17]

The international ramifications of tourism cannot be fully appreciated through an examination of government policies. Tourism entangled the lives of ordinary Americans across the hemisphere. Northerners escaped the responsibilities of the work routine and set off to gaze on the extraordinary.[18] For many southerners, tourism produced a new work routine as they became hotel workers, taxi drivers, tour guides, waiters, and the like. Mass tourism also engaged U.S., Latin American, and transnational hoteliers, labor unions, publishers and publicists, transportation companies, advertising agencies, and banks and credit companies, among many others. Tourism in fact linked all of these millions of Americans, north and south, invigorated the empire's human encounters, and subtly influenced the hemispheric balance of power.

Empire, Tourism, and the Power of Imagination

Exactly what is an empire, and how does tourism breathe life into it? Historian Charles S. Maier has provided a good working definition that connects empire with two features: first, the act of conquest, either by formal military or informal economic and cultural means, and second, the maintenance of loyalties within subordinate societies. Empires deny self-determination to their weaker entities and feature an inherent tyranny that empowers elites at the expense of the masses. The arrangement is often maintained through the categorization of races and ethnic groups. For European peoples, color-conscious racism has typically legitimized white rule over people of color who inhabited the southern half of the globe. Constructions of gender that equate masculinity and strength with the colonizing power and femininity and weakness with the colony have further underscored imperial arrangements.[19]

Historians have fretted about whether the United States is an empire or possesses an empire. In the case of Mexico and the Caribbean, at least, the angst is overblown. A quick review of the history of early inter-American relations suggests a snug definitional fit: U.S. imperialism in the region included the territorial annexation of northern Mexico in the 1840s, the acquisition of Puerto Rico as a colony and Cuba as a protectorate at the turn of the twentieth century, the severing of the Panama Canal Zone from Colombia, and Theodore Roosevelt's famous proclamation of U.S. "police power" in the Caribbean. A devotee of Anglo-Saxon racial superiority and the U.S.

civilizing mission, Roosevelt set an enduring precedent when he imposed financial supervision as well as military occupation of the Dominican Republic. The practice, eventually termed dollar diplomacy and replicated throughout the region, relied on "professional-managerial" functionaries to transfer the manly, scientific ethic of markets and budgetary discipline to weaker, feminine, and less civilized societies.[20]

The question is how the roots and maintenance of the U.S. hemispheric empire can best be characterized and explained. Until recently, scholars of inter-American relations have not delved deeply into the dynamic of cultural interaction, and only a handful have spotlighted tourism as an element of empire.[21] Drawing heavily on positivist discursive frameworks from political science, most depict empire building as a drive for political hegemony and ascribe the life force of empire to hierarchically arranged policymaking mechanisms. Those who adhere to the realist perspective ground their analysis in somewhat ahistorical, universal concepts of power, sovereignty, anarchy, and security. Realists generally ascribe U.S. hegemony in the Caribbean and northern Latin America in the twentieth century to the nation's strategic interests, especially the acquisition of the Panama Canal, the drive to secure adjacent shipping lanes, and a determination to guard the region against internal political instability and European meddling.[22]

Since the realist perspective characterizes hegemony primarily as a defensive posture, it minimizes economic self-interest as a catalyst for the expanding U.S. presence south of the border. During the Cold War, a generation of Keynesian economists, eager to dismiss Marxist theories that linked empire with capitalism, articulated what they called modernization theory. According to their argument, by exporting private and public capital, technology, and entrepreneurial skills, the United States assisted the southern republics in developing and "modernizing" their economies and governments. The theory carried an aura of scientific objectivity but in many ways built on the value-laden ideology of dollar diplomacy. It underpinned the Kennedy administration's Alliance for Progress foreign aid program, which sought to inoculate the region from Fidel Castro's revolutionary ideology. Rechristened "neoliberalism" in the 1980s and 1990s, the prescribed therapy for Latin America's struggling economies stressed privatization, market economies, and budgetary belt tightening imposed by International Monetary Fund conditioning.[23]

Less than halfway through the Cold War, when the realist-based doctrine of anticommunist containment, along with modernization theory, showed wear and tear—most noticeably in battle-scarred Southeast Asia—revisionist historians challenged orthodoxy. They primarily focused on how powerful business groups and their quest for markets and raw materials either determined or prodded U.S. foreign policy. Borrowing from Marxist and progressive Latin American intellectuals, these revisionists rejected modernization frameworks and argued that extensive linkages northward generated economic "dependency" and stunted sovereignty. Although the analysis corrected the misperception that capitalism and empire stood as antithetical forces in U.S. and hemispheric history, it still failed to account for the wide spectrum of individuals and groups enlisted in the imperial project and for the most part categorized Latin Americans as "peripheral" actors in a center-led world system.[24]

This study does not dismiss either the realist or revisionist perspectives. Because tourism centers on the physical movement of peoples across national boundaries and a vigorous exchange of goods and services, it cannot be understood without reference to political economy. But to be fully understood and to serve as a vehicle for a more expansive and probing analysis of empire and international relations, tourism also requires cultural analysis. Never easily defined, "culture" is generally understood as a constellation of symbols that carry societal meaning—textual, musical, cinemagraphic, architectural, collective memories, and common notions of class, race, and gender —that create what the anthropologist Clifford Geertz has famously called "webs of significance." Those signifiers connect individuals to the larger social group, help people make sense of their environment, and publicly order their behavior.[25]

Realist and revisionist scholars are by no means strangers to the study of how ideas influence international behavior. But they have tended to limit their examination to the self-conscious, logically constructed ideologies that policymakers publicly pronounce within the context of state-to-state relations. For realist George F. Kennan, a self-righteous U.S. "moralism," complemented by a belief in the rule of law, led to ill-fated efforts to export U.S.-style democracy and left the nation ill equipped for the harsh realities of power politics.[26] Revisionist William Appleman Williams advanced a more expansive framework when he wrote of empire as a way of life, a weltanschauung or worldview that underpinned the notion that "the City on the Hill has the right to control the world."[27]

By employing cultural theory, contemporary historians have probed how a weltanschauung is constructed and to some extent how it is received. In addition to the worldviews of state leaders, they have directed attention to how nonstate, international actors—organized and unorganized, in both

North and South America—have believed and behaved. Less self-conscious than ideology, culture is more habitual than intellectual, more heartfelt than cerebral, and not easily subjected to self-examination. Societal leaders and much of the public often perceive culture as common sense even when it is based on the least rational of foundations.

Despite the discipline's recent cultural turn, some historians of U.S. foreign relations question the relevance of cultural studies to international affairs, primarily on the basis that the concept of culture is so amorphous that it waters down the awesome reality of national and international power.[28] Power, however, lies at the center of cultural interaction. In the United States as elsewhere, not all web makers are created equal. Dominant cultural discourses have represented the power hierarchies of American life: rich over poor, male over female, white over black and brown—in short, the politically and economically connected over the marginalized. At the same time, these hierarchies have remained subject to contestation, negotiation, and rearrangement. The African American civil rights crusade and the women's movement are just two examples of how modern grassroots struggles in the United States have altered cultural dynamics.

Culture is integral to the process of nation making and identity formation. Benedict Anderson's influential thesis that nations exist as "imagined communities" as well as territorial and administrative units that depend on cultural articulation and construction helps explain the enormous cultural power associated with modern nationalism.[29] The bonds of communion formed by shared belief systems can be so strong that citizens typically respond enthusiastically to the call to fight and die on behalf of other citizens whom they do not know and with whom they share few concrete interests. And when nations experience a dilution of identity through foreign occupation, domestic social change, or civil war, they become increasingly vulnerable to political upheaval, protest, terrorism, revolution, or civil war.

This study demonstrates that empires are also in many ways imagined communities and that tourism and other cultural interactions have allowed ordinary U.S. and Latin American citizens, along with nongovernmental groups, to participate in the meaning-making process.[30] Tourists and hosts have encountered and negotiated variants of racial hierarchies, contrasting constructions of class and gender, and differing conceptions of architectural and natural beauty. At archeological sites and museums, they have shown the malleable nature of historical memory. Gazing on the spectacle of pyramids and temples, visitors may seek to place their modern lives within a larger civilizational context. Host governments and interest groups may use the same artifacts to challenge cultural myths advanced by the external hegemon, negotiate internal political and social conflicts, and revise authenticated views of national heritage.[31]

At bottom, the history of U.S. tourism in Latin America shows that empire is a more nuanced system of inequality, resistance, and negotiation than appears at first glance. Rather than being understood as a series of binary opposites—center and periphery, developed and dependent, modern and nonmodern—the hemispheric empire is in fact a heavily textured and integrated community.[32] This does not mean that hemispheric relations take place on a level playing field. Almost anyone who has studied the U.S. presence in Latin America knows that North Americans have more often than not prospered at the sad expense of local groups. U.S. dollars carry immense coercive energy, as do gunboats that fly the Stars and Stripes. Washington's diplomatic maneuvering, moreover, has rained down on the region a long list of oppressive dictators: Gerardo Machado, Rafael Trujillo, Anastasio Somoza, Jorge Ubico, Castillo Armas, Fulgencio Batista, Augusto Pinochet, to name just a handful. Yet the cultural linkages between the United States and its southern neighbors, including those connections generated by the travel industry, have also produced a myriad of more ambiguous, interdependent relationships. Rather than understanding hegemony, cultural and otherwise, as a fixed condition, it makes more sense to think in terms of what scholar William Roseberry has called "hegemonic process," a term that implies ongoing fluidity, contestation, and bargaining.[33]

In the past two decades or so, numerous historians of U.S. foreign relations have worked to place U.S. foreign policy in its broader social and cultural contexts.[34] One work particularly relevant here is Christopher Endy's *Cold War Holidays* (2004), a study of U.S. tourism in France, especially Paris, during the quarter century that followed the Second World War. Endy explores the cultural dynamics unleashed by visiting Americans whose thirst for "Old World difference" required French hosts to provide the very latest in consumer conveniences. Reluctant to compromise traditional standards of "civilization," the cash-starved French nonetheless evolved a "hip Gaullism" that married reverence for tradition with the building of modern France. Endy demonstrates how Americans smitten by the travel bug not only helped make France the world's leading tourist destination but also facilitated that country's postwar economic reconstruction and contributed to the building of an anticommunist "Atlantic community."[35]

Given the globalizing trends of the past century, parallels not surprisingly exist between U.S. tourism in France and in Latin America. The societies under consideration here similarly mixed old and new in an effort to manip-ulate U.S. hegemony to their advantage. But the Western Hemisphere is not Western Europe. Rather than participating in a transatlantic alliance that implied cooperation among equals, as on the European continent, U.S. tour-ists south of the Rio Grande and east of the Florida Keys became agents of empire. Whereas U.S. "innocents" in Europe sought Old World ambience and perhaps a connection to their ancestral roots, gringos roamed a hemi-sphere where U.S. political and economic domination was long established.

In his two-volume study of U.S. tourism in twentieth-century France, cultural historian Harvey Levenstein has discussed common American pho-bias toward France. Returning travelers often regaled listeners with tales of shady business practices, sexual immorality, disgusting personal hygiene, and revolting gastronomical habits. Yet Levenstein observes that for U.S. travelers, Europe in general and France in particular registered as the epicenter of civilization and sophisticated pleasure. France was at once a place for serious, educational self-improvement and extravagant leisure activity. Much of the conflict in U.S.-European tourist relations sprang from the fact that U.S. cultural influence did not match its political, economic, and military power. Dollar-wielding Yankees might swagger across the continent reliving memo-ries of victorious past wars, but a visit to the Louvre, Big Ben, the Sistine Chapel, or a sidewalk bistro typically produced awe, admiration, and perhaps a touch of status anxiety. And when North Americans behaved in ways that did not mesh with local customs, they often earned the scorn and resentment of their hosts.[36]

In contrast, travel discourse portrayed Mexico, Cuba, and Puerto Rico in more ambiguous civilizational language. To some extent, travel narratives conformed in style to what scholar Edward Said has termed Orientalism, portraying Latin America as backward, exotic, and awaiting the civilizing influence of the United States.[37] Late-nineteenth-century traveler James Bates awoke one morning in the northern Mexican state of Chihuahua and found his environment so unusual that he recorded, "Were I told we were in Pal-estine or Egypt, all about me would confirm it."[38] Other writers marveled at the rehabilitative impact of tourism. The tourist, travel writer John E. Jen-nings noted in *Our American Tropics* (1938), "takes nothing out of the coun-try except a few souvenirs for which he pays extremely well, to say the least, and a coat of tan."[39] These discourses posited two culturally separate but mutually constituted worlds, the West and the Orient, the former superior, masculine, and strong and the latter backward, feminine, and weak.

While Said's thesis provides an innovative tool for exploring the Western imagination, it does not radically depart from traditional representations of empire that juxtapose power and powerlessness. It is too rigid to fully explain the kinetic energy that manufactures culture and the interactive nature of modern hegemony. Although many twentieth-century U.S. travel narratives evoked the theme of masculine power and conquest, the prevailing tone for many others was sentimental—even feminine—in terms of the traveler's fervent hope that universal human impulses would permit a personal bond with the visited "less-developed" society. In such cases, sympathetic tourist writings penned by both males and females might still contribute to the imperial project, and such writings contrast sharply with more deferential views of Europe. Christina Klein's study of Cold War American-Asian relations demonstrates how missionary, philanthropic, and tourist travel accounts often romanced the nobility of America's overseas presence, advanced utopian visions of the U.S.-led global order, and fostered consent for U.S. foreign policy.[40]

Travel literature, tourist testimony, and promotional tracts on Latin America often betrayed similar sentiments. But viewed through the framework of empire, they also carried transformative potential. Tourist guidebooks and magazine articles that heralded the sophistication of the region's indigenous societies, sympathized with the aspirations of postrevolutionary Mexicans or Cuban insurgents, or highlighted Puerto Rico's quest for reform and cultural renaissance prompted some readers to embrace difference, discover new ways to understand self and other, and imagine new, often softer, structures of empire.

Empire, Soft Power, and Tourist Agency

One of the central themes of this study is that the U.S. hemispheric empire has endured in part because the hard power brandished by marine brigades and financial houses has been accompanied by softer power, based on negotiation and suasion rather than compulsion. Victoria De Grazia deploys the concept of "soft power" to explain how a soft resource such as consumerism joined with the hard power of diplomacy and military preparedness to spread what she calls America's "irresistible empire" through twentieth-century Europe. According to De Grazia, the common habits promoted by international Rotarians, chain stores, big brand goods, and corporate advertisers established the United States as a symbol of mass prosperity and social progress.[41]

The precise meaning of the phrase "soft power" remains somewhat elusive. De Grazia notes that the terminology first arose in the context of debates within the U.S. foreign policy establishment of the early 1990s regarding the types of resources available to sustain America's world leadership following the end of the Cold War.[42] Joseph S. Nye, who served as assistant secretary of defense in Bill Clinton's administration, posited that U.S. cultural values, particularly the espousal of democratic government and free enterprise, registered as a third resource, along with the nation's economic and military power, and together they provided the means to success in world politics. His original definition of soft power—the ability to make "others want what you want"—accented the state's responsibility for spreading American values abroad through public diplomacy and assumed that soft power produced a convergence of interests between the United States and those at whom it aimed its soft resources.[43] But soft power might be considered more expansively as an intrusive influence wielded wherever global and local cultures meet by agents that often operate outside the purview of the state. Within the travel industry, agents of soft power include travel writers, artists, intellectuals, hoteliers, labor organizers, entertainers, media moguls, advertisers, and a host of others, all of whom advance their particular interests whether or not they converge perfectly with the interests of host societies.

The tourist's clout as consumer constituted one crucial component of soft power in inter-American relations, but the outward movement of U.S. consumerism played out differently in Latin America than in De Grazia's Europe. Given the hemisphere's profound economic inequalities, relatively few Latin Americans initially found consumer culture and market capitalism "irresistible." By the 1920s, however, rising incomes in the United States expanded worker benefits, and modern systems of transportation facilitated the rise of mass tourism and sent hundreds of thousands of vagabond gringos and modern consumer culture southward. U.S. travelers flaunted their wealth in casinos, brothels, gift shops, hotels, and banks. Their vacation dreams drove transnational and local elites to build new hotels and restaurants; to rearrange the physical environment of cities, mountain villages, and beachfronts; and to import golf courses, swimming pools, and other elements of North American material culture.

Along with consumer power, tourists and the industry that served them possessed the power to interpret and invent cultural identities—that is, the power to define the social meaning of self, other, and empire. As Said might have predicted, many U.S. tourists in Latin America carried a racial identity that elevated whiteness, the same color code that haunted Latino migrant workers in the United States. Chauvinistic images of beautiful, welcoming, brown-skinned women often appeared on postcards, postage stamps, and travel posters. Traveling consumers, moreover, often looked upon their hosts primarily as providers of services whose wares could be snatched up for a pittance. Mayan pottery prominently displayed on the fireplace mantel or Cuban cigars lit up after dinner symbolically and materially conveyed U.S. affluence and domination in world affairs.[44]

Yet travel is also an inherently globalizing experience, and contemporary anthropologists question the idea of coherent or fixed cultures. Rather than a static and knowable phenomenon, culture encompasses a process by which identity-giving symbols and meanings are constantly redefined.[45] In addition to inventing and imposing identities, tourists and hosts enter into a more nuanced process of interpretation and contextualization. Through their purchases of pottery and silver, their personal encounters with both Latin Americans and fellow travelers, and their writing of postcards and travel memoirs, twentieth-century tourists transmitted new webs of cultural significance homeward, altered social, cultural, and political life at the empire's center, and helped millions of U.S. citizens reimagine America's place in world affairs. In short, rather than a simple system of cultural imposition, transnational discourses usually generated difficult-to-predict combinations of culture clash, cultural negotiation, and hybridization.[46] The new terminology does not diminish the reality of empire but does decenter our understanding of it and allows us to see how "others" have globalized America even as the seductive power of U.S. culture has helped to Americanize the globe.

Skeptics have long discounted the intellectual and cultural depth of the tourist experience, a critique that implicitly dismisses the significance of tourists to international relations. Who among us has not encountered the boorish vacationer, American or otherwise, the camera-toting, credit-card-flashing, line-jumping exhibitionist/voyeur who always seems to hold court in the hotel lobby, restaurant, or museum. Commentators from Mark Twain to Senator J. William Fulbright have bemoaned the abysmal behavior of their countrymen and -women abroad. Comedian Steve Martin poked fun at tourists everywhere, not just U.S. visitors to France, when he quipped, "Boy those French, they have a different word for everything."[47]

Conservative historian Daniel J. Boorstin loathed modern mass tourism and the tourist's enthusiasm for the "pseudo-event," the contrived sightseeing itinerary slapped together by commercial agents that shields visitors from the "real" culture, people, and society. He lamented the "lost art of travel," a relic of a bygone era, when the refined and well educated toured abroad with a sense of adventure, a desire to commune with local cultures, and a willingness to take risks. He bestowed on modern travelers the derogatory term "tourist," a species whose thoughtlessness made their international experiences nothing more than a series of prearranged pseudo-events.[48]

The classic critique of the tourist, however, is more anecdotal than analytical and not very helpful to an understanding of tourism and empire. Tourists, in fact, possess historical agency. The word "tourism" is derived from "travail," which means suffering or work. Preparation for that long-delayed getaway requires planning, saving, packing, and a multitude of other chores. While a Hilton hotel provides familiarity and a sense of security, few modern tourists confine themselves to the hotel room and lobby. Many venture into the host's streets and alleyways, explore museums, and seek educational experiences. The popularity of travel guidebooks, street maps, language booklets, credit cards, and traveler's checks indicates that the act of travel is challenging and often anxiety provoking. As historian Rudy Koshar has written, "Tourism finds its meaning through effort, contact, and interaction, no matter how programmed or structured, and if something is learned through tourism, it reaffirms or alters the traveler's sense of self in unpredictable ways."[49]

Nor is there such a thing as an archetypal tourist. Sociologist Dean MacCannell, one of the founders of tourism studies, posits that mass tourism is a product of cultural modernity, a response to the dislocation caused by industrialization and the fragmentation of work from other life activities. Provided structured leisure time, tourists temporarily escape the workplace and scavenge the earth in search of authenticity by visiting ancient Mayan ruins, strolling through colonial Habana Vieja, or lying half naked on a warm, sandy Puerto Rican beach.[50] This thought-provoking thesis may explain why some people travel, but touring Yankees have varied by class, race, gender, and other demographic markers. The hard-drinking North Americans who invaded Mexico's border towns in the 1920s consisted disproportionately of single males; 1930s Mexico City attracted an artistic and intellectually inclined crowd, including students, professors, artists, bohemians, and the middle-aged with a personal taste for edification. Cold War Cuba drew a mix of conventioneers, off-duty sailors, gambling enthusiasts, adventurous singles, and respectable middle-class couples. Sophisticated but pricey San Juan attracted prospective investors and their spouses, well-heeled vacationers, a small, affluent gay clientele, and a collage of sun worshippers and beach bums.

Theorists of cultural reception, moreover, emphasize the numerous ways in which audiences receive and interpret media images.[51] Some travelers lock into the guidebook's rendition of culture. Others absorb the information posted on museum placards. Still others wish to steer clear of intermediaries altogether and become antitourist tourists. "Don't be a tourist, unless you simply must," businessman and travel writer Harry Franck advised in his 1935 guide to Mexico.[52] Some travelers approach the host country as if it were a department store built specifically for their consuming pleasure. Others think of themselves as what historian Lizabeth Cohen has labeled "citizen consumers," practice socially sustainable tourism, and make their purchases with the welfare of the local community and environment in mind.[53] Down through the twentieth century, tourists exhibited a myriad of attitudes and behaviors. The truth of the matter is that travelers, much like nations, define and pursue their own interests.

The voices of soft power usually speak softly and perhaps for that reason often elude scholars of empire. Tourist voices can be found in state papers, but they are more often embedded in travel narratives, personal memoirs, works of fiction and film productions, and other cultural texts. Scrawled messages on the back of picture postcards, correspondence between patrons and travel businesses, and brochures for educational exchange programs reveal at least part of what tourists dream and how they behave. Finally, transnational organizations such as the Hilton Hotel Corporation and Pan American Airlines maintain private depositories that illuminate the inner life of the tourist complex. These voices collectively tell us that tourism is about power, but these expressions of power require careful listening.

Hosts, Cultural Contact Zones, and the Everyday Life of Empire

While tourists are often caricatured as shallow and utterly lacking in agency, critics of modern tourism typically paint hosts with a similar brush. Tourism as a destroyer of cultures is a recurring theme in popular literature. Analysts have coined the phrase "commodification of culture" to highlight how local communities hire themselves out to display representations of native life, mainly for the entertainment and economic benefit of outsiders. Although the practice has historical antecedents, most notably the world's fairs of the late nineteenth and early twentieth centuries with their spectacular presentations of colonial peoples in staged "primitiveness," modern travel has extended the theater.[54] Some representations transmit unambiguously derogatory messages. Floor shows in Cold War Havana were often loosely based on the sexual pantomime of rumba but came to include such preposterous costume and razzmattaz that they reinforced stereotypes of the exotic Cuban other.[55] Others worked harder to straddle the divide between cultural authenticity and commercial opportunity. In 1920s Mexico, the indigenous residents of Teotihuacán resurrected and performed long-forgotten folk dances for visiting North Americans. Government and beer companies in Puerto Rico during the 1960s began sponsoring annual festivals in honor of a rediscovered slave dance known as *la bomba*.[56]

While cultural displays the world over have become subject to commercialization, they do not consistently debase culture. Instead, their meanings usually support multiple interpretations. Thus, another important theme of this study is that host societies and their peoples are not passive victims. They possess their own soft powers and no less than tourists seek to make tourism work in their interest. A wide array of individuals and interest groups within each touristed society—government agencies, political elites, local entrepreneurs, labor unions, artists, tour guides, hotel concierges, and the like—have in fact used the tourist system to advertise their existence and establish their power, although they have not always possessed the political will to do so.[57]

Latin American hosts wielded less economic and cultural power than their European counterparts but developed innovative strategies of resistance and skillfully utilized the tools at hand. They held the advantage of home turf: knowledge of language and mores, familiarity with geography, and access to local contacts. Tour guides often enjoyed the discretionary power to teach history and culture as they saw fit, allowing them to modify the visitor's worldview. At other times, agency came through personalized acts. Service workers might adopt a nonchalant posture toward visitors, respond to tourist queries in Spanish, or slow service down to a snail's pace. Much like James C. Scott's Southeast Asian peasants and their conscious, petty sabotage, or Robin Kelly's inner-city African American fast-food employees and their tactical foot-dragging and dress-code violations, working-class hosts often developed their own system of "infra-politics" whereby they engaged in everyday forms of resistance to domination.[58]

The tourist's soft power, moreover, is neither monolithic nor omnipotent. Indeed, although soft power may not make others want what U.S. policymakers want, its noncoercive essence provides weaker states and their citizens a modicum of negotiating space in which to manage the imperial presence. Tourists, unlike traditional imperialists, do not seek to dominate the production of goods. Instead, they travel with their hearts set on spending, even to the point of accumulating unmanageable debt and squandering their power base. Consumer power is less coherent and unified than the power held by investment firms and traders, less centralized and more easily manipulated than U.S. military muscle. Tourist sentimentality can be exploited to bestow on visitors an idealized version of host identity. To race-conscious and culture-bound U.S. travelers, hosts at various times appeared to be ingratiating or antagonistic, deferential or assertive, dollar hungry or inscrutably oblivious to cash incentives. At those moments, national identity and the meaning of empire became contested terrain.

A few examples at this point suggest the types of cultural encounters that take place inside tourist zones. F. W. Boyd of Baltimore rumbled through Mexico in 1926 in his Maxwell coupe, carrying an empty coffin in the backseat because he was convinced that the macabre accoutrement would ward off "superstitious" Mexican "desperados."[59] At the other end of the relationship, a Mexican vice consul in New York who regularly took inquiries from prospective U.S. tourists complained bitterly to a 1934 interviewer about North Americans who, like Boyd, assumed Mexico to be a uncivilized land of banditos and siestas. Did Mexico City have automobiles "or only burros?," he indignantly recalled one woman asking.[60]

Constructions of race and gender provided ample fodder for culture clash. Many Habaneros resented representations of Cuba as a land of promiscuous, cash-hungry, female sex objects. Luis Conte Agüero asked in the magazine *Bohemia* if tourism was worth the price of "the demoralization of our customs, and the disrepute of the name of Cuba?"[61] Conservative Puerto Ricans expressed dismay when they came upon half-dressed Yankees at local public beaches. In postrevolutionary Mexico, government officials countered chauvinistic representations of Mexican femininity and demonstrated the malleability of cultural constructions of gender with ad campaigns that reconfigured stereotypes. One 1930s Mexican travel brochure featured a mass-produced image of a modernized *indígena* (indigenous woman). Dressed in traditional garb and bedecked in flowers, she extended a generous welcome to foreign guests. Yet her intense gaze, strong cheekbones, and dark skin symbolized resiliency, national dignity, and uncompromising pride in Mexico's multicultural heritage.[62]

Daily cultural negotiations across the empire arose in part from technological innovation. Communications theorist John Tomlinson has explained the impact of modern transportation systems—rail, oceanic, and aerial—on global cultural interaction. Passenger ships steamed U.S. travelers across the Caribbean and Mexican gulf, and railroads transported thousands of others across the Mexican border or to Key West and on to Cuba. Pan American Airlines, along with the Pan-American Highway, provided additional paths southward by the 1930s. These networks not only made long distance travel possible but changed human perceptions of time and space. Distance increasingly became measurable in hours rather than miles, what Karl Marx called the annihilation of space by time.[63] Ports, rail stations, and airports, relatively homogeneous in design and construction, served as departure points and cultural corridors that cushioned the psychological strain of border crossings.[64]

Yankees on holiday imagined Latin America in countless ways while hurtling through thousands of miles of cultural corridor. But once outside the controlled environment of the train station or airport, they entered what Mary Louise Pratt has labeled a "cultural contact zone," a modern social space where disparate cultures met, often in highly asymmetrical power relationships.[65] There, tourists encountered a disorienting world of linguistic, racial, and cultural diversity. Yet like inhabitants of the hemisphere's many borderlands, tourists and hosts also made their contact zones a place where cultural practices blended, where Spanglish idioms proliferated and architectural styles mixed. Indeed, tourists learned that, like themselves, hosts came in a variety of sizes, shapes, and colors.

Cultural contact zones exist throughout the empire. Historians of Latin America are familiar with export enclaves, where U.S. companies penetrate the daily lives of the local inhabitants.[66] Contact zones also pop up in the United States—on university campuses where foreign students matriculate, in art communities, and at vacation spots that attract international visitors. The most common zones of contact in the United States have emerged where demand is strong for cheap, mobile labor: the fertile valley of San Joaquin, the cotton fields of Texas, the rail yards of Chicago and Kansas City, and the urban centers of the Northeast.[67]

Within the tourist districts of Mexico, Cuba, and Puerto Rico, hotels represented one of the more carefully controlled zones. Their grand architectural style bespoke U.S. international power, and in addition to comfortable and in many cases luxurious accommodations, they provided a ritualized introduction to the locality. Concierges, bellhops, bartenders, cashiers, and tour guides served as deferential mentors to their affluent patrons.[68]

Outside of the hotel, however, the tourist's soft power often eroded. Travelers and hosts engaged one another in city restaurants, at bus stops, in museums, at historic and archeological sites, and at musical performances. Within the various contact zones, everything—from constructions of race and gender to the accuracy of historical markers to the price of a taxi—appeared indeterminate and negotiable. Each day of a vacation required 101 interactions between traveler and hosts. They sparred over language, the price of curios, and musical tastes. Gringos might feel discomfort at the sight of Latin America's urban slums, rail-thin children, or union pickets blocking hotel entrances. Local service workers might cringe when the affluent barked commands in English or evidenced white racism. Annoyed cabbies might set the meter and take the long way back to the hotel.

Thus, an examination of U.S. tourism brings to the forefront another overlooked aspect of empire: its everyday life. Traditional historiography organizes the history of inter-American relations episodically. It amplifies the most dramatic political events—revolutions, coups, natural disasters, riots, U.S. military intervention—but leaves routine behaviors, carried out by ordinary people, largely unexamined. Indeed, the preoccupation with national interests, state policy, and global financial institutions tends to marginalize human subjects, be they consumers or workers, female or male, racial minorities, subordinate classes, or the upwardly mobile.[69] The upshot is a perception of empire defined almost exclusively by the metropole's hard power and punctuated by sporadic fits of rarely successful resistance.

Examining the passage of time through the lens of everyday life does not necessarily fracture traditional historical periodization. The interwar era, the Cold War, détente, and the post–Cold War remain helpful devices for analyzing international trends. But the everyday life of the empire, whether it is examined by way of tourist relations or other seemingly mundane activities, places traditional turning points in history into broader context. Events considered to be novel in one era acquire precedence. The cultural distance between the nineteenth-century doctrine of Manifest Destiny and mid-twentieth-century nation building and modernization theory collapses. The linkages between antinationalism and anticommunism are illuminated, and comparisons between the Mexican Revolution and its Cuban counterpart half a century later become more facile. In inter-American relations, the twentieth century acquires new intellectual coherence as an age of empire and resistance, mass culture and national identities, rather than an era fragmented by the Great War, the Second World War, and the Cold War.

Perhaps most important, through the illumination of its everyday life, the reality of empire comes more clearly into focus. More than a quarter of a century ago, when William Appleman Williams speculated that empire might be understood as a way of life, he noted that the word "empire" enjoys "no easy hospitality in the hearts and minds of most contemporary Americans."[70] The national imagination prefers to define the American way of life as involving virtue, democracy, and wealth. The history of cultural contact zones, however, links the pious rhetoric of empire to personal acts of insensitivity, global finance and trade to individual consumption, and the limits of U.S. power to host agency.

Like tourist voices, host voices can be recovered in their respective state archives, in letters to government officials, or through government reports on interest-group activity. But hosts, like tourists, speak through a variety of sources. Letters to both Spanish- and English-language newspapers often feature complaints against offending tourists and sometimes include tourist responses. Editorials commonly address larger policy issues relating to tourism, cultural displays, and national identity. Satirical plays, poetry and fiction, social realist art, and political cartoons provide commentary on vacationing gringos and North American culture.

These indicators show that while host communities may become vulnerable to debasing cultural constructions or might willingly integrate globalized, cultural imports, they are rarely submissive. Host governments and citizens are historical actors whose activities, both ritualized and spontaneous, shape the course of empire. In the modern history of the Western Hemisphere, revolutions, military coups, and elections have at times created serious rifts between hegemon and colonies, as the Mexican and Cuban Revolutions certainly demonstrate, albeit in very different ways. But the everyday life of the empire forms a broader social and cultural landscape whose movements occur more slowly, more ambiguously, over what French historian Fernand Braudel called the "long durée."[71]

Tourism and Foreign Policy

Although the cultural contours of the hemispheric empire have generally exceeded its political dynamics in life expectancy, the two have been inextricably linked throughout the twentieth century. Tourists and other cultural actors, of course, do not formulate or implement policy. Nor do Washington officials make a habit of consulting these actors for advice. Tourists and diplomats nonetheless occupy the same world. Both have exposed the American people to the compression of international distances. While tourists actually experienced the transportation and communications revolutions via the rise of modern cultural corridors, U.S. diplomats have grappled with the security ramifications. Historian Frank Ninkovich has observed that U.S. leaders beginning in the early twentieth century grasped how technology had begun to shrink the world. "We are all peering into the future," President Theodore Roosevelt wrote in 1895, "to try to forecast the action of the great dumb forces set into motion by the stupendous industrial revolution."[72] A generation later, another Roosevelt noted that modern militarism in Europe and Asia threatened the United States. The American people, FDR presciently remarked prior to Pearl Harbor, had "much to learn of the 'relativity' of world geography" and how technology had resulted in the "annihilation of time and space."[73] U.S. officials throughout the Cold War worried that a faraway political crisis might unleash a cascading, domino-like catastrophe that would jeopardize not only U.S. security but civilization itself.

Tourists and policymakers, moreover, have acted as both consumers and producers of culture. Through postcards, souvenirs, photographs, and stories spun around the dinner table, U.S. travelers have bequeathed a multitude of transnational incursions into American life and provoked discussions on history, religion, art, politics, sexuality, race, and national character. The French, according to conventional wisdom, were elitist, short on manliness, and inveterate anti-Americans. Dark-skinned Mexicans enjoyed their drowsy, heat-stricken pace of life.[74] Policymakers may not always contemplate the cultural influences that inform their worldview. After all, most have been trained as foreign policy realists and seek to explain the causes and effects of international events through concrete, empirical evidence rather than the murky lens of culture. Yet through their public pronouncements and their nearly unlimited access to mass media, they have not only articulated U.S. interests but also invented cultural identities and fed cultural myths that filled the political firmament.[75]

In the end, U.S. officials, like the traveling public, are socially engineered beings whose views are drawn from a repertoire of constructed possibilities. The ranks of the U.S. foreign service corps have historically been filled by upper- and upper-middle-class white males educated in private preparatory schools and universities. They read newspapers, listen to radio and television news, take in movies, follow sports, swap jokes and anecdotes, and consume goods and services that reinforce other cultural webs in their daily lives.[76] Among the many influences that have informed policymakers, tourism and travel narratives have ranked high. Most twentieth-century foreign service officers entered their careers already well traveled. Indeed, most modern presidents have taken up residence in the White House with at least some international travel under their belts. Those who have come from upper America—the Roosevelts, John F. Kennedy, and George H. W. Bush—partook of European travel during their youths as a rite of passage. (George W. Bush, whose 2000 campaign handlers told the *New York Times* that the candidate had set foot on foreign soil only a few times, seems to have been the exception.)[77] Even the sons of middle- and working-class America—Woodrow Wilson, Herbert Hoover, Harry Truman, Lyndon Johnson, Jimmy Carter, and Bill Clinton—had seen at least some of the outside world either through business, military service, and college scholarships or through congressional junkets.

Through their travels, these men inevitably contributed to cultural discourses on identity. When Franklin Roosevelt sailed south to take a breather in 1935, he joined other Americans in embracing Mexico's rural tranquillity. He relished the country's Pacific Coast deep-sea fishing and planned to return not for a state visit but to visit picturesque ports at Acapulco and Mazatlán and journey inland to the mountain village of Taxco.[78] Prior to Fidel Castro's ascendancy, Cuba served as a pleasure palace for a handsome, young, and enormously wealthy Senator John F. Kennedy, soon to be America's foremost interpreter of Cuba, who joined his colleague, George Smathers of Florida, for a lost weekend in Havana during the winter season of 1957.[79] Through the first century of mass tourism, the worlds of diplomats, presidents, tourists, and the transnational travel industry increasingly converged.

U.S. officials have certainly granted tourism a great deal of significance. Presidents can be counted among the industry's foremost boosters. "Yes it pays to travel," FDR told a crowd in Fargo, North Dakota, home state of isolationist U.S. Senator Gerald P. Nye, in late 1937. "We get a bigger perspective and a lot of knowledge."[80] Even as the United States faced a deteriorating balance of payments, Dwight D. Eisenhower admonished a group of reporters in early 1960 that it was in America's interest to encourage its citizens to see the world. "The one thing that we don't want to do," he insisted, "is to develop an isolationist practice of staying at home."[81]

The U.S. government gave material as well as moral support to the travel industry. Following World War I, Washington subsidized chosen instruments such as Pan Am World Airways and select oceanic shipping firms, in part to prepare the nation for future conflicts but also to accelerate international trade and travel.[82] During the interwar years, the State Department established the Inter-American Cultural Affairs Division to promote cultural exchanges with the southern republics, and during the Second World War the department launched a campaign to promote "hemispheric solidarity." Immediately following the war, the Export-Import Bank helped finance hotel construction in Latin America.[83] The Marshall Plan advanced much larger loans for the postwar travel industry in Europe.[84]

U.S. tourists did not always behave as budding internationalists or ambassadors of goodwill. U.S. officials expressed exasperation at tourists who escaped the political and ideological Cold War to indulge in Parisian night life and French wines. Foreign policy realists such as State Department planner George Kennan and columnist Walter Lippmann derided thoughtless, consumer-oriented world travelers.[85] U.S. ambassador to Cuba Arthur Gardner found tourist antics in Havana to be for the most part "disgusting." Visitors "are bent only on pleasure and never think of Cuba except in terms of fun, rum, and nightclubs," he complained in a 1956 report to Washington.[86] Still, the government's sustained support for international travel demonstrates how tourism and foreign relations became inseparable.

The history of tourism enriches our understanding of foreign relations in many ways. The flow of interwar U.S. tourists to Latin America and elsewhere calls into question the popular notion that Americans fell into a deep isolationism after the Great War. U.S. travelers south of the border imagined and experimented with competing brands of international behavior. Some flexed their consumer and cultural muscle with little restraint, much as conservative proponents of power politics deploy firepower or dollar diplomats impose financial strings. Their dollars purchased *cerveza* and prostitutes as well as cultural privilege. Others exercised their soft power softly, discerning complexity and variation in the host's cultural practices and using their dollars to support Mexico's postrevolutionary cultural rebirth.

Tourist links to Mexico especially complicate accounts of FDR's Good Neighbor policy. The pledge of nonintervention in the region's internal affairs often meant little more than a free hand for U.S.-backed dictators to enforce order as they wished.[87] But for Mexico it produced a series of major U.S. concessions that resolved revolutionary-era property and debt disputes and transitioned away from dollar diplomacy toward Keynesian financial policies.[88] To explain the rapprochement, historians have listed economic depression and the coming world war as catalysts.[89] But an examination of tourism reveals that numerous transnational actors pressed for improved U.S.-Mexican relations in the 1920s and that bilateral ties warmed prior to the coming of depression and war.

Tourist excesses in postwar Cuba and the resentment they sowed help to explain the coming of the Castro revolution and U.S. officials' failure to see the looming catastrophe. Numerous scholars have expressed puzzlement at the Eisenhower administration's unshakable faith in its client, Fulgencio Batista. Most point to a conflicted bureaucracy and a partially engaged president and explain the policy setback as the outcome of a system failure. Few observers have considered how decades of U.S. tourism had portrayed Cubans as supine and contented and U.S. private enterprise as a force for progress, representations that also informed policymakers' views of the island and helped them to discount the likelihood of an uncompromising grassroots revolt.[90]

After the revolution triumphed in January 1959, both Havana and Washington sensed that a parting of ways was imminent, yet neither abruptly severed relations. Most accounts ascribe the denouement to the positive press the 26 July Movement received in the United States, Castro's lack of clear ties to Cuba's Communist Party, and the absence of viable alternatives to his leadership.[91] But pressure from tourists, hosts, and the travel industry also held the two nations together. Following public protests by hotel and casino workers, Castro attempted throughout 1959 and early 1960 to resuscitate and reform the moribund tourist industry.[92] U.S. firms in turn hoped that the lure of tourist revenue would mellow the new dictator's anti-Yankee fury. Accommodation ultimately proved elusive, but the episode shows that U.S.-Cuban cultural ties, of which tourism stood as a defining component, dissolved less easily than political relations.

Cuba's lurch leftward in 1960 and 1961 made Latin America a principal battleground in the Soviet-U.S. Cold War. But failure at the Bay of Pigs, attempted assassinations of Castro, and nuclear face-off with the Soviet Union demonstrated the limits of hard power. The Kennedy administration's Alliance for Progress represented a softer strategy for blunting revolution via publicly funded modernization programs. The ambitious undertaking included a pledge of ten billion dollars in U.S. public and private investment designed to lift the region out of poverty by the end of the decade. Assuming that Puerto Rico's relative success in industrialization had come about primarily as a result of U.S. tutelage rather than the commonwealth's efforts to contain U.S. hegemony, policymakers and the media seized on Puerto Rico's economy as a model for all of Latin America. Imperial hubris led them not only to underestimate the commonwealth's agency but also to discount the structural and cultural obstacles to development elsewhere in the region.[93] Although Puerto Rico continued to prosper during the 1960s and 1970s, the alliance floundered, to be supplanted in the 1980s by the still more rigid International Monetary Fund policies of privatization, free trade, and fiscal discipline.

This history of twentieth-century tourism is not designed to completely revise our understanding of foreign relations history. Nor does it claim that tourists and hosts ever caused Washington to adopt a specific policy. But the history of the visitor-host relationship adds several layers of knowledge to the history of inter-American relations and provides a new prism or set of tools with which to understand the past. As the United States emerged in the twentieth century as a hemispheric hegemon and world power, U.S. tourists constituted an ever-present force in the nation's foreign relations. Through their exercise of soft power, they heightened international awareness at home, invented identities for others and themselves, helped forge and dissolve strategic alliances, contributed to the coming of revolutions, and participated in international development. They did not merely reflect or symbolize broader political and economic trends but actively shaped and reshaped contexts and created new webs of significance between geographically separated communities.[94] In short, they helped to transform the terrain on which foreign policy and international relations took place.

Tourism and Globalization

The hemispheric tourist-host relationship from 1920 to 1975 belied large transformations in the international setting. During the nineteenth-century heyday of European imperialism, empires developed within bounded geographic spaces organized by powerful, industrialized nation-states. That model dissipated throughout the twentieth century in the wake of world wars, revolutions, and decolonization and the emergence of ever-denser networks of information, mobile capital, trade, and migratory labor that increasingly deterritorialized the international system and spurred globalization. The transportation and communications systems that produced global spatial proximity and helped spur modern mass tourism added to the transnational circuitry.[95]

In the modern world, where tourist attractions are staged and received, consumer power and cultural meanings often become dislodged from their anchors in local and national environments. Identities may be routinely formed and contested in connection to one another, appropriated by hosts and revised for domestic consumption, or commodified and purchased by visitors who lug the newly acquired cultural baggage home for distillation and reinterpretation. Interest groups with a stake in the travel industry spring up not only within host societies but also inside the metropole, establishing new transnational affiliations. This does not mean, as communications theorist John Tomlinson has noted, that we have all come to experience the world as cultural cosmopolitans. But it implies that the global increasingly represents a cultural horizon within which peoples, nations, and empires frame their existence.[96]

The debate over globalization ranks as one of the great controversies of our time. Marketplace ideologues applaud the movement toward a global economy, even in cases where it is painfully clear that global integration deepens inequalities and wreaks havoc on the world's poor. Some observers see the globalization of culture as confirming that America is indeed the world's redeemer, much as Theodore Roosevelt and other jingoists forecast at the turn of the twentieth century. Critics of globalization often equate all internationalizing trends with the financial authoritarianism of the International Monetary Fund or Milton Friedman's shibboleth that rich and poor alike are free to choose. Many people fear that cultural internationalism is a harbinger of a homogenized "McWorld," full of plastic and tinsel and devoid of diversity and authenticity.[97]

Globalization is typically framed from a Euro-American vantage point, as something that the West has done to others. As this book shows, North Americans have throughout the twentieth century consumed Latin America's commodities, natural environments, and cultures. Yet once more, the facile separation of the metropolitan "core" and the colonial "periphery" embedded in much of international relations literature distorts the interactive process of globalization, much as it misrepresents the history of empire. Latin Americans have historically ranked among the world's most globalized peoples, from the sixteenth-century conquests to the era of the transatlantic slave trade to the age of revolutions and throughout the tumultuous twentieth century. They have indeed experienced what sociologist Mimi Sheller calls the "violent embrace of the colonizer and the colonized," but they have also engineered mechanisms of soft resistance, forged a history of their own, and profoundly shaped transatlantic cultures for more than five hundred years.[98]

The history of tourism in the Americas demonstrates that globalization— much like a tourist's destination, a nation, or an empire—is imagined and negotiated. It may be conceived as an international free-for-all where greed dictates the rules—the dominant vision promoted currently by the U.S. government and its corporate allies. Or it can be imagined as a force that generates economic distribution as well as economic growth, cultural sharing rather than imposition, and respect for the rights of all.

This history of U.S. tourism argues that a humane integration of the globe is more likely to occur when the world's less powerful, be they states or private agents, wrest at least a modicum of economic protection, resources, and cultural freedom away from the marketplace. The world's disadvantaged are more likely to succeed if they receive timely support from those who inhabit the globe's more affluent societies. Globalization is a long-term process, much like nation building and hegemony, yet it is carried out on a day-to-day basis. Its trajectory is determined not only by large, impersonal national and international organizations and bureaucracies but also by the decisions and actions of countless ordinary citizens. Globalization does not happen by chance or according to immutable economic laws. It is, in fact, a deeply human affair that engages investors, consumers, workers, and private interest groups as well as diplomats and governments. It disrupts social and cultural norms but also can nurture understanding and cooperation. What follows then, is a story of soft power, cultural contact, empire, and globalization that complicates our understanding of the twentieth century and speaks to the challenges that lie ahead in the twenty-first century.

ONE

Lone Eagles and Revolutionaries

The U.S.-Mexican Rapprochement of the 1920s

President Plutarco Elías Calles and U.S. ambassador Dwight W. Morrow chatted nervously to pass the time. The throng of on-lookers scanned the sky above Mexico City's Balbuena airfield, hoping to glimpse a descending dot in the mid-December sky. Charles Lindbergh's plane had been delayed for two hours by a dense Gulf Coast fog. Then word arrived that the Lone Eagle had been spotted over the city of Toluca, just thirty-five miles east of the capital, and a pilot from Mexico's Ninth Air Squadron now accompanied the Spirit of St. Louis on the last leg of its nonstop flight from Washington, D.C. At 3:49 P.M. on 14 December 1927, twenty-seven hours and fifteen minutes after takeoff, Lindbergh touched down, to the joy and delirium of 150,000 Mexican fans who had turned out to greet him.[1] A tumultuous open-air motorcade through the heart of Mexico City followed, past crowds chanting, "Viva Lindy." "Oh! The crowds in the streets on the way to the Embassy!—On trees, on telegraph poles, tops of cars, roofs, even the towers of the Cathedral. Flowers and confetti were flung every moment," the ambassador's wife, Elizabeth Cutter Morrow, recorded in her diary.[2]

The Lindbergh visit was the brainchild of the recently appointed Morrow, a former J. P. Morgan investment banker and an old Amherst College chum of President Calvin Coolidge. The ambassador hoped that public cultural diplomacy might improve the atmosphere for U.S.-Mexican relations. Morrow had met Lindbergh the previous June in Washington, D.C., shortly after the young aviator completed his historic flight across the Atlantic, and had inquired about the possibility of a goodwill visit. Lindbergh, who had already begun investigating the prospects for a Latin American commercial airline, needed little coaxing.[3]

Appreciative Mexicans also needed no coaxing. Their epic revolution, which between 1910 and 1920 consumed some two million lives, had only recently subsided, and passionate denunciations of U.S. capitalism still echoed across the land. Yet in the days immediately following the landing, President Calles awarded Lindbergh the key to the capital city, and a special session of the National Assembly welcomed the opportunity to bring Mexico and the United States closer together. Anticipating the boost that air travel would give to cross-border exchanges, Senator Alfonso F. Ramirez declared, "On studying our psychology, you will see how the black legend of perversity with which the wicked have represented us, vanishes. . . . [Y]ou will also verify that Mexico welcomes with generous hospitality all strangers of goodwill."[4]

Air travel would not become a major contributor to Mexico's tourism industry and U.S. world power for another decade, but Lindbergh's odyssey dramatized the soft power and globalizing dynamics of modern travel. By 1927, hundreds of thousands of U.S. citizens were already traveling across the border for recreation, many of them encountering Mexico for the first time and reshaping that country's identity in U.S. popular culture. Like Lindbergh, they arrived compliments of innovative transportation technology—mainly rail, auto, and ship—that shortened travel distances. Yet they also savored the adventure of travel and often fancied themselves to be Lone Eagles traversing a vanishing frontier. On the surface, the numbers were not terribly impressive: an official tally of only 12,500 or so in 1928, the first year the Mexican government took a count.[5] In contrast, approximately 300,000 U.S. tourists visited Europe that year.[6] But the Mexican computation included only those who entered the country and stated an intention to travel inland for an extended stay. In fact, the vast majority, thousands daily, either hopped the train or drove their automobiles across the loosely guarded border without showing up on the statistical ledger.

They were a diverse lot. A tidal wave of U.S. tourists, predominantly but not exclusively male, poured across the border following passage of the 1919 Volstead Act, better known as Prohibition, one of the nation's most spectacular social engineering failures. In wide-open border towns such as Tijuana and Ciudad Juárez, rowdy northerners experienced little in the way of modern social reform, just a plentiful supply of cheap liquor and prostitutes, busy casinos, and other manly pursuits. Other Yankees journeyed far beyond the border to explore the rugged Pacific coast, the isolated Baja Peninsula, and the plains of Yucatán. Still others discovered a new world in areas heavily populated by indigenous peoples, such as the southern state of Michoacán. Expatriate artist communities sprang up to partake of Mexico's enchanting rural rhythms. A cohort of leftist intellectuals found in postrevolutionary Mexico City an exhilarating laboratory for revolution and modern socialism.

An undying myth in popular history is that Americans at the end of the First World War were so repulsed by the blood-drenched battlefields of Europe and so disillusioned by Woodrow Wilson's flawed peace treaty that they determined to isolate themselves from the rest of the world.[7] Numerous scholars have deconstructed these notions in recent years, noting that U.S. citizens during the 1920s participated in steadily increasing numbers in internationalist organizations such as the Carnegie Endowment for Peace, the International Relations Council, and the Women's International League for Peace and Freedom; U.S. companies pursued international trade and investment on an unprecedented scale; and an enlarged portion of American workers enjoyed vacation benefits that facilitated travel abroad.[8] The predominant conversation in the United States during the decade in fact did not center on whether the country should engage the world but rather on how to do so: whether to honor America's long-standing traditions of unilateralism and expansionism at others' expense or transition to a softer, more multilateral mode of interaction.

Tourist behavior in Mexico reflected both trends. Some travelers perceived Mexico to be one giant, wide-open town where Yankee consumer power knew no bounds. Others viewed travel as a more interactive endeavor—a manifestation of U.S. power and economic wherewithal, to be sure, but also an opportunity to commune with another culture and return home sporting an international badge of honor. Mexico was conducive to the latter view because it was not an extension of the United States but stood out as culturally different, in many ways even more foreign than Europe. "People accustomed to European travel," writer Frances Toor noted in the 1936 edition of her popular *Guide to Mexico*, "find Mexico more interesting, more invigorating, more of an adventure."[9]

Either way, U.S.-Mexican tourist interaction never became a one-way street. Mass tourism expanded and energized the everyday life of empire, produced new negotiating spaces for Mexican hosts, and modestly altered the hemispheric balance of power. A handful of well-connected Mexican officials played a crucial role in the creation of the border region's adult playgrounds, as did local labor unions. As U.S. tourists trickled south of the border towns, the central government in Mexico City developed cultural attractions that both appealed to roaming Yankees and manufactured a nationalist heritage befitting the postrevolutionary society. At the same time, the U.S. and Mexican governments slowly began to seek common ground. Ambassador Morrow played an important role in the warming trend, but so did tourists, transportation companies, travel agents, and other transnational groups associated with the travel industry.

This chapter examines the origins of mass tourism in 1920s Mexico. It delves into the interior lives of U.S. tourists to explain the multiple ways in which they imagined themselves, Mexico, the empire, and the world. Equally important, the chapter explores how the tourist presence and the travel industry affected Mexico physically and socially and how Mexicans from diverse backgrounds hoped to bend the visitor-host relationship to their advantage. Finally, it shows how tourists and hosts helped lay the groundwork for improved U.S.-Mexican diplomatic relations.

Mexico's Postrevolutionary Setting

As the 1920s commenced, the prospects for U.S.-Mexican relations did not seem bright. Prior to the revolution, dictator Porfirio Díaz (1876–1910) had identified the nation's culture with its European rather than indigenous past and embraced Anglo-American models for economic development and nation building. The Díaz administration welcomed an influx of foreign (mainly U.S.) investment capital and pinned Mexico's future to the global economy as an exporter of agricultural and mining products. Foreign bankers, especially the J. P. Morgan Company, Chase Manhattan, First National Bank, and the National City Bank of New York, rushed to finance railroad construction and electrification.

According to historian John Mason Hart, foreigners held approximately 35 percent of Mexico's land area in 1910, yet 80 percent of the country's population lived in rural locales and landownership constituted the chief measure of welfare. Americans alone possessed 130 million acres, about 27 percent of the surface area.[10] At the other end of the spectrum, Mexico's large population of landless campesinos suffered the loss of their communally owned, food-producing *ejido* (farming cooperative) lands, the majority of which were confiscated by the government, auctioned to private interests, and converted to the production of cash crops. In the U.S.-dominated mining and oil sectors, the labor force suffered low wages and discriminatory hiring practices that awarded supervisory jobs exclusively to white North American workers.[11] Union organizers and dissidents stood little chance of holding out against Díaz's armed posses of *rurales* (rural police).

The bloodshed that followed began as a political rebellion against the government's corrupt authoritarianism and escalated into a decadelong people's social revolution with overt anti-imperialist objectives.[12] U.S. ambassador Henry Lane Wilson's meddling to overthrow the duly elected reformist president, Francisco Madero, in 1913 and install Victoriana Huerta as the new strongman ignited further anti-Americanism. President Woodrow Wilson's penchant for lectures on democracy, his imposition of an arms embargo in 1914, and his gunboat bombardment at Tampico to punish affronts to the U.S. flag alienated nearly all of Mexico's proliferating factions. Finally, the 1916 Pershing Expedition against rural rebel Pancho Villa, which Villa cleverly eluded, made America's hard power look both bullying and ineffective.[13]

The great rebellion culminated in a new constitution, adopted in 1917, that included provisions for land redistribution, the legalization of labor unions, and government ownership of the nation's mineral and oil wealth. The document outraged most U.S. property owners. In addition, the constitution's anticlerical articles, which established civil marriages and secular education, alarmed influential Roman Catholics in the United States. Newspaper reporting on Mexico in the United States heightened concerns by focusing on the revolution's intellectual elites and their infatuation with the recently established Soviet Union. Alarmist headlines evoked fear and loathing in an America still reeling from the anticommunist Red Scare of 1919–20. When the government of Alvaro Obregón established the Comisión Nacional de la Agricultura and began confiscating large estates and redistributing the land to village-based *ejidos*, special interests in the United States launched litigation and lobbied both the Mexican and U.S. governments for compensation.[14] Historian Daniela Spenser has described how U.S. business leaders and the communications industry raised the specter of Bolshevik agents boring from within Mexico's government to provoke Washington's intervention.[15] U.S. and Mexican officials momentarily came to terms in 1923 when they signed the Bucareli Accords, which granted diplomatic recognition to the Obregón government, resolved the property and financial disputes, assured U.S. oil and mining firms that subsoil rights granted prior to 1917 would be respected, and set up mechanisms for U.S. bankers and the Mexican government to reschedule debt payments for loans extended prior to the revolution.

Bucareli brought only a brief respite. Land seizures continued, Mexico fell behind on its debt payments, and in July 1924, the Obregón government established diplomatic relations with Moscow. Obregón's successor, President Calles, balanced his more conservative economic policies with a heightened anticlericalism. Morrow's predecessor in Mexico City, James R. Sheffield, made the worst of a difficult situation, sending disparaging communications back to Washington. When Calles voiced his support for Augusto Sandino's uprising against the U.S. military occupation in Nicaragua, Sheffield painted the Mexican government as a Marxist pariah.[16]

In actuality, Mexico's revolution never fulfilled its radical potential. Revolutions, like empires, have an everyday life shaped by countless acts of resistance, repression, and negotiation. Leaders and members of the rank and file joust, localities and regions compete for influence, and over the long haul all contribute to a reframing of state and identity. The Obregón government won the admiration of leftists internationally for its land reforms and tolerated the presence of Marxist intellectuals and labor proponents but also worked to soothe U.S. financiers. Calles moved Mexico further to the right, slowing agrarian reform, co-opting labor through state-sanctioned unions, and establishing Mexico's Central Bank for national commercial and industrial development. During the 1920s, a U.S.-based General Electric subsidiary, American and Foreign Power, came to dominate Mexico's electric power generation, and International Telephone and Telegraph controlled the country's telephone systems. As scholars of the revolution have emphasized, the new order accented production over redistribution, industry over agriculture. It preferred to dole out favors to a new Mexican business elite whose membership overlapped that of the new governing elite but also turned to North American entrepreneurs when necessary.[17]

The government, however, balanced economic pragmatism with an identity politics that recognized the dynamism of the country's popular culture and sought to unify Mexico's mosaic of local and regional communities around a common national sentiment. Departing from Porfirio Díaz's national vision, Mexico's new leaders downplayed the country's Spanish inheritance and celebrated its Indian and mestizo (mixed-race) identities and spoke to grassroots demands for social justice. Indigenism found expression in music, art, and education. The government's Ministry of Education, led by José Vasconcelos, advanced an innovative program of basic education geared toward the rural poor. The ministry also gained notoriety by subsidizing talented muralists, including Diego Rivera, David Siqueiros, and José Orozco, whose works both evoked and manufactured a public memory that repudiated conquistador Hernán Cortés and idealized pre-Columbian and contemporary rural life. The artists consecrated a new pantheon of national heroes: Cuauhtémoc, the last Aztec emperor; Miguel Hidalgo, the early-nineteenth-century crusader for independence; Benito Juárez, the Indian-born liberal who faced down the French intervention in the 1860s; and Emiliano Zapata, the recently martyred messiah of the rural poor. In 1925, Vasconcelos published *La Raza Cosmica*, a veritable indigenist manifesto that inverted European racial constructions by celebrating mestizos as harbingers of a new aesthetic age.[18]

The state's cultural politics ultimately dovetailed nicely with the tourist's thirst for difference and foreign encounters. But the revised identity initially challenged prevailing North American constructions of the southern neighbor. At least since the days of the Mexican-American War (1846–48), when Mexico had been forced to forfeit half of its national estate, the ideology of Manifest Destiny had underpinned conventional perceptions of the Mexican other. The expansionist doctrine combined beliefs in white Anglo-Saxon racial superiority, patriarchy, providential Christianity, and a democratic mission to legitimize a U.S.-led hemispheric empire. These ideas still resonated in North American thought in the 1920s.[19] Popular writers Richard Harding and Jack London, along with Hollywood cinema, played on stereotypes of Mexico as a "half-breed" nation in dire need of regeneration by northern benefactors.[20] Conservative commentator H. L. Mencken pondered in his *New York World* column whether a reservation system would be needed after the United States asserted itself and spread south. "If anything is plain in this world," he elaborated, "it is that the United States is gradually sweeping the weaker republics of the southward into its net. . . . We can no more escape taking Mexico, sooner or later, than we could escape taking California."[21]

Ethnocentrism permeated popular responses to the recent spike in Mexican immigration to the United States. During the 1920s, when America's golden door closed to Europe's dispossessed, roughly fifty thousand Mexican laborers migrated to the United States annually, where they typically found low-wage employment in urban rail yards, meatpacking, and cannery factories in the Midwest and Southwest or tended crops in rural Texas and California's San Joaquin. By the end of the decade, Los Angeles had become home to about one hundred thousand Mexicans and Mexican Americans. In many localities, Mexican immigrants and their families felt the sting of racially based Jim Crow laws that forced children to attend separate schools, denied equal access to public facilities, and fostered an environment conducive to police harassment and vigilante violence.[22]

A small number of adventurous Yankees had carried these cultural constructions with them to Mexico during the late nineteenth and early twentieth centuries. The building of a modern rail system, mainly with U.S. investment capital, had facilitated an infant tourist industry in Mexico patronized mainly by upper-class U.S. citizens. They joined a growing North American community, some forty thousand strong by 1910, that consisted of property owners, businessmen, miners, petroleum engineers, farmers, and ranchers.[23] Travel writers of the era typically adopted Orientalist language to describe the country, accenting its backwardness while extolling its exoticism. James Bates, who traveled to Mexico during the 1880s, wondered why "our painters go to Tangiers and the distant Orient for subjects" when they were amply present in the Americas. Maturin Ballou commented on Mexico's "tragic history quite as picturesque and absorbing as that of any portion of the East."[24] Nahun Capen, a Boston capitalist and publisher who visited Mexico in 1870, highlighted the racial inferiority of Mexico's people: "In view of the real character of the Mexican people, it will be necessary to enlist large numbers of the superior race. To save that nation, you want a solid foundation of character, and what you cannot find there, it will be necessary to carry with you."[25]

Tourist travel to Mexico prior to 1920, however, failed to catch on. By the time Mexico's national railway system reached completion at the end of the Porfiriato and a handful of hotels had opened, violence and banditry had subsumed the nation, and Mexican culture brimmed with resentment toward Yankee financial power. When the fires of revolution finally cooled, U.S. tourists once again looked south across the border for travel adventures. But a booming postwar U.S. economy, a spreading consumer culture, and a growing curiosity regarding other nations and peoples assured that Mexico would attract and engage a broader cross-section of the North American population than in the recent past.

The Border Wars

The tourism boom of the 1920s was fueled in part by what might be best termed primordial impulses of conquest and possession. The earliest point of tourist-host contact occurred immediately south of the binational border. Spurred by Prohibition, Mexican towns such as Ciudad Juárez, Matamoros, Mexicali, Nogales, Nuevo Laredo, and Tijuana and their legendary open-air saloons, brothels, and casinos became magnets for pleasure-seeking gringos, most of them male. The Progressive reform era of the early 1900s, along with the Great War that followed, had accustomed many Americans to a larger, more interventionist federal government, financed by taxpayer dollars and charged with monitoring corporate malfeasance, urban housing standards, labor conditions, and other features of modern industrial life. But many who made the pilgrimage south deeply resented the extended reach of the law into their daily lives, especially the prohibition on alcoholic beverages and the Nineteenth Amendment, which granted women the vote. Both measures threatened traditional male culture. Despite the penetration of U.S. consumer power southward, tourist-host relations in the borderlands demonstrated that power relationships within the empire's cultural contact zones might fall subject to sudden realignment.

Porfirio Díaz first legalized gambling at the turn of the century. The establishment of rail links and cross-border businesses, along with inordinately dry conditions north of the Rio Grande, encouraged U.S. citizens to cross the border in record numbers during the 1920s. Mexican officials estimated that by 1930, approximately twelve million people headed south through entry stations each year.[26] It is impossible to tell how many of the millions were tourists. Many U.S. and Mexican citizens who lived close to the border regularly crossed the boundary for business and personal purposes. Still, wine, women, and song undoubtedly retained a strong allure.

Two border towns—Tijuana, sixteen miles south of San Diego, California, and Ciudad Juárez, below El Paso, Texas—held special status as sites of North American hedonism. On 4 July 1920, Tijuana, a town of only 1,000 inhabitants, hosted more than 65,000 U.S. Lone Eagles and their 12,650 cars, most of which parked along the Avenida de la Independencia in front of the town's standing-room-only saloons.[27] Tijuana lay just forty-five minutes away from San Diego by train and typically teemed with sailors on leave from the U.S. naval base there. *Terry's Guide to Mexico* (1927) described Tijuana as a town famous for its horse races "and for the ease with which the purple goddess beloved of Bacchus is obtainable."[28] Ciudad Juárez began its ascent as a pleasure zone at the turn of the century when Texas reformers shut down El Paso's notorious entertainment district. The cross-border culture transfer rapidly made the Mexican city a mecca for tourists and U.S. soldiers on leave from their base in El Paso, and the era of Prohibition solidified Juárez's standing. The city's main street, one local newspaper reported, had more bars than any other thoroughfare in the world.[29]

State governors in Nuevo León, Chihuahua, and Sonora amassed fortunes by catering to casino interests and American vice lords. The governorship of General Abelardo L. Rodríguez (1923–29) in the Distrito Norte of Baja, California (home to Tijuana), stood as a case in point. Rodríguez, who had served in Obregón's revolutionary army and enjoyed the president's strong support, partnered with U.S. "border baron" investors Wirt G. Bowman, Baron Long, and James N. Crofton to build and manage the Agua Caliente

Hotel and Casino on the eastern edge of Tijuana. Far more opulent than the vast majority of dives and gin mills, the Agua Caliente was constructed of white plaster and red tile, the rage in California at the time, and its interior consisted of a collage with Mexican, Mediterranean, and art deco elements. The hotel offered its guests an Olympic swimming pool, tennis courts, horse and dog racing, and a golf course. State officials exempted its casino, frequented by Hollywood celebrities such as Al Jolson, Clara Bow, Buster Keaton, and Jimmy Durante, from the local midnight curfew on gambling.[30] The Agua Caliente, which opened in June 1928, became the flagship of a vast leisure complex that made Tijuana one of Mexico's fastest-growing cities and one of the most significant cultural contact zones where Mexicans and outsiders, primarily North Americans, met, clashed, and negotiated.

Most of all, the border region stood out in the imaginations of visiting Anglos as a remnant of a mythical Old West, where meddling reformers and the Cult of the New Woman had not compromised male prerogatives. "All who visit San Diego, must see Tia Juana," wrote Stephen Chambers of the *New York Times* at the outset of Prohibition. There, "you forget yourself in what strikes you at first as a recrudescence of a Bret Harte mining camp or a Wild West main street in the movies."[31] "I am in Mexico today drinking one for you," one cowboy boasted to his buddy back in the States on a postcard with a photo of Juárez's infamous Owl saloon, complete with bartender and half a dozen Anglo patrons. Another young hombre scribbled, "This is the life for me. I'm taking it easy," across the back of a postcard that featured an attractive señorita and a large foamy glass of "Cerveza Mexicali."[32]

Despite their official backing, the casinos, particularly those owned by North Americans, aroused local discontent. Mexican entrepreneurs complained bitterly that state officials granted preferential treatment to foreign owners and that the well-connected border barons stifled competition. Favors did not come cheap. Carl Withington, owner of the popular Tivoli bar and casino, paid local authorities sixty thousand dollars a month for gambling rights. Still, the glaring favoritism inspired nationalist as well as financial resentment. Local unions, moreover, decried the wholesale hiring of foreigners to work in casinos, bars, and hotels. In fact, most establishments employed few Mexicans, and the locals who did land jobs usually took up menial positions.[33]

Many of the businesses also enforced Jim Crow. African American soldiers from El Paso could not gain entrance to numerous bars in Ciudad Juárez. Even light-skinned prostitutes gained higher status and often remained out of bounds for black patrons. African Americans who found themselves in

THE QUEENS OF TIJUANA

This postcard trumpets the manly pleasures to be enjoyed along Tijuana's bar-, brothel-, and casino-filled streets, ca. 1920. A parade adds to the celebratory ambience. DeGolyer Library, Southern Methodist University, Dallas, Texas, AG2000.1333.

Tijuana looking for a good time ambled to the Avenida Madero's Main Event saloon, owned by boxing legend Jack Johnson. Ironically, Johnson had sought exile in Mexico following trumped-up charges that he had illegally transported his white lover across U.S. state borders in violation of anti-prostitution laws. Johnson praised and exaggerated the racial progressiveness of Mexico's postrevolutionary regime and used Mexico as a platform from which to denounce white supremacy up north.[34]

Johnson judged the popular mood in Mexico more astutely than he did the country's official policies. The recently concluded revolution and the 1917 constitution that sanctioned unions and land reform had mobilized rural peasants and urban workers for participation in what for Mexico was a new phenomenon: modern mass politics. On the union front, anarcho-syndicalists, communists, trade unionists, and a potpourri of other ideologically based movements blossomed, and during the early 1920s, they often operated outside the government's purview.[35] In Tijuana, local authorities succumbed to public pressure: on 12 September 1923, police raided and shut down the Tivoli on the grounds that the establishment discriminated against Mexican job applicants. The legal action turned out to be mild compared to the subsequent attack on the Tivoli by a union-led mob, which busted up chairs and overturned gaming tables. Governor Rodríguez attempted to punish the mob's leaders, but public sympathy rested squarely with the protesters. In July 1925, the municipal government decreed that Mexican employees must constitute at least 50 percent of the workforce at local businesses. Within a decade, Mexican nationals accounted for more than 80 percent of the city's workforce.[36]

Initially caught off guard, Rodríguez proved adept at capitalizing on the anti-Americanism. During the years that he and the border barons had run the Agua Caliente horse racing track, his U.S. partners had invested some $285,000 in improvements. The establishment had become renowned for its elegance and its high-rolling clientele, despite persistent rumors that the races were fixed. In November 1929, state and federal authorities seized the lucrative track. The governor's North American business partners were summarily shut out of the business before the government restored the property to Rodríguez's sole proprietorship.[37]

The Tijuana episode exposed the inconsistent nature of the tourist's soft power. Even soft power might take a predatory turn. But local groups, organized labor, and opportunistic government officials possessed the means to alter the visitor-host relationship and strike back at the empire. For most of the 1920s, however, the policing of tourist activities remained the exception rather than the rule. That was exactly the point for many North Americans smitten with an appetite for exploration and discovery.

Beyond the Border: Lone Eagles as Internationalist Vanguard

Beyond the raucous border, Mexico acquired a more complex set of meanings for North Americans. Most of the early Lone Eagles who descended into the country's interior did not leave behind a written record of their experiences. But travelers published a handful of narratives, often printed privately with fewer than one hundred copies. Over the years, postcard collectors, fascinated by the pictorial representations of travel, have helped preserve additional snippets of the cultural space inhabited by U.S. tourists who engaged in the travel ritual of postcard correspondence. The imperial discourse for the most part assigned Mexico a romanticized identity: a place of transcendent beauty, elemental rusticity, unadulterated nature, and picturesque peasants working the fields.

Some of the narratives represented Mexico as part of the natural world that awaited the civilizing habits and financial help of the manly Anglo-Saxon race, a characterization that testified to the enduring appeal of Manifest Destiny as ideology. The tourist gaze of the 1920s, however, produced a second set of perceptions that complicated the empire's cultural landscape. Tourism promoters in the western United States had already begun to cash in on the Anglo public's deep but problematic fascination with Spanish, Mexican, and indigenous imagery. Phoebe S. Kropp has shown how local boosters advertised San Diego, California, and surrounding environs as a slice of a mythical Hispanic West where Spanish cultural conquest, embodied in the region's colonial Catholic missions and sprawling ranchos, had helped civilize the original, savage inhabitants. When the Panama Canal first opened in 1915, San Diego's community leaders sponsored the Panama-California Exposition, which attracted hundreds of thousands of visitors to exhibits designed to popularize a regional identity based on Spanish architecture and ambience and to celebrate Southern California's pivotal position in the burgeoning American empire.[38] In the southern Rocky Mountains, the Santa Fe Railroad and its partner, Fred Harvey, caught essentially the same wave of public enthusiasm and contracted with local Indian reservations to commodify their handcrafted pottery and blankets for sale to easterners en route to Santa Fe and Taos, New Mexico.[39]

For many Yankee travelers, postrevolutionary Mexico conveyed an even more intriguing amalgam of old and new, in no small part because it lay beyond the nation's border and beckoned as a safe house for authentic Indian folkways. Many travel narratives waxed sentimental over the southern republic's ancient Mayan, Aztec, and Toltec archeological sites, its colonial-era missions and cathedrals, and the simple rhythms of peasant life. A wave of expatriate artists and intellectuals found Mexico alive with creative impulses and the location for innovative social reform in landownership, education, and popular art.

The competing northern and southern visions of the Hispanic world in many ways connected to long-standing currents in U.S. international thought. The first accented spread-eagle unilateralism and conquest, a tough, go-it-alone approach to world affairs that in many ways underpinned Washington's antagonism toward Mexico's postrevolutionary government and still resonates in U.S. diplomacy and culture at the turn of the twenty-first century. The second illustrated a vision of soft power and multilateralism that had informed Woodrow Wilson's blueprint for the League of Nations, spurred the creation of interwar peace organizations and the United Nations after the Second World War, and still stirs contemporary discourse on America's place in the larger global village. Many North Americans in fact have blended the two perspectives. Discourses on America's role in the world and the globalizing trends of the twentieth century have by no means been confined to the halls of Congress or State Department offices. They also have found expression in travel literature, postcard writing, fiction, and travel posters.

Ralph Fletcher Seymour, who sailed from New Orleans to the Yucatán port of Progreso, sounded the call of the wild and evoked the pioneer spirit in his 1928 travelogue. "I could not resist the pull of mystery and romance surrounding a country of this nature," he noted. Seymour especially relished the lonesome journey from Progreso to the capital at Mérida and then the ancient Mayan ruins at Chichén Itzá. For the most part, he slept in hammocks, admitting to only two overnight stays at hotels, "and very modest hotels at that." The untamed contours of the land and its thoroughly unmodern Indian population served as the narrative's dominant theme. "The population is as largely Indian as there ever was," Seymour exulted, and the "tropical jungle, like the Indian, is not kind to civilization."[40] Approximately 750 miles to the west, George Hugh Banning scoped out Guadalupe Island off the Baja coast and invoked a similar language of unilateralism and discovery. "I followed Robinson Crusoe and John Silver," he wrote, "to small bodies of land surrounded by so much more than water."[41]

Another would-be buccaneer, John Cudahy, similarly emphasized the Baja's remoteness. "It is an unknown land, untracked country. . . . Precious few trophy hunters have ever crossed its sandy wastes or climbed its rocky, waterless mountains."[42] Adding a large dose of gendered and racial discourse to his narrative, Cudahy heaped praise on antebellum filibusterer William Walker and groused that the conquerer's scheme to annex Lower California as a slave state had been aborted by "antislavery Bolsheviks like Lincoln."[43] Cudahy also proudly toasted the extralegal U.S. presence in the border town of Mexicali: "Old fashioned vice walking the broad day unmolested, financed by American capital and directed by American talent. Old friends before we knew Mr. Volstead's blighting shadow," he editorialized. Historian Amy S. Greenberg has analyzed how nineteenth-century martial ideals of manhood underpinned the U.S.-based filibustering expeditions of the 1850s. Those same swashbuckling traditions certainly remained alive in male travel culture during the 1920s.[44]

Another frontiersman, Harry Carr, lionized Mexico as "the mother of our West" and the source of "our earliest heroes." Gendering Mexico female, he elevated the exploits of its hypermasculine Spanish conquistadors, especially Francisco Vázquez de Coronado, who arrived in the New World via Mexico's west coast in the sixteenth century and extended the Spanish empire north to the present-day United States. Carr retraced the steps of the great conquerors, and his travelogue meditated on his country's history of territorial aggran-dizement. "The charm of exploring this old gateway to the West," he wrote, "is that it remains in many essentials as it was in the past."[45]

Harry L. Foster and his travel buddy, Eustace, visited what was at the time the small West Coast village of Mazatlán. Foster's memoir also assigned Mexico a feminine identity but blended elements of Manifest Destiny and Progressive reform ideology. The two young men claimed to have spent evenings lingering about the town plaza observing the courtship rituals of the single young men and women who promenaded past one another under the watchful eyes of parents and relatives. Foster boasted that he struck up "an accidental engagement" with two "slim girls," Herminia and Lolita, who confidentially complained to the travelers how native traditions restricted their freedom. In one purple passage that must have tantalized readers back home, he described how the two "dark eyed señoritas" had inquired excitedly about "petting parties" and "female freedom" in the north.[46] The author then lamented the inequality under which the local women lived. The average Mexican man, Foster reasoned, had little interest in intellectual companion-ship with his future spouse but desired her solely for "animal sex." "The barriers that surround the girl," Foster surmised, "prove to interested males that others have not been able to reach her."[47]

Although Mexican women had played immensely important roles in the revolution as political activists and *soldaderas*, the modern sexual revolution had not become a feature of rural Mexican female culture by the interwar era. In the countryside, dating and kissing were not practiced, although courtship was beginning to replace arranged marriages. Sociologist Oscar Lewis re-ported in his study of rural Mexico in the 1940s that adolescent girls believed that sexual intercourse was painful and thought that sexual organs were ugly. Women commonly described pregnancy as being "ill with child."[48] Foster nonetheless ended his story with a twist, reporting that after parting ways with Eustace and returning to the United States, he received a letter out of the blue from his old friend with news of the latter's relocation to Mazatlán and marriage to Herminia.[49]

Whether the tale was true, fabricated, or perhaps loosely based on reality, it reflected a North American male's ambivalence toward modern gender con-ventions as well as his sense of racial superiority to Mexican men. The story line allowed male readers to have it both ways: a sense of moral outrage directed at gender inequality in Mexico, couched within a titillating sexual fantasy that featured shy, brown-skinned women. It also allowed U.S. expansionists to marry competing yet complementary colonizing impulses, the drive to acquire and possess and the irrepressible urge to suppress "barbaric" native practices.

Some Lone Eagles even discovered the primitive in Mexico City. Stephen Graham, working on his travelogue in 1922–23, took a room at the downtown Hotel Iturbide and remembered it as clean and pleasant, noting, "By no possibility could we have been shot from the street whilst standing at the window."[50] He found the city inviting by day but "sinister at night." "The underworld of the city is terrible, and no student of life could shut his eyes to it—poverty widespread and staring, a morose, drunken male population, women who suffer more than most women."[51] Despite the stated concern for Mexican womanhood, he inverted the standard gendered language of imperial discourse. "It is difficult to find much feminine beauty among the Aztecs," he recorded. "There is a moment of unearthly beauty, just a moment, in the early teens, and then the Aztec girl goes heavy and repulsive looking, her coal-black hair becomes coarse as a horse's mane, her bosom spreads, dirt gets the better of her body."[52] Still, he labeled Mexico "the most romantic country of the New World" and "a country marked for conquest."[53]

While the muscular rhetoric of Manifest Destiny rang loud and clear in the travel literature of the 1920s, it was joined and increasingly overshadowed by the less aggressive, softer brand of internationalism, often espoused by women travelers. Kristin L. Hoganson has analyzed the important linkages between turn-of-the-century American domesticity and the nation's growing contact with the outside world. Home furnishings, women's fashions, and the commodification of immigrant folk culture signified the growing "global production" of American domesticity. The widespread popularity of middle- and upper-class women's travel clubs and travel tours also spoke of the international sensibilities inherent in U.S. women's culture. A trip beyond the nation's geographic boundaries allowed women to transcend the boundaries of culturally prescribed restraints on female behavior and join their male counterparts in enjoying the fruits of empire. For some women, international travel meant identifying with white privilege and national power. But for others, it offered a tutorial in internationalism.[54]

Clare Sheridan, a British writer, recorded her impressions of Mexico in *My American Diary*, published in New York for a U.S. readership. Her realistic female voice contrasted with the romantic masculinity of Cudahy, Graham, and others. She humorously owned up to her misplaced expectations of finding in Mexico an Eden-like, pastoral paradise. Traveling by train from Veracruz to Mexico City during the summer of 1921, she and two companions arrived late "in a town that is wide-avenued, full of motors, and disappoint-edly civilized." "For people who looked for and hoped for something primi-tive, disordered, and tropical," she confessed, "to find order, dullness and coolness, is ridiculous. [A companion] and I, comparing notes on our expec-tations and realizations, simply laughed."[55]

Well connected and a serious student of Mexico, Sheridan arranged meet-ings with President Obregón and his minister of foreign affairs, Alberto J. Pani, discussing the country's plans for land reform and education, with which she sympathized. At odds with both adventure-seeking male travel writers and Washington's official antagonism toward the Obregón govern-ment, she imagined Mexico as an international compatriot rather than an object of conquest, a partner within an increasingly interconnected world. She also worked to place Mexico's political and economic problems in a larger comparative and historical context. Mexico merited the chance to solve its social ills in its own ways, she observed, and should not be coerced to adopt an agenda imposed by others.

Women tourists by no means monopolized these internationalist im-pulses. George Mertz Slocum, editor of the *Michigan Business Farmer*, left the snow behind in March 1927 to see Mexico on the Third International Tour of the American Agricultural Editors Association. He returned home to write another sympathetic portrait of the southern neighbor. Interwar Michigan, home of isolationist Republican senator Arthur Vandenberg, is often por-trayed as one of the most parochial of states, and numerous historians have depicted Midwest farmers as having been particularly prone to an intolerant and nativist populism.[56] Slocum defied such stereotypes. His group traveled by train, stopping frequently to meet with Mexican farmers, local officials, and even President Calles. Slocum drew parallels between Mexican and U.S. agriculture but resisted the common inclination to view vastly different social conditions through a single, universal lens.

Slocum recalled visiting the town of Aguascalientes, north of Mexico City (not to be confused with the Tijuana resort of Agua Caliente), where he observed working-class women barely subsisting by hand sewing embroi-dery. He seemed haunted by a memory of returning to the dining room of the train that night and eating "Long Island duckling, while hungry faces peered at us from the station platform."[57] He struggled with the issue of land redistribution, so much at variance with the U.S. creed of private property, especially when the Mexican government confiscated land that had been owned and improved by North Americans. Yet he ultimately sided with Mexico's campesinos. "No one who has been to Mexico," he wrote, "can be

Lone Eagles and Revolutionaries | 45

without sympathy for the present government and what they are trying to accomplish in breaking up these gigantic estates."[58] In his generous assessment of both Mexican and U.S. reformers, he described Calles as "Rooseveltian," a man of the people who was willing to meet with North American farmers and entertain their thoughts on Mexico's programs.[59]

The Arts and Letters and Postcards

Sheridan and Slocum were not alone in their rethinking of Mexico. For many Americans, postrevolutionary Mexico, somewhat akin to France after the Great War, held considerable cachet. Historian Helen Delpar has explained that young intellectuals and artists, disaffected by modern war and the provincialism of middle-class U.S. life, found creative inspiration in Mexico. Rustic indigenous songs and dances, "primitive" folk art, and the spontaneity of village life appealed powerfully to the vibrant artist community that settled in Mexico's central valley, including notables Witter Byner, Hart Crane, John Dos Passos, D. H. Lawrence, Mabel Dodge Luhan, and Katherine Anne Porter.[60] Liberal social commentators and academics, including Stuart Chase, Ernest Gruening, and Frank Tannenbaum, wrote approvingly of Mexican reformism. This outspoken contingent of artists, social critics, and travel writers not only showed affinity for Mexico's cultures and communities but also dissented from Ambassador Sheffield's rigid anticommunism. Collectively, they softened the sharp polarization that had characterized U.S.-Mexican relations.

Porter's story is illustrative. In the wake of family discord and broken relationships, the twenty-seven-year-old southern writer drew energy from the Mexican artists she met in New York City after the war and connected emotionally to the idealism of the Mexican Revolution. She abandoned plans to expatriate to Europe in favor of resettling in Obregón's Mexico, which she later described as "the most marvelous, natural, spontaneous experience of my life."[61] In Lone Eagle fashion, she was exhilarated by the element of danger in train travel across Mexico, still plagued by factional fighting and uprisings, and arrived in Mexico City in December 1920 to take up the task of writing articles on the political scene for publication in the United States.[62]

Porter soon grew distant from politics and settled into her fiction writing, interspersed with a great deal of procrastination, socializing with other expats, and even sampling the local marijuana. Her enthusiasm for the Mexican Revolution withered as a consequence of its mixed record of reform and the rise in official corruption.[63] But she maintained a deep admiration for the minister of education, Vasconcelos, and his support for artists and intellectuals who promoted Indian and popular art, "not the bourgeois art of the mid nineteenth century."[64] Among her Mexican friends she counted Diego Rivera, for whom she used to mix paint: "Everyone did—it was the thing to do—go and grind paint for Rivera," she reminisced.[65] In 1921, she worked with the North American–Mexican Institute to arrange the shipment of some eighty thousand objects, including many pre-Columbian pieces, for exhibit in Los Angeles, a project that helped cultivate interest in Mexico and Mexican art north of the border.[66]

In addition to artists, a cadre of leftist and left-leaning journalists and scholars emigrated southward during the interwar years to observe a society in ferment. Tannenbaum, a U.S. specialist on Latin America, first traveled in Mexico in 1922 to collect data on the Mexican labor movement and contribute articles to *The Survey*. A devoted labor activist, he fell in love with Mexico, describing it as "the country of the future. There is no wonderful spot on the face of the globe that can compare with this."[67] Gruening, a former physician and future U.S. senator, famous for casting one of only two dissenting votes against the 1964 Gulf of Tonkin Resolution and President Lyndon Johnson's war plans for Vietnam, ranks as one of the best known of the political pilgrims. He first journeyed to Mexico by steamship in 1922 as the managing editor of the *Nation*. Gruening befriended Presidents Obregón and Calles and wrote favorably, although not uncritically, of their policies in his well-received book, *Mexico and Its Heritage*.[68]

The left-liberal attraction to Mexico grew not only from a fascination with quasi-socialist policies but from a long-standing tradition of U.S. anti-imperialism. In 1916, a group of missionaries, academics, and activists under the leadership of Samuel Guy Inman, perhaps the nation's leading scholar of Latin American history and culture, had organized the Committee on Cultural Cooperation with Latin America. The committee dedicated its early years to opposing U.S. military intervention in Mexico's revolution. During the interwar era, the group embraced the cause of international cooperation and advocated greater economic equality and cultural exchange between the two neighbors. In the 1930s, Inman became an adviser to Secretary of State Cordell Hull on hemispheric affairs.[69]

The cast of North Americans who championed cultural exchange with Mexico also included Hubert C. Herring, a graduate of the Union Theological Seminary and a leading interpreter of Mexican society and history. Herring and several fellow clergymen traveled to Mexico in 1926 and initiated what proved to be a long series of annual summer seminars at the National

University in Mexico City. The three-week colloquia typically included lectures on Mexican history, culture, and society; meetings with Mexican officials, religious leaders, artists, and intellectuals; and excursions to points of interest outside the city. A long list of binational notables participated in these seminars as either students or instructors, among them Herbert Croly, John Dewey, Rivera, and Tannenbaum. By the end of the 1920s, the seminar attracted close to two hundred participants annually.[70]

During the interwar era, numerous Mexican artists, performers, and intellectuals also journeyed to the United States, where they enjoyed an environment conducive to free expression. Poet José Juan Tablada, artist Miguel Covarrubias, and composer Julián Carrillo ranked among the many illustrious Mexican artists and performers to achieve notoriety in New York as that city gained prominence as an international cultural center. Art shows such as the one organized by Porter and a much larger 1930 exhibit sponsored by the Carnegie Foundation at New York's Metropolitan Museum of Art exposed North American audiences to modern Mexican art with its aesthetic and social importance grounded in the folk culture of the revolutionary era. The Carnegie collection included more than three hundred pieces, including paintings by twenty-four leading painters, among them Rivera, Orozco, and Siqueiros.[71]

In addition to the artists and intellectuals, ordinary voices from Middle America contributed to the discourse on Mexico. They transmitted their observances, thoughts, and meditations not via published novels and political tracts but by a modern means of communication known as the picture postcard, an invention of the late nineteenth century. The number of these artifacts left behind is small, and the writings are often hurried and cryptic, yet they demonstrate that Mexico's place in the North American imagination derived from the observations and insights of middle-class travelers who hailed from the likes of Michigan, Indiana, Oregon, and California as well as eastern universities and art galleries. The senders and the recipients alike have remained anonymous in the history of U.S. foreign relations yet merit recognition as significant international actors.

Some postcard messages reeked of ethnocentrism. One correspondent put a photo of quaint, traditionally dressed, street vendors in the mail, but her written annotation highlighted the annoying noises that she associated with the local street life. Early that morning, she complained, an army regiment had paraded down the street on which their hotel was situated. "Then, all the dogs—barking—for hours. . . . Never know what next. Queer."[72] Another tourist sent along a picture postcard of a peasant "vendadore de petates" (mattress vendor, actually selling woven mats), observing, "Here's a fine looking man tempting you to purchase this flamboyant '*patete*,'—a mattress without the Simmons Approval, but a mattress nevertheless to these Indians."[73] Another correspondent chose a photo of a young mother and her children in front of their straw house to represent Mexico, remarking, "This is a typical habitation when they don't live in caves or roll upon the ground anywhere."[74]

Yet in most cases, postcard storytellers relished Mexico's premodern ambience and spoke in a vein similar to that of better-known internationalists. Such photographic images as tall, candelabra cacti, homely looking burros, young women in colorful dresses and lace, and straw huts increasingly symbolized Mexico in the North American mind.[75] One female traveler in April 1925 sent home a colorized photo of a *mercado* (marketplace) in the small city of Colima in the central-western state of Jalisco, explaining the barter system, praising the artistry of the products on sale, and savoring the "delicious enchiladas."[76] Another wanderer sent a postcard depicting a Mexican man in sombrero laboring in a village pottery shop. The didactic explorer explained, "This is a bit of a huge pottery factory and this man is packing up bowls and other useful articles in straw and crude crates and soon they will be moving to open markets on the backs of Indians and burros. . . . It is all very primitive but they make beautiful and useful things."[77]

Many tourists considered a visit to the mountains of the central cordillera to rank among the ultimate experiences. A couple from Fort Wayne, Indiana, sent a postcard that featured a simple rural village situated under the shadow of the eighteen-thousand-foot Orizaba peak. "This is certainly different," they scribbled to fellow Hoosiers Bill and Lucille; "we went through the tropics today with plenty heat, but having a delightful trip and making good time."[78] The southern state of Michoacán, with its indigenous Tarascan population, provided Lone Eagles with another favorite retreat. A Californian sent home a photo of a campesino and his burros and scribbled, "Having a good trip down here where everyday is bright and sunny, and time takes its time."[79] Tourists raved about the capital city of Morelia, with its narrow cobble-paved streets and Indian markets. The picturesque lake at nearby Pátzcuaro, a sleepy little mountain town of eight thousand, also won accolades.[80]

The internationalist vanguard that ventured into Mexico's hinterland played an important role in U.S.-Mexican cultural relations. By the mid-1920s, the multilateralists, who disdained the language of confrontation and conquest, had begun profoundly to influence U.S. cultural discourses on Mexico. Their idealized interpretations of village life and their optimistic

This postcard showcases a quaint rural village in the gulf state of Veracruz, ca. 1925. Orizaba Peak (Citlaltépetl in the native Nahuatl language) looms in the background. The base of the dormant volcano lies in a lush, tropical setting, while the peak, eighteen thousand feet above sea level, is encased in ice. DeGolyer Library, Southern Methodist University, Dallas, Texas, AG2000.1370.1.

readings of the revolution often fell short of accuracy. But their tolerance of difference and their sympathy for Mexico provided a strong counterweight to the harsh intolerance voiced by Ambassador Sheffield, Mencken, and the angry community of recently dispossessed U.S. property owners. The new postrevolutionary state and its private sector allies, moreover, discovered in the new imperial discourse a marketing tool to propel Mexico more fully into the age of mass tourism and a mechanism for displaying and disseminating a reinterpretation of historical memory and national identity.

Tourism and Transnational Interest Groups

Backstage of Mexico's authentic, remote settings, an array of individuals and transnational interest groups coalesced. To be sure, Mexico's tourism infrastructure suffered from numerous shortcomings during the 1920s. The country's travel industry during the Porfiriato had catered to a small number of upper-crust tourists and business travelers drawn mainly from Europe and North America. The tourist infrastructure had hinged on foreign investment, primarily small-scale, often family-run European concerns, a far cry from the requirements of mass tourism. Modern hotels remained in short supply, even in Mexico City, and many potential destinations still lay beyond reach of roads and trains. The country also suffered more than its share of bad press. Many leading U.S. newspapers continued to amplify Ambassador Sheffield's take on Mexico's drift toward leftism and dictatorship. When opponents of the constitution's anticlerical provisions organized an armed uprising, the Cristero Rebellion, from 1925 to 1928, the new government faced yet another serious challenge to its survival. Factional fighting, government repression of armed pro-Catholic forces, and a spike in banditry encouraged cautious Yankees to stay home.

Developers and promoters nonetheless pressed ahead, determined to ease the fear and burden of travel without overpolishing Mexico's rough-hewn finish. The largest and most effective spokespersons for Mexican tourism consisted of the network of U.S.-owned railroad companies that had first won entry to Mexico during the Porfiriato. As early as 1908, brochures distributed by the St. Louis–based Missouri Pacific Railroad spoke to the North American thirst for international adventure while highlighting the ease and efficiency of modern travel with the slogan "Mexico, a foreign land a step away."[81] The revolution dampened the impact of the ill-timed ad campaign, but by the early 1920s the Missouri-Pacific was back at it, popularizing the southern neighbor as "a land of contrasts, a land of surprises."[82]

The Missouri Pacific's Sunshine Special established itself as the premier link between the two countries. It transported many a Lone Eagle from St. Louis to Mexico City in sixty-two hours, passing through connecting points at Little Rock, Austin, and San Antonio before reaching the border at Laredo, Texas. Along the way, passengers experienced the wonderment of a modern cultural corridor: air-cooled temperatures, U.S.-style soda fountains, and living-room-like Pullman cars. From Nuevo Laredo, across the border, travelers hopped aboard a National Railways of Mexico train, operated by the Mexican government, and sped across the northern desert to the industrial city of Monterrey, climbed 3,478 feet in sixty-seven miles through the city of Saltillo, and reached a peak altitude of 9,000 feet at the village of Carneros. "Persons from the lower countries are greatly benefited by going to Mexico, owing to a decided change in the functions of the lungs," the railroad informed its patrons; "the decreased atmospheric pressure causes an expansion of the lungs and a more vigorous heart action."[83]

Following its completion in April 1927, the Southern Pacific railroad provided a popular route down the California coast from Los Angeles, east to Tucson, across the border to Nogales, south along Mexico's Pacific shore to

Mazatlán and Guadalajara, and then inland to Mexico City, a total of 1,101 miles of standard-gauge track.[84] "In Mexico," one Southern Pacific ad declared, "every stop is a fiesta."[85] "Millions of Americans know Europe," read another advertisement, "but relatively few realize that their southern neighbor affords a rich field of interest and pleasure, different from anything seen before."[86]

The National Railways of Mexico and the Mexican Railway also fed the tourist trade, not only transporting Yankees to Mexico but connecting them to attractions within the country.[87] The two systems had been consolidated at the end of the Porfiriato and nominally nationalized, though the U.S. firms that had established the network received generous compensation and maintained a controlling interest over large sections of line.[88] The system would not be fully nationalized until the 1930s. In the meantime, the Calles administration (1924–28) concentrated on restoring and modernizing rail stock and cars. In 1925, the Mexican government contracted with General Electric to electrify the popular Mexican Railroad from Veracruz (on the country's east coast) to Mexico City, making it the republic's first electrified railroad.[89]

The government's drive to develop an efficient rail system arose primarily from its aim to industrialize Mexico's economy, but the nation's leaders also coveted the touristic revenue stream. One early-1920s National Railways guide highlighted the nation's readiness for foreign visitors, calling attention to the presence of modern hotels and tourist-friendly restaurants in Mexico City, the excavation and restoration of pre-Columbian ruins at Teotihuacán (just north of the capital), and the thrills to be had at Sunday-afternoon bullfights at Mexico City's Plaza de los Torros, "the equivalent to American baseball in cultural appeal."[90]

In the fall of 1925, the Missouri-Pacific teamed up with its Mexican railway partners to sponsor a two-week Mexican excursion for members of the American Association of Traveling Passenger Agents. The junket coincided with the organization's forty-ninth annual convention in Mexico City. Intent on selling Mexico as a vacation destination, the convention booklet waxed ecstatic about the country's "sunshine and flowers, its animated life and romantic people, its grand cathedrals and ancient ruins." "Mexico," promoters boasted, "is more charming than Europe, more picturesque than the Old World, more beautiful than the gardens of the Orient."[91]

The group's first official meeting took place in Monterrey at the Casino de Monterrey, complete with a luncheon, compliments of the city's chamber of commerce. The party then chugged across the mountains, stopping briefly at the future tourist and expat retreat at San Miguel d'Allende, "interesting for its beautiful gardens and notable for the fine Gothic Cathedral," before attending a reception at the state governor's palace at Guadalajara. The highlight of the trip centered on a whirlwind of activities in Mexico City, including meetings and luncheons with government representatives and chamber of commerce officers and a dinner paid for by the Montecuma Brewery.[92]

While rail ranked as the most popular mode of mass transportation to Mexico, other cultural corridors also served the traveling public. Cruise ships remained a favorite for those with a taste—and the pocketbook—for relaxation and luxury. The New York and Cuba Mail Steamship Company's Ward Line sailed from New York City to the port of Progreso in the Yucatán, a four-day journey. Visitors might then journey to nearby Mérida, the state capital graced by colonial architecture and stately mansions built from the profits of henequen trade. From there, travelers could choose a trip to the Mayan ruins at Chichén Itzá and Uxmal or push east to Veracruz, from which most caught the train to Mexico City. The Standard Fruit and Steamship Company, popularly known as the Vaccaro Line, made weekly runs from New Orleans to Veracruz, a trip that took two days. The Grace Line sailed from New York to the Gulf Coast and San Francisco to Mazatlán. Regardless of itinerary, all the vessels offered a tropical voyage, complete with fine dining and dancing, luxury cabins, and evening strolls along the Promenade Deck.[93]

Automobile travel through Mexico flourished in the latter half of the 1930s, after the Laredo-to–Mexico City highway, also known as the Pan-American Highway, had been completed. During the 1920s, a road trip to Mexico usually ended just a few hours across the border in a parking space outside a bar or casino.[94] But a handful of Lone Eagles outfitted their automobiles for backcountry conditions and rumbled deep into Mexico. Among the more eccentric was Baltimore's F. Morrison Boyd. In addition to selling plumbing supplies, Boyd contracted with the Michigan Automobile Association as a "motor scout" to explore road trips for members. Between 1922 and 1926, he, his wife, and their pet dog traversed North America from Mexico to Alaska in their specially designed Maxwell coupe with a Chrysler motor. The vehicle's three custom-made trunks stored not only the couples' clothes but a supply of replacement car parts and lubricants.

Boyd sought neither conquest nor possession, but his commentary often spoke to unflattering stereotypes of Mexico as an unruly frontier populated by primitives. Although he reported that banditry had declined in recent years, he drove across the country with a used coffin sticking out of his car's jump seat, a precaution, he said, to ward off superstitious desperados, who "would not come near a corpse if it was humanly possible to avoid doing so." His colorful exploits received press coverage throughout the United States.[95]

At the same time, the Mexican government worked to hack out a modern road system. In 1925, the Calles administration established the Mexican National Highway Commission and launched a massive road-building project that promised to buttress internal economic development and create an interlocking system of tourist destinations. By 1930, the commission had expanded the country's 90 miles of all-season roads to more than 750 miles of either surfaced or paved byways. The effort concentrated on four principal highways. Two ran coast to coast. The southern route connected the Pacific port of Acapulco, a sleepy little fishing village at the time, to Mexico City and the gulf city of Veracruz. The northern route linked the Pacific port of Mazatlán to Matamoras on the gulf. Two other roadways cut north to south, including the beginning of what would become within a decade's time the Pan-American Highway.

For a country with an area of 762,000 square miles, the bare-bones highway infrastructure still left much of the nation isolated, and even many of the improved roadways suffered from steep grades, potholes, and rock slides.[96] But the network had begun to tie together much of the central Mexican valley, facilitating the formation of a tourist district in the heart of the country. Ford-loving Yankees driving out of Mexico City could easily access the capital's suburbs to view the floating gardens of Xochimilco, a remnant of the Aztec canal system, or visit Guadalupe Hidalgo and the shrine of the Virgin of Guadalupe, where an apparition only ten years following the Spanish conquest inspired Mexico's most fervent religious cult. Curious travelers could also sail south along the highway to the old cathedral-filled colonial capital of Puebla, travel west to the mountain retreat of Cuernavaca, and follow the descending sun to the arms of Acapulco.

Tourism, Government, and Identity Formation

Government road projects and rail modernization facilitated tourist travel to and within Mexico, but both came as spin-offs from initiatives designed primarily to promote other postrevolutionary objectives—namely, industrial development and nation building. Private transnational interest groups— railroad companies, chambers of commerce, artists, philanthropic organizations, and automobile enthusiasts—rather than the Mexican government rated as the most active promoters of the travel industry during the 1920s. But the central government in Mexico City took its first tentative steps toward more active engagement in tourism promotion, setting the stage for more vigorous government sponsorship in the 1930s.

The development of historical and cultural tourist attractions stood as the central state's most significant contribution. Restoration and display of pre-Columbian sites not only attracted tourist revenue but also addressed Mexico's quest for a postrevolutionary national identity through the celebration of indigenous cultures. The interwar era represented a golden age of sorts in Mexican archeology, when government and private interests combined to recover and restore renowned pre-Spanish Indian cities at Teotihuacán (in central Mexico), Chichén Itzá (in the Yucatán), and Monte Albán (in the southern state of Oaxaca).

The heritage projects also assisted U.S. identity formation. North American fascination with Mexico's ancient artifacts reflected an ongoing tendency to exoticize and Orientalize the non-European "other." But it also embodied the spirit of internationalism, the yearning to learn of other peoples and civilizations, to place modern societies in context, and to locate the United States in world history. The discovery of Aztec and Mayan Mexico coincided with the wave of U.S. publicity for the 1922 discovery of the tomb of the child king, Tutankhamen, in Egypt.[97] The exaltation of the distant past also eased adaptation to modern consumerism, another key impulse that drove mass tourism. Visiting archeological sites in Mexico—or, for that matter, the pueblos of Taos, New Mexico; the medieval cathedrals of France; and countless other tourist treats—could be counted as self-improvement rather than indulgence and facilitated the shift from a Protestant ethos of self-denial to a consumer ideal of self-fulfillment.[98]

Nor did the tourist's taste for the elemental and the authentic conflict with the secularized and scientific values of the modern age. Sociologist Dean MacCannell has explained that "the best indication of the final victory of modernity over other sociocultural arrangements is not the disappearance of the nonmodern world, but its artificial preservation and reconstruction in modern society." The maintenance of a reconstructed past and the elevation of rural settings to "vacation getaway" status created entertaining diversions, or a set of "modern playthings" that reaffirmed rather than denied the forward march of progress.[99]

The restoration of the pre-Aztec city at Teotihuacán ranked as Mexico City's premier project. Located about thirty miles north of the city, the site's main attractions included the acclaimed Pyramids of the Sun and the Moon, the former some 215 feet in height and 735 feet along the base and a favorite

Yankees gather around the Adosado Platform at the pre-Aztec site of Teotihuacán, just north of Mexico City, and observe a reenactment of an ancient native dance, ca. 1925. The temple of Quetzalcoatl, the plumed serpent, god of wind and dawn, can be seen to the right, behind the performance. Victor A. Blenkle Postcard Collection, Archives Center, National Museum of American History, Behring Center, Smithsonian Institution, Washington, D.C.

tourist climb. Running down the middle of a series of ancient tombs, the haunting Avenue of the Dead led to the Temple of Quetzalcoatl, the mythical plumed serpent and symbol of Mexico's ancient past. Published travel guides and magazine articles marveled at the city's mysterious origins, predating the presence of Aztec and earlier Toltec tribes. Archeologists agree that the community rose to preeminence contemporaneously with the Roman empire, roughly 200 B.C. through 600 A.D. But in the absence of written records, little is known of its origins or demise. As with the ancient Egyptian pyramids at Giza, interwar commentators speculated at the skill, technology, and human muscle that made construction possible. The origins of the structures at Teotihuacán were "buried in the remote past," one travel guide noted, "and the traditions referring to them throw but scant light on their history or of the people who erected them."[100]

While curious North Americans utilized the site to position themselves in the context of modern global change, the Mexican government juggled cultural, financial, and social objectives. At the direction of Dr. Manlio Gamio, a Columbia University–trained anthropologist and head of the Mexican Bureau of Anthropology, the project's staff undertook a sweeping study of the area's indigenous culture. A champion of rural reform and national uplift,

Gamio won presidential authorization to use tourist revenue to found a school based on what he called "integral education." The school featured instruction in diet and hygiene, a prenatal clinic, training in agricultural techniques, and the teaching of recovered indigenous arts and crafts traditions.[101] Gamio collaborated with *teotihuacanos*, the local inhabitants, to develop a highly saleable style of pottery based on native designs but altered for improved durability and enhanced appearance. Like the staging of regional folk plays, the pottery sales can be interpreted as a crass commodification of local traditions, yet they also empowered the local population and transferred consumer dollars from the empire's metropole to a needy indigenous community.[102]

Gamio lobbied the Calles administration for a larger nationwide program, but the president appointed his campaign manager, Dr. José Manuel Puig, as secretary of education and designated Gamio as subsecretary. Five months later, the administration eliminated Gamio's position altogether.[103] Despite the political infighting, government development of premodern sites continued. In 1923, Mexican authorities joined with the Carnegie Foundation to establish a field station at Chichén Itzá, a fifteen-hundred-year-old Mayan/ Toltec city. British explorers John L. Stephens and Frederick Catherwood, who explored the region in the 1840s, had been the first foreign travelers to describe the spectacular ruins to European and American audiences. A string of archeological projects followed, including the dredging of the ancient sacred cenote (a natural underground elliptical well used for human sacrifice ceremonies). In violation of Mexican law, precious stones, pottery, and other valuables from the well wound up at Harvard University's Peabody Museum.[104]

The Carnegie Foundation project sprang from the imagination of a young Harvard-trained archeologist, Sylvanus G. Morley. Prior to the opening of diplomatic relations with the United States, the Obregón administration embraced the partnership, partly as a result of Morley's public assurances that no objects would be spirited away to the United States. Chichén Itzá's famed El Castillo pyramid (also known as the pyramid of Mayan deity Kukúlcan), the Temple of the Warriors, the Nunnery, the Ball Court, and the oddly modern-looking Observatory, today viewed by thousands daily, stood enshrouded in mounds of soil and tropical greenery when the Carnegie team launched its work. Indeed, the site appeared on the itineraries of only the most dedicated Lone Eagles, willing to stay overnight in Mérida and travel 140 kilometers by train to a nearby town and then hire an automobile to drive the rest of the way. Morley and associates cleared away the brush and painstakingly restored deteriorated structures. A well-connected local entrepreneur, Fernando Barbachano Peón, lobbied the Yucatán state government to develop roads to the remote location. State officials supplied the pavement, and Barbachano Peón, followed by his sons, built an empire of hotels that today extends to the megaresort of Cancún. By the early 1930s, Chichén Itzá began to swell with tourists who marveled at the architecture's mathematic precision, the alignment of many structures with astronomical cycles, and the ancient meaning of sport and ritual.[105]

The government's role in tourism expanded only marginally beyond historic preservation during the 1920s. In July 1928, President Emilio Portes Gil established the Mixed Pro-Tourism Commission, the country's first government-led tourism planning board. The initiative, however, came at an inauspicious moment. After amending the 1917 constitution to allow presidential reelection, Obregón, a national hero, stomped his opponent, Vasconcelos, in the 1928 election. But the assassination of the president-elect by a *Vasconcelista* threatened the nation with chaos. Acting as power broker, President Calles stepped in and appointed Portes Gil to lead a caretaker government until new elections could be held.

Historian Dina Berger has examined Portes Gil's mixed public-private partnership in depth. Much of the initial activity centered in the offices of the Bank of Mexico, which established its own tourist bureau and dipped into public funds to produce attractive travel brochures and other promotional materials. Several new private associations augmented the government's promotional campaign, including the U.S.-based Mexican American Automobile Association, founded in 1929 and later renamed the Mexican Automobile Association, and the Mexican Tourist Association, a coalition of U.S. transport companies headquartered in New York.[106]

The government initiative, however, suffered from duplication, disorganization, and a dearth of funds.[107] The most important policy departure came when the president instructed border officials to reduce the red tape and shorten the prolonged process of baggage inspection that frequently entangled travelers crossing the border. U.S. tourists were no longer required to present passports but allowed entry with tourist cards, valid for six months.[108] The loosening of restrictions coincided with the passage of legislation that allowed the federal government to track entry and exit through the country's borders and designated for the first time a category for foreign tourists. The head count still excluded most border crossers but nonetheless detected the trend, recording increases from 12,586 in 1928 to 13,892 in 1929 to 23,769 in 1930.[109]

For Mexicans—at least those in government and those associated with the budding travel industry—tourism presented a series of opportunities. Elevating the country's Indian identity allowed political leaders to pay reverence to the revolution's strong anticolonial impulses, advance rural reform, and generate revenues to revitalize the country's commerce and pursue state-guided industrialization. Finally, tourism gave Mexicans a chance to establish their presence, trumpet their proud past to others, and begin to alter North American preconceptions of the less affluent neighbor. As organized labor's protest against tourist power in Tijuana earlier in the decade had also demonstrated, Mexicans were gradually learning that hosts as well as visitors held bargaining power.

Tourist Soft Power and U.S. Diplomacy

While U.S. tourists and Mexican hosts engaged in increasingly friendly interactions, their governments made little progress toward a resolution of the highly charged diplomatic controversies of the era. Following the failure of the Bucareli Accords, the Calles government and its successors continued to seize U.S.-owned private property, especially in regions close to coastlines and the border, citing both agrarian reform and national security as rationales.[110] President Calles also continued to press the clerical issue by deporting dissident clergy, intruding on the church's health and education programs, and adopting a hard line against the proclergy Cristero insurgency.

Despite the radical posturing, Calles wanted improved relations with United States and better access to U.S. investment resources. By the late 1920s, Mexico's revolutionary elite had grown increasingly disenchanted with the Soviet Union, whose Mexico City embassy had clumsily interfered in the country's volatile labor politics. In Washington, the probusiness Coolidge administration, prodded by congressional critics of Ambassador Sheffield's confrontational tactics, came to view Calles as a willing partner in reconciliation.[111] If any U.S. diplomat possessed the ability to mend fences, it was newly appointed ambassador Dwight W. Morrow. Morrow maintained a close friendship not only with President Coolidge but also, and probably more important, with his former associates at J. P. Morgan, the banking and investment firm that managed the portfolios of U.S. investors with a stake in prerevolutionary Mexico. After arriving in Mexico City in September 1927, Morrow went out of his way to assure the Calles government and the Mexican press of his good intentions. In addition to planning the Lindbergh spectacle, he helped inaugurate Mexico's new U.S.-installed telephone system and arranged a congratulatory call from Coolidge to Calles. The new communications systems not only connected U.S.

and Mexican diplomats but also ultimately became an important tool of the travel industry and other commercial endeavors.[112] Morrow deescalated the war of words, pledged to seek loan assistance for Mexico's struggling economy, and established a warm rapport with Calles. Morrow, who spoke Spanish, even gained occasional invitations to the Mexican leader's ranch, twenty miles outside of the capital city.[113]

Despite his personal efforts, Morrow's concrete accomplishments remained few. He played an instrumental role in persuading Calles that his war with the church undercut Mexico's political and economic stability. After the Mexican army had worn the rebels down, the ambassador played go-between in brokering the end of the Cristero Rebellion.[114] But resolution of more difficult property and debt issues proved elusive. Mexico remained badly in need of financial aid, but prior to the creation of the Bretton Woods system of publicly financed multilateral banking after the Second World War, Washington relied on private bankers, especially J. P. Morgan, to assist capitalism abroad. The doctrine of dollar diplomacy, first implemented at the turn of the century, was based on the premise that Latin American leaders lacked the manly discipline to manage their economies and dictated conservative lending policies that attached numerous strings to U.S. loans. Morrow's old associate, Thomas Lamont, head of J. P. Morgan and chair of the International Commission of Bankers on Mexico, intended to use any loan arrangement as leverage to make Mexico pay generous compensation to former U.S. property owners and insisted that Mexico make good on its Porfiriato-era debt of roughly $1.5 million. Morrow, who had hoped to arrange for loans on a more liberal basis prior to a settlement of outstanding disputes, was stymied.[115]

The ambassador, however, possessed one innovative diplomatic card—tourism. Christopher Endy's study of tourism in Cold War France emphasizes how U.S. foreign aid assisted France's travel industry and strengthened Franco-American political relations. In interwar Mexico, the U.S. embassy's promotion of tourism worked differently. The arrangements remained informal, contingent on the ambassador's initiative and support from private interests rather than official foreign aid.

Like the best-selling travel narratives of the age, Morrow sprinkled his public speeches—before business groups, college commencements, and private philanthropic organizations—with allusions to Mexico's ambience. "It is a very beautiful place and they are a remarkable people," he told a London audience. "They are in the household industry stage, it is almost like turning back one's history three or four hundred years and seeing how we lived then. . . . They make rugs on looms which they have constructed themselves, and they use old vegetable dyes. . . . They make wonderful pottery, not for sale but for use." Abandoning his predecessor's contempt for revolutionary change, he also underscored Mexico's vision of the future: "It is a lovely country and a lovely climate and a lovely people who are struggling with modern civilization four hundred years behind the times, and you cannot live down there without getting a tremendous feeling that they are entitled to a chance."[116]

In early December 1927, just two weeks before the Lindbergh extravaganza, President Calles invited Morrow to join him for a railway tour across Mexico's northlands, the country's most heavily touristed region. Never one to downplay the soft power of public relations or to dismiss the importance of tourist relations, Morrow invited comedian Will Rogers to join the entourage. Rogers described the trip in a series of articles in the *Saturday Evening Post*, telling readers that he had come to Mexico to "enjoy the people and the Country and get some real Chili con Carne and Tamales, see the Mexican Ropers—the best in the world—see the Señoritas dance, and mebbe, if fortunate, see 'em shoot a Presidential Candidate." He balanced his political barbs with lavish praise for the country's tourist attractions and endorsement of Calles's agricultural and legal reforms.[117]

Morrow's purchase of a country retreat in Cuernavaca, the capital city of the state of Morelos, located about two hours' drive southwest of Mexico City, also boosted the country's image. Cuernavaca, today a major metropolitan center, was at the time a small town of seven thousand inhabitants, known for its year-round temperate climate, its poinsettia-filled gardens, the summer palace of conquistador Hernán Cortés, and the American-owned Casino de la Selva. Dwight and Elizabeth Morrow hired a local artisan to build a home based on photographs of Spanish architecture. The couple then commissioned a U.S. expatriate and self-trained expert on Mexican crafts, William Spratling, to furnish the home with collectible pottery, handwoven textiles, and jars.[118]

With the help of a ten-thousand-dollar commission, Morrow even persuaded Diego Rivera, the celebrated painter of Marx, Engels, and Lenin, to paint a mural for the front portico of the Cortés Palacio.[119] Spratling joined Morrow's secretary, Allen Dawson, as interpreter, accompanying Rivera, who dressed in a sharkskin suit and sported a revolver, to the ambassador's residence for tea.[120] The completed mural panels, a visual survey of Mexican history from conquest through the revolution, did not compromise Rivera's Marxism. One panel portrayed the notorious Spanish conquistador subduing the Aztecs, and a second glorified the rural hero of Morelos, Emiliano

Zapata, and the cause of land reform.[121] Cuernavaca soon became a favorite North American haunt. U.S. visitors who took in the Palacio gained a pictorial lesson in revisionist Mexican history.

By the time tourism showed signs of surging late in the decade, the bitter discord in U.S.-Mexican relations mysteriously trailed off. Although multiple long-standing disputes remained unresolved, the two governments had abandoned the confrontational tactics of the past. More often than not, U.S. and Mexican officials simply agreed to disagree. At the same time, cross-border transportation systems expanded, the significance of geographic distance to both travel and diplomacy eroded, and growing numbers of U.S. and Mexican citizens met each other on a daily basis inside Mexico's proliferating tourist districts.

Throughout the 1920s, the United States and Mexico failed to resolve the nagging economic and political disagreements that had arisen out of Mexico's revolution. From a realpolitik perspective, the two states pursued strikingly different interests: Mexico asserted its nationalist power, while the United States sought to uphold its hemispheric hegemony. Mexico worked to address the problems of rural poverty, health, and education while forging an industrial base, whereas the United States vigorously defended the sanctity of private property and denied Mexico badly needed financial assistance.

Yet the acrimony that had been so apparent during the revolutionary and early postrevolutionary years—the U.S. military interventions under Woodrow Wilson, Wall Street's financial threats, and Calles's aggravating anticlericalism—slowly and almost imperceptibly gave way to quiet diplomacy. Morrow's determined effort to put a new face on U.S. relations with Mexico, along with his innovative exercise of cultural diplomacy, undoubtedly improved the climate. Calles's relatively conservative orientation, his slowing of agrarian reform and emphasis on private investment, qualifies as another factor. But the reversal of almost two decades of animosity begs for additional explanation.

Tourism's soft powers by no means single-handedly caused the modest U.S.-Mexican rapprochement, but the growing cultural and consumer interaction inherent to travel brought the two nations closer together culturally. By the close of the decade, the neighbors found themselves connected by modern cultural corridors, a growing roster of transnational interest groups, and a set of cultural discourses that had begun to change the way North Americans thought of Mexico as well as the way North Americans perceived their place in world affairs. Mexican hosts at the same time had discovered new ways to establish and assert their power.

Cultural discourses rarely undergo sudden and thorough transformation. Popular pressure had rearranged employment practices in Tijuana, but rowdies still filled border-town saloons and bordellos on most weekends, and the ritualistic reenactment of Wild West myths continued unabated. North of the border, Mexican immigrants and Mexican Americans continued to suffer frequent poverty, hardship, and venomous racial hatred in the cultural contact zones of the United States. And many travel writers continued to spin out discourses that reinforced long-standing stereotypes of Mexico as a land of male depravity, female vulnerability, and racial and civilizational backwardness.

The growing collection of tourists, hosts, travel writers, railroad companies, and pressure groups that drove the travel industry, however, complicated U.S.-Mexican cultural relations. Growing numbers of northern visitors gained exposure to Mexico's illustrious past and its aspirations for the future. Many had begun to imagine themselves as international collaborators rather than conquerors, and they changed the policymaking context in subtle ways. The increased cultural interaction of the 1920s enhanced each side's ability to endure disagreements, wait out petty irritations, and seek solutions through diplomatic channels rather than public ultimatums. The incremental shift in cultural discourse did not constitute the kind of epic-inspiring upheaval that usually catches the diplomatic historian's eye. It did not result in a sudden diplomatic realignment, a bold power play, or the collapse of an empire. But U.S.-Mexican relations had entered an era of good neighborliness years before Franklin Roosevelt used the phrase to define his policy toward Latin America.

It remained to be seen how long the neighborliness might last and how far it might extend. At the end of the decade, Stuart Chase, a leftist social commentator, undertook a five-month visit to Mexico to study its rural folkways and write a book accessible to the general reading public. The result was *Mexico: A Study of Two Americas*, published in 1931, at the onset of the Great Depression. The heart of the book involved a comparison of the village of Tepoztlán, just north of Mexico City, and the industrialized community of Muncie, Indiana, immortalized by Robert and Helen Lynd in their 1929 classic, *Middletown: A Study in Modern American Culture*. Like many Progressive writers of the era, Chase expressed personal alienation from capitalist modernity and disparaged the soulless routine of mechanized existence in the industrialized north. In contrast, he lauded Tepoztlán's "machineless men," their handcrafts, their vibrant fiestas, and the timelessness of the village way of life. "Time is measured by sun and climate, not by clocks," he rhapsodized.[122]

Like many discerning travelers, he used harsh words to describe fellow tourists: "They do not like Mexican hotels, and their conversation turns mainly on indignities suffered therein; that and their customs greviances."[123] Worst of all, he predicted, with the completion of the Pan-American Highway in coming years, their numbers would multiply. "Clouds of Buicks, swarms of Dodges, shoals of Chevrolets—mark my words, they will come."[124] The age of mass tourism had already descended on Mexico when Chase penned his premonition, but modern mass tourism creates its own momentum. Once the travel corridors were in place, word was bound to spread, and the trickle of Lone Eagles soon became an unstoppable, cascading current.

TWO

Containment and Good Neighbors

Tourism and Empire in 1930s Mexico

The banquet room of the swank Hotel Regis did not seem a likely place for talk of war in early 1934. For the gathering of California businessmen and their spouses, the trip to sunny Mexico City provided relief from the dreary February cold that had gripped the homeland. The Mexicans present, mainly city officials, had greeted the visitors warmly, eager, no doubt, to lure more Yankees southward for their dollars. Thus, the luncheon speaker, State Senator Ralph H. Clock of Los Angeles, took his audience by surprise when he turned to the subject of military history and in blunt language recounted the valor of U.S. servicemen who had stormed the heights of Chapultepec Hill during the Mexican-American War of the 1840s. "We whipped" the Mexicans, the visiting politician exclaimed, "and made them like it!"[1]

The next day's *La Prensa*, a leading daily newspaper, characterized the address as lacking "the most elementary courtesy." Most of the Mexicans present, including Mexico City's chief of police, had walked out of the room in protest, as did a few embarrassed North Americans. The U.S. ambassador, Josephus Daniels, wasted no time investigating. Talking to a reporter from his hometown *Los Angeles Times*, Clock denied having made such statements, but Daniels's contacts testified otherwise. The ambassador gained assurances from most Mexican newspapers that they viewed the slight as an isolated incident and would not report it. As an additional safeguard against unwanted publicity, the U.S. embassy obtained a statement on behalf of eighty of the visiting Californians that expressed their collective regret and apology for the senator's "ill-spoken words."[2]

"Why will some Americans leave their manners, if they have any, at home when they go abroad?," Daniels wrote to President Franklin Roosevelt. "I have had little trouble with Americans here," he told FDR; "nearly all are high-class people who deport themselves in a way to cause respect for our country-men."[3] Still, the incident was actually not at all isolated, and it is revealing for a number of reasons. First, Clock's jeremiad demonstrated that the tourist's power, although soft, often manifests itself in very public and embarrassing spats. Second, despite their position of relative weakness within the empire and their need for revenue, hosts are unlikely to tolerate overt cultural slights. Third, Daniels's feverish activity to squelch the story illustrates that U.S. diplomats recognized early in the history of mass tourism that travelers could as easily be diplomatic liabilities as assets and that visitor-host encounters had emerged as an important element of bilateral relationships.

The challenges grew with each passing year. Despite the global depression, the Mexican travel industry continued to grow during the 1930s. In fact, the financial crisis, along with the appearance of goose-stepping armies in Germany, Italy, and Japan, magnified popular doubts about modern life and amplified Mexico's image as a land of rural calm. The country's geographic proximity to the United States and its affordability, especially compared to pricey transatlantic travel, further bolstered its appeal. The annual tally of visitors, overwhelmingly from the United States, rose to 75,000 or so by 1935 and by decade's end topped 127,000, still not taking into account the countless thousands of tourists who sprinted across the border each year.[4] As the Second World War approached, Mexico attracted more U.S. visitors than any other foreign destination in the hemisphere.

Numerous commentators noted the growing presence of dollar-wielding, non-Spanish-speaking North Americans below the Rio Grande. In July 1935, the New York Times reported that Mexico's annual tourist revenues surpassed $314 million. The presence of U.S. oilmen south of the border, the paper observed, "had been replaced by a swarming army of tourists."[5] Two years later, travel writer Howard Vincent O'Brien commented that Mexico City "is full of Americans, yet they say the season has not really started. . . . [T]here is a convention of lady horticulturalists, a convention of hotel managers, a gathering of serious minded folk intent on a study of Latin America, and heaven knows how many others besides."[6] New tourist hotels sprang up, international restaurants opened for business, and travel agencies sprouted new offices around the country. The number and variety of cultural contact zones where North Americans and Mexicans brushed shoulders multiplied.

The rapid growth of mass tourism invigorated the everyday life of the empire. Incidences of culture clash, similar to the Hotel Regis episode, escalated. Overbearing northerners who found themselves in unfamiliar surroundings might assign the presence of Mexican beggars to a national propensity for laziness, link postrevolutionary labor activism to communist intrigue, and assign other unwelcomed behaviors to Mexican skin color and machismo. The atmosphere was at times made more contentious by the nationalism that continued to permeate Mexican society. Artist Diego Rivera, who had profited handsomely from Ambassador Dwight W. Morrow's promotion of Cuernavaca, found a market for paintings that poked fun at tourist antics. Local police, especially near the border, happily took the wind out the sails of many a drunken Yankee. And Mexican investors maneuvered to prevent large U.S.-based travel firms from snapping up the prime prospects.

The Mexican government exercised the most vigilant eye. In July 1934, Lázaro Cárdenas, governor of the state of Michoacán and a former revolutionary general, assumed the presidency. The new chief executive had established unusually strong credentials as a supporter of organized labor and a champion of agrarian reform. Although many scholars have emphasized the relative moderation of Cárdenas's initiatives, his presidency (1934–40) in many ways marked the high tide of revolution-inspired social reform and national renewal. The government seized more than forty-three million acres of land, including millions of acres of American-owned properties along Mexico's coasts and frontiers, and dispersed the largesse to peasants, village *ejidos*, and Mexican investors. The regime encouraged unionization of the urban workforce, implemented populist literacy and educational programs, and particularly rattled Uncle Sam in 1938 when it nationalized the Mexican oil industry.[7] Cárdenas also devised innovative techniques to manage the bourgeoning tourist industry. He effectively contained the disreputable border trade on New Year's Day 1935 with an executive decree that outlawed casino gambling. He then pumped funding into archeological projects that extolled Mexico's ancient indigenous heritage and doled out tax breaks and subsidies to Mexican hotels and restaurants.

Despite the constant sparring, U.S.-Mexican relations had become more cordial than ever by the end of the decade, and the two nations finally settled their long-standing debt and property disputes. Traditional historiography holds that the trend arose solely as a consequence of issues of international political economy. The anxieties stirred by global depression and the shadow of global war motivated Washington to patch up old animosities and avoid new ones.[8] The argument carries considerable explanatory power but suggests that relations improved almost overnight in response to a specific international crisis. It downplays the globalizing trends of the previous two decades, the rise of powerful new transnational interest groups (including those tied to the travel industry) that linked the United States and Mexico, the enhanced transportation and communications systems that connected the two nations, and the gradual but steady U.S.-Mexican rapprochement of the 1920s.

This chapter examines the U.S. tourist invasion of the 1930s and Mexico's efforts to contain it. It explains how the cultural dynamic inherent to tourism redistributed power within the empire, improved relations between Mexico and the United States, and helped both countries adapt to an increasingly ominous and interdependent world order.

Transnational Elites Expand the Tourist Infrastructure

Mexico's revolution underwent increasing institutionalization during the early 1930s. Following Alvaro Obregón's assassination in 1928, retiring president Calles loomed as the power broker behind Emilio Portes Gil's caretaker presidency. Calles organized the Partido Nacional Revolucionario (PNR, the National Revolutionary Party), the precursor to the long-standing Partido Revolucionario Institucional (Institutional Revolutionary Party), which dominated Mexican politics for the rest of the century. In 1930, Pascual Ortiz Rubio received the PNR's seal of approval and easily defeated José Vasconcelos, most likely with the assistance of modestly reimbursed election officials. Rubio resigned in 1932, after a falling out with Calles, to be replaced by Calles crony Abelardo L. Rodríguez, the former governor of the Distrito Baja and feudal lord of Tijuana's gambling industry. Whoever wore the presidential sash during these years never strayed far from Calles's party line. Official rhetoric lauded land reform and the rural ideal, while government policy positioned the nation for rapid industrialization. More substantial reform awaited Lázaro Cárdenas's ascendance to the presidency, his public break with Calles in 1935, and the PNR founder's exile to the United States. Even then, the fundamental structures of the postrevolutionary era remained intact: single-party rule, a mixed economy, and populist appeals to working-class consciousness, indigenism, and national greatness.

Mexico City's travel promotion efforts sputtered early in the decade, undergoing occasional restructuring but failing to gain much traction. Part of the problem arose from bureaucratic duplication and inefficiency. In early 1930, Portes Gil reshuffled offices, replacing the Mixed Pro-Tourism Commission with the National Commission on Tourism and assigning the new agency the task of developing an advertising campaign. At the same time, the Mexican National Bank, the National Railroad of Mexico, and the Mexican

National Railways pursued their own agendas. The way in which different interests worked at cross-purposes became apparent at the first National Congress on Tourism in Mexico City in April 1930. Eduardo de León, representing the chamber of commerce of the border city of Nuevo León, made a pitch for further reducing paperwork and requirements for border crossings. Other delegates endorsed federal funding for hotel construction, not only in the border regions but throughout Mexico, a responsibility that de León insisted belonged at the state and local levels.[9]

The crux of the difficulty, however, lay in the country's dire financial straits. While the depression helped make Mexico more attractive to cash-strapped tourists and provided Mexico City a chance to chip away at Europe's domination of the international travel market, it also constrained public investment. In late 1931, after Ortiz Rubio had assumed the presidency, a report on "Como Reparte el Dollar del Turista" (How to Deliver the Tourist Dollar) circulated through government offices. The author noted that the U.S. Department of Commerce calculated that American travelers spent more than four billion dollars annually and observed that Mexico, with its climate, scenery, and history, stood poised to benefit. Referring to tourism as "las industria mas moderna de nuestra época" (the most modern industry of our time), it pointed to Cuba, Canada, and France, where modest investments in advertising had generated impressive revenue. In Cuba alone, which had attracted 163,252 tourists the previous year, a one-hundred-thousand-dollar investment in advertising had yielded more than fifty million dollars in new income. The Rubio administration praised the report as "concise and insightful," but the national treasury was in no shape to make the recommended investment.[10]

Thus, private groups whose constituents often lived on both sides of the border filled the void in much the same manner as they had during the 1920s. Joining railroad companies and shipping lines, automobile enthusiasts for the first time flexed real muscle, especially as the Pan-American Highway neared completion. The 766-mile Laredo–Mexico City highway stretched from the Texas border town across Mexico's dry, barren northlands, through a succession of subtropical sugar-producing valleys, and then upward and over the towering Sierra Madre Mountains before descending into the Valley of Mexico and the capital city.[11] The sixty-three-million-dollar road officially opened on 1 July 1936, but the newly formed Mexican Automobile Association, with its mixed Mexican and North American membership, had long since recognized that the project would constitute a major boon to the tourist trade. The group lobbied Mexican local, state, and federal governments to create a gasoline tax for road construction, ease entry and exit regulations, and gain backing for the construction of roadside lodges and restaurants.[12]

The Mexican Automobile Association, like other promotional agencies, also combated depictions of Mexico as a land of revolutionary lawlessness and social backwardness. In addition to publishing a magazine and brochures, it broadcast its upbeat message through friendly travel writers. In the foreword to Michael and Virginia Scully's *Motorist's Guide to Mexico* (1933), the association's president touted his country as a land "rich in romance and history" yet "young and vital," with freshly constructed highways, modernized agriculture, and shiny new industries. Even before the completion of the Nuevo Laredo Highway, he asserted, more than twenty thousand U.S. tourists had driven by auto to the city of Monterrey, about 175 miles south of the border.[13] The Scullys echoed the news: "These highways, taking the tourist close to the heart of Mexico, should change the American mental picture of that country within a few years."[14] The book stressed and to some extent exaggerated the ease of border crossing and customs inspections, the absence of banditry, the safety of road travel, and the availability of comfortable hotels.[15]

Tourism boosters recognized the importance of providing visitors with first-class accommodations, but Mexico's hotel industry lagged. Revolution and economic depression combined to make public and private investment scarce, and nationalism made the government and its private sector allies averse to overreliance on U.S. capital.[16] Mexico's Ministry of Foreign Affairs gathered data on international tourism from consulates in the United States, Canada, Cuba, and Europe and viewed Cuba's policies as a cautionary tale. There, Gerardo Machado's U.S.-backed dictatorship had cast the island's tourism destiny with that of U.S. hotel interests, travel agencies, and shipping companies. Free of impediments to U.S. consumer and cultural power, Havana had already gained a reputation as a tropical speakeasy, much like Mexico's border towns, dominated by bars, brothels, racetracks, and mobsters.[17]

Activity in the Mexican hotel industry during the early 1930s centered on refurbishing the small number of establishments, most owned by Europeans and Mexican nationals, that had opened before the era of mass tourism. The Grand Hotel Ancira in Monterrey led the way. The Ancira had been built by a Mexican entrepreneur early in the century as a grand, European-style inn, complete with imported French glass and furnishings. Located directly across from the city's central plaza, it enjoyed a solid reputation for service and comfort but experienced a significant spike in business as the Nuevo Laredo–Mexico City Highway neared completion.[18] A major renovation followed, including the addition of a premier restaurant and bar, wine cellar, and parking garage.[19] A handful of hotels in Mexico City, Cuernavaca, and Acapulco underwent similar renovations.

Although not many U.S. firms gained entrée to the Mexican hotel business, a variety of U.S. interests contributed other vital components to the tourist trade. The Missouri Pacific Railroad linked up with several other U.S. rail companies to expand its connections from the Northeast and Midwest to Mexico City. U.S.-based cruise companies expanded service and arranged package deals with Mexican hotels. In addition to more established transit companies, Pan American Airlines entered the race for the tourist dollar in the 1930s, offering same-day flights from Brownsville, Texas, and two-day excursions from Miami via Havana to Mexico City.

William Spratling, the expatriate art collector who had mediated the negotiations between Diego Rivera and Ambassador Morrow for the murals that hung in Cuernavaca's Cortés Palace, gained recognition as one of the more eccentric U.S.-Mexican tourism promoters. According to his autobiography, Spratling took the two-thousand-dollar commission he received from Morrow for facilitating the Rivera deal and in early 1929 purchased a house in the village of Taxco, a colonial-era mountain town located not far from Cuernavaca in the state of Morelos (about 110 miles southwest of Mexico City).[20] With Morrow's encouragement, Spratling set out to revive Taxco's long-lost silver industry, initiated by conquistador Hernán Cortés and later expanded by French entrepreneur Francis Borda.

Spratling hired a corps of local workers and trained them in the art of silversmithing. In some cases, he resurrected traditional jewelry designs, but he also pioneered new styles in necklaces, bracelets, rings, and earrings geared to urbanized, gringo consumers. Mindful of the importance of authenticity—or at least its aura—he rented an abandoned smelter across town and maintained ancient smelting practices. He exhibited both respect for the country's craft skills and a condescending attitude toward his workers. "In Mexico," he recorded in his autobiography, "silversmithing has always been considered a folk art [and] over the years I have arrived at the conclusion where the people of Mexico have sufficient simplicity of outlook, or one-mindedness, which makes the production of handcrafted goods here possible."[21]

Taxco soon acquired celebrity status, appealing especially to avant-garde consumers who held Mexican folk arts and crafts in high esteem. Its aged white-stucco and red-tile-roofed buildings; hilly, winding cobblestone streets; and overhanging balconies gave the town Iberian charm. Its central plaza and cathedral bespoke of a bygone era of colonial grandeur. The completion of the highway from Mexico City to Cuernavaca, Taxco, and Acapulco in 1931 delivered tourists by the busload.[22] Spratling added to the town's luster by hosting an eclectic group of artists and writers at his home, including Rivera, John Dos Passos, Katherine Anne Porter, Hart Crane, and exiled Russian revolutionist Leon Trotsky. He even claimed to have invented a predecessor to the margarita at Doña Bertha's local cantina, a blend of lime juice, sugar, and tequila he dubbed the Tequila Limonada.[23] Mexico's National Department of Colonial Monuments stepped in and officially recognized the town as a historic district.

The U.S. embassy in Mexico City continued to support the promotional effort. President Franklin Roosevelt designated his former boss from the Navy Department, Josephus Daniels, ambassador to Mexico City. As navy secretary in 1914, Daniels had coordinated Washington's gunboat showdown at Tampico. Although Mexican nationalists initially viewed his appointment with disbelief, Daniels quickly made amends, openly declaring his personal antipathy toward U.S.-based oil trusts, publicly comparing Mexico's social reforms to FDR's New Deal, and launching a new round of cultural diplomacy. Borrowing a page from Morrow, Daniels encouraged artistic exchanges, welcomed movie stars—Helen Lamarr, Dorothy Lamour, Tyrone Power, Bob Hope, and others—to Mexico City, and traveled widely within the republic.[24]

Like his predecessor, Daniels rarely missed an opportunity to plug the benefits of international travel and Mexico's attractions. Addressing the tenth seminar on Mexico in July 1935, he delivered his typical stump speech: "Mexico is becoming more and more the Mecca for people of the United States," renowned for its "climate, history monuments, flowers, and beauty."[25] The ambassador celebrated the Laredo–Mexico City highway not only as a feat of engineering but also as an avenue of cross-cultural understanding. To inaugurate the road, Daniels joined a three-day auto convoy of U.S. and Mexican officials along the roadway's entire length. The party paused at the route's highest point, the small mountain enclave of Zimapán, north of Mexico City, before a small monument donated by the American Chamber of Commerce. "In the form of an open book this monument is placed to remind passing travelers that the history of progress is the history of transportation and communication," Daniels sermonized, "and on its pages will be inscribed a record of the present friendship, of the future deeper and broader mutual understanding between Mexicans and Americans."[26]

President Roosevelt traveled to Mexico in the fall of 1935, not for an official state visit but to fish the waters of Magdalena Bay off the Baja Peninsula's west coast, an expedition that required a special security clearance from the Mexi-

After receiving special permission from the Mexican government, U.S. president Franklin D. Roosevelt took a break from his White House duties and indulged in some deep-sea fishing at Mexico's Magdalena Bay in October 1935. The president is seated on the right, admiring the catch of the day. The ladder on the left ascends to the deck of the USS Houston. Franklin D. Roosevelt Presidential Library, Hyde Park, New York.

can government.[27] But the president's interest in Mexican travel extended beyond marlin and yellowfin tuna. Following the grand opening of the Laredo–Mexico City Highway, Roosevelt wrote to Daniels to express delight at the project's completion and compliment the ambassador's participation in the ribbon-cutting ceremonies. FDR also shared some public relations ideas: "Even a small advertising appropriation of perhaps $25,000 would bring lots of results but the ad ought to be sure to mention adequate hotel facilities between the U.S. border and Mexico City and also reasonable prices."[28]

The Mexican travel industry in fact was already fast becoming a full-fledged magnet for North American consumer culture. While a combination of transnational elites and Mexico's government cobbled together a tourist infrastructure, the flow of tourists accelerated and drew the United States and Mexico more fully into collision-prone cultural orbits.

Tourist Insecurities and Tourist Power

Typically less adventurous than the Lone Eagles of the previous decade, U.S. travelers during the 1930s demanded more of their Mexican hosts. Despite their affluence and privilege, the new crop of tourists often felt pangs of personal insecurity, not utterly dissimilar from the national insecurities that foreign policymakers have articulated while negotiating the vagaries of twentieth-century power politics. Most U.S. travelers, for example, gained their first introduction to Mexico via the cultural contact zone known as the railroad station. There they faced the challenge of arranging the transport of baggage from train to hotel, a task that might be assigned to an onboard agent or might be put up for bidding to licensed *cargadores*, who typically waited en masse at the point of disembarkation.[29] The latter could be a disorienting experience for visitors, with the crowded cacophony of Mexican workingmen's voices and grimacing faces, supposedly identifiable by government license and photograph, competing for dollars. "My God," exclaimed one indignant Anglo as her train approached the Veracruz station, "those wolves!"[30]

To navigate the cultural maze and augment their soft power, tourists relied on a veritable arsenal of travel accessories. Among the many tools, the published travel guide enjoyed prerequisite status. Popular travel literature originated in seventeenth-century Britain, but the literary genre came into its own in the United States beginning in the mid–nineteenth century. International exhibits at world's fairs later in the century, the Thomas Cook travel agency, women's travel clubs, and the growing presence of travel-related articles in popular journals and magazines testified to the increasing demand for touristic guidance.[31]

Among guidebooks to Mexico, no single volume exceeded *Terry's Guide to Mexico* in thoroughness and authoritativeness. Author T. Philip Terry's book first appeared in 1909—bad timing in light of the coming revolution and the cessation of tourist activities. But after tourism recovered, the book underwent regular revisions to keep up with the rapidly changing travel scene. Nearly six hundred pages in length, the 1927 and 1935 editions were encyclopedic, including an extensive section on "history and races" that reeked of Euro-American centrism and white privilege, covering tourist attractions geographically from north to south and addressing practical matters such as transportation, accommodations, and eateries. In appearance, the guide resembled a holy book, hard-covered with a gilded, engraved title and ribbon markers to help readers highlight the most illuminating passages.

A map to the empire, *Terry's Guide* was in some ways the tourist's State Department research office. It included threat assessments as well as a list of preventative measures. The 1927 edition dwelled on the health dangers posed by water, spoiled food, and climatic conditions. Some of the advice proved worth heeding, but the didactic tone reflected the self-important voice of the metropole. "In Mexico City pulmonary and bowel troubles form the largest items in the mortality list," it admonished.[32] Antidotes included boiled water and milk and avoidance of street vendor food and drink. "The prudent traveler," *Terry's* dryly commented, "will never eat food served at wayside stands or in cheap *figones* or *mesones* favored by the *peones*, as in some of them decayed vegetables, the meat of defunct burros, horses, cats, dogs, and other dubious stuff may be served, and their high flavor disguised by hot chiles and pungent sauces."[33] The book droned on with two pages of definitions for various Mexican dishes, including guacamole, tacos, and tortillas.

Not all travel guides adopted *Terry's* master narrative style. Anita Brenner was born in Mexico in 1905 but migrated to the United States with her parents during the revolution. She returned to her country of birth in the early 1920s and became one of the first writers to publicize Mexico's artistic renaissance in the United States.[34] Brenner published *Your Mexican Holiday: A Modern Guide* in 1932, and it quickly became a best seller. She painted a less romanticized but more realistic portrait of the country: "Mexico and Central America having been the focus of ancient civilization in the new world have been called 'America's Egypt' . . . 'America's Babylon' . . . etc.; but those are silly names to give things which have their own names, even though they may be, as they are, worthy of the comparison."[35] She sought most of all to deliver a book more appropriate than *Terry's* for the age of mass tourism. "If your visit is prompted by a wish to understand this country whose complexity is fascinating serious minds," the author warned, "you will not find the explanation in this book." Instead of a list of "must sees" and admonishments, she offered a series of suggested sites, activities, and itineraries from which travelers might pick and choose.[36]

Edith Mackie's popular *Mexican Journey* (1935) took a similar tack, asserting that only one rule applied to Mexican travel: Yankees needed to lighten up. "The trait persists, to a greater or lesser degree, in most of us: as soon as we are deprived of some small amenity, we miss it. The coffee is stronger; the service is slower; the bathrooms are not the same. . . . So, relax. Knock the chip off your own shoulder, dismiss your fussiness, and have a really grand time."[37] Like most travel guides of the era, Mackie emphasized that Mexico's revolution had long since subsided and that travel was both safe and convenient. "Far from being barbarous, the country has a great deal to show in the way of both our type of civilization and that civilization which the Indians have inherited from their own race," she wrote. There is "complete material comfort (inner-spring mattresses, tiled bathrooms and all the rest) for those who want it."[38]

In addition to consulting travel guides, most North Americans devoted time and energy to logistics. The age of the credit card remained in the future, making a spontaneous splurge and payment at a later date impossible. Instead, much like U.S. foreign policymakers or business leaders, tourists determined their budgets, plotted their priorities, and developed strategies for engaging their travel world. Yankees in interwar Mexico increasingly relied on the expertise of travel agencies to help them arrange and finance their wanderings. In Mexico City, the Creed Travel Company, led by Mrs. M. E. Creed, a member of American Chamber of Commerce, opened its office in 1923 and represented numerous hotels in Mexico City and Cuernavaca.[39] But most North American tourists turned to U.S.-based agencies such as American Express. An offshoot of Wells Fargo, American Express issued its first traveler's checks in 1891. The transportation revolution after the Great War transformed the firm into one of the world's leading travel businesses, and the American Express office on Mexico City's Avenida Madero became a major security checkpoint for visitors.[40]

Despite the continuing romance with Mexico's countryside, Mexico City gained status on the tourist itinerary during the 1930s. With a population of a little less than one million, it offered the advantages of a major metropolis, including transportation and communications connections, travel offices, and a potpourri of shops and markets. Situated at an altitude of seven thousand feet, the city boasted a climate that travelers found alluring, with daytime temperatures averaging in the seventies and low eighties, followed by a brisk cooling off at night.

The city also exuded a rich heritage. Its downtown *zócalo* (central square) was the largest in Spanish America and featured the hemisphere's oldest Catholic cathedral, built atop the ruins of the Aztec Templo Mayor. Diagonally across from the cathedral sat the presidential palace and city hall. Few tourists missed a visit to Chapultepec Castle and Park, erected in the eighteenth century and refurbished by Maximilian and Carlota during the French intervention in the 1860s.

Despite its sophistication, Mexico's capital rattled the confidence of many visiting Yankees. Thus, in addition to purchasing guidebooks and consulting travel agents, growing numbers of North Americans sought the most modern and secure inner-city hotels. As the decade progressed and tourist numbers mounted, new hotel construction and openings became more common in Mexico's leading contact zones. Expensive North Americanized hotels served as the tourist's equivalent to forward military bases, bastions of comfort and security to which empire-exploring gringos could safely retire at the end of the day. *Terry's* voiced unequivocal advice: "Usually the personal discomforts in any but the best hotels are so many that the wise traveler will lodge only at the best."[41]

The 250-room Geneve Hotel, located in the city's diplomatic quarter, stood out among Mexico City's some sixty-two hotels as a top-notch lodge, a blend of history and modernity that thrilled most tourists. Opened in 1907 by Canadian-born Sinclair Gore, the hotel featured elegant furnishings: tasteful crown moldings surrounded a ceiling whose skylight filled the lobby with soft sun rays, Spanish columns hinted of the Old World, and leaded glass windows and oriental rugs added refinement. Concrete and fireproof, outfitted with steam heat and electricity, and offering pure, artesian water from a well on the premises, the building represented "the last word in hotel design."[42]

The city's modern hotel infrastructure gradually thickened with the opening of the Regis, the Ritz, and the Mancera.[43] The city's flashiest hotel, the Reforma, opened its doors in 1936. Built by investor and former minister of foreign affairs Alberto J. Pani, the ultraposh 250-room hotel equaled any state-of-the-art accommodation in the United States in conveniences and frills and stood as a testament to the tourist's consumer power. "The Reforma is Mexico's deluxest hotel," one guidebook commented, "and it is about as

Mexican as the Ziegfeld Follies." Waiters in the hotel's restaurant and bar wore dress suits, spoke English, and recited the extensive wine list flawlessly. Bathrooms included separate faucets for cold and hot water, and in-room phones matched room color and decor.[44]

Even in the hinterland, which the travel narratives of the 1920s had celebrated as drowsy and remote, old hotels received facelifts during the 1930s. Still relatively undiscovered, Acapulco offered the cliff-edge Hotel Mirador, with private rooms and baths and open-air dining.[45] And in Mazatlán, described in the 1935 edition of *Terry's Guide to Mexico* as "rapidly coming into its own as one of the most delightful Winter Stations on the continent," Hotel Belmar, unusual in that it was U.S.-owned, won accolades for comfort. "The Belmar appeals more strongly to Americans" than did other local options, *Terry's* noted, with its "ocean view rooms, Talavera-tiled patio, and excellent food." Only one warning accompanied the endorsement: "*Tequila*, a potent cactus distillation for which the region is celebrated, should be approached with caution and accorded the respect due to powerful forces."[46]

Elite restaurants also served as colonial outposts. In light of the average American's excessive fear of food poisoning, akin to Ambassador Sheffield's ill-informed fear of communism, tourists favored the most renowned eating establishments, most of which served U.S.-style comfort food. The Lady Baltimore in downtown Mexico City gained fame for its ice cream and desserts. Zahler's tea room and restaurant, also in the city, won the endorsement of most travel guides. A "must see" for both cuisine and atmosphere was the restaurant at the San Angel Inn, located just south of the capital city. The Mexican-owned San Angel specialized in local dishes and offered patrons seating on a flower-drenched outdoor patio. It had originally been a seventeenth-century Carmelite convent and had functioned in previous incarnations as a gathering place for Mexico's revolutionary elite.[47]

Sanborn's restaurant, situated just a stone's throw from Mexico City's *zócalo*, easily ranked as the most popular dining experience for North Americans. Known as the Casa de Azulejos (House of Tiles) for its mosaic tile exterior, Sanborn's was housed in an ornate seventeenth-century building that during the Porfiriato had been home to the city's prestigious Jockey Club. The revolution ended the club's glory days, and in 1919 the owners remodeled the building and leased it to U.S.-based Sanborn Sons. Tourists replaced Mexico's conservative ruling elite as the building's most numerous patrons. The breakfast menu featured cornbread, hotcakes with maple syrup, hot biscuits, and North American coffee.[48] Gringos also appreciated Sanborn's gift shop and pharmacy.[49]

Mexico's interwar tourism boom did not bring about a large-scale recon-figuration of physical space or entire blocks of newly constructed U.S.-style architecture. With a handful of exceptions, Mexico City and other tourist sites retained their architectural personalities. But the Geneve, the Reforma, and Sanborn's still stood as outposts of U.S. culture and manifestations of U.S. power. Only the wealthiest Mexicans found the U.S. consumer empire both irresistible and affordable. Those who did might have behaved like Artemio Cruz's estranged wife, Catalina, and soon-to-be-wed daughter, Teresa, in Carlos Fuentes's epic novel, *The Death of Artemio Cruz* (1964). After an exhausting morning of shopping for wedding finery, the two snooty women dined at Sanborn's:

> The waitress appeared, a woman wearing a Tehuantepec native costume, and the daughter ordered nut-waffles and orange juice and the mother, unable to resist, asked for raisin bread with melted butter. . . .
> "Joan Crawford," said the daughter. "Joan Crawford."
> "No, no, it isn't pronounced like that. Crow-fore. Crow-fore. They pro-nounce it like that."
> "Crau-fore."
> "No, no. Crow, crow, crow. The 'a' and 'u' together are pronounced like 'o.' I believe that's how they pronounce it."[50]

Tourist outposts such as Sanborn's simultaneously delivered Mexican and North American authenticity to its high-society Mexican patrons.

Collision: The Everyday Life of Empire

Despite the steam heat, dance bands, and fine food, most U.S. visitors even-tually ventured outside their hotel fortresses. Some wandered in groups; others resembled the Lone Eagles of the previous decade. Some hired tour guides, while others pursued a less mediated exploration. More and more regions of Mexico and more of its cities sprouted tourist districts that not only benefited investors and merchants but also functioned as zones of cul-tural contact. Even more than during the 1920s, tourism and the transna-tional cultural exchanges it engendered brought peoples and societies into new, unpredictable relationships and did so on an everyday basis.

In many ways, the cultural rapprochement of the 1920s expanded and blossomed during the 1930s. Artists, poets, and travel writers continued to express an affinity for Mexico's countryside, fine arts, and socialist renewal. At the same time, many travel narratives contained subtexts that exposed overlapping levels of cultural and economic skirmishing wherever tourist power exerted itself. For many observers, Mexican and foreign, Mexico seemed awash in wealthy U.S. tourists. One commentator wrote of the capital, "At times the city, now that the dollar is down, is as full of Americans as Paris. The nicest Americans cannot be beaten by anyone in the world but it is mostly the others who go to Mexico. They walk through the streets like bulls charging a flock of lambs."[51]

Set adrift within Mexico's contact zones, a good many North American travelers fell back on harsh constructions of the Mexican "other" to interpret their surroundings. Back home, promoters continued to trumpet the southwest's Hispanic heritage. In Los Angeles, second only to Mexico City in Mexican population in the Americas, Anglo visitors flocked to the famed Olvera Street marketplace, several blocks long and featuring Mexican vendors in colorful costume. But the exhibit also bespoke of an idealized multicultural past that conveniently glossed over the city's growing ethnic residential segregation. Mexican immigrants were still more often than not labeled outsiders, people of color set apart by their Catholic crucifixes, Spanish language, and willingness to labor long hours for next to no pay.[52] And when times got tough economically, Mexicans became America's most expendable newcomers, or at least the most susceptible to deportation en masse. More than a few middle- and upper-class northerners on holiday relied on those same cultural constructions to interpret life south of the Rio Grande.

Some viewed the host country through the lens of class. U.S. middle-class culture traditionally associated joblessness with moral failure and labor agitation with communism. Both could be found in abundance in interwar Mexico. O'Brien warned of pickpockets in Mexico City and advised tourists to carry few valuables and hold tight to their handbags and cameras.[53] Famed world explorer and radio commentator Carveth Wells promoted car travel to Mexico but admonished, "One of the small inconveniences to the motorist in Mexico City is to have things stolen from his car when it is parked in a busy thorough fare."[54] Others commented wryly on the "national vice" of stealing gas caps from parked Chevys and Fords.[55] The possibility that theft might constitute, even in part, a form of resistance to tourist power did not enter the discourse.

Although the 1930s constituted a breakthrough decade for the U.S. labor movement, with the rise of the Congress of Industrial Organizations and New Deal labor legislation, well-to-do North Americans on holiday often complained of Mexico's combative unions. As he pursued rapprochement with U.S. bankers, Plutarco Calles had struggled to corral the nation's unions. Empowered by the revolutionary constitution and inspired by working-class militancy in Western Europe, the Soviet Union, and the United States, organized labor made work stoppages and strikes a regular feature of Mexican national life. Bus and taxi drivers tangled Mexico City in 1923, trolley car workers followed suit in 1925, and in late 1926 and early 1927 the Confederation of Railway Societies threw down the gauntlet against the national rail system.[56] Calles, in turn, gave lip service to labor's rights but reined in radicals by making Luis Morones, chief of the moderate Confederación Regional de Obreros Mexicanos, secretary of labor and head of the government's Board of Conciliation. The Cárdenas administration followed a similar policy of co-optation but chose to favor Vicente Lombardo Toledano's more aggressive Confederación General de Trabajadores de Mexico. Since wages remained low under both regimes and political alliances stayed fluid, work disruptions remained endemic through most of the interwar era. Indeed, during the first six months of the Cárdenas presidency alone, various unions organized more than five hundred strikes.[57]

Many U.S. tourists viewed the class struggle primarily as an annoying inconvenience. One visitor bragged that in spite of a taxi strike, he worked a memorable bargain with a driver willing to take him and his companions to a small town outside Mexico City. What seemed to the author to be a benign deal, however, turned "sinister." After the party returned to the city, strike organizers surrounded the car and harassed the beleaguered driver. In the midst of the squabble, the occupants emptied out of the cab, walked the remaining few blocks, and left the driver to contend with the pickets. "It is very pleasant to get anything so cheaply and we took advantage of it, ignoring the strike, which we could always do as there were many drivers who preferred working to starving," the author gloated.[58]

Harry A. Franck, a prolific travel writer and contributor to the *Saturday Review*, held little sympathy for either local labor or local businesses. In his 1935 guide, *Trailing Cortes through Mexico*, he related his troubled journey to the Yucatán. He denounced the wharf workers' union in the port village of Progreso because the men "charge one peso for landing even if you carry your own baggage." And he decried the newly established and Mexican-owned Mayaland Tours and its Mayaland hotel, a quaint former hacienda and Chichén Itzá's only major commercial accommodation, as "tourist exploiters."[59] A particularly rabid antilabor diatribe spewed forth from the pen of Max Miller: "The two word phrase, Labor Trouble, so common throughout today's world as well as yesterday's world and the day before yesterday's world also predominated in Mexico while I was there. . . . [S]ome of the strikers' demands border on the burlesque: ponies, world travel, etc."[60]

Elise Haas, whose privately published travelogue was limited to a run of seventy-five copies, described her visit to a rural school where she found "Communistic" classroom frescoes. "The hammer and the sickle of Soviet Russia [and] Labor's clasped hands" covered one wall, and another featured a union poster with the caption "Martyrs of Chicago," complete with a list of the names of those who had been killed in the Haymarket Riots of 1888. While her guide dismissed the significance of these decorations, Hass expressed her fear that the doctrine of class struggle had replaced the church as "the religion of the future, at least in Mexico."[61]

Without question, popular British writer Graham Greene ranked as one of the grouchiest visitors. Greene traveled to Mexico in the late 1930s to write a book about religion and politics. He hated Mexico and seemed to enjoy his dislike. The country's educational reforms were fascist. Agrarian rebel Emiliano Zapata had been nothing more than a failed opportunist. Hawkers of food at railroad stations were pests. "How one begins to hate these people . . . the hidden inexpressiveness of brown eyes. . . . People never seem to help each other in small ways, removing a parcel from a seat, making room with their legs. They just sit about."[62]

Greene even despised Mexican food: "Just a multitude of plates plucked down on the table simultaneously, so that five are getting cold while you eat the sixth; pieces of anonymous meat, a plate of beans, fish from which the taste of the sea has long been squeezed away, rice mixed with what look like grubs . . . a little heap of bones and skin they call chicken."[63] Most of all, Greene held the country's revolution in contempt. It had nurtured authoritarianism and militarism rather than reform and had encouraged a breakdown in law and order. A devout Catholic, Greene deeply lamented the prosecution of priests and other voices of God. The discriminating author could hardly keep his impressions to himself and published his scathing critique in his 1939 book, *The Lawless Road*. The volume received a mixed response, but a reviewer for the *New Yorker* magazine echoed many when he wrote, "A Catholic view of Mexico by an Englishman who can write extremely well but whose perspective is somewhat limited by his constant indignation at what he conceives to be Mexico's anti-clericalism."[64] Kingsley Martin of the *Nation* put it more bluntly, writing that Greene "uses hatred as a barrier against beauty."[65]

In addition to class, revolution, and religion, the everyday life of empire featured antagonistic Anglo commentary on matters of race and gender. Perhaps the most common expression of North American disappointment with travel to Mexico came from those who idealized the country's rural folkways but despised urban Mexicans. Haas waxed poetic on the virtues of Mexico's village culture: the Indian marketplaces, the peons along the roadside, the "women with their soft voices," children "well behaved and never slapped."[66] But she excoriated Mexico City: "I do not relish its mixed flavor of Europe, mongrel Mexico, and North American big business. It is sad to see the beautiful Spanish colonial buildings making way for modern architecture of the Teutonic school. Traffic is noisy and hazardous, the shops do not tempt me, nor is the night-life alluring. In short, I am not happy here—it is not what I came to see."[67]

Traveling North Americans, accustomed to Jim Crow's relatively simple black/white racial distinctions, often found unsettling Mexico's complex system of racial mixing and more subtle color hierarchy, a legacy of Spanish-Indian unions and the colonial-era enslavement of African workers along the Gulf Coast. Larry Barretto echoed Haas's romantic view of indigenous cultures and her disdain for urban centers but spiced his analysis with color consciousness. Visiting the city of Puebla, renowned for its colonial architecture, handcrafted tiles, and culinary arts, he took a dim view of the traffic, the congestion, and most of all the city's Hispanic male population. "I did not like the people on the streets, and I was particularly annoyed by the young men," he explained. "Their skins were too light—and I had become used to copper—although compared to myself they were for the most part a positive bronze. . . . They hung around street corners in small groups, cigarettes dropping from their lips, and eyed the women with a sort of searching reptilian stare. I wondered if they ever worked."[68]

African American travelers might also be confounded by Mexico's color line. While many border-town honky-tonks enforced Jim Crow, other venues promoted racial tolerance. Boxer Jack Johnson was not the only U.S. sports figure of color to praise Mexico for racial enlightenment. Many African American baseball players, confined to the Negro Leagues in the United States, enjoyed interracial play south of the color barrier. The game was most likely introduced to Mexico during the Porfiriato by employees of U.S. railroad companies but became entrenched in Mexican urban culture during the postrevolutionary years. By the 1930s, the Mexican Leagues attracted professional black players, first from nearby Cuba and then from the Dominican Republic, Panama, and the United States. The legendary Satchel Paige became the first African American to take to the mound in a professional game in Mexico City in 1938. "Everywhere I went in Mexico I ran into Negro League players," he later recalled; "with all those guys I knew, it was real friendly down in Mexico."[69]

Not all African American visitors found Mexico to be a land of milk and honey. Renowned scholar and civil rights activist W. E. B. Du Bois wrote a long letter to social scientist Frank Tannenbaum recounting "extraordinary difficulties" encountered in crossing the border. The previous summer, three Atlanta University staff members had gone to Mexico separately, he explained. One was a white man who simply paid the $1 tourist tax and gained entrance. The second man, "a brown man of Negro descent," was compelled to post a $250 cash bond in New Orleans and was nonetheless refused admission at the border. The third was "a yellow man of Negro descent, a doctor of philosophy from Harvard"—presumably Du Bois himself. He applied at the Mexican consulate in Washington, D.C., and was continuously "put off." Du Bois had friends in the U.S. State Department, however, and after some delay, and when he was already in California, he received a document that permitted him to enter as a tourist "in spite of the fact that person is of Negro descent."[70]

Interpretations of Mexican gender relations might also carry multiple meanings. O. A. Merritt-Hawkes, author of *High Up in Mexico*, made a special point of visiting Ciudad Juárez, a "dirty, revolting town of gambling dens and dancing halls . . . presided over by dirty men, fat men, sinister men, all having guns of no mean size, not hidden, but obtruding from their pockets." A harsh critic of Mexican male culture, she complained, "The first Spanish I learnt was 'No me molesta.'" But Merritt-Hawkes supposed that sexual harassment was a more serious problem for Anglo women than for their Mexican counterparts: "If you are beautiful and blonde I imagine a super-megaphone is needed to call those few little words aloud as you progress through the city, where dark women are common and beautiful ones, in spite of propaganda pictures, are rare."[71]

A more nuanced critique of Mexican patriarchy came from the pen of Emma Lindsay Squier, author of *Gringa: An American Girl in Mexico* (1934). Squier journeyed south in the early 1930s to make a film about Mexican life that would counteract insulting northern stereotypes. Along the way, she recorded her thoughts on the status of Mexican women, informed partly by an understanding of class and race. She recalled a visit with a wealthy Mexican widower and his family in the state of Sonora, on the Pacific Coast. The father's two daughters appeared "shy, and eager eyed." When the author inquired if the young women might travel and study in the United States, as their older brothers had done, the patriarch replied that no proper woman would be permitted to undertake such a journey. "Their destinies are clearly outlined from birth," Squier surmised; "they will marry someone approved by their father; they will then go into the retirement of their husbands' homes. They will raise many children—just as many as possible."[72]

In contrast, Squier observed and admired the entrepreneurial skills of working-class Mexican women, especially their ability to hold their own against the tourist's consumer power. Masculine visitors might think of commerce as factories and auto sales statistics, she commented, but polite, dark-faced mestiza *vendadoras* came to hotels to sell clothing, shoes, and jewelry: "It takes time to buy correctly, but it is worth it. For if you pay the first asking price, you are immediately classed as a bloated plutocrat, one of the capitalistas whom it is a joy to overcharge."[73]

Gender issues became further complicated when North American women inconsistently practiced assertiveness. Marcene Riley's entourage of female tourists from San Francisco imbibed an ethic of women's agency and comradeship, and Riley's narrative of the trip, published in 1939, is filled with references to the group's spirit of adventure. But all did not go as planned. Hotels in smaller towns lacked hot water, breakfast coffee was sometimes "unsatisfying," and service was slow. The greatest inconvenience occurred in the town of San Miguel, where the group's much-delayed train arrived at 3:30 in the morning. Riley expressed relief when a young man dressed in white trousers greeted them at the station. "The Señor was charm and gallantry itself, apologizing profusely that the train was so late, as if it were his fault. He was certainly a shining knight to damsels in distress."[74]

Finally, culturally constructed gender norms collided in Mexico's underground commercial sex industry. North American males who fantasized about brown-skinned female submissiveness sometimes underwent a reality check. Writing for the National Travel Club in New York, Henry Albert Phillips described an early morning romp through the capital city's lower-stratum bars and dance halls. "In my opinion," he reported, "it is the most atmospheric and colorful center of conscious depravity in the world," complete with cheap liquor, gambling, marijuana, "homos," and "a few inquiring foreigners." The escapade's capstone came at one "local dive" where the hostess, a Yaqui Indian whom the other women seemed to fear, tried to pick the pocket of the author's friend. When the men accused her of theft, she gruffly revealed a tattoo on her bared breast and readied for a fistfight. The men fell silent and slunk away.[75]

The clash between U.S. tourists and Mexican hosts can be overstated. For every example of class, racial, and sexual conflict cited, countervailing cases of friendly cooperation can be referenced. Most travel guides noted that despite persistent complaints regarding bad service, bumpy train rides, labor unrest, racial antagonism, and sexism, most North American visitors seemed pleased with Mexican hospitality and genuinely wished to learn more about the lives of their southern neighbors. One writer scoffed at the idea that Mexico would be "ruined" by travelers. "What the conquistadors couldn't do," he predicted, "the Yankee will do no better."[76]

The consumer and cultural power of northerners nonetheless rang out palpable and clear. Anthropologist Oscar Lewis visited Mexico in 1947 to examine the terms of life in Tepoztlán, a village just north of Mexico City that had become a favorite community for academic study. Lewis reported that on first impression, the village seemed to have changed little from what others had described previously: adobe houses, men wearing ancient white *calzones*, barefoot women with long braids. But on closer inspection, signs of change appeared. Main roads had been paved, tourist buses came and went, Coca-Cola signs dotted the highway, new stores had opened in the central plaza, and a few women wore bobbed hair and high heels. The change was not entirely welcomed by the inhabitants. The issue of tourism evoked particularly strong reactions. "We have a new road and many tourists, but our children are still dying," one astute villager observed.[77]

Containment; or, The Colony Strikes Back

Coca-Cola, high heels, and tourist buses can be counted among a growing number of symbols of U.S. life that had begun to insinuate themselves into the everyday life of Mexico's tourist zones. But the infiltration of North American culture did not go unchecked. Instead, Mexican hosts—vendors, taxi drivers, police, artists and writers, and the government—devised tactics to manage and contain the tourist's consumer and cultural power and realign visitor-host arrangements to Mexican advantage.

Taxi drivers appear to have been among the first to contest tourist power. In addition to inconveniencing tourists with periodic work stoppages, Mexico City's cabbies proved to be shrewd bargainers of rates. O'Brien explained in exasperated tones the ritual of taxi negotiations. He understood that if the passenger uttered the word "tostón" when entering a taxi and the driver responded with "Sí," the fare would be entered at half price, or half a peso—pocket change for most U.S. tourists. But "if, as happens often, [the driver] says nothing, it means you are likely to have a row when it comes time for a settlement." Filled with indignation when charged the full peso by a sullen cabbie, he bemoaned, "The passenger may call a policeman, but all he can tell you is that one peso is the legal fare, and any discount must be negotiated beforehand."[78]

One U.S. couple underwent a similarly baffling experience but handled it with greater aplomb. Arriving in Mexico City by train, they steadfastly determined to avoid the country's "tourist traps." When two taxi drivers approached, eager to provide transportation, they conveyed through a mishmash of simple English and broken Spanish that they desired a hotel that catered to natives instead of tourists. The two drivers conferred, and their choice of "a clean, simple one with shared bath" very much pleased the discriminating Yankees. The next afternoon, however, much to the surprise of the female half of the couple, one of the taxi men accosted her as she tried to enter a different taxi in front of the same hotel. The animated airport cabbie informed the new driver that the woman was his "patrona." She was dutifully relinquished without a struggle, "and the old family retainer of almost a week beamed on me as if I were a kidnapped child returned to hearth and home."[79]

Labor carried more clout when organized, and state-sanctioned unions during the 1930s refused to concede Mexico's contact zones to tourist ownership. Despite the scorn of many roaming northerners, labor unrest not only brought improved wages and working conditions but also enhanced host power. Taxi strikes, undertaken to obtain less expensive gasoline, higher rates, and lower taxes, regularly triumphed in Mexico City and other urban areas where local officials feared the impact of such stoppages on commerce and tourism.[80] Other strikes benefited from the tourist presence as well. Riley's group arrived in Mexico City in 1938 in the middle of a workers' strike against the power company. She described her party's annoyance and the jubilant celebration in their hotel lobby when the strike was settled.[81]

In some industries, labor organizers might even take action against gringos considered *muy simpatico* to Mexican culture. In the summer of 1931, not long after Taxco's silver industry had begun to attract notice, about half of Spratling's labor force of 144 workers struck for improved wages. Better versed in Mexican labor practices than most U.S. expats, Spratling relied on loyal workers to peacefully persuade their friends to abandon the strike. To appease the remaining strikers—17, by Spratling's count—he followed the advice of a friend in the legal field and deposited an indemnity for each man in a local bank. The strike ended in two days.[82]

Mexicans sometimes asserted agency through creative expression and at times constructed visitor identities rather than conceding the identity game to the tourists. In the mid-1930s, financier and former diplomat Alberto Pani commissioned Diego Rivera to paint a mural for the banquet hall of Pani's chic Hotel Reforma, then under construction in Mexico City. The assignment presented the artist with an irresistible temptation. When completed, the mural consisted of four panels, the third of which depicted Yankee travel writers, complete with jackass ears and fat fountain pens, interpreting the country for the outside world. The image of a slender blond-haired woman, a demonic group of masked figures holding bags of gold, and a plucked chicken representing Mexico rounded out the display. Aghast at the representations, Pani paid for the work and then hired his brother to alter the images. Indignant, Rivera sued, and the court awarded him two thousand pesos in damages and ordered Pani to restore the original paintings. Pani, however, remained the owner of the art and placed the murals in storage. They were eventually sold, and today they grace the walls of the Mexican Tourist Agency in Mexico City.[83]

Like laborers and artists, local authorities often sought to one-up the visitors. Touring Nuevo Laredo, sister city to Laredo, Texas, in 1934, Ambassador Daniels reported a veritable laundry list of tourist complaints against border and law enforcement officials. While the problems might be ascribed to government corruption or incompetence or simply to an onerous bureaucracy, the frequency with which disputes arose and their recurring nature suggest a more complex cultural tug of war.

The grievances were legion. In some cases, police imposed hefty fines for minor infractions, as one couple in their seventies learned when they stayed after their tourist card expired. Local officials slapped the pair with a one-hundred-peso fine; when the man and woman refused to comply, they found themselves confined to what they described as a "crude hotel." Rowdy Anglos arrested for disorderly conduct at a bar or nightclub—a common transgression along the border—might gain their release only to walk free minus some of their personal belongings. A common infraction, punishable by a fine of up to fifty pesos and confiscation of many a traveler's most prized possessions, involved photographing "saloons, burro carts, and beggars"—subjects regarded by identity-conscious authorities as "unfit for exhibition in other countries." In addition to zealous policing, U.S. tourists might experience a loss of items during baggage inspection, and those driving south by automobile often waited months for the return of their tourist immigration deposit, a serious problem for those on tight budgets.[84]

Visitor-host disputes eventually percolated up to the federal government level. A Mexican vice consul in New York confided to one interviewer in 1934 that he was endlessly amazed and appalled by the questions posed by U.S. citizens planning to visit his country. Are there stores? Does anyone speak English? Is there anything to eat other than tamales? "Don't people read newspapers and magazines?," he exclaimed.[85] "We have suffered as a nation from misrepresentation," Mexico's education minister told the questioner, "from the pictures that tourists have taken of the worst features of our country poverty, illiteracy, we are working on these problems but it takes time . . . and it is no more just to take a picture showing our worst qualities and label it 'Mexico' than it would be for us to bring back a photograph of the slums of New York and call it 'America!'"[86]

True to its nationalistic agenda, the Cárdenas administration mobilized state power to refashion the country's travel industry. On New Year's Day 1935, one month after taking office, Cárdenas delivered a nationwide radio address in which he promised that his government would "pay special attention to exercising vigilance against vices and gambling houses prohibited by law." Later that day came the presidential decree that banned casino gambling across the nation. The initiative reflected the president's personal distaste for the bourgeois excesses associated with the Porfiriato and his determination to uplift Mexico morally as well as economically. It also made for good politics since in a matter of months Cárdenas would officially break with former president Calles, and the new president's handlers cherished his image as a corruption-free crusader of the people who offered Mexicans a new leadership style. Indeed, the antigambling initiative was also probably intended as a thrust against Calles and his ally, Abelardo Rodríguez, the former president and casino-friendly Tijuana governor.[87]

The administration did not immediately enforce the initiative uniformly. State and local officials in Tijuana skirted the dictate for nearly a year and a half, and Rodríguez's hotel and casino complex at Agua Caliente gained temporary dispensation as well. But by August 1936, the *New York Times* reported, Tijuana resembled a "ghost city." In February 1937, Cárdenas removed General Rafael Navarro Cortina as governor and military commander of the Northern District of California as a result of complaints of resumed gambling near the border. The following summer, the Agua Caliente shut down. The new law, coupled with the repeal of Prohibition in the United States, slowly choked the border trade and diminished the tourist presence along the border.[88]

While Cárdenas put the kibosh on the casino business, he showed no intention of stifling tourism as a whole. Instead, his administration worked to channel the cavalcade of visitors into the nation's interior and toward Mexico's cultural attractions. José Quevado, director of the government's newly created Department of Tourism, spearheaded the effort. Beginning in 1936, he invited representatives from private industry to participate in what became the National Tourism Committee (Comité Nacional de Turismo, CTNT). The group encompassed the leaders of the Mexican Automobile Association, the National Railways of Mexico, the Mexican Railways, the Missouri-Pacific, the Ward Line and Grace Line steamship companies, the Mexican Aviation Company (a subsidiary of Pan Am), the Mexican National Bank, both the American and Mexican Chambers of Commerce, Wells Fargo, a representative group of hoteliers, and numerous other firms.

Dina Berger has described the CTNT's role in designing a tourism policy that reinforced postrevolutionary identity formation. Quevado in particular viewed Cuba as a place where tourism had degenerated into a destructive cultural predator. The CTNT sought to build on earlier efforts to stage an authentic ancient Mexico, generate tourist dollars, and reinforce the country's indigenous identity. In the southern state of Oaxaca, federal assistance funded the excavation of the recently discovered pre-Columbian city of Monte Albán, and to the east, across the Yucatán, federal assistance for restoration at Chichén Itzá increased.[89] Further north, the government supported efforts of the Society of Friends of San Miguel to restore and preserve the town's picturesque colonial architecture, shaping the community as a North American art and retirement colony. On the initiative of Friends member Felipe Cossío and with vital assistance from state officials in Guanajuato, San Miguel's School of Fine Arts was founded where the Convent of the Nuns had formerly stood. One Foreign Office official explained to a gathering of hotel investors the government's calculation that the town's "fine taste and aristocracy, so characteristic of the Mexican colonial period," would attract a contingent of intellectual and artistic tourists and expatriates.[90]

The government's tourism plans hinged most of all on strengthening public-private partnerships and upgrading travel infrastructure. Rejecting Cuba's reliance on U.S. investment, Mexican officials in the latter half of the 1930s built a nationwide system of hotels and restaurants, financed in part by the state and owned wholly by Mexicans. A new federal agency established in 1938, the Crédito Hotelero, became a clearinghouse for the distribution of subsidies and loans for Mexican-controlled projects.[91] Many of the new accommodations popped up in Mexico City, but key cities along the Pan-American Highway and other heavily touristed locales underwent more subtle face-lifts.

In addition to espousing cultural and economic nationalism, the subsidies strengthened the PNR by rewarding loyal former government officials and party leaders. Former president Ortiz Rubio, who had joined forces with Cárdenas against Calles, received roughly $1.5 million in subsidies and tax breaks to help finance the opening of hotels in Monterrey and Acapulco.[92] Rubio in turn used his influence to secure government financial support for fellow investor Carlos F. Osuna for a rustic-style resort, Casa Grande en Valles, located along the Pan-American Highway, outside the city of San Luis Potosí. Osuna sought not only a peso subsidy but special licenses to allow him to circumvent the country's currency controls and import the kitchen equipment, furniture, and machinery he needed.[93] Another party stalwart, Manuel del Valle, received a concession for his new restaurant, Manolo, which he planted strategically on the beach in Acapulco, a town that would soon become a Mexican gold mine sans conquistadors.[94]

The Cárdenas government publicized these and other attractions with a penny-pinching but effective promotional campaign. It turned down offers from advertising and travel agencies in the United States to orchestrate expensive advertising campaigns. Instead, the government sponsored low-budget film series in the United States, invited travel writers and travel agency executives to visit Mexico, and opened a tourist agency in New York City.[95] Cárdenas expended considerable personal energy on the tourism project and frequently took time out of his busy schedule to meet and correspond with influential visiting Americans, including college and university groups, authors, newspaper and magazine editors, union leaders, and big-city mayors.[96]

The campaign weathered some serious strains in U.S.-Mexican diplomatic relations. The rapprochement between the two countries that had inched along since the early 1920s nearly derailed in late 1937 and early 1938. In response to prolonged labor unrest in Mexico's oil fields that affected some 18,000 oil workers, Cárdenas expropriated 350,000 acres of Standard Oil land in November 1937, the first step in the comprehensive nationalization of the oil industry.[97] Nationalist and leftist Mexicans, especially organized labor, thundered their approval, but the initiative provoked indignation among U.S. oil executives, certain factions in Congress, and numerous U.S. newspapers. Standard Oil affiliates Continental Oil (Conoco) and Texas Oil (Texaco) undertook a rigorous public relations offensive to discourage travel to Mexico, publishing warnings of gas shortages, dangerous road conditions, and widespread hostility toward Americans. In addition, a short-lived armed May 1938 uprising in San Luis Potosí led by the local caudillo, General Saturnino Cedillo, Cárdenas's former secretary of agriculture, gained coverage in the *New York Times* and led the U.S. State Department to issue a travel warning.[98]

A coalition of public and private agencies from both sides of the border effectively outmaneuvered big oil and Mexico's other critics. The Mexican Automobile Association broadcast a widely played radio program that reassured motorists that gas, paved roads, and highway safety still prevailed south of the border.[99] The Hotel Greeters of Mexico, led by Antonio Perez O., manager of the Hotel Reforma, orchestrated a July 1938 "Caravan of Good Will" from Mexico City to Atlantic City, New Jersey, meeting with the U.S. press and government officials along the way to publicize the security of the cultural corridors connecting the two countries.[100]

The Cárdenas regime, moreover, stepped up its outreach efforts with the U.S. press. One series of government-approved articles on "romantic old Mexico" that appeared in the *Miami Herald* in mid-1938 highlighted the growing availability of "modern" hotels and lavished praise on "the peace-loving" nature of the Mexican people.[101] An advertisement jointly sponsored by the Mexican and U.S. governments accompanied the first entry and featured letters signed by Cárdenas and Ambassador Daniels. "I am happy to say to you," the president announced, "that the Mexican government is not and cannot be indifferent to anything tending towards an active cultural and economic exchange."[102]

Although tourist numbers dipped slightly from just over 130,000 in 1937 to 103,000 in 1938, they shot back up to 127,822 the following year.[103] The slump may have resulted from the bad publicity that accompanied oil nationalization but may also have been a response to a hurricane that swept across Mexico in late August 1938, knocking out bridges, washing out roadways, and leaving hundreds of U.S. tourists unhappily stranded. At any rate, the government redoubled its promotional efforts. In late 1938 and 1939, Pemex, Mexico's new national oil corporation, launched its own campaign to lure North Americans southward. The *Pemex Travel Bulletin* promoted auto trips to Mexico, calling attention to the country's many tourist attractions and distributing road maps that specified the convenient locations of Pemex filling stations.[104]

In 1938, the government organized yet another public-private partnership, the Mexican Tourist Association (Asociación Mexicana de Turismo, AMT). A transnational coalition of hoteliers, railways, travel agencies, auto clubs, and chambers of commerce again buttressed the travel industry. Whereas the CTNT had plotted to define Mexico's identity, the AMT advertised it. Taking advantage of the war in Europe and a decline in transatlantic travel, the organization solicited donations from private firms and government ministries to produce pamphlets and posters, booklets, and press releases. In 1939, the AMT took a step that the Mexican government had long resisted when it contracted New York advertising firm Hamilton Wright to choreograph a full-fledged ad and press campaign. Hamilton Wright had gained fame in the advertising world for its successful selling of Egypt's pyramids as vacation destinations.[105] The marketing of Mexico, the land of pre-Columbian mysteries, colonial architecture, and modern travel conveniences, got fully under way.

The government's travel advertisements fused tradition and modernity and addressed the ongoing domestic quest for national identity. Hired artists adopted the modernized *indígena* (indigenous woman) as the nation's symbol, and she was emblazoned on the front of each year's AMT-published *Mexico: The Faraway Land Nearby* brochure. Sometimes she appeared as a dark-skinned Aztec princess. At other times, she bore indigenous and Anglo features and personified the nation's feminine mestizo identity. Either way, her beauty—youthful face, long black braids, intense eyes, and inner self-confidence—drew attention to the nation's pre-Spanish roots and contrasted sharply with that of a 1920s border-town barmaid. She typically appeared in traditional garb in front of a detailed backdrop of volcanic mountains, plants, burros, and churches that represented Mexico's mosaic of regional identities. Thus, for Mexicans, her appearance resonated national unity in the tradition of the postrevolutionary art form known as Mexicanidad. For travelers, she promised foreign adventure and a visit to the past as well as the benefits of modern development: miles of paved highway, up-to-date hotels, and assurances of personal security.[106]

Beyond Rapprochement: Accommodation

The amorphous visitor-host relationship of the 1930s exhibited a pendulum-like quality, first defined by Yankee consumerism and cultural power, then refined by the public policies of the Cárdenas administration. The Mexican government played its hand skillfully. The growing thirst for foreign experiences and Mexico's cultural allure and affordability assured an ample supply of visitors. Grassroots laborers and law enforcement officials demonstrated that hosts as well as visitors wielded soft power. Cárdenas understood that tourists could not be clumped together under one label and determined to attract certain species and discourage others.

As had been the case in the 1920s, tourism brought ordinary Americans and Mexicans into closer proximity and integrated their lives and identities.

This 1938 Mexican Tourist Association poster announced Mexico's pride in its feminized, indigenous identity and beckoned U.S. tourists to participate in the country's reawakening. Getty Images.

In July 1935, the *New York Times* reported that tourist expenditures in France had dropped by ten million dollars from 1933 to 1934 but had risen to more than forty-one million dollars in Mexico, giving the southern neighbor the third-largest expenditure after France and Canada. "Mexico City, with more than a million inhabitants, is a place where the old and new meet, the civilized and the primitive," the *Times* proclaimed.[107] Hubert Herring, founder of the annual summer seminar at the National University in Mexico City, wrote of the U.S. "rediscovery" of "the unconquerable Mexican" in the June 1937 issue of *Harper's Monthly*, applauding the nation's land reform and economic modernization as well as its receptiveness to North American visitors.[108] "Mexico is a land where the American tourist will find much old romance of a typically Spanish country," the *Review of Reviews* noted, "yet equipped with modern hotels in the large cities, comfortable modes of travel and a genuine hospitality on the part of the populace."[109]

Many travelers wrote to President Cárdenas in praise of Mexico and in recognition that their two countries shared a common destiny. The president's staff diligently sent polite replies and filed away the fan mail. James L. Calaway of Dayton, Ohio, returned home from his first journey to Mexico in August 1939 eager to share his impressions with the country's president: "Mexico is truly a Land of Charm, a Land of Romance, a Land of Sunshine and Song. . . . We enjoyed every minute of our stay there."[110] M. F. Sessions of Chattanooga, Tennessee, conveyed his compliments: "I am more impressed with the happiness and contentment prevailing among your people . . . who have found work to do and enjoy it."[111] Oliver Babcock of Los Angeles, a self-described "ordinary businessman," contacted Cárdenas prior to departure. "I have admired very much the things you are doing for the common people of Mexico," Babcock commented, and "in that respect you are very much like our President Roosevelt."[112] Michael and Virginia Scully, authors of one of the first guides to automobile travel in Mexico, wrote extensively on the country's social reforms, including its "New Deal" in rural education.[113]

As visitors and hosts clashed, sparred, and negotiated, they increasingly found commonalities. U.S. and Mexican governmental officials pursued a similar tack and searched for ways to retire the diplomatic controversies of the revolutionary era. In his March 1933 inaugural address, President Roosevelt articulated his famous Good Neighbor policy toward Latin America, giving a name and a public face to Washington's willingness to negotiate differences rather than settle them with gunboats: "I would dedicate the nation to the policy of the good neighbor, the neighbor who resolutely respects himself, and because he does so, respects the rights of others."[114]

The Good Neighbor proclamation did not revolutionize U.S. policy in the region and most certainly did not disassemble the foundations of empire. In many cases, especially in the turbulent and strategically vital Caribbean, economic and military support for pro-U.S. dictators replaced direct military intervention as a tool of control. But in Mexico, the doctrine of the Good Neighbor meant a willingness to pursue a peaceful settlement of ongoing property and debt disputes, to fend off oil company demands for retribution against Mexico's nationalist government, and to enhance cultural exchanges, including tourism. The Roosevelt administration's policies toward Mexico in many ways mimicked already established trends in the visitor-host relationship. Like U.S. tourists, U.S. diplomats learned to yield some of their privileges and accommodate Mexican interests.

A number of factors enabled a U.S.-Mexican accommodation. The war clouds that swirled across both oceans and the expectation that the United States would soon need access to Mexico's resources, ports, military bases, and air transit rights gave Roosevelt and Daniels reason to persevere. As tourists well knew, the world was not as large as it had previously been, and the United States could not survive and prosper on its own. Under the rubric of "hemispheric solidarity," Washington extended an olive branch to the Latin American republics prior to and during the war and promised assistance for postwar modernization in exchange for wartime collaboration. U.S. diplomacy paid handsome dividends when Mexico followed the United States in declaring war against the Axis powers and became a valued military ally.

Mexico had its own reasons for improving relations. Historian Stephen Niblo has shown that the Cárdenas administration began to moderate its reformism by the late 1930s, calculating that Mexico's industrial future depended on healthy relations with the regional superpower. The implementation of land reform slowed, cooperation between Mexican and U.S. investment and import firms increased, and Mexico City welcomed Ambassador Daniels's proposal to resolve the issues of debt and compensation in one fell swoop. The 1940 election to the presidency of Manuel Ávila Camacho, an avowed centrist and anticommunist, accelerated the moderating trends.[115]

In early 1941, Daniels and his Mexican counterparts under the newly formed Camacho government finally resolved the long-standing disputes over land, oil, and debt in a comprehensive "global settlement." The deal reaffirmed Mexico's sovereign rights over its land and resources and signaled Washington's willingness to treat Mexico generously. Mexico City pledged to pay forty million dollars in indemnities to U.S. property holders whose agrarian lands had been seized, but the United States government in return provided a forty-million-dollar peso stabilization plan that provided the Mexican government the wherewithal to fund the compensation. In addition, the United States agreed to purchase six million dollars worth of Mexican silver per month, provided a thirty-million-dollar Export-Import loan to assist road building, and agreed to establish a joint board to determine the indemnity to be paid to U.S. oil companies, later assessed at a modest twenty million dollars.[116]

As heavily as political, economic, and military considerations weighed on officials of both countries at the end of the 1930s, the steady expansion of transportation and communications links, the growth of business and cultural contacts, and the tourism boom of the previous twenty years had nurtured profound changes in the everyday life of the empire. The settlement in many ways reflected a redistribution of power that had already occurred in Mexico's tourist districts, its gaming houses, and archeological sites. Deeper than the political adjustments carried out in the closing months of the decade, the changes generated by two decades of tourism had rearranged consciousness and identities. By 1940, U.S. perceptions of Mexico had become increasingly nuanced. The language of Manifest Destiny had by no means disappeared, but it was increasingly complemented by an appreciation for Mexico's past civilizations, its rural lifeways, its indigenous and mestizo peoples, and its struggle to form a modern state and a unifying national identity.

The tourist-host relationship, moreover, had engaged both governments and demonstrated culture's growing significance to international relations. While President Cárdenas deployed state power to make tourism better serve the national interest, President Roosevelt embraced tourism as a diplomatic tool. The U.S. executive declared 1940 the Travel America Year and stepped up his public support of the travel industry. The newly established Office of the Coordinator of Inter-American Affairs, led by Nelson Rockefeller, launched a well-funded public relations campaign to counter Axis propaganda in Latin America. Washington partnered with Hollywood to finance and distribute films that portrayed Latin American countries in positive, even romantic, tones to U.S. audiences. *Holiday in Mexico* and *Weekend in Havana* swept moviegoers from prewar and wartime theaters to the hemisphere's most idealized palm-laden vacation destinations. To avoid inadvertent cultural slights, the script for the musical *That Night in Rio* (1940), in which starlet Carmen Miranda sang "Chica, Chica, Boom, Chica," was reviewed and approved by Brazilian authorities. Rio, Havana, and Mexico City acquired increased status in U.S. popular culture as urban centers that blended modernity and tradition and provided the backdrop for erotically charged European encounters with the non-European other.[117]

Softening the financial conservatism of dollar diplomacy and in some ways foreshadowing the postwar promotion of European travel under the Marshall Plan, the Roosevelt administration fine-tuned its bureaucratic apparatus to encourage U.S. tourists to travel south. New Deal planners had established the Export-Import Bank in 1934 to provide loans mainly to dollar-producing extractive industries in Latin America. The goal had been to stimulate Latin economies, create markets for U.S. goods, and give the Good Neighbor policy a tangible financial dimension. During the early 1940s, looking ahead to the end of the war, FDR began to envision tourism as another economic sector worthy of Ex-Im assistance and encouraged Treasury Department officials to entertain loan applications for hotel construction.[118]

FDR proved susceptible to his own rhetoric. In March 1938, at the height of the U.S.-Mexican oil controversy, he penned an expansive letter to Daniels about a possible presidential visit to Mexico. The trip would afford the opportunity to meet with President Cárdenas and conduct state business, but the chief executive devoted considerably more attention to sightseeing itineraries. Noting that Congress would adjourn by early June, he laid out two options: rail to San Francisco, followed by travel by cruiser to Acapulco, or overnight train to Mexico City, with side trips by automobile to Iguala and Acapulco. The three-day excursion to Mexico City, he noted, might be too strenuous. But then again, he had heard there was a "fairly good hotel" in Iguala. For that matter, "there is, of course, a good hotel at Taxco," but "that is 185 miles from Acapulco and that is a long distance on a dirt road." Roosevelt admitted his preference for sailing, explaining, "I could stop on the way down the Mexican coast and do some fishing." But in a postscript he added, "On looking at the Mexican railway map, I find there is a railway from Mexico City to Manzanillo but I do not know if a special heavy train could run over it. If it could, we could go there to join the cruiser instead of Acapulco."[119]

In the end, the tête-à-tête with Cárdenas never came about, and FDR settled on a second fishing trip to Magdalena Bay. But Roosevelt's personal engagement in the matter and his knowledge of Mexico's hotels, transportation, and recreational offerings suggest that he inhabited the same cultural space as many tourists. Josephus Daniels became no less enamored of things Mexican. Two years earlier, he had visited the famous ruins at Chichén Itzá and used his official status to arrange extended conversations with Carnegie Foundation archeologist Sylvanus Morley. The ambassador's record of the visit conveyed his sense of awe at antiquity. "I had heard Dr. Sylvanus Morley, the scholar and archeologist, tell of the history and mystery of Mayan architecture and learning," he wrote, "but it seemed like being carried back centuries to stand upon the ancient site and hear Dr. Morley tell the transcendentally interesting story; it was like being transported into another world."[120]

The world of the tourist and that of the policymaker increasingly revolved around the same constellation of hopes and fears during the 1930s and early 1940s. Both travelers and diplomats possessed an irresistible urge to explore and to spread their influence, yet each looked upon the shrunken globe with foreboding. Each tended to perceive world affairs from the center of the empire looking out, yet each learned to appreciate the perspective of the "other" and the advantages of dialogue. Tourism relationships, not just in Mexico but around the world, had already accustomed a significant segment of the U.S. public to international engagement and erected a larger context in which Americans perceived and interacted with the outside world.

FDR understood the linkages between tourism and political internationalism. On an October 1937 visit to Fargo, North Dakota, home state of Senator Gerald P. Nye and the cradle of political isolationism, the president remarked extemporaneously on the globalizing effects of tourism and the psychology of fear: "Yes, it pays to travel. . . . [W]e get a bigger perspective and a lot of knowledge," he declared. He then related a story: "One day [Ambassador Daniels] got a letter from a friend of his in Chicago, who wrote, 'I am contemplating a business trip to Mexico City. Do you think it would be safe for me to come and bring my wife and daughter with me?' A few hours later a Mexican friend came to the Embassy and said, 'Mr. Ambassador, I would like to go to the Chicago Exposition. Do you think it would be safe for me to take my wife and family to Chicago?'" FDR concluded, "The Ambassador told the gentleman from Chicago and the gentleman from Mexico that both trips would be eminently safe, so they went and they had a wonderful time."[121]

Roosevelt finally made his long-awaited visit to inland Mexico in April 1943, a highly secretive jaunt across the border by train with his wife, Eleanor, to meet with wartime ally President Camacho. The U.S. president left his sightseeing itinerary at the White House, limiting his stops to the northern industrial city of Monterrey. But FDR still relished his taste of Mexico. As he rode through the pennant-bedecked streets, señoritas threw flowers and confetti from the balconies. That night, he and Camacho sat down to a seven-course dinner. While Eleanor Roosevelt tried her newly learned Spanish on the Mexican First Lady, the two presidents conversed through an interpreter.

Then they rose to address their countries by radio. Their speeches were filled with Good Neighborliness and a mutual pledge to fight the war through to a complete victory over the Axis powers. The two governments, Roosevelt observed, had "recognized a mutual interdependence of our joint resources" and "know that the day of the exploitation of the resources of one country for the benefit of any group in another country is definitely over." Both chief executives declared that they looked forward to the postwar years, when the hemispheric Good Neighbor policy could be extended to the entire world.[122]

The globalizing trends of the interwar era produced many unexpected outcomes. Some registered as nothing short of horrific: the mass death of total war, extermination camps, and holocaust and widespread economic havoc. But the dynamic also enhanced economic interdependence, spawned increased cultural exchanges, and of course stimulated international tourism. During the years that separated the U.S. rejection of the League of Nations and its embrace of the United Nations, the country's citizens engaged the rest of the world as never before through commerce and travel. In many cases, Americans broadened their horizons, came to know others, and imagined themselves as members not only of a national community but of a larger, world community.

The story of the world's drift toward the Second World War is usually told with the benefit of hindsight. The outcome was less evident at the time. If rising tariffs and rearmament represented one response to global depression, the growing cooperation between the United States and postrevolutionary Mexico occupied the other end of the spectrum. Six decades out from the Second Great War, in an age of shrinking distances and accelerated globalization, the complex legacies of interwar transnationalism take on additional meaning. The era not only paved the way toward a mammoth battle between geographically based and industrialized nation-states but also carried within itself technological, economic, and cultural forces that helped produce the deterritorialized, postindustrial international system of the early twenty-first century.

By the time Lázaro Cárdenas stepped down as president, the basic structures of Mexico's modern tourist industry had been established and the country had undergone a stunning expansion in tourism. In 1935, Mexico City boasted a total of twenty-two registered hotels; by 1942, that number had risen to fifty-five, with more than thirty-five hundred rooms. Restaurants and nightclubs proliferated as well. On the eve of the Second World War, the Cocoanut Grove at the new Hotel Waldorf, where waiters in tuxedos served dinner to patrons on a patio shaded by coconut trees, enjoyed a reputation as the capital's most fashionable bistro. But it faced stiff competition from the Bottoms-Up restaurant and bar, Club Venus, the El Patio, and Raffles night-club. Acapulco, perhaps postwar Mexico's most exclusive and renowned tour-ist retreat, had also begun to sculpt a modern personality with the opening of the large and opulent Hotel La Marina. In Cuernavaca, the new all-inclusive Hotel Marik featured swimming, horseback riding, tennis, and golf.[123] The war temporarily slowed the boom, but after four years of sacrifice, U.S. citizens were anxious to hit the road again, and in 1946 the tally of U.S. tourists in Mexico surpassed 245,000.[124]

Since the end of the Second World War, the North American passion for Mexican spaces has only intensified. The outcome has not always been equi-table. Acapulco evolved from quaint fishing village to a exclusive megaresort for affluent Yankees and Mexican elites. In the 1980s and 1990s, Cancún and the Mayan Riviera boomed with hotels and gated retirement communities—what critics have termed "other-directed" landscapes because they have been developed with the interests of foreign tourists primarily in mind. Yet at the same time, several of the more carefully regulated travel destinations of the interwar era, including San Miguel, Taxco, and Oaxaca, continue to thrive. Even sprawling, pollution-plagued Mexico City, like the country's other ur-ban centers, has preserved its *zócalo* as a site for community activity and political protest as well as for history-minded tourists.

Along the border, the red lights have been relit. The low-wage maquiladora factory system, first established in the 1970s and expanded with the passage of the North American Free Trade Agreement in the 1990s, feeds the U.S. pub-lic's seemingly insatiable appetite for low-priced consumer goods and repre-sents one troubled outcome of hemispheric integration and globalization. At the same time, migratory labor patterns, cross-border trade, and tourism have created a transfrontier metropolis where languages, cuisine, and music have blended and blurred, even in the face of militarized border patrols.[125] For better and for worse, interwar tourism helped to transform the everyday life of the empire and lay the groundwork for today's cross-border networks. It inspired and made profitable the building and extension of cultural cor-ridors and new cultural contact zones. It empowered transnational elites but also bestowed a variety of soft powers on ordinary tourists and hospitality workers. It allowed U.S. capital and diplomatic influence to regain admission to Mexico's nation-building project but also empowered the Mexican gov-ernment selectively to blunt those influences. It extended U.S. consumer and cultural power southward and spawned new forms of conflict yet produced new partnerships and acts of collaboration, from cross-border business alliances to artistic and scholarly exchanges to the bond that might develop serendipitously between a Mexico City taxi driver and his *patrona*.

It is significant that the rapprochement occurred in the immediate aftermath of one of the twentieth century's landmark social revolutions, a revolution that severely tested the durability and flexibility of the U.S.-led hemispheric empire. During the latter half of the 1940s, following the end of the war, international tourism experienced another major growth spurt, not only in Mexico but across all of Latin America and the world. Immediately to the east of Mexico's Yucatán coast, across the turquoise Caribbean, Cuba beckoned. Long a U.S. dependency, Cuba, much like Mexico, had first tapped into the mass tourism market during the 1920s. But whereas the travel industry in Mexico had facilitated the institutionalization of social revolution and accommodation with the United States, in Cuba it fueled the outbreak of a second twentieth-century upheaval that unraveled the visitor-host relationship and utterly broke the bonds of empire.

THREE

The Safe Bet

Batista's Cuba

The crowded casino of the stately Hotel Nacional reeked of smoke, liquor, and perfume. The fashionably dressed clientele excitedly watched the repetitious toss of the dice. It was January, the height of the 1958 winter season. Nearly six years after coming to power through a military coup, Cuba's dictator, Fulgencio Batista, felt reasonably secure. Constitutional rights had been suspended, the press censored, and the official story ran that a rural insurrection led by a pesky, twenty-eight-year-old rebel, Fidel Castro, represented little more than a nuisance. Jake Lansky, brother of celebrity gangster Meyer Lansky, worked as the casino's pitman, a "technician" who ruled over games of chance at the craps table, surrounded by the deep carpeting of the Nacional's game room. "We are getting bigger bets than Las Vegas," a dice man bragged to a *Time* magazine correspondent. "All the real big Eastern crapshooters are coming down here to take a crack at us."[1]

The outlook had not always been rosy. Five years earlier, Havana's casinos had been castigated in the press for fast dealing and fixed games, largely a consequence of an eight-die game called razzle-dazzle, so complex that most players never learned the rules before being fleeced. The swindling of Dana C. Smith, an influential Republican contributor to California senator Richard M. Nixon's campaigns, prompted letters from Nixon to the U.S. State Department and the Cuban government in Havana. In March 1953, the *Saturday Evening Post* ran a widely noticed article, "Suckers in Paradise," that exposed Cuba's crooked casinos.[2]

A month after the article appeared, Batista's military intelligence forces, the Servicio de Inteligencia Militar, arrested and deported a dozen North Americans, mostly lower-level mobsters, for running fixed games at some of Havana's leading establishments: the Tropicana, the Sans Souci, and the Jockey Club.[3] Facing a downturn in both gambling and tourism, the second-

Mobster Meyer Lansky operated the Hotel Nacional Casino in partnership with his old friend, Las Vegas hotelier Wilbur Clark. Well-dressed, sophisticated visitors hover around the gambling tables and the adjacent Starlight Terrace Bar in this 1958 postcard. Cuban Heritage Collection, University of Miami Libraries, Coral Gables, Florida.

most-important factor in the Cuban economy after sugar, Batista turned to an old associate, the Russian-born Meyer Lansky, a longtime presence in Havana's casino world whom the U.S. Senate's Kefauver Report on organized crime described as one of the six top hoodlums in the United States, to manage Havana's hottest gambling joints. Lansky received a dream decree—a waiver on corporate taxes for ten years, cancellation of customs duties on imported gaming equipment, and permission to grant two-year work visas to mob-trained roulette stickmen and craps pitmen. Batista acquired a no-nonsense gambling czar who ran an honest but lucrative game and delivered the revenue—some two thousand dollars a month from each gambling room plus 20 percent of profits—to the presidential palace.[4]

Lansky restored "integrity" to Havana's plush casinos, but Cuba's corrupt tourism industry—a razzle-dazzle of private interests, conspicuous consumption, vice mongering, government bribes, real estate scams, and shady underworld players—remained intact. In contrast to postrevolutionary Mexico's heavily regulated public-private arrangements, prerevolutionary Cuba's tourism industry replicated the capitalist structures of the island's agriculture-dependent export economy and catered almost wholly to private interests.

Private enterprise is not necessarily free enterprise. The Batista government studiously planned Cuba's tourist sector, but this form of planning looked to well-connected elites—U.S. investors, banks, organized crime, select allies within the transnational travel industry, and the dictator's favored business and military loyalists—to run the island's hospitality trade. They deployed their host power to reconfigure Havana's built environment and popularize cultural constructions of Cuban identity that fed tourist fantasies of pleasure and entitlement. Postwar consumer capitalism shaped U.S. cultural relations and helped spread an "irresistible empire" in Western Europe, but in Cuba it helped foment an irresistible revolution.

Cuba's tourism binge came at an inopportune moment in international history. First, the United States, which had exercised hegemony over the island since the turn of the century, ascended to world leadership following the Second World War. The onset of the Cold War with the Soviet Union and decolonization in the Third World did not alter the foundations of U.S.-Cuban relations—Washington had drawn a line in the sand against communism in Latin America long before the Soviets and Americans divided postwar Europe. But the global Cold War reinforced Washington's inclination to support conservative Latin American regimes, including Batista's, that protected U.S. interests. Second, the world fully entered the aviation age, shrinking the planet's girth and multiplying the cultural corridors that linked peoples and nations. Third, the early years after the Second World War marked a turning point in the history of U.S. consumerism, when the New Deal's demand-side policies and their wartime spin-offs bestowed on middle- and working-class Americans unprecedented prosperity.[5] Big business and big labor negotiated progressive wage and benefits packages, the dollar ruled the global economy, and Americans succumbed to the travel bug as never before.

Cuba occupied a special place in the global picture. Ninety miles out to sea from Key West, Florida, it enticed tourists and policymakers alike. It had long fed U.S. dreams of empire—as a prospective sugar-producing slave state during the early republic, a site for naval bases at the time of the Spanish-American-Cuban-Philippine war, and a U.S. protectorate after Congress adopted the 1901 Platt Amendment that secured Guantánamo as a U.S. outpost and permitted U.S. military intervention. Louis A. Pérez Jr., the leading historian of U.S.-Cuban relations, has explained how North Americans inscribed the island into their imaginations by means of metaphor. The U.S. system of domination rested on self-congratulatory notions that Cuba could be best understood as a neighbor in need, fruit ripe for the picking, a damsel in distress, a hemispheric Armenia, or an orphaned child.[6] By the 1950s, Cuba had emerged as an investor's utopia, a bastion of anticommunism, and the second-most-popular U.S. tourist spot in the hemisphere, trailing only Mexico.

U.S. citizens poured across the Straits of Florida by plane and ferry, some three hundred thousand annually by the end of the decade. Yankees visiting Cuba might be likened to latter-day colonials. They could be spotted strolling Havana's breathtaking seawall promenade, the Malecón, with the sparkling Caribbean as backdrop; downing daiquiris and *mojitas* at Sloppy Joe's bar; and stopping in for a nightcap at the Floridita, where Ernest Hemingway drank. They plopped down their credit cards and travelers checks and dined on delicious crab morro at the venerable Zaragozana restaurant, ogled the flesh and feathers at the Tropicana nightclub, and placed their bets at more than twenty major Havana casinos.

Some found in the Antillean retreat a refuge from the monotony of their postwar corporate offices. Others fled the insecurities of the nuclear age. Still others yearned to escape the confining sexual mores of Cold War domesticity, which, while hardly universal, characterized the lives of many middle-class Americans.[7] In a short time, tourist soft power transformed the everyday life of empire in Cuba. Whereas negotiation and compromise became the norm in interwar Mexico's tourist zones, Yankees in Cuba tended toward unilateralism. They demanded that less affluent Cuban hosts bow to North American racial and sexual domination, expansive consumer demands, and desire for control and possession.

North Americans have historically been willing to gamble to expand their opportunities in Cuba and have taken pride in nearly always placing the sure bet. President William McKinley initially resisted the "yellow press" and jingoists in Congress in the late 1890s but finally caved in to pressure and handily defeated Spain in a "splendid little war."[8] During the 1930s, when Cuba experienced a powerful but short-lived social revolution, the Franklin Roosevelt administration bet that a Cuban military sergeant named Fulgencio Batista and his political allies would send reformist president Ramón Grau San Martín packing. Batista's regime secured Washington's vital hemispheric strategic interests through most of the Second World War before stepping aside.

This chapter examines the sergeant's return to power in 1952 as a full-fledged dictator and the five-year tourism boom that followed. The high rollers from the mainland again lined up, not just Washington officials and U.S. military leaders but a long list of banks, corporations, mobsters, media moguls, and tourists, all of whom were complicit in bolstering the authoritarian regime. This time the wager went sour. Fused with U.S. political, military, and financial power, tourism played a major role in the coming of the Cuban Revolution.

Prelude to Paradise

Cuba's postwar status as a pleasure paradise did not arise overnight. As in Mexico's border towns, the arrival of modern mass tourism in metropolitan Havana coincided with Prohibition in the United States. During the previous two decades, following Cuba's "liberation" from Spanish colonial rule, U.S. and Cuban entrepreneurs had begun to snap up oceanfront properties in Marianao, a suburb just west of Havana, and to lobby the newly sovereign Cuban government to finance sewers, harbor dredging, and other public works.[9] Lavish ocean-side homes, a small cluster of beach cabanas, and a golf course soon popped up, but the construction of the Gran Casino Nacional gained the most notice. Real estate speculators, including Gran Casino owner and future public works director Carlos Manuel de Céspedes, proved instrumental in the passage of the Casino and Tourist Bill of 1919, which legalized gambling in establishments where at least $1.5 million had been invested.[10] The omnibus bill also provided financing for construction of a bridge over the Almendares River to connect Mariano to downtown Havana and established the Cuban Tourist Commission.[11]

Casinos and booze immediately became Cuba's main tourist draws. The tally of annual visitors rose from 44,000 in 1916 to 56,000 in 1920 to 90,000 in 1928 and 178,000 in 1937. Havana also duplicated the interwar Tijuana model by adding cheap sex to its tourist itinerary. Prostitution in Cuba was not a Yankee invention; poverty, machismo, and the ingrained patriarchal standards of Roman Catholicism played a part as well.[12] Still, the estimated number of prostitutes working in Havana steadily grew with the increased U.S. presence, jumping from 4,000 in 1912 to 7,400 in 1931.[13]

Although an infant air service to Havana commenced in 1928, ports and cruise ships served as the cultural corridors of choice for most U.S. visitors. Some steamed south from Manhattan on vessels operated by New York and Cuba Mail Steamship, better known as the Ward Line, 1,171 nautical miles in sixty hours at a round-trip cost of $160.[14] Others sped by rail to the docks of Key West, Florida, and crossed the open Atlantic via the Peninsular and Occidental Steamship, a six-hour float at $30 round-trip.[15] If they wished, Americans could sign their automobiles on as passengers with the Florida East Coast Ferry.[16]

Despite a vigorous debate over the social and moral impact of legal gambling, Cuban elites viewed tourism as a hedge against the unpredictable export market for the island's economic mainstay, sugar. In contrast to Mexico's nationalistic planning and state-private partnerships, however, Cuban leaders followed the familiar path, organizing the travel industry by doling out lucrative deals to foreign, mainly U.S., investors and relying on U.S. markets for customers.[17] John Bowman, founder of the Biltmore hotel chain in the United States, got in on the ground floor. In May 1920, he purchased Havana's leading hotel, a 250-room Spanish-inspired architectural gem, and christened it the Sevilla Biltmore.[18] The hotel sat in the heart of Old Havana (Habana Vieja), the formerly walled portion of the city, a treasure trove of narrow, cobblestone streets, colonial churches and cathedrals, old homes with enclosed courtyards, and Iberian-style plazas. The Bowman empire expanded rapidly and helped make tourism a central feature of the U.S. empire in Cuba. He leased with an option to buy the Gran Casino Nacional in Marianao, then acquired the Oriental Park racetrack, the Havana Biltmore Yacht and Country Club, and Bowman's Cuban-American Realty, which monopolized private home sales along Marianao's increasingly pricey oceanfront.[19]

A cadre of Cuban politicians won licenses for gaming houses, jai alai franchises, kickbacks on construction projects, and partnerships in lucrative real estate ventures. A turning point came in 1924 with Gerardo Machado's election to Cuba's presidency. Machado campaigned on a platform of agrarian reform and economic nationalism, but after his electoral victory, he cultivated U.S. investors and bankers, especially the Chase National Bank, for loans to finance public works, road building, and tourism. His administration initiated construction of an eighty-million-dollar *capitolio* building modeled after the neoclassical domed structure in Washington, D.C., an extravagant expenditure for a poor country. A large chunk of public works funds went to Machado's construction company and to his closest political ally, Carlos Manuel de Céspedes.[20]

Machado's management style foreshadowed Batista's, especially after 1927, when Machado unilaterally extended his term of office to 1935 and showed no tolerance for dissent. Washington's support for Machado nonetheless remained unbending, and U.S. investment in Cuba's economy soared. Between 1925 and 1929, mainland interests invested $1.5 billion in Cuba, more than a quarter of the total invested across all of Latin America. The sugar trust, led by New York's Horace Havemeyer, had steadily consolidated its hold on the island's mills and refining capacities since the late nineteenth century. Applying industrial methods to cash-crop production, the sugar trust systematically deforested large swaths of Cuban landscape, introduced hydraulic and steam technology to the milling process, and subjected local farmers to a system of sharecropping and a cycle of debt. By the end of the 1920s, foreigners owned 78 percent of the island's arable land, much of it devoted to either sugar or tobacco cultivation. Deepening the dependency, U.S. consumers purchased more than 50 percent of Cuban sugar annually.[21]

The travel industry further accelerated Cuba's economic development and its dependence on the United States. Havana welcomed several new tourist hotels, including the El Presidente (1927), the Palace (1928), and the jewel in the crown, the Hotel Nacional (1930). The hybrid art deco and neoclassical Nacional, located just west of Old Havana at Twenty-third Street and the Malecón in the emerging central-city Vedado neighborhood, sat majestically on a bluff overlooking the ocean.[22] About the same time, Du Pont interests began to develop Varadero Beach, about one hundred miles east of Havana, as an upscale ocean resort. Milton Hershey built an electric rail system east to Matanzas Province, where he transformed his giant sugar estate into a Cuban version of his chocolate theme park in Pennsylvania.[23]

Back in metropolitan Havana, Bowman's Gran Casino Nacional reopened in 1928 after undergoing an extensive refurbishment. In addition to its gambling rooms, it featured a restaurant nightclub with seating for one thousand, suitable for the growing number of Yankees who had discovered the sensuous magic of Cuban rumba performances. The Gran Casino Nacional became identified internationally by its exotic outdoor Fountain of Youth, which featured eight alluring nymphs dancing, grapes in hand, in a circular chain.[24] A new boulevard, Quinta Avenida (Fifth Avenue), connected Habana Vieja to the western suburbs and their beach homes, racetrack, and casino.

Havana increasingly took on a North American look and feel. Crisscrossing streets and avenues connected urban core to suburbs and created snarls of automobile traffic. A U.S. architectural firm, Schultz and Weaver, redesigned Bowman's Sevilla Biltmore and drew up plans for the Concha Beach club in Marianao. New Yorkers McKim, Mead, and White determined the lines of the Hotel Nacional. Popular stateside bands entertained tourist audiences in ballrooms and restaurants. *Terry's Guide to Cuba*, published in 1926, approved the trend. "The Present Day Cuban is rapidly becoming Americanized," the guide explained; "thousands act, think, talk, and look like Americans; wear American clothes, ride in American autos, use American furniture and machinery, and many speak English."[25]

Still, the North Americanization of Havana remained constrained during the 1920s and 1930s. The elegant Iberian *danzón* was not eclipsed by the

Charleston or the foxtrot. Habana Vieja, graced by colonial-era architecture, remained central to the city's cultural life and identity. City fathers promoted suburbanization and assisted the movement of shops and government buildings outside the periphery of Old Havana to a transformed Prado, a nineteenth-century boulevard. The advent of modernity did not altogether uproot the old, but the balancing act soon entered a new phase.

The Dawning of the Batista Era: Planned Corruption

Machado's hold on power grew tenuous with the arrival of the depression in the early 1930s. In September 1933, a revolution erupted that, much like Mexico's earlier rebellion, fused demands for economic transformation with anti-Yankeeism and anti-imperialism. Around the world, economic planning came into vogue. Only the Soviet Union maintained a thoroughgoing command economy, but most capitalist states, including FDR's United States and of course neighboring Mexico, intervened massively in the marketplace. Strong support from university students and striking workers helped bring reformer Ramón Grau San Martín to power in Cuba. Grau promised to abrogate unilaterally the odious Platt Amendment and implement a new regimen of national economic planning to diversify the island's economy and reduce dependence on sugar and the United States.

The reformist moment proved short-lived. The Roosevelt administration's Good Neighbor policy left little room for compromise with nationalism in Cuba and the rest of the Caribbean, a sharp contrast from Mexico. Although Washington avoided resort to gunboat diplomacy, traditional tools of hegemony proved sufficient to maintain North American supervision over the island. The U.S. ambassador in Havana dismissed Grau as a communist and worked both publicly and privately to oust him. In early 1934, Sergeant Fulgencio Batista, originally a supporter of the revolution, withdrew his backing for the outspoken president. Grau wisely stepped down and retreated into exile in postrevolutionary Mexico.[26]

Batista ruled from the shadows from 1934 to 1940. He won election to his own four-year term of office in 1940 in relatively honest polling held under the auspices of the country's new democratic constitution. The future strongman retired from public life in 1944 and moved to Daytona, Florida, to enhance his personal fortunes, already quite handsome after a decade at Cuba's helm. During an eight-year interregnum, the island was ruled by a chastened and thoroughly corrupted Grau (1944–48) and then by Carlos Prío Socarrás (1948–52), leaders of the Auténtico Party. The two won election as economic nationalists but by most accounts fleeced the national treasury and left Cuba's economy firmly in the North American grip.[27]

In accordance with provisions of the 1940 constitution, Prío established the Banco Nacional de Cuba to promote domestic savings, bolster private banks as a guarantor of loans, and spur economic diversification.[28] The public institution theoretically could have weaned Cuba from its dependence on sugar. A national bank might also have redirected the island's tourism industry from a Yankee-owned and -managed concern to an enterprise that favored local hosts and trumpeted Cuban culture. But the financial institution's impact was dwarfed by massive government corruption. As the Korean War neared its stalemated conclusion, the international price of sugar collapsed. At the same time, Auténtico misrule reached the breaking point. Having returned from Daytona and won election to the Cuban Senate, Batista sensed that the moment was his. In March 1952, three months prior to a scheduled election, he and his military allies staged a coup that installed him in the presidential palace and subsequently suspended the country's young constitution.[29]

Like most Cuban leaders before him, Batista advertised himself as an economic nationalist. He surrounded himself with a group of advisers who had lobbied during the Grau and Prío presidencies for public investment and diversification. Historian Ramiro Guerra, journalist and travel writer Armando Maribona, and engineer Victor Santamarina became outspoken advocates of a planned travel industry, patterned to some extent on the Mexican example, to serve as a "segunda zafra" (second harvest)—that is, as a backup for the volatile sugar market. Not long after seizing power, Batista created the Instituto del Turismo Cubano (ITC) and staffed it with reformers who not only advocated economic planning but also hoped to infuse Cuba's travel industry with nationalistic cultural content. Maribona, who served as the ITC's vice president, emerged as an especially eloquent champion of developing attractions that accented the island's Cubanness. Hundreds of miles of beaches, mineral springs, and colonial-era city plazas and churches represented an irreplaceable but barely acknowledged "national patrimony" that would easily draw inquisitive visitors. "On the other hand," Maribona wrote, "the cabarets, the hotels, the theatres of variety, the horse tracks, the roulette table, etc., are not sufficient in the list of attractions of a city or country that respects itself and pretends to conserve an honorable place in the concert of civilized nations."[30]

Batista selectively appropriated the ITC's ideas. Maribona's cultural nationalism promised little immediate return and ran counter to Cuba's modern dependence on U.S. investment funds and consumer demand. Linking tourism with identity formation was thus relegated to low-priority status. At the same time, Batista had no problem with economic planning as long as the process enriched him and his small camp of Cuban and U.S. business tycoons. The dictator accordingly set to work upgrading the island's tourism infrastructure rather than its tropical luster. Indeed, Cuba's hotels and restaurants had grown shabby during the depression and world war. While Mexico's tourism industry forged ahead during the 1930s and 1940s, Cuba's suffered from lack of investment and overall neglect. An early-1953 ITC report found that since the early 1930s, hotel construction had all but ceased in Havana; seven older accommodations had actually been torn down. Eleven other hotels had shut down their restaurants. Outside Havana, only three provinces hosted first-class hotels.[31]

The report observed that with the end of the Second World War, rising incomes in the United States, Europe's reconstruction, and the availability of abundant air travel, international tourism had begun to surge. According to an American Express report, U.S. citizens spent more than $19 billion traveling abroad in 1953, but only $50 million or so landed in Cuban coffers. Worldwide, Europe led the competition for tourist dollars, absorbing 23 percent of the market. Mexico took first place in the Americas, generating about $300 million in 1952. Canada plucked about $258 million from slightly over 26 million visitors, although the lion's share came from day-trippers to Niagara Falls.[32]

One striking trend was Cuba's loss of ground to its closest neighbors. Between 1949 and 1954, the island's share of the regional trade fell from 43 percent to 31.4 percent. Puerto Rico, Nassau, and Jamaica ranked among Cuba's staunchest competitors.[33] But the state of Florida, just a stone's throw across the sea, gave Cuba its most serious run for the money, with beaches, hotels, and casinos that rivaled those of Havana, Marianao, and Varadero. The Sunshine State relieved U.S. vacationers of approximately $100 million in 1952. It also attracted large numbers of middle- and upper-class Cubans— more than eighty thousand in 1952 alone—eager to appropriate northern culture and incorporate it into their own.[34]

The Batista government set out to restore the island's former glory. Hotel Law 2074, adopted in 1953, granted tax exemptions to all newly constructed hotels and motels.[35] The Banco Nacional de Cuba, which sprouted several satellite banks, most notably the Banco de Desarollo Economico y Social and the Banco de Fomento Agricola e Industrial, replaced National City Bank as the foremost supplier of investment capital. The Banco Nacional and its subsidiaries chipped in more than $80 million in public loans for private companies willing to build hotels, restaurants, and other tourist attractions.[36] Plans went into effect to expand Havana's international airport to accommodate larger planes and heavier traffic.[37]

Batista's planners approached the challenge mathematically, much as casino managers might. Their data told them that contrary to myth, Americans were not millionaires. Ninety-five percent of the U.S. population of 150 million earned less than $10,000 annually. That economic reality, along with Cuba's geographic proximity to the mainland, placed the island in a position to attract more new tourists than either Europe or Cuba's Caribbean competitors. The effort would be well worthwhile, for even those who earned less than $2,000 annually spent an average of $156 during their yearly vacation. Those in the median group of roughly $5,000 spent nearly double that amount.[38]

To lure those Yankees across the sea, the government planned to update urban sanitation, train English-speaking tour guides, and even hire a public relations firm, Guastella–McCann Erickson, to coordinate a "citizen education" program to teach Habaneros the benefits of tourism and make them more congenial hosts.[39] Much like Mexico during the interwar era, Cubans had developed a love-hate relationship with U.S. visitors. Hotel and restaurant workers, musicians, bartenders, and taxi drivers had regularly exercised their host power and either struck for higher wages or organized work slowdowns that disrupted or threatened to disrupt life in the tourist districts. During the post-Machado years, the government's Department (later Ministry) of Labor often backed union demands, much to the chagrin of island's Hotel and Restaurant Association.[40] During his first stint in power, Batista too had been considered friendly to labor, but back at the helm in the 1950s, he sought to bridle worker unrest by securing an alliance with Eusebio Mujal, secretary-general of the moderate Confederation of Cuban Workers, which oversaw some eighteen hundred unions.[41] The strategy succeeded in that it promoted economic growth and left many workers with little choice but to back the Batista regime. By the end of the decade, however, disenfranchised unionists constituted a core constituency within Fidel Castro's 26th of July Movement.

To top off the tourism makeover, Batista's planners also ratcheted up advertising in the United States via radio, film, and the new medium of television to accent Cuba's climate, nightlife, colonial architecture, and friendliness to English-speaking northerners. With Batista seemingly in charge and a postwar world conducive to travel, Cuban planners had a strategy in place by early 1953 to resurrect paradise.[42]

Cold War Internationalism, Transnational Interests, and Tourism

As Batista and friends plotted Cuba's tourism future, the global setting underwent multiple transformations that profoundly impacted international travel and the U.S.-led hemispheric empire. The Second World War had demonstrated once and for all that modern transportation and communications technology had collapsed the planet. While a shrinking world made mass tourism flourish, it also made possible the Japanese attack on Pearl Harbor and drew the United States into dangerous global conflicts. In a world recently shattered by war and nuclear nightmare, international peace seemed a distant dream. Reflecting on the Nazi killing machine and postwar Soviet expansionism, Protestant theologian Reinhold Niebuhr questioned the optimism of the Christian social gospel and rediscovered moral contingency in human affairs. Billy Graham, the most popular postwar U.S. evangelist, carried his message of sin and redemption to major cities across the country, denouncing communism's godless materialism along the way.[43]

Toward the end of the war, U.S. military planners speculated about where the next major threat might arise and how U.S. defenses might be organized to forestall catastrophe. All signs pointed to the Eurasian landmass, where dictator Joseph Stalin, the Soviet Red Army, and communist ideology appeared to represent a colossal danger. If the Second World War demonstrated the destructive potential of modern aviation and aerial bombardment, military planners reasoned, the deployment of U.S. air and naval power at forward bases around the world would provide "defense in depth."[44] In addition to the system of bases, the Truman administration pronounced its commitment to contain Soviet power in Eastern Europe and advanced more than twelve billion dollars to reconstruct war-torn Western Europe through the Marshall Plan.

Alert to the interconnectedness of economic and military security, U.S. leaders built new multilateral institutions aimed at preventing a repetition of the disastrous 1930s. The United Nations provided a semblance of collective security, subject to great power veto. The trade regime ultimately known as the General Agreement on Tariffs and Trade and the banking system created at Bretton Woods—featuring the International Monetary Fund and World

Bank—spurred reduced tariffs, stabilized currencies, and allocated loans for postwar reconstruction and economic development.[45]

The Marshall Plan represented a major exercise in soft power but gave way in short order to an emphasis on armaments. With the outbreak of the Korean War in June 1950, the Truman administration redirected the bulk of U.S. foreign aid to military assistance to anticommunist allies, first in Europe and subsequently in East Asia and the oil-rich Middle East.[46] The uneven process of political decolonization convulsed the latter two regions, spurring revolutions and civil wars, fueling aspirations for economic and social transformation, and raising the specter of superpower intervention. As the 1950s progressed, strategically placed Cold War partners such as South Korea and Taiwan became the leading recipients of U.S. economic assistance.

U.S. hegemony in Latin America (not technically a recently decolonized region) also seemed ready to loosen. A national security policy paper written in the early 1950s observed, "There is a trend toward nationalist regimes in Latin America." Indeed, whereas Cuba remained under the control of the pro-U.S. Batista regime, a nationalist regime critical of U.S. imperialism took power in Guatemala in 1954, and an assassin's bullet felled Nicaraguan dictator Anastasio Somoza in 1956. One of the more dramatic expressions of anti-Yankeeism occurred when protesters mobbed Vice President Richard Nixon's motorcade in downtown Caracas in late 1958. An aide to Secretary of State John Foster Dulles advised his boss, "The preponderance of U.S. influence in Latin America is being challenged."[47]

Despite the warning signs, the Truman and Eisenhower administrations reasoned that the Western Hemisphere remained relatively secure under U.S. leadership and therefore required only modest economic assistance. This assumption sat at odds with Latin American expectations, buoyed by FDR's wartime pledge of hemispheric solidarity and forcefully expressed at the first postwar inter-American conference in Chapultepec, Mexico, in 1945. Representatives from the southern republics insisted that they had delivered critical raw materials to the Allied war effort over the previous four years and that payback time had arrived. Latin American delegations specifically called on the United States to provide massive aid to ignite industrialization. The U.S. delegation countered that the region's developmental needs could be best met through "trade, not aid" and counseled local governments to eliminate tariffs and other impediments to foreign trade. U.S. aid remained restricted mainly to military assistance for "internal security," provided under the terms of the 1947 Rio Pact military alliance, and small doses of technical aid and loans.[48]

U.S. policymakers still placed considerable faith in soft power, including the benefits of international travel, which they believed made the American people less parochial and more aware of the U.S. stake in world affairs.[49] But while the Marshall Plan provided public funds for an ailing travel industry in Cold War Europe, official funding for Latin America's travel industries dried up. In 1946, the Export-Import Bank kept the Roosevelt administration's commitment and extended eighty million dollars in taxpayer money for hotel construction in Latin America, but bank officials resisted entreaties for more robust government support.[50] U.S. diplomats had long been accustomed to saddling Latin American nationalists, including Mexico's Plutarco Calles, Nicaragua's Augusto Sandino, and Cuba's Grau, with the "communist" label. They rushed to the same conclusion regarding the social democratic regime of Guatemala's Jacobo Arbenz Guzmán, whose reformist government the Central Intelligence Agency helped overthrow in 1954. But in contrast to Europe, the Middle East, and East Asia, the postwar Cold War seeped into the social and cultural life of Latin America without fanfare and most certainly without huge outlays of U.S. foreign aid. Instead, the Cold War slowly enveloped the preexisting edifices of empire and amplified Washington's antagonism toward Latin American nationalism.

Absent a hemispheric Marshall Plan, Cold War tourism in Latin America, including Cuba, relied on a roster of transnational interest groups. In some ways, the Rockefeller brothers, Nelson and Laurance, provided a bridge from the modest government activism of the war years to the private sector initiatives of the postwar era. Fascinated by the prospects for profit in Latin America and a true believer in hemispheric cooperation, Nelson Rockefeller easily transitioned from coordinator of inter-American affairs under FDR to postwar travel industry booster. Even before war's end, he opened the world-class Hotel Avila in 1942 in Caracas, Venezuela. Rockefeller targeted stateside employees of U.S. petroleum companies with interests in Venezuela, along with cruise ship tourists, as the most likely clientele. Laurance Rockefeller preferred nature-centered retreats. He organized a company called RockResorts and opened the company's first establishment in the Teton Range in Wyoming, where his family had been active in support of the U.S. National Park system. The first Caribbean RockResort arose at Caneel Bay on the island of St. John in 1952, with the upscale Dorado Beach Resort in Puerto Rico following in 1958. Both retreats featured a simple, low-density design meant to complement the natural surroundings but brimmed with modern amenities and luxury. "The whole idea," Rockefeller explained, "is to keep beauty simple and unspoiled. . . . But you know simplicity can be a very expensive thing."[51]

Hemispheric travel became synonymous with Juan T. Trippe's Pan American World Airways, which pioneered air travel during the 1920s in the Caribbean and gulf region. The company initiated flights from Key West to Havana in 1928; the first aircraft, piloted by no less than Charles Lindbergh, was greeted at the U.S. military's Camp Columbia airport by President Calvin Coolidge, in town for a pan-American conference. Pan Am enjoyed monopoly status in the region until the Roosevelt administration encouraged an "open skies" policy to spur competition and assist war mobilization.[52]

Despite increased competition from carriers such as Braniff, Trans World Airlines, and Eastern Airlines during the 1940s and 1950s, Pan Am's postwar public relations materials projected a gung-ho spirit that espoused an unshakable faith in modern technology and progress. "From the very beginning, there has been no end, no limit, to what mastery of the air could mean to living," a 1958 company publication pronounced. The Caribbean represented "an immense operational testing laboratory . . . a water-filled bowl between two continents, a bowl dotted with large and small islands."[53] Pan Am's place in the international travel industry expanded beyond aviation. Although U.S. public funds for the promotion of Latin American tourism remained limited during the early postwar years, Trippe used his immense influence in government to land a twenty-five-million-dollar Ex-Im Bank loan for Pan Am's subsidiary, the Intercontinental Hotel Corporation, the "hotel chain with wings." By 1950, the corporation had plans for one hundred million dollars in hotel construction in Bogotá, San Juan, Mexico City, and Santo Domingo and had established package air and accommodation arrangements to woo customers.[54]

Among the postwar promoters of international travel, Conrad N. Hilton had few equals. Son of a Norwegian immigrant father, he began his career in 1919 with a small hotel in Cisco, Texas. Borrowing capital and striking partnerships, he opened hotels across Texas and New Mexico, weathered the Great Depression, and began scouting additional opportunities. During the war years, when blackouts and travel restrictions crimped the hotel industry, Hilton bought out worried competitors nationwide, and when the postwar travel industry boomed, Hilton methodically acquired a series of prestigious U.S. hotels: the Waldorf-Astoria in New York; the Mayflower in Washington, D.C.; and then the entire Statler chain. He actively supported the Marshall Plan and its funding for European travel. In 1946, he created a subsidiary called Hilton International Corporation and sat former secretary of state Edward Stettinius, who had led negotiations on the United Nations charter, on the board of directors. In 1949, Hilton International opened its first overseas hotel in San Juan, Puerto Rico, the sumptuous Caribe Hilton, the center-piece of Puerto Rico's emerging tourist district.[55]

Hilton International was soon on a roll with shiny new hotels in Istanbul, Rome, Cairo, and Paris. The Havana Hilton opened in March 1958 and ranked as one of the world's most modern and glamorous and provided the Batista regime with a tremendous source of pride. As for Conrad Hilton, he aspired to celebrity status. "Hotels are not just buildings," one Hilton associate reminisced, "they are show business too. . . . Conrad Hilton loved the entertainment business."[56] His marriage to Zsa Zsa Gabor captured head-lines, and his appearances on television broadcasts included Edward R. Mur-row's *Person to Person*, Art Linkletter's *House Party*, the 1950s hit *This Is Your Life*, the *Ed Sullivan Show*, and the *Merv Griffin Show*. Each Hilton hotel opening featured a mix of government officials, television personalities, and second-tier Hollywood stars, along with a philosophical oration delivered by the corporate chieftain himself. A devout Roman Catholic, he regularly at-tended President Dwight D. Eisenhower's well-publicized prayer meetings. In addition to Gabor, Hilton's close friends included Norman Vincent Peale and Billy Graham.[57]

Hilton's trademark slogans, "Trade, Not Aid" and "Peace through Interna-tional Travel," embodied the internationalism of the age. His management team hailed mainly from Europe, and each new hotel featured multiple res-taurants and a veritable United Nations of cuisines. He cast a spotlight on the hotel industry's soft power in one speech: "Rather than assume the role of invaders intent upon siphoning back all profits to the United States, we have joined in a business fellowship with foreign entrepreneurs." "Each of our hotels," he declared on another occasion, "is a 'little America,' not as a symbol of bristling power, but as a friendly center where men of many nations and of good will may speak the language of peace." He naturally connected his overseas ventures to the Cold War: "Our Hilton house flag is one small flag of freedom which is being waved defiantly against Communism exactly as Lenin predicted. With humility we submit this international effort of ours as a contribution to world peace."[58] Historian Annabel Wharton has observed that Hilton even designed his hotel buildings to reflect the Christian, capital-ist, materialist values he espoused. Their sleek, modern lines, glass facades, and shopping arcades expressed the ethos that material comfort offered a ticket to personal freedom and international security.[59]

Additional interest groups contributed to the drumbeat. American Express represented the cutting edge in postwar travel financing with its innovative "travel now, pay later" schemes. By 1961, the company operated 271 offices worldwide and sold more than two billion dollars' worth of its famous traveler's checks annually.[60] The American Society of Travel Agents, founded in the 1930s, underwent rapid growth in the late 1940s as insecure travelers increasingly turned to professionals for trip-planning services. The society's trade journal, the *Travel News*, included regular updates on hotels, air travel, and rates. The organization also lobbied in Washington for legislation friendly to the travel industry. Its ideological message echoed Hilton's and Trippe's populist Cold War internationalism. Ironically, the group held its annual meeting in Havana in October 1959, ten months after Fidel Castro came to power.[61]

Publishers hopped on the bandwagon as well. The magazines *Travel* and *National Geographic*, founded at the turn of the century, and *Holiday*, established in 1946, especially catered to restless Americans. Both the *Saturday Review* and *Reader's Digest*, the former a liberal mainstay and the latter steadfastly conservative, espoused a postwar internationalism through what Christina Klein has called their "middlebrow" genre of travel and foreign news stories. *Reader's Digest* ran its popular "Armchair Travelogue" series and served as an outlet for members of the anticommunist China lobby who lionized Chiang Kai-shek's defiance of Communist China on the island of Taiwan. The *Saturday Review* featured a regular column by travel author Horace Sutton, a frequent flier around the Western Hemisphere, and regularly published articles and reviews on world religions and cultures. Readers of travel reviews and digests typically imbibed an ethos that identified the United States as a nonimperial agent of international integration and cooperation.[62]

The film and television industries also plugged global travel. The 1950s surfer girl Gidget (Cindy Carol) visited the eternal city in *Gidget Goes to Rome* (1962), Phileas Fogg (David Niven) orbited the planet in *Around the World in Eighty Days* (1951), and the Reverend Dr. T. Lawrence Shannon (Richard Burton) and Maxine Faulk (Ava Gardner) introduced Americans to the Mexican seaport of Puerto Vallarta in John Huston's rendition of Tennessee Williams's *Night of the Iguana* (1962). With each week's television broadcast, Gale Storm sailed into America's living rooms aboard a cruise ship on the *Gale Storm Show*, and Mayberry met Tenochtitlán when Aunt Bee of the *Andy Griffith Show* won a vacation to Mexico. Like passages from a travel book, Hollywood-constructed national identities helped Americans navigate the world's cultural systems.[63] Gidget's Rome shone as a city of fountains and high fashion; steamy Puerto Vallarta seemed exotic and sexually seductive, especially after Elizabeth Taylor joined Burton on the *Night of the Iguana* set.

Self-interest and the profit motive no doubt served as high-octane fuel for the postwar international travel machine. At the same time, Americans yearned to see the world. Their reasons for doing so ran from the profound to the mundane. Still, the U.S. government and many of the nation's opinion leaders believed in their hearts that what was good for the travel industry was good for the United States. In a 1953 speech on foreign trade, President Eisenhower beseeched U.S. sightseers to "portray America as he believes it in his heart to be: a peace-loving nation, living in the fear of God, but in the fear of God only."[64] The following year, the State Department inserted into every passport a pamphlet that instructed travelers how to behave as politically useful actors. The department amplified this message in 1957 by including a letter from the president that advised all U.S. tourists that wherever they ventured, they represented the nation, and their behavior and attitudes would "help to mold the reputation of our country."[65]

Tourist Soft Power and the Physical Construction
of Cuba's Contact Zones

In Latin America, Batista's Cuba stood as a prime example of the type of privately financed economic development that Washington encouraged, and the island's tourism potential seemed boundless. On the statistical surface, Cuba's economy showed up as one of the most prosperous in the region, with a per capita income of $374.[66] Although the U.S. stake in sugar production had declined since the 1920s, direct investment in Cuba totaled approximately $1 billion by 1958. U.S. companies held monopolies in public utilities, petroleum, mining, and steel, and U.S. brand-name consumer goods—Ford, Chevy, Colgate, Palmolive, General Foods, and General Electric—flooded Cuba's markets. The lion's share of Cuba's sugar exports, moreover, still went to the United States as a consequence of Washington's allocation of a lucrative sugar quota to its Caribbean ally.[67]

Foreign policy "realists" in Washington saw little to be gained from quibbling over Batista's means to power. The U.S. Navy maintained control over the strategic base at Guantánamo, and the Eisenhower administration lavished military aid on the dictator, with amounts rising from four hundred thousand dollars in 1953 to three million dollars by 1958, Batista's last year in office. Vice President Nixon visited Havana in early 1954 and judged Batista a "master politician."[68] If anyone could stabilize Cuba's corruption-filled politics, State Department officials reasoned, Batista could. As the new government's plans for tourism became known, most U.S. officials applauded the measures. As had been the case in interwar Mexico, the worlds of the diplomat and that of the traveler converged, but with very different outcomes.

The soft power wielded by tourists and the travel industry extended U.S. influence in Cuba far beyond the realm of political economy and military security. Tourism in fact helped to reconfigure Cuba's built environment, especially in heavily visited Havana. The transformation of the city's material culture—its street system, its skyline, its sense of place—was not entirely unique. The early postwar era witnessed the rebuilding of bombed-out cities around the world. In response to tourist demand, Europeans as well as Latin American societies integrated U.S.-style hotels, department stores, and retail outlets into their urban settings. But in Cuba, an authoritarian government and its business allies took North Americanization to unusual heights.

One of the intriguing aspects of Havana's increasingly North American facade is that so many Cubans embraced it. For fifty years or more, the cultural corridors connecting North America and the Antilles had served as two-way streets, with as many Cubans heading north as U.S. vacationers going south. Middle- and upper-class Cubans sent their children to the States for higher education, Cuban professionals employed by U.S. firms often headed north for training, and in popular Cuban culture a vacation to Miami or New York represented the penultimate in cultural enrichment and fun.

Indeed, the North American proposition of progress and modernity saturated Cuban consciousness and culture to the point that postwar Cuba stands as the foremost case in Latin America where soft power most nearly conformed to its textbook definition—that is, a force that made others want what U.S. leaders and citizens wanted. "I've been pro-American all my life," Alfredo Berrera Lordi told sociologist Oscar Lewis. "Even though we are proud of our old Spanish traditions," Alberto Candera, head of the Banco Nacional de Cuba, declared in 1958, "we think and act as modern Americans." Years later, Ofelia Schutte looked back on her childhood in 1950s Cuba: "Occasionally my family would travel to Miami," she remembered; "I went to as many movies as I liked without going through a bodily search or fearing a bomb might explode. . . . Seeing everything bright and rosy in the tourist zones of Miami Beach, I quickly reached the conclusion that the United States was a land of democracy, freedom and personal opportunity and that no other place in the world was the equal of it. . . . Before the revolution my identity was already split."[69]

Not surprisingly, Cuban tourism planners possessed a keen comprehension of things North American. First and foremost, they grasped the northerner's love of velocity and comfort. While some Yankees still hopped aboard the train and headed for Key West's ferries, modern passenger planes served as the premier cultural corridor to Cuba during the early postwar years. The Batista regime adapted and made the expansion and modernization of the Rancho Boyeros (José Martí) International Airport a priority. Completed in fall 1956, the main terminal building had grown a whopping 551 percent, from 1,366 square meters to 7,500 square meters, and newly refurbished passenger salons, restaurants, and customs areas claimed additional space. Most important, extended airstrips accommodated the larger planes that had become a mainstay of the travel industry. The total cost of the renovations amounted to nearly $1.5 million.[70]

Air travel to Cuba became not only increasingly convenient during the 1950s but also affordable for most middle-class North Americans. By the middle of the decade, five-hour flights from New York to Havana averaged $123 round-trip. Pan Am flew six flights daily from Miami and back for $36, and Delta offered regular round-trip flights from New Orleans for $114.[71] The number of visitors nearly doubled from 119,702 in 1946 to 234,200 in 1954. Cuba's Institute of Tourism estimated that each tourist dropped approximately $250 on the island. Cruise ship passengers, who accounted for 38,505 of the visitors, spent an average of $50, meaning that tourists spent a grand total of $50,849,000 in Cuba in 1954.[72]

Cuban elites also understood and shared the northerner's love of the automobile, drive-to shopping centers with parking, and other accoutrements of modernity. Since Havana served as the primary point of tourist interest, Cuba's urban planners undertook to create contact zones that enhanced the visitor's comfort and sense of familiarity. In less than a decade, a city sculpted centuries earlier by Spanish plunderers and religious zealots and long considered one of the most beautiful in the hemisphere emerged reinvented as a mishmash of cobblestone and modern highway. In contrast to interwar Mexico, where local officials and interest groups had gone to great lengths to preserve and display antiquity, the Batista regime's determination to update Havana jeopardized the city's heritage.

According to scholars Joseph L. Scarpaci, Roberto Segre, and Mario Coyula, the completion of three underwater highway tunnels, two under Havana's Almendares River and one under Havana Harbor, eased traffic congestion in the city but also spurred urban sprawl and suburbanization. Along the old city's western perimeter, trendy Vedado in central Havana sprouted a crop of new high-rise hotels, condominiums, department stores, and restaurants. Farther west, the suburbs of Marianao and Miramar gained population, supermarkets, and retailers. The bay tunnel opened areas east of Havana that had been immune to development for four centuries and provided a boon to real estate interests.[73]

Many of the new buildings rose high enough to block the city's natural coolant, the Antillean breezes, and left working-class Habaneros to contend with stagnant tropical heat. Commercial buildings and affluent homeowners installed air-conditioning, which kept more people inside and diminished street life. The problem would have certainly been exacerbated had planner José Luis Sert had his way. During the late 1950s, the Batista regime actively considered Sert's idea of building an artificial island in the Straits of Florida within earshot of central Havana and filling it with hotels and casinos. To accommodate yet more car traffic, several blocks of Habana Vieja would have been razed to make space for tourist parking. Before the proposal could win official approval, however, the Cuban Revolution intervened.[74]

Still, the influence of North American material culture on Batista's Havana ran deep. Baseball had been a chief U.S. export since the days of the Platt Amendment, but in 1946 Havana's Gran Stadium opened with a seating capacity of thirty-five thousand. U.S. minor league teams drew large and enthusiastic Cuban and U.S. crowds, as did Cuba's four professional teams. Even Fidel Castro came up through the ranks as a pitcher, known among the pros—in both baseball and politics—for his hard-to-read curveball. Cuba baseball player Tommy Lasorda, who went on to become manager of the Los Angeles Dodgers, reminisced that Castro even had a tryout with the Washington Senators but failed to make the team. "Instead of becoming a Senator," Lasorda quipped, "he became a dictator."[75]

Jim Crow also maintained a foothold in Cold War Havana and helped shape the city's spatial geography. Cuba had historically maintained a racial hierarchy not entirely dissimilar from Mexico's: less rigid than the black/white divide in the United States as a result of the extensive blending of racial groups but still color conscious and discriminatory. The arrival of U.S. troops, civil administration, investors, and expatriates at the turn of the century brought new demands for racial separation. The result was a patchwork system in which certain hotels and public beaches barred blacks and mulattos. In the days of the Negro Leagues in the United States, African American players who played winter baseball in Cuba relished the opportunity to play with and often outperform visiting white Major Leaguers. When Brooklyn Dodgers owner Branch Rickey set his sights on integrating the U.S. Major Leagues in 1947, he took his team to Havana to let Jackie Robinson get the feel of integrated play. Rickey nonetheless segregated his players, placing white team members in the elegant Hotel Nacional and Robinson and other African American prospects in less expensive quarters, separate and unequal.[76]

African American writer Langston Hughes visited Cuba in 1930, his third trip to the island, and commented on the intricacies of the color bar. Nearly "all the clerks in the bigger shops were either white or near white," and "in the daily papers almost all the photographs of society leaders are white, or light enough to pass for white," he observed. Yet darker-skinned officials, who would have been categorized "Negro" in the United States, were by no means absent from positions of authority. When Hughes was arrested for attempting to access a segregated Havana beach, the judge before whom he appeared turned out to be "a kindly old mulatto gentleman" who reprimanded the beach attendants and let Hughes go free.[77]

The hit-or-miss nature of racial indignities remained a fixture in Cuban life through the Batista era. Ann Terry, an African American traveling from St. Louis in June 1957, arrived at Havana's Siboney Hotel, where her American Express agent had booked her a room. Her dream vacation went awry when the management made clear that it did not particularly desire her to stay at the establishment. The removal of her luggage from the lobby to the outside walk proved an effective message.[78]

The most conspicuous change to Havana's built environment during the 1950s consisted of the proliferation of grandiose hotels. During Batista's six-and-a-half-year reign, no less than thirteen new ultramodern hotels with a total of 2,258 rooms realigned Havana's skyline. The Capri, Havana Riviera, Havana Hilton, St. John, Flamingo, and Colina all occupied a lively, hilly strip in Vedado known as the Slope.[79] The Capri and the Riviera stood out as two of the most stunning, completed in time for the 1957–58 winter season. The Cuban-owned Hotel Capri opened on Thanksgiving weekend and featured 250 rooms along with an innovative rooftop swimming pool.[80] Its flashy casino was leased to Santo Trafficante Jr., a well-known Florida-based mobster who years later was implicated in Central Intelligence Agency plots to assassinate Fidel Castro.[81]

Not to be outdone, Meyer Lansky opened the Riviera the following month with twice as many rooms, an equally stylish casino, a rooftop pool, central air-conditioning, and the swankiest nightclub in town, the Copacabana. Lansky hired two Toronto-based hoteliers, Ben and Harry Smith, to manage the Riviera Hotel Corporation, a holding company with numerous dubious investors and brilliantly shabby recordkeeping. The Smiths arranged for all 440 rooms to be prebooked for the entire winter. The opening show at the Copa

The Batista building boom, December 1958. On the eve of the Cuban Revolution, downtown Havana boasted multiple high-rise towers. To the left stands Meyer Lansky's Riviera Hotel; to the right is the Hotel Capri. Both opened for business in late 1957, just in time for the Batista era's last winter season. Cuban Heritage Collection, University of Miami Libraries, Coral Gables, Florida.

featured Ginger Rogers and seats scalped for hundreds of dollars.[82] The inventor of late-night talk-show television, Steve Allen, took his show to the Riviera in January 1958. The cameras scanned the casino room and the pool and beamed performances by singer Steve Lawrence and comedian Bud Costello at the Copa back to U.S. viewers.[83]

A third new hotel, the granddaddy of them all, suffered cost overruns and delays that caused it to miss out on the Batista era's last lucrative winter. The planning of the Havana Hilton earlier in the decade had initiated the spate of hotel building that refashioned the city's physicality. Conrad Hilton's first overseas hotel had opened in December 1949 on an idyllic rockbound perch overlooking the sea in San Juan, Puerto Rico. Owned by the commonwealth government but managed by Hilton International, the hotel garnered financial success beyond expectations. The following April, Hilton wrote that he "would like to have a hotel in Havana, as the one in Puerto Rico is doing wonderfully."[84]

Hilton developed an industrial model for hotel management that relied on time-and-method studies and innovative technology to reduce labor costs, daily business forecasts to keep inventories low, and mass purchasing to keep costs down.[85] He also had a knack for structuring deals in which host country investors put up the bulk of the investment. Whereas Puerto Rico's commonwealth government had been the main source of capital for the San Juan hotel, Hilton turned for help to a labor union in Cuba. After months of negotiations, Hilton International signed a contract in November 1953 with Francisco Aguirre, president of the Culinary Workers Union, locally known as the Gastronómico Union and an affiliate of the pro-Batista Confederation of Cuban Workers. The union provided about fourteen million dollars from its pension fund, and the Banco Nacional de Cuba lent the union another eight million dollars for the project. Hilton chipped in only two million dollars. The pro-U.S. and pro-Batista *Havana Post* toasted the partnership: "One faces the temptation to wax lyrical in praise of this arrangement in which capital goes to work for labor."[86]

In reality, the scheme required considerable wheeling and dealing. Batista pushed through legislation to allow labor unions to invest their pension funds in private undertakings, a practice previously prohibited because of its inordinately high risks. Hilton, the union, and the Batista government also won approval from Havana's board of aldermen to waive all municipal restrictions and regulations that interfered with the thirty-story building's construction.[87] Finally, Hilton International received tax exemptions for ten years, waivers on import duties, permission for a casino, and additional guaranteed loans from the Banco de Desarollo Economico y Social.

The building boom soon spread beyond Havana. The government completed the long-planned Central Highway across the expanse of the island, and in 1955, Cuba's National Planning Board drew up plans for regional tourist development.[88] Eastern and southern cities, including Trinidad and Santiago de Cuba, gained new hotels and public funds to develop historic and cultural attractions. Off the southwest coast of Cuba lay the Isle of Pines, today known as the dwelling place of Castro's most unfortunate political opponents. Batista and numerous private investors, including Mafia kingpin Lucky Luciano, exiled to Sicily to escape the reach of U.S. authorities, entertained plans to develop the tiny island into a major attraction.[89]

Despite its beautiful oceanscape, Cuba did not specialize in beach tourism. Havana's beaches were pleasant enough, as was the popular oceanfront in Marianao. But unlike Honolulu, Miami, San Juan, and the new Mexican resort at Acapulco, beach sand remained an afterthought for Cuban tourism planners. The town of Varadero, 114 miles east of the capital and serviced by bus and air, was the exception. In January 1955, the Blue Beach Law created the Planning Commission of the Varadero Tourist Center to promote the town's beautiful Playa Azul, and the Varadero Tourist Center Authority developed the area commercially. Investment surged from $245,000 in 1951 to $2,589,000 in 1956.[90]

North Americans flocked to Varadero during the winter season. Small and medium-sized hotels and guesthouses, many modestly priced, dotted the beachfront. But the plush Varadero International Hotel, which according to one guide offered "Florida attractions at Florida prices," gained prominence as Cuba's most opulent hotel. Its extensive grounds offered shops, a cabana-surrounded swimming pool, a poolside bar and dining service, a spacious private beach, tennis, golf, deep-sea fishing, and sailing.[91]

Around Havana and beyond, the North American flavor had become unmistakable by the late 1950s. Although many Cubans cheered the arrival of modernity, the new built environment empowered tourists and local elites at the expense of the local populace. While the constructed contact zones reaffirmed many people's successful appropriation of North American identity, U.S. visitors constructed Cuban identity in far less generous terms.

Tourist Soft Power and the Construction of Cuban Identity

Before the vacation destination is experienced—indeed, well before departure—travel is turned over in the mind. The power to imagine and to manipulate the imagination is a soft power that lies at the heart of visitor-host negotiations. In postrevolutionary Mexico, the host government, an array of private and public organizations, and freelancing service workers engineered ways to alter U.S. perceptions of Mexican society and reconcile the hunt for tourist dollars with the production of national identity. Batista and his U.S. associates, in contrast, invented and imposed a Cuban identity based on the most self-serving North American daydreams.

In 1945, the United States stood as the world's wealthiest and most powerful nation. Yet its citizenry perceived multiple threats to their well-being, real and imagined, abroad and at home. Depression, alien ideologies, world war, holocaust, Cold War, brainwashing, and the dawning of the nuclear age had connected Americans to the rest of the world by means of trauma. Social and cultural change at home generated additional foreboding. The Second World War unleashed powerful demands for African American equality and sent millions of women into the workforce. During the early postwar era, grassroots activists pumped life into the civil rights movement in Montgomery, Little Rock, and Greensboro, and the aggregate numbers of women in the labor force continued to grow.[92] To tamp down demands for change in race and gender relations, Washington implemented modest civil rights reforms and helped returning servicemen reestablish prewar standards of family life through educational and housing benefits. Madison Avenue and other producers of mass culture promoted what historian Elaine Tyler May has called "domestic containment," a cultural arrangement that pressured middle-class women to embrace a life of marriage, child-rearing, home management, and mass consumption and to see their male breadwinners off to work each morning. Premarital abstinence, early marriage, and erotically charged monogamy would "contain" female sexuality. Still, as Joanne Meyerowitz and others have shown, numerous U.S. women—be they racial or ethnic minorities, working-class or professionals, community activists or free-spirited bohemians—bucked these trends and continued to complicate postwar domestic life.[93]

U.S. tourists traveled to Cuba to enjoy the very latest in creature comforts, but they also yearned for a foreign experience and a vacation that would release them from the constraints that ordered life at home. A *Welcome to Havana* brochure prepared by the Cuban Institute of Tourism in the mid-1950s promised that "the colonial atmosphere; genuine antiques, and a luxury that surrounded the nobility of past centuries will enchant you while enjoying the world's best cocktails and most exquisite cuisine."[94] One travel writer described colonial Old Havana, the El Morro fort, and the ancient Iglesia de Paula: "Close to the harbor Havana reminds you first of Venice; next it looks like Alexandria; it even has the feeling of Rome in the area of the capitol."[95] Travelogues and guidebooks commonly referred to Havana as the "Paris of the Caribbean" and the Casino Nacional as "the Monte Carlo of the Americas."[96] Postwar U.S. consumers delighted in swilling rum, ambling through the humid, midnight air, welcoming the morning in air-conditioned hotel comfort, and soaking up sun and trade winds at poolside during the day.[97] Standard vacation cuisine might include cocktails and appetizers, locally harvested seafood, dessert, café con leche, and after-dinner drinks. Evening rituals might include a test of one's luck at a casino or taking in a big-name nightclub show. U.S. recording artists Tony Bennett, Nat King Cole, and Frank Sinatra regularly performed at the city's many venues, as did jazz legends Cab Calloway, Benny Goodman, Woody Herman, and Sarah Vaughn.[98]

The imagined Cuba represented more than an amalgam of old and new, familiar and foreign. It registered in the North American mind as a place where pleasures forbidden or frowned on at home could be indulged. Travel writer Harold C. Lanks observed of travelers to Cuba, "The airplane night clubber forgets he is a bald-headed businessman from Manitowoc; he is swept away by the tropic night."[99] Of all the elements of U.S. cultural life at the time, gender, sexual, and race relations ranked among the most conflicted. Cuba offered a site where North Americans might exempt themselves from the rigid rules of Jim Crow and Cold War sexuality, where males and females, single and married, might flirt and fling with the Latin other.

The tourist's sexual habits often involved spectatorship and fantasy at dozens of clubs that showcased Afro-Cuban rumba dancers. The rumba and its offshoot, the mambo, were dance performances based on the *son*, a fusion of African and Andalusian rhythms with a syncopated beat. Traditionally performed by a man and a woman, rumba featured sexual innuendo and pantomime and was scorned by polite, upper-class Cuban society. Yankees loved it.[100] Lanks's enthusiastic description of a rumba performance reeked of white privilege: "A high yaller gal swirls out on the patch of floor and melts into an ultra-seductive version of the sensuous rhumba. A high yaller gal, bathed in colored lights, swathed in obvious abundance of close fitting bronze skin. . . . [N]o costume is as beautiful as bronze skin. . . . High yaller gal! dancing to savage music, the breath of the jungle."[101]

If a floor show at the Tropicana, the Sans Souci, or the Montmartre failed to satiate desire, a chance meeting at a lively bar or dance hall might. But numerous manly Yankees also relied on the power of the dollar to purchase sexual authenticity in Havana's multiple red-light districts, home to a thriving commercial sex industry that employed an estimated 11,500 prostitutes.[102] As had been the case in Tijuana, with its nearby U.S. naval base in San Diego, Havana's brothels normally swarmed on weekend nights with U.S. sailors visiting the port of call or on leave from Guantánamo. But the sex business also captured a segment of the recreational tourist trade. One of the most striking features of Cuba's sex tourism was the openness with which North Americans participated in and discussed it. Travel books addressed the matter frankly. "The triangular pocket nearest the wharves," *Terry's Guide* informed its readers as early as the 1920s, "is a prurient spot resorted to by courtesans varying in complexion from peach white to coal black; 15 year old flappers and ebony antiques."[103]

Male patrons published accounts of their exploits. Historian Neill Macaulay, who served as a young volunteer in Castro's army in the late 1950s, accompanied visiting friends to a Havana whorehouse. Macaulay turned down offers to participate but observed that the establishment served as "a place where American high school and college boys of the 1950s came to relieve their sexual tensions in surroundings that were not forbiddingly for-

Tourists flocked to sexy floor shows at metropolitan Havana's many fashionable nightclubs. The Tropicana, pictured here in November 1955, dished out some of the most spectacular performances. The strikingly beautiful female dancers wore scanty outfits and pain-inducing high heels. Cuban Heritage Collection, University of Miami Libraries, Coral Gables, Florida.

eign."[104] British writer Graham Greene, who detested 1930s Mexico for its anticlericalism and corruption, visited Havana in 1958 to gather materials for his spoof on Cold War espionage, *Our Man in Havana* (1959). He fondly remembered an evening on the town that began with a marijuana high, included a live porn show at the seedy Shanghai Theater in Havana's Chinatown, and ended with the purchase of cocaine from a taxi driver. Demonstrating agency even in the context of the grossly unequal U.S.-Cuban relationship, the purveyor slipped the famous author a small amount of harmless white powder instead of the potent illegal stuff.[105]

Mob lawyer Frank Ragano recorded his impressions: "As a soldier, I had seen decadence in postwar Japan, but Havana was wilder. Prostitution was wide open and casino gambling went on almost twenty-four hours a day. . . . I have old fashioned conservative notions about taking respectable women to places of debauchery, so I decided never to return to Havana with my wife."[106] Like many married U.S. males, Ragano returned to Havana without his spouse. Trafficante, Ragano's client, treated him to a special performance by "Superman" at a private home in Havana. Superman, also known as El Toro, did not leap tall buildings in a single bound but astounded audiences with his fourteen-inch erection and sex acts performed with female accompanists.[107]

Havana catered to female as well as male imaginations. The Cunard Cruise line estimated in the mid-1950s that roughly 65 percent of its U.S. passengers to Cuba were women. Many, of course, came with spouses in tow. Havana's upper-end nightclubs and floor shows attracted a respectable clientele of well-to-do couples as well as unattached males. But single, working women, often secretaries, retail personnel, nurses, and the like, also made their presence felt in Cuba's tourist districts. Popular accounts of Havana's commercial sex establishments do not mention significant female patronage. But women might drop their dollars at popular bars, casinos, restaurants, hotels, and department stores. Their cultural power often could be found on display along Cuba's handful of popular beaches during the winter months, when locals for the most part disdained the jacked-up prices for accommodation. Varadero Beach in particular provided a coveted sunbathing destination for pale-skinned northerners.

The notion of single women taking a break from the workaday world for a weekend in romantic Havana ingrained itself in U.S. popular culture. In the 1941 film *Weekend in Havana*, Nan Spencer (Alice Fay), a salesclerk at Macy's, travels to the Antillean city and makes the rounds of bars and nightclubs. The hit television series *I Love Lucy*, starring comedienne Lucille Ball as Lucy Ricardo and her Cuban-born husband, Desi Arnaz, as Ricky Ricardo, premiered in 1951 with a viewing audience fifty million strong and remained spectacularly popular for the rest of the decade. In "Lucy Takes a Cruise to Havana," a 1957 flashback episode of a successor series, the *Lucy-Desi Comedy Hour*, viewers learned that Lucy had first met Ricky when she was a young secretary sailing to Cuba with her friend, Susie McNamara (Ann Sothern), giddy about the romantic possibilities.[108]

The Lucy-Ricky relationship spoke volumes about soft power, gender, and empire. The Lucy character, cast as a 1950s housewife and ultimately happy mother, tried to live up to the ideals of domestic containment. Many of her escapades, however, comically turned the tables on established gender roles, whether she outsmarted Ricky with a prank or a credit card. Without a Cuban Ricky, the show would probably not have worked as popular entertainment in postwar America. Viewers deemed Lucy's antics comedic in part because the male on the receiving end was foreign, heavily accented, non-threatening, and of color. The rumba bandleader had rhythm but appeared vulnerable and childlike, an inversion of the male ideal, and like Cuba itself was a happily subordinate colonial ward. Even Ball once commented of her husband, "Beneath that dazzling charm was a homeless boy who had no one to care for him, worry about him, and love him."[109]

The messages and cultural symbols embedded in *Weekend in Havana* and *I Love Lucy* found expression in other popular media as well. Hit movies such as *Guys and Dolls* (1955) instructed potential tourists that Havana was a place of bars, casinos, and sexual seduction, as protagonist Sky Masterson (Marlon Brando) pursued romance with the virginal Salvation Army worker Sarah Brown (Jean Simmons). Brown caught the fever but in 1950s good-girl fashion kept her virginity, at least until her presumed marriage to Masterson at the film's end. U.S. moviegoers encountered Havana's romance and rhythms again and again in *Moonlight in Havana* (1942), *Club Havana* (1946), *Cuban Pete* (1946), *Havana Holiday* (1949), *Havana Rose* and *Cuban Fireball* (1951), *Santiago* (1956), *Affair in Havana* (1957), and *Pier Five Havana* (1959).[110]

Cuba also transcended North American rules and regulations when it came to gambling. Even before the 1953 casino scandal, Batista had smiled on Lansky's residency in Havana. A 1920s bootlegger, Lansky had initially linked up with the dictator in the 1930s as a post-Prohibition distiller and manager of the lucrative Gran Casino Nacional.[111] The U.S. Senate's 1950–51 Crime Committee, led by Tennessee Democrat and presidential aspirant Estes Kefauver, exposed Lansky for failing to keep tax records, at which point he transferred operations to Cuba just in time to lead Batista's gambling "reforms."

A consolidation of mob rule followed, not only in the casinos but also in the unfettered prostitution and narcotics rackets. Batista allowed gambling houses to run twenty-four hours a day, with no restrictions on amounts wagered. Lansky managed the Montmartre casino and the gaming room at the Hotel Nacional until 1958, when he transferred operations to the brand-new Riviera Hotel. Trafficante ran the casinos at the Sans Souci nightclub and the Capri, Commodore, Deauville, and Sevilla Biltmore hotels.[112] The Associated Press reported that a battalion of investors from shady backgrounds in New York, Cleveland, Detroit, and Las Vegas ran gaming businesses along the Malecón. Professional gambling crews, granted two-year visas, set up schools to teach Cuban employees how to handle dice, deal cards, and run roulette wheels.[113]

The massive web of corruption in some ways constituted a covert U.S. foreign aid program. A gambling license, for example, required an original payment of $25,000 to the Cuban government, a monthly flat fee, and a percentage of the profit. But Trafficante confided to Ragano that the "expected amount to be paid under the table for a lucrative concession" ran in the neighborhood of $250,000, accompanied by an understanding that construction contracts would be directed to Batista's business allies.[114] A chunk of the casino fee wound up reinvested in the island's National Lottery, whose weekly sales provided another cash cow for the president's henchmen.[115] The payoff system even trickled down to petty officials and street cops. In January 1958, the *New York Times* ran a story on corruption in Cuba that described the daily routines of government "collectors" who picked up payments from small shop owners, restaurateurs, and brothel operators. Even cabbies had to cough up a dollar to park at prime pickup spots.[116]

U.S. travelers often perceived themselves as observers of Cuban hedonism rather than inventors and participants. Batista's Tourist Institute fed the delusion. According to one government brochure, Havana was a female "modern deity. . . . With open arms she greets her visitors, and inviting them to her banquet of pleasure, she frolics, dances, sings, and plays as few Sirens have ever done, and plants in their hearts the undying desire to come, again and again."[117] Commentators similarly attributed a love of gambling to the Cuban psyche. "Gambling is a major passion among Cubans," W. Adolphe Roberts observed in his early 1950s travel guide. "Serious efforts to stamp it out have been made from time to time, but these have never been successful nor maintained for long."[118] In short, Cubans were a happy and gregarious nationality. "The night life is one of Havana's strong points," Lawrence and Sylvia Martin observed in their travel guide, "and the Cuban, whether a performer or a spectator, flings himself into it with untrammeled spirits."[119]

Cubans had been accustomed to discrepancies between North America and Cuba. Among those who traveled north, the presence of wealth, efficiency, technology, and liberty had been an immense attraction as well as a source of inhibition and insecurity. By the late 1950s, in a homeland riddled with corruption and vice, the incongruities mounted. Despite the currents of soft power that had attracted Habaneros to northern cultural norms, tourist and travel industry renderings of Cuban character and identity had so skewed the soft power equation that even many of the most avid admirers of Yankeedom had begun to feel pangs of disillusion and resentment.

The Everyday Life of Empire and the Coming of the Cuban Revolution

Unlike Mexico, where the visitor-host relationship helped to foster political as well as cultural communion, tourism in Cuba created a vast cultural chasm conducive to polarization. The story of the M-26-7 insurgency, or the 26th of

July Movement, and Fidel Castro's ascendancy has been told many times. Most accounts center on the now-famous string of events and the activities of a handful of young, bearded rebels who operated for the most part in Cuba's impoverished rural areas. The traditional narrative emphasizes young Castro's impulsive raid on the Moncada army barracks on 26 July 1953; his trial and riveting oratory; his imprisonment and exile to Mexico; his death-defying voyage aboard a rickety yacht, the *Granma*; and his run for cover in the Sierra Maestra wilderness in eastern Oriente Province. Then came promises of agrarian reform, guerrilla war, and finally the triumphant march into Havana on New Year's Day 1959.[120]

The familiar turning points remain of profound significance. But comprehending the Cuban Revolution's full dynamics requires examining M-26-7's complex internal structures and the central role played by activists far away from the Sierra in urban centers such as Santiago de Cuba, the capital of Oriente Province, and of course Havana, located in the country's lowlands, or Llano. The 26th of July attracted a heterogeneous group of young men and women: members of the opposition Orthodox Party, social democrats, intellectuals, nationalists, disgruntled unionists, and socialists. Although most rejected communism, the core leaders appropriated the anti-imperialist stance of Cuba's Communist Party, the Popular Socialist Party. Historian Julia E. Sweig, who gained unprecedented access to Cuban archives, has documented the essential role played by the 26th of July's National Directorate, led by a twenty-one-year-old Santiago-based schoolteacher, Frank País, who made the urban underground far more than a rear guard for the gritty guerrilla movement in the mountains. The Llano provided Castro's soldiers with weapons, medicine, clothing, food, and recruits.

The central strategy revolved around the clandestine organization of a nationwide general strike aimed at bringing down the Batista government. Although the movement failed to achieve a united front, the 26th of July also reached out to other urban oppositionists, including the Student Revolutionary Directorate, the Popular Socialist Party, and elements of the opposition Auténtico Party. In addition, the Conjunto de Instituciones Civicas (Federation of Civic Institutions), a coalition of nearly two hundred professional and civic organizations representing approximately three hundred thousand Cubans, usually refrained from directly participating in armed insurrection but assumed an important role as a respected critic of Batista's repression.[121] Pepín Bosch, president of the renowned Bacardi rum company and icon of civic responsibility in Cuba de Santiago, not only publicly rebuked the government but funneled tens of thousands of dollars to Castro's forces.[122]

While they never achieved a lasting alliance, most members of these various groups sprang from similar backgrounds: Cuba's urban middle and professional classes, precisely the groups most likely to aspire to North American lifestyles. This cohort also ranked as most likely to suffer from Cuba's anemic economic growth rates—about 1 percent annually during the 1950s. For all the progress displayed in Americanized Havana, Cuba remained addicted to agricultural exports for its livelihood. In 1956–57, sugar alone still accounted for about 80 percent of all exports, while its international price swung unpredictably. With a quarter of its workforce in the seasonal sugar industry, Cubans endured 16 percent unemployment plus 7 percent underemployment. The lack of economic diversification in spite of decades of promised modernization left the aspiring professional and middle classes increasingly bereft of hope. Batista's corrupt patronage system, which rewarded loyalty over merit, only exacerbated the problem.[123]

Cuba's urban professionals also stood out among their fellow countrymen and -women as those most likely to have had daily encounters with the tourist presence in Havana and other cities. Tourism cannot be counted as the leading impetus for revolution, but the unchecked soft power of tourists and the travel industry, especially in Havana, aroused deep animosity toward the Batista regime and dependence on the United States. This animosity strengthened Cuban nationalism, especially among those elements of the Cuban population most likely to support the insurrection, and did so well before the Fidelistas began to gain traction in rural Oriente Province.

For all intents and purposes, tourists had replaced the Platt Amendment as the most noxious U.S. presence in the everyday lives of Habaneros. Yankee commentators might insist that gambling, narcotics, and prostitution were favorite Cuban pastimes, but indignant Cubans disagreed. "We can not help but notice," Eladio Secades wrote in the newspaper *Bohemia* in November 1955, "that the city is filling with bars. We are creating a capital of bars." Many Cubans denounced the narcotics trafficking. Others deplored the pornography and prostitution. Journalist Hernández Traviesa, writing for *El Mundo*, derided North American depictions of the island that encouraged arriving Yankees "to think that Cuban women are waiting for them on the beaches." Baptist minister Nemesio Garcia Iglesias struck a Billy Graham–like tone in a March 1955 meditation in *El Mundo*: "If we continue like this . . . I believe that it will not be long that we will become worse than Sodom and Gomorrah."[124]

The omnipresence of casinos and mobsters also aroused shame and indignation. Andrés Valdespino lamented in the magazine *Bohemia*, "The most prominent representatives of the . . . North American underworld, owners and managers of gambling establishments . . . have transferred their operations to Havana. . . . It is said that this will promote tourism. . . . Is this objective worth staining the national panorama even more, converting Cuba into a center of major scandals?"[125] The representation of Ricky Ricardo in *I Love Lucy* also came under fire. Many Cubans knew that Desi Arnaz was a child of the island's old elite whose father had been a staunch Machado supporter in the 1920s. Havana television producer Joaquín Condall went so far as to label Arnaz an "enemy of all Cubans" and a source of "humiliation for Cuba."[126]

Urban discontent spread beyond the professional classes. Between 1920 and 1958, as thousands of U.S. tourists came and went each week, the metropolitan population swelled from 600,000 to more than 1,360,000. Although the metro constituted only .3 percent of the island's land area, it held nearly 20 percent of the nation's people.[127] Despite a decade of breakneck construction and modernization, almost half of the city's housing stock remained in poor condition. Old Havana in particular had grown dilapidated, and multiple-family boardinghouses known as *solares* and *cuarterías* proliferated. *Barrios insulabres* (shantytowns) sprouted on the city's edges as dispossessed rural migrants came to Havana in search of low-end work, often seasonal, in the service sector. While fashionable Vedado and Marianao flourished, approximately a third of the capital city suffered water shortages. Many residents could not afford to pay their monthly utility bills to subsidiaries of large U.S. corporations.[128]

In addition to housing and job shortages, the tourist-inspired urban makeover had muted Havana's indigenous Caribbean cultural rhythms. Small family-owned bodegas still dotted working-class neighborhoods, but modern-style supermarkets dominated in suburban areas. Northern pop and rock steadily replaced the impromptu music of the streets.[129] Even the rumba took on a U.S. tone, as New York clubs and recording companies appropriated the popular sound and refashioned it to northern tastes. U.S. audiences preferred crooner Perry Como to Cuban traditionalists such as Antonio Arcaño and Arsenio Rodríguez.[130]

North American tourists occupied a privileged social space that immunized them from Cuban sentiment. In February 1957, however, *New York Times* correspondent Herbert Matthews began to rearrange popular thinking when he filed a headline-grabbing interview with Fidel Castro. Sought out by M-26-7 agents in Havana, Matthews and his wife, Nancie, demonstrated how soft power can quickly mutate. They disguised themselves as a middle-aged tourist couple and traveled by car to the charming colonial city of Santiago de

Cuba in Oriente Province. Courage, tactical smiles, and tourist luck got them through government roadblocks to their first stopping-off point, and while Nancie Matthews stayed behind with M-26-7 sympathizers, her fifty-seven-year-old husband headed by jeep and by hoof deep into the Sierra Maestra. The journalist evaded army platoons and informers and rendezvoused with the rebel leader. The two conversed in Spanish, smoked cigars, and took photos.[131]

Castro's troops repeatedly marched in, out, and around the camp, leaving the journalist with the impression that M-26-7 possessed an army larger than it actually did. But the three articles Matthews wrote after the interview exposed Batista's fiction that Castro was a meaningless annoyance, snuffed out months earlier along the southern Cuban coast. The pieces also disputed the president's campaign to paint the insurgency as a communist conspiracy. Instead, Castro premiered in the U.S. media as a rural reformer determined to stamp out Cuba's corruption. Batista censors deleted the series from copies of the *New York Times* sold on Cuban newsstands, meaning that Cubans learned that the government's official story was a fabrication only after U.S. tourists carried the paper with them to Havana.[132]

Cuba's political theater captured headlines again on 13 March 1957 when forces from the Student Revolutionary Directorate and the Auténticos attacked the Presidential Palace. The conspirators hoped to assassinate Batista and accelerate the revolution, but the assault ended in the deaths of forty insurrectionists. The government summarily arrested four hundred or so suspected participants, dealing a harsh blow to several urban insurrectionary organizations. Still, the protest drew the rotting regime's legitimacy further into doubt. Tourism worked its way into the story when word came that a U.S. tourist, Peter Korenda of Illinois, had been killed in the cross fire while observing the shootout from his hotel window.[133]

For the next year, the insurrection gained momentum in the Sierra and the Llano. To discredit the ruling regime, 26th of July forces stepped up sabotage against private property, especially the burning of sugarcane fields and mills. The urban militias accelerated bombings in Havana and the metropolitan area. Still, many U.S. writers and travelers clung to their notion of contented Cubans. "The Cuban likes his huge good-natured 'uncle,' for almost alone among Latin Americans he senses no covetousness in our attitude toward him. He believes the United States his awkward, bungling, but sincere champion," Sydney A. Clark commented in his popular Cold War travelogue, *Cuban Tapestry*.[134] "The bombings and bomb scares were part of the most casual revolution I ever saw," a writer for *Holiday* magazine observed, "The guards around Batista's palace carried their rifles in a relaxed manner, smoked cigars and talked incessantly even on duty."[135] During the previous winter season, Senator John F. Kennedy had joined in the fun when he visited Havana with his buddy, Florida Senator George Smathers, and according to mob sources was "set up with three gorgeous prostitutes" for a private sex party at the Commodore Hotel.[136]

While JFK and friends romped, U.S. policymakers pondered the insurrection's significance. Most reacted angrily to the Matthews articles. U.S. ambassador Arthur Gardner, acting assistant secretary of state for inter-American affairs R. Roy Rubottom Jr., and secretary of state John Foster Dulles lined up behind Batista. Although he expressed concern regarding Batista's abuse of presidential power, Rubottom viewed the Sierra Maestra uprising as a "backdoor harassment," unlikely to alter the fundamentals of the U.S.-Cuban relationship.[137] Batista increasingly attached the "communist" label to the uprising, despite the lack of any significant communist presence in the M-26-7 movement, hoping to transform Latin America into a Cold War battleground and leverage additional U.S. military assistance. But most of official Washington did not go for the Red bait and did not evidence alarm. President Dwight D. Eisenhower's National Security Council met twenty-six times as the insurrection escalated between April and December 1958, and Cuba did not make the agenda once.[138]

The new U.S. ambassador, Earl E. T. Smith, a well-connected Republican businessman who assumed his duties in Havana in July 1957, was the only high-ranking American official to buy Batista's charges. Insisting, without any plausible evidence, that communists had indeed infiltrated the insurrection, Smith bitterly complained when embassy officials, including the Central Intelligence Agency's mission chief, contradicted him.[139] Realist scholars often use the term "misperception" to explain foreign policy failures such as that which unfolded in Cuba in the late 1950s. In Cuba's case, U.S. diplomats underestimated Batista's liabilities, failed to grasp the meaning of the growing anti-Americanism, and certainly lowballed Fidel Castro. The question is why U.S. officials, rigorously trained to assess interests and threats, proved so prone to misperception.

Hegemonic habits and the misperceptions they breed are not forged solely by political leaders, military officers, capitalist robber barons, and yellow journalists. Assumptions and perceptions of the Cuban other as a weak but happy dependent pervaded U.S. postwar culture. Travel writers, American Express, Pan Am, Hilton Hotels, and many other groups had peddled the image. Millions of U.S. tourists who visited Cuba during the decade sent postcards, wrote letters, and returned to regale family and guests with the wonders of Havana. Hollywood further layered the discourse, as did television and record producers.

Most North Americans knew little about Cuba—its culture, its history, its political factions, its derailed constitution, and most of all its people—in spite of the large-scale contact. U.S. tourists descended on the island on a daily basis. Some soaked up the sun on beaches that remained closed to Cubans. Others claimed the casinos and gambling rooms as their battle stations and lost more money in a single night than most Cubans earned in a year. More than an occasional U.S. sailor delighted in Havana's brothels. Cubans generally liked and admired their northern neighbors but observed them with increasing incredulousness. By late 1957, Cubans had begun to contemplate inviting their guests to leave.

Tourism is about many things, but its core significance to international relations is that it facilitates the negotiation of cultural identities, spurs the creation of physical and imagined communities, and helps determine the direction and velocity of globalization. After surviving the cultural border wars of the 1920s, Mexican hosts discovered a variety of means by which to contain tourist soft power. In so doing, they helped determine the everyday life of the empire and shaped a context conducive to cultural and diplomatic rapprochement. Batista's Cuba devoted more energy to containing an imagined communism than to containing tourist imaginations.

Cuba's authoritarian regime auctioned off Cuban real estate, cluttered Havana's urban spaces, and refused to empower middle- and working-class elements that might have negotiated a more equitable visitor-host relationship. They indulged Yankee consumer privilege and fed visitor fantasies of benevolent, colonial stewardship. In alliance with U.S. corporations and organized crime leaders, they exacerbated the island's social and economic inequalities, imposed U.S. cultural norms, and eroded Cuba's pre-Yankee identity.

To be fair to Cuba's policymakers, postwar international trends placed new constraints on host power. In part, the aviation revolution, U.S. affluence, and global marketing integrated the world as never before and brought new pressures to bear on local sociocultural arrangements. The tourist invasion, moreover, can hardly be said to have constituted the principal impetus for Cuba's revolution. Tourist excesses joined with a multitude of other grievances not simply as a symbol of U.S. power but as a major element of an onerous U.S. presence and a spur to anger over the dilution of Cuba's national identity.

U.S. leaders maintained that the turmoil in Cuba remained of the sort that had periodically characterized the island's politics since the first U.S. military intervention in 1898. U.S. hegemony had previously weathered internal disturbances in Cuba, and history showed that they could best be handled by the local proxy. As the insurrection in Oriente Province gained momentum, U.S. policymakers continued to encourage U.S. vacationers to head southeast for a good time. "Tense internal political conditions have prevailed in Cuba for a protracted period," Secretary of State Dulles instructed the U.S. embassy in Mexico City to advise tourists planning the jaunt across the gulf in early 1958, "but not a stage of gravity to prompt the Department to discourage American tourists from visiting the Havana area."[140] Support for the Batista regime still seemed a worthy gamble.

| **Paradíse Lost**
Castro's Cuba

The "magical charm of a tropical night, the rollicking rhythms of the Cuban countryside," the 23 March 1958 *Havana Post* gushed, "colorful dances that range from the African-derived '*guaguanco*' to the dignified '*danzon*,' dinner and dancing climaxed the opening of The Havana Hilton Hotel."[1] The long-delayed extravaganza drew an eclectic crowd. In addition to the Tropicana Club's corps de ballet, the three hundred invited guests included television and radio talk show host Tex McCrary, gossip columnist Hedda Hopper, *Time* magazine's Frank Shea, Serafino Romnaldi of the AFL-CIO, and William H. Bowe from the Brotherhood of Sleeping Car Porters. Hilton executives even arranged for an "official blessing" of the new building by Havana's Manuel Cardinal Arteaga.[2]

Located in fashionable Vedado, the Hilton towered over the city. Some thirty stories high, it ranked as the tallest building in all of Latin America and attested to Cold War Cuba's special claim on modernity. The twenty-four-million-dollar edifice boasted 588 rooms and 42 suites, all equipped with circulating ice water and three-channel radios. Central air-conditioning, a ballroom with banquet facilities for twelve hundred, multiple restaurants with shiny, stainless-steel kitchens, including the street-level Trader Vic's and the rooftop Sugar Bar cocktail lounge, bespoke the hotel's lavishness. Designed by the Los Angeles–based Welton Becket and Associates, it blended suburban U.S. and European motifs more than Cuban, with its imported Italian blue mosaic glassworks, courtyard graced by a Spanish fountain, and California-inspired swimming pool surrounded by cabanas.[3]

At a gala dinner held on 27 March for Cuban and foreign dignitaries, Conrad Hilton delivered one of his signature histrionic orations: "To say that Christopher Columbus was a world traveler must be something of an understatement," he remarked, "I am very happy today that four hundred and sixty six years later Hilton Hotels has discovered Cuba." Addressing the ideological fissures of the Cold War and in a veiled way Cuba's unrest, Hilton spun his reliance on the Gastronómico Union's pension fund for investment capital into an act of social consciousness. He explained, "The usual thing is for employees to work for employers. . . . But here in the building and operation of our new Havana Hilton, we have reversed the picture: Capital is working for Labor; the Employers for the Employees."[4]

The firm's leading executives were less sanguine in private. Keenly aware of the growing strength of the 26th of July Movement and the recent spate of bombings in Havana, they had considered postponing or canceling the grand opening. Company vice president and general manager Robert J. Caverly later recalled that State Department officials had expressed concern that a major U.S. company's failure to move ahead on schedule would reflect badly on the Batista regime, which the U.S. government "recognized and sponsored." Thus, the company decided somewhat reluctantly to go ahead, but only after hiring a hundred or so private security guards to mingle among the guests, arranging for local police to post guards at hotel entrances, and deploying marksmen on nearby rooftops to protect visiting dignitaries.[5]

It turned out to be a bad decision. In February and March 1958, explosions occasionally broke Havana's nights, marking the beginning of what historian Julia E. Sweig has termed the "golden age" of the Llano insurrection. By December, tourist traffic to Havana plummeted, and the Hilton operated deeply in the red.[6] Over the same period, Castro's Sierra Maestra–based insurrection spilled out of Oriente Province. In December, M-26-7 forces took the strategic city of Santa Clara, more than halfway along the central highway to the capital. On New Year's Day 1959, the Fidelistas, now popularly celebrated as the *barbudos* (bearded ones), entered Havana hours after Fulgencio Batista boarded a plane and took flight to Rafael Trujillo's Dominican Republic. On 8 January, Fidel Castro arrived in the capital to an outpouring of exuberance. In an act of considerable irony, he took up residence and established working quarters in the Havana Hilton.

Prospects for tourism in Castro's Cuba seemed dim. The revolutionary leader reserved special venom for the industry, which he held to be inherently corrupt and dehumanizing. In addition to an unbending nationalism, he displayed a pronounced puritanical streak. He relished Havana cigars but shied away from Bacardi rum. He viewed gambling as a moral vice that preyed on human frailty, especially that of the working poor. In his legendary "History Will Absolve Me" speech following the Moncada Barracks attack, Castro lamented that foreign interests, including the travel industry, had bled

Conrad N. Hilton choreographed each of his international hotel openings to resemble a Hollywood premier. At the grand opening of the Havana Hilton in March 1958, Hilton and a former Miss Minnesota posed before a replica of the ultramodern hotel. As celebrities mingled, marksmen took up positions around the building's exterior as a precaution against insurrectionist attacks. Conrad N. Hilton College Library and Archives, Houston, Texas.

Cuba of millions of dollars, including "losses of all types due to gambling, vice, and the black market."[7]

Despite the animosity, U.S.-Cuban tourist relations hobbled along after January 1959, as did bilateral diplomatic ties. For the next year and a half, the Castro and Eisenhower administrations snapped at one another and visitors and hosts waited for a moment of decision, yet both Washington and Havana sought to avoid a sudden rupture in relations. Historians and political scientists have offered a number of explanations for this uneasy state of limbo. The media undoubtedly played a role. In the wake of Herbert Matthews's stories, a parade of journalists tramped through the jungle to report on the youthful revolutionary army at war with a repressive dictatorship. As even the seasoned *New York Times* reporter had done, many exaggerated Castro's commitment to political pluralism and raised hopes for the establishment of warm U.S.-Cuban ties.

In addition, U.S. government leaders had difficulty deciphering the new leader's intentions. Castro derided Washington for its past support of Batista but insisted that the new regime wanted normal relations with the United States. He ran show trials and executed several hundred Batistianos but showed no stomach for a massive, Stalin-like purge of political enemies. He denounced U.S. capitalism but nationalized private property in spurts. Ambassador Earl E. T. Smith, who left the Havana post soon after Castro took charge, maintained the anticommunist drumbeat. But most State Department officials wagered that Castro led a revolution he did not fully control and that the new government would mellow in time as more elderly and moderate elements within M-26-7 assumed command.

While the U.S. press and Castro's unpredictability helped prevent an abrupt U.S.-Cuban collision, the tourist-visitor arrangement and the long-established everyday habits of empire played a critical role as well. As debased as the industry had been, it produced a web of interest groups, many of whom proved willing to cooperate with the new regime. Throughout the first two years of Castro's rule, travel agents still booked vacations for clients, U.S. airlines maintained a schedule of regular flights, and print and broadcast media continued to entice U.S. tourists to visit the island. Of the U.S. players in the travel industry, the Hilton Hotel chain made one of the most sustained efforts to accommodate the revolution and keep its Havana hotel afloat. Important elements within the host society, especially recently unemployed hotel, casino, and restaurant workers, also pressured Castro to nurse the industry back to health. Cuban and North American familiarity died a slow death.

While the U.S. government devised policies to contain Cuba's revolution, Castro's government evolved a tourism program that promoted travel while containing its antisocial and anti-Cuban impulses. In the end, the two containment strategies turned out to be incompatible. In Cuba, unlike postrevolutionary Mexico, Washington refused to accept any erosion of U.S. political and economic hegemony, and Castro moved steadily leftward toward a populist authoritarianism. Nonetheless, the tourism bond remained strong during many months of upheaval, and U.S. and Cuban tourist interests came close to preventing a political rift. This chapter examines the collapse of Batista's tourist paradise in 1958, Castro's efforts to build a revolution-friendly alternative, and the many ways in which cultural dynamics shaped the U.S.-Cuban political crisis.

Things Fall Apart: Tourist Agency and Official Paralysis

For the tourist industry and the Batista regime, the grand opening of the Havana Hilton constituted one last bright, shining moment. By late winter 1958, one or two bombings per night had become the norm in Havana, regularly knocking out power stations and disrupting electrical service. In February, M-26-7 "action" and "sabotage" teams set fire to four hundred thousand gallons of jet fuel stored in Regla, outside of Havana, at the Belot oil refinery owned by Esso corporation. Three weeks later, underground units kidnapped but subsequently released unharmed a famed Argentinean race car driver, Juan Manuel Fangio, who had come to Havana to participate in the annual carnival week auto race.[8] In light of the Hilton hoopla, Herbert Matthews recorded in his notes that visiting North Americans "must have gone back believing that all the stories in the U.S. press were exaggerations or false." "It is . . . somewhat like visiting a Volcano that is not going to erupt for some days or weeks," he mused, "There are no explosions to be seen."[9]

Matthews was not alone in depicting U.S. tourists as a clueless lot. Although U.S. policymakers and opinion leaders generally praised tourism for its internationalizing power, numerous voices acknowledged that tourist behavior could as easily undermine as buttress the nation's foreign policy.[10] The publication of the 1958 novel *The Ugly American* just as Batista's regime neared collapse played on such concerns. The popular and widely discussed Cold War narrative chronicled U.S. diplomatic missteps in a Southeast Asian embassy but included a Havana-like scenario in which an ambassador's fondness for the local dictator placed the United States at odds with a local insurgency. The novel ends on a positive, melodramatic note when a civic-minded embassy employee helps shift U.S. policy toward more humane support for the country's peasant population and thus prepares the country to reject communism. Although the book did not directly address discourses on travel or tourists, tourism critics picked up the term "Ugly American" and began to use it to characterize loud, ill-mannered U.S. visitors abroad.[11]

Havana had certainly hosted brutish Yankees over the years and continued to do so from 1958 through the early 1960s, but as the Batista dictatorship crumbled, the holidaymakers demonstrated an awareness of the changing political and cultural scene and showed up in greatly diminished numbers. In the weeks immediately following the Hilton's christening, hotel occupancy limped along at less than 50 percent.[12] The State Department regularly issued assurances to prospective travelers that the danger in Cuba remained confined to rural Oriente Province and that Havana vacation plans faced few threats.[13] But more than U.S. national security managers, U.S. tourists seemed to understand the seriousness and immediacy of the revolution and exercised caution.

Hoping to quiet his critics and divide the opposition, Batista briefly lifted censorship in February and early March and scheduled elections for June. Assuming that the elections would be fraudulent and sensing that the time was ripe for a final islandwide uprising, M-26-7 accelerated its military operations. The strategy centered, however, on the organization of a general strike, which in revolutionary parlance meant not only work stoppages but a sustained campaign of violent sabotage, bombings, kidnappings, and assassinations. Although planners envisioned the strike as a national event, success hinged on breaking Batista's authority in Havana.[14]

Havana's organizers, however, lacked weapons and failed to reach out to important potential allies, especially the worker-based Communist Party. After several delays, the strike came and went on 9 April. Badly coordinated and infiltrated by Batista agents, the failed strike left forty dead, mostly M-26-7 activists, and represented a serious setback for the insurrection, especially its urban wing.[15] Dead bodies on the streets of the capital only deepened the tourism recession. Although the prospects for success had been shaky from the start, Havana Hilton manager Rodolfo Casparius later traced the enterprise's financial woes to the blood spilled during the general strike. One day in May, he later recalled, the six-hundred-plus-room hotel registered only nineteen guests. Company offices in New York directed him to cut the staff of fourteen hundred by some eight hundred.[16]

Unlike U.S. tourists, U.S. policymakers and the Batista government took the failure of the general strike as a sign that the Fidelistas were on the ropes. In May, Batista launched his final summer offensive and promised to quash the insurrection once and for all. He sent ten thousand crack troops into Oriente Province to hunt down the rebels and deployed aircraft to bomb suspected rebel fortresses. M-26-7 guerrillas, however, countered with highly effective sniper attacks and devastating hit-and-run tactics. They killed and captured government troops, confiscated their weapons, and sapped the army's morale. Aerial bombardments that killed innocent civilians alienated the local population from its own government.

The insurgency grabbed headlines worldwide in June when M-26-7 operatives kidnapped some fifty North Americans, most employees of U.S. firms operating close to the Sierra Maestra. Although the White House and U.S. State Department condemned the hostage taking, newspapers reported that the action had been intended as a protest against the continuing flow of U.S. military aid to Batista's army in spite of a U.S. arms embargo announced the previous February. The crisis ended a few weeks later, following diplomatic intervention by the U.S. embassy in Havana, and Castro ordered the prisoners released. The gesture gained more favorable press for the rebels, since journalists reported that the hostages had been well fed and cared for and that the group had even enjoyed a Fourth of July baseball game and roast pig with their captors.[17]

Not all of Havana's turmoil arose from the revolution. Throughout 1958, rival mobsters battled one another. The 25 October 1957 gangland-style murder of racketeer Albert Anastasia outside New York's Park Sheraton Hotel set off the feuds. The details of the slaying remain unclear, but the *New York Times* reported that Anastasia had been trying to elbow into the Havana casino market.[18]

Conrad Hilton's new hotel in Havana seems to have been a principal catalyst for the war. New York district attorney Frank S. Hogan had questioned Hilton executives regarding their lease of the hotel's casino. The company had gone to considerable lengths to keep the mob out of its establishment, including hiring former Federal Bureau of Investigation and Kefauver Committee investigators to weed out underworld applicants.[19] But crime syndicate lawyer Frank Ragano later recalled that his client, Santo Trafficante Jr., had teamed up with Anastasia to bid on the Hilton lease, an initiative that did not sit well with Meyer Lansky, who had an agent, Joseph Silesi, make an offer. Trafficante told Ragano that he met with Anastasia in New York the night before the murder.[20] At the time, Hogan sent out nationwide alerts for both Silesi and Trafficante for questioning, but both men dropped out of sight. Trafficante claimed to have no knowledge of the matter and not to remember whether he had been in New York at the time of the killing. Silesi was more candid: Hogan "could drop dead," he told the *New York Times*.[21]

Taken together, the gang wars and the insurrection drove Cuba's travel industry into the ground. The Statistical Office of the Cuban Tourism Commission reported a decline in tourist numbers from summer season 1957 to summer 1958. More ominous, the prospects for winter 1958–59 were "not encouraging." Data for winter 1957–58 showed 258,789 arrivals on the island; tourism planners predicted that the totals for 1958–59 would not crack 200,000.[22] The *Wall Street Journal* noted in early November 1958 that the big hotels in Havana were reeling from all the bad press. Occupancy at the Hilton had plunged to only 15 percent, and Thomas Kelley II, the resident manager of Pan Am's Intercontinental Hotel, estimated that "business is running about half of normal"—most likely a rose-tinted guess. Even taxi drivers complained of a serious business slump.[23]

One new cohort of U.S. tourists did arrive on the scene, but their presence carried little economic impact. Historian Van Gosse has analyzed Fidel Castro's rise as a cultural icon in the United States in the late 1950s. The image of courageous *barbudos* locked in battle against the forces of repression struck a chord with many young Americans who had been raised on swashbuckling movie heroes such as John Wayne and Errol Flynn. The latter, a Castro sympathizer, lived in Havana with his underage girlfriend, whom he cast in his poorly directed and miserably acted movie, *Rebel Girls*. The flow of positive press on Castro in 1958 and 1959 helped North Americans, liberal and conservative alike, imagine Fidel and his ragged band more as republican reformers than the hardened revolutionaries they aspired to be.[24]

The infatuation with Castro led what appears to have been a small group of mainly high-school- and college-age males to rush off to Havana over spring break to learn more about Cuba and its revolution. For those seeking a truly masculine adventure and an escape from the boredom of suburbia, signing up with M-26-7 carried considerable panache. Most romantics never quite followed through on the dream. Gosse tells the story of two Connecticut teenagers who stole a service revolver, one hundred dollars, and the family sedan and headed down the parkway to join the *barbudos*, only to be apprehended by authorities at one of those bothersome Connecticut tollbooths.[25] But an undetermined number of more clever young men hooked up with M-26-7 operatives in the United States and navigated their way to Havana through a maze of 26 July Movement contacts and eventually reached Cuba's militarized zones.[26]

In time, North Americans on both the left and the right encountered what Matthews called the "real revolution," a top-to-bottom overhaul of Cuban society, not a Cuban New Deal. But as revolution descended on the island throughout 1958, the insurrectionists' image and that of Cuba as a whole seemed something that could be molded and shaped at will. Perhaps for that reason, Batista decided that the time was right for a new public relations program. His New Cuba Pro-Tourism Committee, composed of representatives from hotels, airlines, travel agencies, and local chambers of commerce, hired a U.S.-based advertising firm to coordinate a "gigantic promotion plan" in the eastern United States for the summer and fall of 1958. The group issued press releases, hosted cocktail parties for travel agents, and even composed a manifesto. "This Committee looks upon the travel and industrial future for the country with extraordinary optimism," one pamphlet declared.[27]

The unreality of the effort was newsworthy, but press censorship in Cuba stifled investigative journalism. In October, Batista personally welcomed five hundred Gibson distributors, dealers, and salesmen to the presidential palace. Insisting that reports of unrest had been greatly exaggerated in the United States, he thanked them for their loyalty: "We are highly pleased that you chose Havana for your meeting."[28] That same week, the Hotel Capri took out ads in the English-language *Havana Post* to persuade tourists to come watch the World Series baseball championship on its new "Giant 27 inch TV Screen." "Next to seeing the World Series in the flesh, what could be better than the elegant air conditioned comfort of the Casino de Capri and its very large TV screen?"[29] Under the government's watchful eye, the *Post* ran no articles on the insurgency but continued to feature ads from Havana's finest shops peddling blue, white, and pastel mink coats, muskrat wraps, and white and blue fox stoles as winter in the tropics approached.[30]

It was as if reason had been suspended and hegemonic assumptions of Cuban identity transcended all wisdom. The publicity played on long-held U.S. perceptions that Cubans were a happy and contented people who had benefited greatly from association with the United States. *Holiday* magazine informed its readers that the "mass of [Cubans] are as bourgeois as Parisians —most families in all but the lowest classes can afford a servant, so the housewife is relieved of burdensome work." The author of the piece described a birthday bash held at a private residence for Ambassador Smith, with dinner prepared by fifteen chefs, a band that played "Happy Birthday," and a late-arriving Batista who appeared "completely at ease."[31]

The tourists still did not bite. Yet a handful of travelers and certainly elements of the North Americans travel industry found it hard to fathom that Cuba, that seductive, submissive, dark-skinned siren, would turn her back on Uncle Sam. Nor could they believe that the insurgency would sacrifice dollars for principle. Americans seemed to assume that every Cuban had a price. Trafficante, who represented the tourist industry's darker side, insisted, "Castro is nothing. . . . I'm sure Fidel Castro will never amount to anything. But even if he does, they'll never close the casinos. There is so much damned money here for everyone."[32]

Happy New Year: International Hotel Diplomacy

Official Washington seemed at a loss in late 1958 when Castro's rebel forces closed in on victory. Some State Department officials, cognizant of Castro's independence from local communists, began to reconcile themselves to the idea of a Castro government, hopeful that moderate elements in the 26th of July Movement and on the Cuban political scene as a whole would in time prevail over more radical factions. Others took heart in the election of a new constituent assembly in November, reasoning that although the balloting had been rigged, Batista might take the opportunity to step aside and make room for a "third force." Others looked to the Cuban military to remove Batista, preferably by suasion, and establish an acceptable anti-Castro military junta.[33]

It was too late for any of these schemes to work. By December, dispirited government troops had been thoroughly routed, and rebel forces took the Oriente capital of Santiago. On the day after Christmas, M-26-7 forces launched the siege of Santa Clara in central Cuba. Havana's hotels, restaurants, clubs, and tourists braced themselves for the revolution that Washington had so badly underestimated and for an unusual New Year's celebration.

Matthews was back in town, this time not on official assignment but to ring in the New Year with friends at the Riviera Hotel. Although the Copa Room of the Riviera was about only a quarter filled, he and his party—his wife, Nancie; his *Times* colleague, Ruby Hart Phillips; and Ted Scott of the *Havana Post*—"had the traditional dinner: paper hats, horns, champagne, and what not." Matthews later remembered that "the vacation ended during the baked Alaska." "Young Arvey," son of Jake Arvey, a notable Chicago politician, dropped by the Matthews table and casually remarked that he had glanced out his hotel room window overlooking the military base and landing strip at Camp Columbia and seen "a number of cars, women, children, and luggage streaming toward the airfield." "This is it," Scott exclaimed.[34]

At the Hilton, the rumors began to fly at about 2:00 A.M., but most of the 325 guests heard the news on the morning radio after they had retired or gone home. Batista and his coterie had fled the country by plane, leaving a motorcade of Cadillacs on the tarmac at Camp Columbia. New Year's Day brought a rush of Habaneros onto the streets, thousands dressed in the red and black colors of the insurrection. The Hilton manager reported to corporate headquarters that jubilant crowds drove past the hotel in convertible cars and other vehicles, shouting, "Long live Fidel Castro and the Movement of 26 July." Radio Rebelde, the rebel station, broadcast instructions for people to decorate houses with Cuban flags, and Castro called for a general strike to bring down the last remnants of the ancien régime.[35]

The celebration took a violent turn here and there, with looting, shootings, and the destruction of hotel property and casinos. Matthews astutely observed in the next morning's *New York Times* that "although the rioting may seem aimless, it was noteworthy that the places chosen were owned by known sympathizers of former president Fulgencio Batista." The Trafficante-run casino at the Sevilla Biltmore sustained more than $250,000 in damage. The Plaza Hotel, connected in Cuban minds with Joe Rogers Stassi, a protégé of Anastasia, the murdered gangster, also received special attention. "Rightly or wrongly," Matthews commented, "the casinos and slot machines are connected in the public mind with gangsters, police protection, and the corruption of the Batista regime."[36]

The Havana Hilton's Casparius, on his second assignment for the international chain, called a special personnel meeting and requested that workers man the entry doors and help protect Havana's most extravagant building. Rioters dropped by the hotel but turned away after sizing up the defenses. Some desperate Batistianos took up positions outside Trader Vic's, where a volley of gunfire left one of them wounded. Meanwhile, unionists identified by Hilton managers as communist used the general strike as a pretext for toppling the hotel's Gastronómico Union, perhaps hoping to outmaneuver M-26-7 unionists. The leaders demanded that Casparius close the hotel and expressed irritation when the young manager recruited "volunteer" workers to attend to the two hundred or so mostly U.S. and Canadian guests.[37]

The art of inn keeping imitated the art of international diplomacy the next morning, 2 January, when rebel forces poured in from the countryside and the Hilton lobby filled with more than six hundred soldiers. Casparius arranged sleeping quarters for the *barbudos* in the ballroom. North American tourists appeared intimidated at first, but the tension quickly eased, and some patrons even began "making friends" with Castro's soldiers. Casparius told his supervisors in New York that the Fidelistas were "full of respect, humility, and simplicity." The militant unionists refused to allow food service to the guests, insurgents and tourists alike, but when the Hilton management staff obtained a written order from the M-26-7 commander in chief of Havana that exempted the hotel from the general strike, the insurrectionists allowed the Hilton staff to return to work.[38]

By nightfall on 2 January, about twelve hundred soldiers had come and gone from the hotel; the last of them transferred to Fort Columbia after its

Troops from Fidel Castro's 26th of July Movement pose in triumph outside the entrance to the Havana Hilton on 1 January 1959. Castro arrived in Havana a week later and established his offices and residence on the hotel's twenty-third floor. The building was seized by the revolutionary government and rechristened the Habana Libre a year and a half later. Cuban Heritage Collection, University of Miami Libraries, Coral Gables, Florida.

fall to the rebels. Casparius reported that the soldiers had been "in dirty condition and the lobby smelled like a stable," but not even an ashtray had been broken.[39] Similar reports came from Hotel Nacional, the Riviera, and the Capri, where rebel soldiers had been temporarily housed. By contrast, chaos enveloped most of the city's tourist districts, where approximately two thousand U.S. citizens waited impatiently to depart. Cruise ships kept arriving at dockside bearing additional visitors, while those seeking to evacuate found the ferry to Key West temporarily shut down and commercial air traffic snarled. The general strike added to the confusion: banks shut down, and everyday business ground to a halt.[40]

Impatient U.S. hotel guests vented frustration at their embassy for delays in evacuation. Hilton clients complained that "the Embassy did not seem to know what they were doing, making the guests take their luggage out, then back again, and then out again."[41] Wayne S. Smith, a young vice consul at the embassy at the time, remembered making the rounds to the big hotels to try to soothe tempers. There was no real danger, he later wrote, and no shortages of food and water. M-26-7 authorities agreed to permit charter flights to assist the evacuation, but the flights departed irregularly.[42]

The worst of the tumult subsided within a day or so. At 7:00 P.M. on 4 January, Castro took to the radio airwaves and announced the end of the general strike. Unidentified unionists at the Hilton continued to obstruct routine, but the bulk of the staff got out the vacuum cleaners and mops, and by the next day the building looked much as it had on the day of its grand opening, except that the casino, Trader Vic's, and two smaller public rooms remained closed.[43] Pockets of counterrevolutionary resistance held out across the city, and leftist and moderate unionists jockeyed for advantage, but arrival in Havana of Manuel Urrutia, Castro's hand-chosen noncommunist president, signaled a return to order. Urrutia organized a presidential cabinet consisting of respected professionals and political moderates, and M-26-7 troops patrolled the streets and quelled the unrest.

Castro took the first week of the New Year to conduct a "victory parade" to the capital. Along the way, he encountered crowds of admiring Cubans, eager to glimpse the triumphant underdog. He seemed enthralled by the public euphoria, although his intentions remained vague and contradictory. Press censorship would be lifted, and elections were a possibility. He insisted that he wished the United States no ill will but railed against U.S. support for Batista during the insurrection's final days. He was clear on one matter: Batista's leading cronies would be executed.[44]

Castro entered Havana on 8 January to a thunderous welcome. Exhausted, running on adrenalin, and savoring his astonishing success, he spoke excitedly but incoherently to the admiring throngs. He spent his first night in Havana as a Hilton resident, and over the next week the entire twenty-third floor was transformed into the headquarters of the provisional revolutionary government. On any given day, the lobby held more uniformed *barbudos* than vacationers. The Fidelistas imposed tight security around their chief, but only one frightful moment occurred. Errol Flynn, who lived in the apartment below Castro's, more often than not in a vodka-induced haze, fell asleep one night while smoking and set off fire alarms. Castro came and went with ease. He delighted the kitchen staff by occasionally popping in during the wee hours of the morning to chat and chow down his favorite late-night snack, a Hilton steak.[45]

Revolution and Tourism: Host Agency

Castro came to power determined to bring the visitors back but to do so on terms more beneficial to the host society. No set blueprint existed, and certainly no preconceived formula. Battlefield tactics, U.S. aid to the established government, and the possibility of U.S. intervention had been Castro's main preoccupations during the preceding months. The new government nonetheless quickly set to work to negotiate a redistribution of power inside the island's touristed cultural contact zones.

The effort did not produce immediate results. Fighting for his life in the Sierra Maestra, Castro had adopted a harsh stance not only toward U.S. military aid to Batista but also toward foreign tourism, especially its sponsorship of rampant vice. The Castroites infused Cuban nationalism with a strong moral tone, a response no doubt to the demeaning constructions of identity imposed on Cuba by fun-loving tourists. Matthews remembered Castro and his young officers as provincials when it came to gambling, narcotics, and prostitution. "Fidel was so old fashioned when he first reached Havana," he told a student audience at the City College of New York in 1961, that "he argued that interest on money was a sin."[46] Even prior to Castro's arrival in Havana, victorious rebels began to interrogate and arrest some casino operators and seize their daily receipts. Thus, few observers expressed surprise when President Urrutia ordered the closure of casinos and gaming houses on 5 January.[47]

Revolutionary morality, however, had to be reconciled with conflicting interest group pressure and the need for tourist revenue and employment. Even Ernesto "Che" Guevara, the ideological firebrand among the bunch, tempered his idealism. "I am for total planning as a matter of principle as well as theory," he told Matthews in early 1959; "however, I am only one person in the government and I realize that in the present state of the Cuban economy, there must be a mixture of planning and private enterprise." Nor did Guevara sense rabid anti-Americanism among the revolution's rank and file, especially when compared to postrevolutionary Mexico. "You know Mexico. In Mexico I have seen crowds showing hatred of Americans as Americans. You have never seen that here and you never will."[48]

U.S. travel industry officials representing Pan Am, American Express, Hilton, and other firms struck a pragmatic pose, undertaking ad campaigns to lure visitors back to the island and seeking support from the new government.[49] Just a few weeks following Castro's victorious arrival in Havana, representatives of the American Society of Travel Agents (ASTA) met with President Urrutia and assured him that they still looked forward to holding their annual meeting in Havana later in the year.[50] Coming just days after the closing of Havana's casinos, ASTA's gesture not only promised an influx of some two thousand conventioneers into the Cuban capital but also affirmed that one of the U.S. travel industry's most influential organizations wanted to do business with the Castro government.

After hearing of Batista's New Year's morning flight from Havana, Hilton's Caverly hopped a plane and headed directly for the Havana Hilton. Through the intercession of a former hotel building engineer who served on Castro's staff, Caverly arranged to meet with Castro on his first morning in Havana. The corporate executive ordered breakfast, and the two sat with an interpreter and talked on the balcony of Castro's suite for about an hour. "I had the feeling he was not anti-American," Caverly later remembered. Castro stated that he was "interested in maintaining tourism as it was a principal source of hard currency and also created a significant amount of employment." When Caverly commented that gambling was a major attraction for tourism, Castro replied that while he personally opposed gambling, he "recognized its importance as a tourist attraction and would consider leaving the hotel casinos open for tourists, but would discourage casino patronage by Cubans."[51]

Advancing beyond generalities, Caverly noted that Hilton International, already reeling from postopening losses, anticipated continued low occupancy and operating deficits in the coming months. To maintain operations, the company would need to arrange credits. After some discussion, Castro expressed interest in keeping the hotel open and its staff employed and asked how large a credit would be needed. Caverly estimated that one million dollars would get the hotel through the troubled times. The meeting ended amicably at 7:00 A.M. About noon the next day, Caverly received a message to go to the Banco Nacional de Cuba at 3:00 that afternoon to meet with Fidel's brother, Raúl, and Guevara. In less than an hour, they arranged a one-million-dollar loan to the credit of a Cuban corporation, a shell company with no assets that the Hilton people had formed on behalf of the hotel.[52]

The Hilton loan demonstrated Castro's authoritarian inclinations, especially his willingness to act without consulting Urrutia and his cabinet. But it also revealed his initial desire to develop a mixed rather than a command economy. In fact, Castro surrounded himself with liberal economic planners, foremost among them Felipe Pazos, who headed the Banco Nacional. The group strenuously urged economic diversification but advocated only modest nationalization. On 13 January, less than a week into the revolution, Castro appealed to tourists and investors to come "back to Cuba . . . which can now be counted among the countries where democracy is a reality."[53] *Cuba Magazine*, a publication of the Cuban Tourist Commission, put out a special postrevolutionary issue touting Cuba as the "Land of Opportunity, Playland of the Americas" that explained that "the Cuban revolution has eliminated the atmosphere of the police state which greatly restricted the number of tourists who visited our shores in recent years." Below a smiling photo of Fidel Castro, the issue announced a new appropriation of six million dollars for tourism projects.[54]

As Hilton and other companies regrouped, Havana's more than ten thousand hotel, casino, and restaurant workers asserted themselves as well. In late January, several thousand unemployed hospitality workers took to the streets to voice their discontent with the forced closure of Havana's casinos. The prohibition on gaming not only cost casino workers their jobs but also jeopardized the livelihoods of all hotel workers. Since most of the city's large luxury hotels carried heavy overhead expenditures and depended on casino dollars to turn a respectable profit, gambling rooms provided the key to employment opportunities throughout the hospitality industry. In response to labor as well as business pressure, the revolutionary government formed the new Cuban Tourist Commission on 26 January, and its chair, Oscar Ramírez Torres, paid public homage to "the importance of the foreign tourism to Cuba's economy."[55]

Conceding that large, deluxe hotels needed casino income, the government eased its gambling ban. On 6 February, Castro announced that although he remained opposed to games of chance and hoped eventually to ban them permanently, he had accepted a special government commission's recommendation to legalize gambling "since it provided jobs to Cubans."[56] The text of the new law, enacted on 19 February, reflected the leader's mixed feelings. It began with an extended preamble that read in part: "WHEREAS: Gambling is a vice. WHEREAS: Of all forms of gambling the worst is that which feeds itself on the scarce resources of the most humble classes of the people, impoverishes the citizens in a material way and prostitutes them morally."[57] Further along, following several pages of qualifiers, the document reluctantly allowed for the reopening of casinos to foreign tourists as a measure to relieve unemployment. The new law expressly restricted gambling to larger luxury nightclubs and hotels, and legal games included only roulette, blackjack, craps, baccarat, and big six. The law prohibited slot machines.[58]

The government also announced the return of the country's National Lottery, a popular but corrupt program of lucky numbers and weekly drawings that catered to locals more than tourists. Castro viewed the old lottery as a source of "vice and enrichment of political cliques" and charged that under Batista, the system had employed more than sixteen hundred salaried employees who essentially did no work. The revised lottery sold tickets in the form of bonds; even losing numbers could be redeemed for 40 percent of their original value. Holders who retained their tickets for between one and six years qualified for 50, 60, 70, 90, or 110 percent reimbursement. In short, the new arrangement encouraged savings over risk taking. The awarding of fewer prizes (the weekly grand prize still totaled one hundred thousand dollars) and a reduction in staff and graft enabled the government to finance the program.[59]

Newsweek reported happily in early March that roulette wheels were whirling again in Havana's luxury casinos, "as much a fixture in the landscape as skyscrapers in New York City," and that the new government was "bubbling over with bright new ideas" for tourism.[60] Havana's gambling impresarios, however, expressed skepticism regarding the new laws because they required casino operators to pay significantly heftier taxes and fees than had previously been the case. The reopening of a casino required the posting of a fifty-thousand-dollar surety, a new fee to be deposited with the Instituto Nacional de Ahhoro y Vivienda (National Savings and Housing Institute). License fees remained at the prerevolutionary rate of twenty-five thousand dollars, but monthly taxes ranged from five thousand to thirteen thousand dollars, depending on the number of tables in use and hours of operation, a series of flat fees that replaced Batista's more skimmable 20 percent of profits quarterly. The government funneled its share of the take to low-cost housing programs and tourism promotion.[61]

It is difficult to gauge the long-term impact of the revised gambling legislation. While many of Havana's gaming houses decried the new system as highway robbery, others predicted that when tourist numbers bounced back to prerevolutionary levels, the percentages still ran with the house. Hilton legal counsel Sidney H. Willner, who had negotiated the Havana Hilton's original casino lease to an outside company, estimated that the new taxes would amount to approximately $120,000 annually for the hotel and concluded that the "terms of the new contract can fairly be said to be much better from our point of view than the terms of the [hotel's] original contract." Since the Hilton leased out its casino, it would still be assured of at least $22,500 per month in rent.[62]

The return of gambling by no means harkened back to the Batista-Lansky era. In mid-March, the Havana press carried a United Press International dispatch that quoted U.S. narcotics commissioner H. J. Anslinger's testimony before Congress that the Cuban government had requested his office's assistance in putting an end to the "enormous drug trade" in Cuba. Anslinger asserted that he had laid down as a condition that Havana deport "foreign hoodlums" in the casino business. Castro unleashed a blistering reply in *Prensa Libre*. "We are not only disposed to deport gangsters but to shoot them," he bellowed. "What happened is that the Commissioner has not heard that there has been a Revolution here and gangsterism, racketeering, interventionism and similar things have stopped."[63]

Nor did Castro intend to grovel before the U.S.-led international travel industry and allow tourist power to trump his fundamental egalitarian goals. No North American had better access to the liberator's thinking at the time than Matthews. The journalist made several trips to Havana during the early stages of the revolution and seemed to occupy a special place in Castro's heart. One day in mid-February 1959, after Castro had arranged to have himself appointed prime minister, he traveled with Matthews to the small fishing village of Cojímar, just east of Havana. They visited a small house on a hill overlooking the ocean that the new head of state intended to fix up and use as a retreat. As they strolled around the modest property, Castro pointed to the expansive beach below and told Matthews of his plans to transform it into public space. "Four kilometers of beach," he said in a shocked tone, "and all of it privately owned. Yet the people of Havana have so few places of recreation to go."[64]

Matthews and Phillips, his colleague from the *Times*, met Castro on another occasion at the Hilton at about 2:00 in the morning. They began the interview in the coffee shop so that Castro could quickly chow down a steak "to keep him going." The three then drove out to a stretch of beach between Havana and Varadero where the sand was fine and the water blue, clear, and calm. Cuba's chief revolutionary enthusiastically shared his vision of a public beach equipped with a low-cost hotel, bathhouses, sports fields, and restaurants. The government would create sixty such beaches around the island's coast, he forecast, designed with Cuba's working-class specifically in mind. The concept was to "get the people out of Havana and give them and their families an inexpensive, pleasant, and happy place to go."[65]

Castro expressed hope that foreign tourists would also be attracted to the recreational areas. Recalling the humiliating discriminatory practices of the Batista era, he insisted that recreational facilities would be open to anyone, without discrimination by nationality, race, color, or economic status. "All this was my idea," Castro said proudly. "I used to think of it when I was up in the Sierra Maestra. Beaches and their clubs used to be for the rich; now they will be for all. Habaneros never had anywhere to go before. Isn't it better to go to a beach on a Sunday afternoon than to stay in at a movie?"[66] The proposal was hardly radical. Matthews compared Castro's model seashore to Jones Beach, a public facility located on Long Island near Manhattan. But it did run against the grain of decades of U.S.-Cuban tourism practices and challenge the interests of an angry cohort of private landowners.[67]

Despite its clarity of vision and its willingness to compromise, the Castro government had difficulty reconciling competing interests that blocked tourism's recovery. Although business firms and Cuba's hospitality workers shared an interest in restoring the trade, they clashed regarding wages, employment policies, and other operational issues. The Havana Hilton and other hotels struggled to reduce expenses in light of shrinking revenue and ballooning debt. Facing two million dollars in losses after one year of operation, Caverly developed plans to reduce the Hilton's labor force, close down unprofitable hotel shops and restaurants, and scale back utility costs. Union workers, however, persuaded the labor ministry, which contained the revolution's most militant leftists, to reject the package and brand the proposed layoffs "anti-revolutionary."[68]

The new tourist commission, staffed by a series of representatives from different ministries, added to the confusion. Its officials seemed to loathe making decisions in the face of pressure from labor, management, and government. "Every time we talk to these people," Caverly groused, "they listen carefully, profess sympathy, but then say that tourism will return to Cuba and our problems will be solved."[69] The disinclination to chart a consistent course arose in part from the political minefield that the revolution had sown. In early February, the M-26-7 newspaper, *Revolución*, reported that the former head of Gastrónomico, Francisco Aguirre, was in jail. He was accused of receiving large sums of money related to the Havana Hilton's construction.[70] Whether by design or accident, the arrest signaled to tourism officials that they needed to tread carefully.

In mid-June, Castro established a revamped Board of Tourism Development with himself at the helm and integrated into its operation all preexisting tourist agencies. The new board allocated two hundred million dollars to fund tourism initiatives across the island, but the ambitious agenda would have intimidated the most seasoned travel industry experts. Among its many responsibilities, the board was charged with improving transportation facilities, converting private beaches to public recreational areas, promoting tourism to less heavily visited areas outside of Havana, and scrutinizing the business practices, especially the underreporting of profits, of Havana's large hotels and popular restaurants.[71]

Operating under trying conditions, the revolutionaries nonetheless refused to give up on North American travelers. All signs pointed to the ASTA's annual meeting, scheduled for October in Havana, as the moment when things might turn around. The Cuban Tourist Commission accordingly undertook a "crash program" to scrub up the city for the travel agents. More than twelve hundred workers, working in eight-hour shifts, hustled to complete renovations on the José Martí International Airport. The local press reported that out of "revolutionary zeal," the construction workers donated an extra hour's work daily to the project.[72]

Completed on schedule, the modernized terminal boasted central air-conditioning. Its new ceiling board, curtains, and drapes had been manufactured in Cuba, and the fluorescent lighting was of the most recent design. Press reports claimed that the finished product compared favorably with New York's Idlewild Airport. The U.S. embassy described the work as "impressive." "The front of the terminal building has been modernized by the construction of 'flying' carport-type roofing to protect passengers leaving the airport from inclement weather, and a long line of 'royal' palms, many as tall as forty feet or more, have been newly planted along the approach road to the airport from the Rancho Boyeros Highway, presenting an impressive view to the visitor to Cuba."[73]

The government's efforts to revitalize tourism on the host's terms yielded at best mixed results. Throughout 1959, with the exception of an occasional convention crowd, the travel industry crawled along. The most obvious explanation for the stagnation is probably the best: U.S. tourists, either rightly or wrongly, viewed travel to Cuba as risky. Despite Castro's proclaimed democratic intentions, his government behaved much as a revolutionary regime might be expected. Promised elections were delayed, and the trials and executions of "war criminals" went forward, including that of a marijuana dealer whose appearance before a firing squad was justified by Cuban officials as "a social benefit."[74] Late-night television comedian Jack Parr, who had broadcast from Havana just prior to the revolution, acted much like other tourists when he canceled a planned vacation to Cuba in early 1959. "I don't look good in a blindfold," he quipped.[75]

Yet while the visitor-host relationship could not be characterized as healthy after months of revolutionary governance, it was alive. Fidel Castro and his government remained weary of the travel industry's antisocial impulses but had consistently shown a willingness to play host. The government leaders had been joined by thousands of Cuban hospitality workers and an array of cooperative transnational business firms. Although many potential U.S. tourists remained gun-shy, some still could not resist Havana's call. The

Hilton and other hotels continued to book conventions on a semi-steady basis, preventing the complete evaporation of hope for recovery. An October 1959 list of Havana Hilton conventions included the ASTA, the Amateur Softball Association, the American National Insurance Company, the Prairie Farmers Association, Rotary International, Sealy Mattress, and perhaps most telling of all, Optimists International.[76]

Cultural Relations versus Political Relations

While U.S.-Cuban cultural relations held out at least a semblance of hope, political relations aroused no optimism whatsoever. Although Castro quickly established order across the island and demonstrated ideological flexibility toward tourism and other industries, Washington never relaxed its furrowed brow. While U.S. officials agreed throughout 1959 that Cuba's new leader was not a communist, sympathetic to communism, or supported by Moscow, he clearly represented revolutionary change. Soon after assuming power, Castro nationalized the Cuban Telephone and Telegraph Company, a subsidiary of AT&T, and lowered rates; lowered housing rents by 50 percent; denounced U.S. imperialism and support for right-wing dictatorships in Latin America; and offered support to opponents of pro-U.S. dictators Rafael Trujillo of the Dominican Republic and Luis Somoza Debayle in Nicaragua. In short, Castro refused to submit to U.S. hegemony and overtly threatened the foundational structures of the U.S. hemispheric empire. Cuba's newfound independence, rather than its possible embrace of communism, drove U.S. policymakers to contest Castro's rule.[77]

Yet U.S.-Cuban relations drifted along through 1959 and well into 1960 without abruptly imploding. Realist scholars, who attribute the conduct of international relations to systems of power, have been hard-pressed to explain the strange interregnum between the revolution's triumph and Washington's active efforts to overthrow it. The North American hegemon possessed an array of mechanisms with which to bridle upstart dependencies, including marine brigades, covert operations, economic embargoes, and preponderant influence in organizations such as the United Nations and the Organization of American States. In time, U.S. leaders resorted to variants of all these tactics but did so in a gradual and reactive manner rather than through coordinated and deliberate action.

Historian Thomas G. Paterson has used the metaphor of a beached whale, powerful but helpless, to describe the waning of U.S. hegemony in Cuba. To explain the U.S. system failure, he cites internal bickering in the U.S. embassy in Havana—driven largely by Ambassador Smith's lone insistence that Castro was either a communist or a fellow traveler, the myopia of the Eisenhower White House and National Security Council, Washington's preoccupation with Cold War crises in Berlin and the Taiwan Strait, the polarization of Cuban politics that eliminated moderating influences and allowed Castro to increasingly monopolize power, the global process of decolonization that undercut hegemonic systems worldwide, and a culturally based "imperial hubris."[78]

Alan McPherson, who has written a penetrating history of anti-Americanism in Latin America, has posited that Castro and many other Cubans harbored contradictory attitudes toward the United States. Aspiration to North American lifestyles throughout the twentieth century juxtaposed resentment toward the structures of dependency that limited Cuban economic development and political democracy. Thus, a deep ambivalence toward the United States colored much of modern Cuban political life. McPherson argues that Castro both imbibed and manipulated these attitudes and shifted gears when necessary. He espoused a willingness to engage Washington when it suited his needs but adopted a staunch anti-Americanism as conditions allowed. Ambivalence is certainly the watchword when it comes to U.S.-Cuban relations during the revolution's first year or so. But McPherson dates Castro's firm, self-conscious intransigence toward the United States from mid-1958 on, whereas tourist-host relations suggest that Castro remained ambivalent at least through the fall of 1959 and even into early 1960.[79]

Louis A. Pérez Jr. has described a slightly longer interlude in which U.S. relations with the Castro regime evolved as a "state of affairs in continuous flux as developments with portentous implications seemed to gather momentum from one day to the next in vertiginous succession."[80] He attributes the surreal time lapse to cultural factors, especially the Americans' inability to adjust long-held perceptions of a dependent island neighbor to the new reality of an assertive Cuba. Castro's defiance left Washington officials and a good part of the U.S. public amazed and disoriented. In part, the ailing hegemon suffered symptoms of cognitive dissonance. Still more complex, having viewed Cubans since the early twentieth century as wards of the American state, U.S. observers took Castro's hostility as a severe blow to their self-esteem. Severed from historic U.S. understanding of Cuba and Cubans, U.S. policy drifted for months until Cold War labels, especially the communist tag, placed Castro and Cuba within a familiar narrative.[81]

For months, the cultural connections that bound together the United States and Cuba in fact proved more powerful than the political discord that ultimately drove them apart. The linkages generated and sustained by U.S. tourism and the travel industry stood near if not at the center of the stage and shed considerable additional light on the slow and emotionally agonizing deterioration of diplomatic relations. While the exploitative tourist-host relationship had helped fuel the revolution, it had also produced a mutual familiarity and a collage of habitual behaviors. The deeply embedded intimacy enabled vestiges of the everyday life of the empire to survive the empire's obvious political disintegration and momentarily suggested that U.S.-Cuban relations might survive the revolution.

The visitor-host relationship during the first months of Castro's rule certainly lacked warmth. Tourist numbers remained stagnant, and Cuba's revolutionary hosts often appeared less than cordial. The State Department received numerous complaints from U.S. travelers of mistreatment by officials at the José Martí Airport. The most frequent grievance arose from "brusque searches" of incoming passengers, which the Cubans understandably viewed as a necessary precaution against the smuggling of arms and cash to active anti-Castro groups on the island.[82] Manifestations of popular anti-Americanism also increased. Conrad Hilton received an indignant letter from a Spanish-speaking patron named Godofreda Torres Neda who had stayed at the Havana Hilton and noticed that all of the employees seemed required to speak English: "I consider this an error on behalf of hotels in Latin American territory where the national idiom is Castellian."[83] Longtime Havana resident John Snook expressed "shock" when he was standing in line at a bank and overheard a Cuban teller remark, "Deja el Americano esparar hasta el última" (Leave the American waiting until last).[84]

The case of Hilton International, however, illuminates the lasting binational bond. Conrad Hilton and his top executives by no means welcomed Castro's populism and early in the crisis considered bailing on the Havana Hilton. But company lawyers learned that the contract with Gastronómico and the Cuban government could be abrogated without penalty only in the event of "force majeure." Company official Gregory R. Dillon acknowledged that the term lacked precise definition but generally implied a natural disaster or an "act of God." Since the U.S. government recognized the Castro regime, it technically constituted a government rather than an insurrection and could hardly be termed a supernatural phenomenon.[85]

Company officials consequently decided to stay and hope for the best despite the challenges of working with a revolutionary regime and in spite of a steady thinning of the tourist population. Conrad Hilton made the call, confiding to colleague Willner, "I, like you, don't know what is going to happen. This is a gamble, and we will have to see."[86] Despite the healthy skepticism, leading executives soon found themselves believing that a working relationship with Castro was feasible. In an early February letter to Hilton, Caverly estimated the hotel could break even financially if it could reach 43 percent occupancy, a target he thought could be obtained by April or May. Other hotels were in worse shape, he noted. Castro and other government officials still resided at the Hilton, and on Saturday nights the lobby, bar, and restaurants hosted about 150 customers. Caverly had visited the Rivera and observed perhaps "no more than twenty people" in its public spaces.[87]

Some of the company men even became disenchanted by Washington's drumbeat of hostility toward the new regime. Caverly vented his frustration: "Certainly some of the things the new Castro regime has done are beyond the limits of human decency," he told Hilton. But "a lot of the trouble has been stirred up by the American press and some of our Congressmen." Aware that tourists possessed the power of choice, he maintained that it would be "extremely difficult to develop any substantial amount of travel to the Island until the press and the politicians leave Cuba alone and let the average person make up his own mind as to whether or not he wishes to go to Cuba."[88] Dillon pinned responsibility for Castro's bad press to Miami's media moguls, who viewed Cuba's travails as good news for the Florida travel industry that subsidized the Miami press.[89]

Hilton officials expressed renewed hope when Castro traveled to the United States and Canada in April. To convey his displeasure with the regime's anti-American diatribes, President Eisenhower snubbed the visiting dignitary but arranged for Vice President Nixon and State Department officials to meet and assess Castro. The Hilton chain rolled out the red carpet to welcome the Castro party. Caverly instructed hotel management in New York, Washington, Montreal, and Houston "to extend all possible courtesies to this group." Accommodations were discounted 25 percent, although the Cubans insisted on paying regular rates for meals. When he arrived in Washington, Castro discovered a complimentary bottle of Bacardi Carta Oro, a box of Cuban cigars, and a courtesy card from the Havana Hilton manager in his suite; his minister of the treasury, Rufo López Fresquet, received the same royal treatment except that a bottle of good scotch substituted for the rum. Local management plastered each hotel with advertising for the luxuriously appointed Havana Hilton.[90]

The trip allowed Castro to bolster the positive press he had received during the insurrection. The media for the most part continued to paint him as a reformer, and an admiring public soaked up his charisma. After returning to

Cuba, he signed into law what represented at the time the revolution's pinnacle reform, the May 1959 Agrarian Reform Act that nationalized latifundia (large plantations) of more than 472 hectares (approximately 1,000 acres). While U.S. property owners decried the measure, large numbers of small and medium-sized farms remained in private hands, and many observers remarked on the measure's moderate nature.[91] From Hilton International's perspective, agrarian reform certainly did not constitute reason to panic. In June, the former rebels made good on their promise, and the Banco Nacional de Cuba released the first of two half-million-dollar installments in credits for the Havana Hilton. Hilton officials could draw on the funds through 31 December at a rate of 7.5 percent interest.[92]

Willner reported to Conrad Hilton that the government's "mood" had steadily improved over time and speculated that the hospitality extended to Castro on the recent trip had improved atmospherics. But "underlying all of the foregoing specific changes in the situation," Willner observed, "is the development of an attitude toward tourism in general and Hilton organization in particular, without which most of the specific steps could not have been accomplished."[93] Dillon returned from ten days in Havana and reported the rumor that Fidel had summoned his brother, Raúl, a self-proclaimed Marxist, to a meeting in Houston where he "laid down the law" against alignment with the communists.[94]

Even a raucous rally marking the anniversary of the founding of the 26th of July Movement failed to dull the capitalists' upbeat assessments and in fact produced sympathy for the government's objectives. Cubans turned out en masse to hear their beloved leader deliver a passionate defense of the revolution. On hand as Castro's guest was Mexico's former president, Lázaro Cárdenas, who had combined land and labor reform with tourism and friendly ties to the United States. "We Mexicans know that revolutions are not imported or exported," he told the cheering throngs. He then summoned Franklin Roosevelt's policy of "mutual respect" and declared that Latin American nations possessed the right to "live freely and independently, without intervention."[95] Arthur E. Elmiger, the executive vice president and steward of Hilton's Latin American assets, was in Havana at the time. He wrote to the head of his company of the hundreds of thousands "wild machete-bearing campesinos from western Cuba" who made the Havana Hilton a meeting place for their rally. "They came from early in the morning till late at night, some in shoes, some with hats, some without.... Most of them had never seen a city, nor electricity, nor the wonders of the Havana Hilton." Hilton management put hundreds of them up on cots in the hotel garage and fed them in the employees' kitchen, and although the visitors caused wear and tear on the hotel, the event took place without incident. "I have never seen anything like it in my career in hotels," the astonished Elmiger noted.[96]

Although business remained in the doldrums, the Hilton's diplomatic efforts continued. After staying away from the island earlier in the year, Parr took his popular television show to Havana in early October, the week before the ASTA convention, and broadcast from the Hilton. Briefly dropping his wisecracking persona, Parr pleaded with his audience, "Tourists have stopped going to Cuba in the most part," yet this "is one of the most beautiful hotels in the world. It's because of the scare. I can tell you that I saw nothing but friendship and a welcome out to all Americans. . . . But they need tourism very, very badly." He went on to note that Castro could be observed coming and going, eating late-night dinners with kitchen workers, and even mediating employee disputes. Although the revolutionary opposed gambling and drinking, Parr assured his viewers that Castro tolerated such practices among North American visitors.[97]

Thus, while Washington and Havana hurled insults at one another and talk of covert intervention filled the air, tourists and hosts pursued a quiet series of diplomatic exchanges. Castro, his travel officials, labor unions, and the transnational travel industry worked steadily to establish a new visitor-host system. The new system's success, however, hinged on the tourist response, and visitors required time to digest the changes, weigh the accuracy of government and media representations, reimagine Cuba as a sovereign state, and reconstruct a Cuban culture sans prostitution, narcotics, gangsters, and subservience.

A Messy Divorce: Culture Meets Politics

Identities are never permanent but always remain subject to contested discourses on race, class, gender, national identity, and other cultural constructions. Cuba's identity in the United States in 1959 and early 1960 emerged as a major point of cultural and political contention. Leftist academics and youth embraced the new Cuba, while conservatives gasped at the tumult, the expropriations, and the executions. The business community stood divided. Those who had invested in sugar and land tended to perceive Castro as an implacable Bolshevik, while most of those in the hospitality industry believed political conditions to be fluid.

U.S. policymakers momentarily waited for Castro to moderate his nationalism but ultimately proved less adaptable to Cuban aspirations than did the travel industry. Washington officials had grown accustomed to and even fond of the familiar images of the island and the convenient identity of subservience assigned to its people. Many U.S. leaders expressed the sentiment that the island nation under Castro would most likely continue to resemble the Cuba of lore: swaying palm trees, energetic rumba dancers, and mischievous, childlike natives. "I think the boy means to do right," former president Harry S. Truman said of Castro in April 1959; "let's wait and see."[98]

The wait did not last long. The image of an army led by a bearded Ricky Ricardo clone whose arrested development left him in a state of prolonged adolescence quickly became a dominant theme in official conversations. At a February 1959 National Security Council meeting, Central Intelligence Agency chief Allen Dulles expressed strong skepticism of Castro's abilities as a leader and insisted that the new Cuban officials had to be "treated as children."[99] Vice President Nixon met Castro during his April visit to the United States to address the American Society of Newspaper Editors and concluded that he was "either incredibly naïve about communism or under Communist discipline—my guess is the former."[100] Hopeful that Castro could be disciplined and educated, Nixon reported that he talked to the Cuban "like a Dutch uncle." (Robert Stevenson, Nixon's interpreter, later recounted that the vice president "had talked to Castro like a father.") Secretary of State Christian Herter advised Eisenhower that Castro was "very much like a child" who became "voluble" and "wild" when he spoke.[101] From the halls of Congress, Senator Allen J. Ellender, a Democrat from Louisiana, advised that Cubans saw North Americans as "big brother," suggesting a need for tough love.[102]

Yankee tourists and the transnational travel industry had not been the sole inventors and popularizers of these stereotypes. But from the 1920s forward and with overwhelming intensity during the 1950s, tourism had become the most common means of interaction between North Americans and Cubans. It had nourished difficult-to-dissolve cultural linkages but had also served as the principal means by which distorted perceptions of Cuban identity had been transmitted north and the conduit through which ordinary Cubans had come to know their "big brothers."

Following Castro's April visit to the north, U.S.-Cuban political relations entered a period of increased confrontation even as Hilton and other hoteliers expressed cautious optimism. In July, to protest the Agrarian Reform Act's expropriation of some U.S.-owned sugar mills with compensation based on tax value rather than market worth, the Eisenhower administration threatened to suspend Cuba's sugar quota. Castro answered by expropriating the remaining 105 U.S. mills.[103]

Throughout the summer, the U.S. business community in Cuba increasingly chastised Castro. "The American colony is emotionally anti-Castro," Herbert Matthews jotted down in his notes in July, and "sees communism everywhere."[104] Although the regime simplified the country's tax code and in some cases lowered taxes on investment, many U.S. analysts decried the government's intervention in the affairs of the Cuban Telephone Company, mandatory reduction of utility rates, slashing of rents in Havana and elsewhere, and refusal to rein in union demands. *Fortune* magazine editorialized that by "mid-August, Fidel Castro had led his tragic nation a long way down the road toward economic chaos."[105]

The hospitality industry remained among the last to give up on Castro, and in many ways its inability supply the Cuban leader with the dollars he craved marked the point of no return for U.S.-Cuban relations. Castro invested heavily in the ASTA meeting scheduled for 17–19 October. The extravaganza began on an upbeat note. The organization's president, Max T. Allen, strongly urged his membership to attend the big meeting: "A peaceful Cuba is vital to all Caribbean travel," Allen announced; "Cuba is the gateway to all the other islands and its hospitality and gaiety set the stage for every Caribbean tour."[106] More than two thousand travel agents descended on Havana, filling up several hotels and clinking glasses in numerous restaurants and bars. Castro addressed the happy group: he unhooked his gun belt in a symbolic gesture of friendship, laid it on the floor, and declared, "Never mind political propaganda. . . . [H]elp your friends to the happiness which travel to Cuba can give."[107]

But the meeting coincided with the public airing of two divisive internal disputes in the Castro government. One centered on complaints lodged by Major Húber Matos, the heroic former rebel army chief, that the Agrarian Reform Institute had undertaken numerous illegal land seizures. Castro struck back quickly, cutting off arms and ammunition to Matos and then jailing him as a "traitor" and an "ingrate."[108] As ASTA conventioneers digested the news of the Matos confrontation, they received an earful from another disgruntled former military officer. On 21 October, the former chief of the air force, Major Pedro Luis Díaz Lanz, made an unauthorized flight in a DC-3 aircraft from Miami to Havana, where he bombarded the tourist-agent-infested capital with anti-Castro leaflets. Accounts varied, but a flurry of military antiaircraft fire left two dead and several wounded. Castro immediately accused Díaz Lanz of firing on the city and denounced the action as having been orchestrated by the Eisenhower administration. "This is our Pearl Harbor," he thundered on television, and he called for a public mass rally to protest U.S. aggression.[109]

Castro produced no evidence that Díaz Lanz had deployed either rifle fire or explosives, and over the next several weeks, the Cuban leader reluctantly acknowledged that the incident had constituted an "air incursion" rather than a bombing. But Díaz Lanz's actions nonetheless soured U.S.-Cuban relations. Top U.S. officials speculated that Castro had deliberately inflated the violation of airspace to justify a further clampdown on internal dissent and severing relations with the United States. Herter reasoned that the exaggeration had been "deliberate and concerted."[110] The new U.S. ambassador, Philip Bonsal, labeled Havana's condemnations "Goebbels-type propaganda."[111] The dismissal of Castro's grievance, however, seems at least mildly disingenuous. Castro, after all, had gone to great lengths to prepare Havana for the ASTA meeting and had appeared in person before the large gathering to seek help strengthening the tourist industry. To choose the same event to let loose a concocted accusation and move Cuba into a permanent state of anti-Americanism seems an unlikely tactic.

Castro regularly referenced Washington's machinations against his drive for power during the final weeks of the M-26-7 insurgency. He took special umbrage that a possible U.S.-backed propaganda ploy appeared intended to undermine his efforts to revive the travel industry. Although he had moderated the gambling ban, loaned funds to Hilton and other hoteliers, reorganized the tourism bureaucracy, and brought ASTA to Havana, the travel business remained stalled, much to Castro's frustration.

To some extent, the problem was Castro. He wanted tourists in Cuba and relations based on equal terms with Washington, but he made inflammatory statements and took actions that aggravated ill feelings and scared tourists and U.S. officials alike. The majority of U.S. tourists, their diversity notwithstanding, had shown that they were not mindless consumers of goods and services but alert international players who assessed threats as well as pleasures and shied away from danger zones. The dilemma, however, was multilayered and certainly implicated U.S. policymakers. *Time* magazine and other news outlets regularly characterized Castro's behavior in terms of rant, emotion, and paranoia.[112] Press representatives, however, likely remained in the dark when the U.S. Department of State approved plans to work with anti-Castro groups in Cuba to "check" or "replace" the revolutionary regime, an action that took place in early November, just weeks after the ASTA convention. The line between paranoia and security awareness in international relations is often thin.[113]

Regardless of Washington's or Castro's intentions, U.S.-Cuban relations deteriorated steadily after the ASTA meeting. Castro went shopping for new sugar customers, including the Soviet Union, and commenced arming his supporters to deter expected U.S. aggression. For the first time, Castro appeared on the verge of abandoning the tourist industry. In November, his government seized and nationalized the Riviera Hotel following a prolonged conflict over labor policies.[114] Even Hilton executives grew gloomy. On 23 November, Elmiger told Hilton, "All tourist trade is being choked by the Cuban government" and advised that the Havana Hilton should be run for the rest of the year on a "day to day basis." "We should not put another nickel into the hotel," he counseled. He closed with the curious suggestion that there might be hope for a new government in January.[115]

President Osvaldo Dorticós Torrado, recently appointed to replace the moderate Urrutia and give the government a more nationalist profile, attacked the hoteliers and travel agents head-on. In his welcoming remarks to an April 1960 gathering of Latin American travel agents, he laid out his government's position: sluggish tourism "isn't our fault nor is it due to our negligence but simply due to a disloyal campaign of lies and defamations which wanted to cut our breath short."[116] A month later, the National Institute for the Tourist Industry hosted the Hemingway International Marlin Tournament. Castro not only led the welcoming ceremony but showed up armed with a fishing pole and ready to compete. During three days of deep-sea fishing, he reeled in four marlin, enough to earn the individual prize for pound points. He accepted the honors and predicted that the Americans would probably ask, "Who put the marlin on Fidel's hook?"[117]

Washington did not appreciate Castro's sarcasm and chalked up Cuban angst to emotion and irrationality. Bonsal observed that Castro suffered "mental imbalances."[118] Eisenhower dismissed the fiery leader as "a madman."[119] The discourse helped the administration dismiss the possibility of additional diplomacy and justified covert intervention in Cuba's internal affairs. Ike took a giant leap toward a political divorce in March 1960 when he ordered the Central Intelligence Agency to train Cuban exiles for an invasion of the island, the beginning of what would become the Bay of Pigs Invasion a year later.[120]

U.S.-Cuban relations did not deteriorate solely as the result of a political game of tit for tat involving economic sanctions, retaliation, escalating rhetoric, covert operations, and armed preparedness, although all of those behaviors contributed. Nor did the impasse arise primarily from strategic miscalculation, misperception, tactical propaganda, Soviet intrigue, or realist-based geopolitics. Over the preceding half century, the ninety miles that separated Cuba and Florida had become an integrating corridor, connecting two countries culturally as well as politically and economically. Cubans had emulated North American lifestyles and value systems, and tourism had played an essential role in extending the U.S. presence on the island and forging Cuba's identity.

The revolution gave Cubans new ways of imagining themselves or a new way of becoming "Cuban." The new Cuba challenged the identity forms that had been invented from the outside. It found expression in the regime's domestic reforms—tax simplification, lower utility rates, agrarian reform, expropriation—but also manifested itself in popular culture. The era of Cadillacs surrendered to the era of rent controls. The aesthetic beauty of desegregated public beaches rivaled that of high-rise hotels and swimming pools. Prostitution, practiced openly in public spaces, became a rarity, and Cuban leaders espoused a new ethic of sexual equality. In men's fashion, the suit coat and tie gave way to the guayabera (shirt jacket). Cuban musicians found employment once more in clubs and hotels. As Castro explained in April 1959, "We have been Cubanizing Cuba, because although it may appear paradoxical, Cuba was not Cubanized, and we ourselves lived with that type of complex of doubt, or resignation and where we undervalued the interest of our nationality before things foreign."[121]

As in postrevolutionary Mexico, tourism in Cuba blurred the line between politics and culture. In contrast to the Mexican experience, where visitors and hosts had negotiated ways to mesh tourism, Mexican identity formation, and the Good Neighbor policy, Cubanization under Castro could not be reconciled with Batista-era tourism and U.S. assumptions of political and economic hegemony. In the end, Castro's cooperative but inconsistent efforts to reimagine and restructure the Cuban tourist trade and the Hilton Corporation's exhaustive diplomatic efforts could not overcome half a century of history and popular memory quickly enough to stave off the imperial relationship's demise.

In June 1960, after depleting the million-dollar credit extended by the Cuban government a year earlier, the Havana Hilton informed Cuban authorities it could no longer make payroll and maintain employment. On 10 June, Castro's Ministry of Labor nationalized the hotel and renamed it the Habana Libre.[122] State takeovers, or "interventions," quickly followed at the Hotel Nacional, the St. John's Hotel, the Rosita de Hornedo Hotel, and the Tropicana nightclub. The group of enterprises joined the previously intervened Hotels Riviera, Commodore, and Sevilla Biltmore.

Castro adopted the metaphor of war as he clamped down on the country's once thriving cultural contact zones, openly acknowledging tourism's relevance to diplomacy. Hotel managers, he told a packed meeting of service workers, had acted in complicity with counterrevolutionaries by failing to cooperate with government efforts to bring U.S. tourists to Cuba. Without mentioning the U.S. government by name, he reviewed a list of affronts initiated from outside Cuba to weaken his regime: the attack on the sugar quota, a suspension of bank credits, and a slowing of fuel deliveries. In addition, he charged, "a pretense was made to use tourism as a weapon of economic pressure and all efforts were made to keep American tourists from coming to Cuba." "If what they want is to ruin our tourist industry," he carped, "if their desire is to starve our hotel workers, they won't succeed because their efforts will crash against the spirit of our workers and noble people." Cuba, he promised, would "win the tourist battle."[123]

Hilton's managers had taken precautions against the government takeover of the hotel. The lion's share of the company's initial investment in Havana had come from Gastrónomico's retirement fund. The million dollars in loans provided by the Castro government had been made to a local subsidiary and were slated to be repaid from the future profits of the Havana Hilton. Thus, after the hotel had been nationalized, Hilton Hotels International had no liability. During the eighteen months of the hotel's operations, moreover, management heavily promoted customer use of the company's Carte Blanche credit card so that charges incurred at the Havana hotel were received through credit card banking channels and held in a special account instead of being transferred back to Havana. In the end, credit card income of $300,000 stood against approximately $2 million in unpaid preopening and operational costs. In the context of Hilton's extensive international operations, the total losses of a little more than $1.8 million registered as a pittance. Indeed, the company's public annual report for 1960 showed a record net profit of $9,792,010.[124]

By mid-1960, tourism, popular culture, politics, and war had crossed paths in a manner that made reconciliation impossible. Instead of helping to heal political rifts, as in Mexico decades earlier, tourism's soft power had become identified with meanings of Cuban nationhood that Cubans could no longer find acceptable. For Cuba, the era of the "high yaller gal," Superman, Ricky Ricardo, cocaine, Meyer Lansky, Santo Trafficante Jr., suburban sprawl, Jim Crow beaches, Anglicized rumba, daiquiri-induced hangovers, porn theaters, brothels, spring break revolutionaries, and mink stoles was coming to an end. Many Cubans and North Americans longed for a way to refashion the relationship—either to start from scratch or to renegotiate terms that had grown obsolete. Agents were many, but none proved capable of capping a volcano.

As the two nations headed toward persistent animosity, U.S.-Cuban popular culture produced one more bombshell. On 3 March 1960, Lucille Ball filed for divorce from her husband of nearly twenty years, Desi Arnaz, on grounds of mental cruelty. The couple had just finished the final season of *I Love Lucy* (renamed the *Lucy-Desi Comedy Hour*), but their ability to work and live together had been diminishing for several years. Much like the Eisenhower and Castro administrations, the two engaged in very public shouting matches on the set of their show as well as around Tinseltown. Regardless of the merits of the case, Ball's court testimony is noteworthy because her portrayal of Arnaz, the living icon of Cubanness in the United States, so closely paralleled the way U.S. officials described and discredited Fidel Castro. Arnaz was subject to fits of anger in private and public, even in front of the children, she told the court. He possessed a "Jekyll and Hyde" personality.[125] Art imitates life, according to a popular saying. It might also be said that politics imitates culture.

The punishing U.S. trade embargo that Washington imposed on Cuba in January 1961 included severe restrictions on citizen travel to the island. The tourist presence had already dwindled to the point of economic irrelevance, and most of the once-thriving entertainment districts resembled ghost towns. Castro had again lashed out at the North American travel industry in December 1960 when his government announced that visiting Yankees would be required to carry official passports, eliminating the more casual tourist card system that had helped define the 1950s travel boom.[126] The State Department's initiatives limited legal travelers to those deemed to advance the U.S. national interest. With implementation left entirely to Foggy Bottom, the regulations reduced travel mainly to journalists and businesses with ongoing interests in Cuba.

The government's effort to put a choke hold on the Castro regime did not go unchallenged. ASTA established itself as a staunch defender of travel to all destinations, and a trickle of private citizens and groups continued to ply their way south across the Straits of Florida during the first half of the 1960s. Some were political activists who still admired Castro's revolutionary zeal and thrilled to the dictator's public conversion to Marxism-Leninism in late 1961. Most made the trip simply out of curiosity, perhaps tempted by the forbidden fruit or intrigued to witness the famed island's transformation into a communist state. At any rate, appeals against government policy ultimately landed before the U.S. Supreme Court. In 1958, Chief Justice Earl Warren and the Court had technically established a constitutional right to travel by striking down the government's denial of passports to Communist Party members on the grounds that the ban violated the First Amendment right to freedom of expression. In May 1965, however, the liberal court upheld the Cuba restrictions on the grounds that Castro's efforts to export his revolution since 1961, much like European and Asian aggression in the 1930s, posed a direct threat to U.S. national security and justified sanctions reminiscent of the war years. Justices Hugo Black, Arthur J. Goldberg, and William O. Douglas dissented. Douglas voiced an eloquent defense of those who wished to visit Cuba and other communist regimes to better understand them: "The First Amendment presupposes a mature people, not afraid of ideas."[127] In light of ongoing court challenges and a temporary lifting of the travel ban under President Jimmy Carter (1977–81), the government supplemented State Department "travel restrictions" with "currency restrictions" enforced by the Department of the Treasury.[128]

Tourism and culture clash caused neither the Cuban Revolution nor the collapse in U.S.-Cuban relations that followed. But the cultural discourses that arose from the visitor-host relationship ran through both societies and shaped the way their citizens perceived, analyzed, and dreamed of each other. These discourses lay behind the identities that each nation assigned itself and even infiltrated the articulation of political and economic interests, a process that policymakers typically assume to be rooted in objective reality.

In Batista's Cuba, tourism both invented and reinforced U.S. cultural assumptions that inspired architects to give Havana a new physical appearance. The same discourses fastened onto the Cuban people an identity that accorded them all the rights that the United States bestowed on North American blacks, women, and children at the time. African-inspired rumba and forbidden sex gave the island's image a romantic gloss. Capitalist ideology infused the project of empire with redeeming social value.

When Cubans rebelled against the U.S.-backed authoritarian government that sponsored and profited from the tourist arrangement, North Americans lost their bearings. Some demonized the new regime as communist. Others idealized its reformist zeal. For the most part, tourists recognized the magnitude of the revolution's destabilizing impact before U.S. diplomats did so and consequently laid low. Castro's new government proposed a new way of hosting Cuba's guests and a new way of imagining Cuba. But as political tensions escalated between Washington and Havana and their respective visions of empire collided, the chances for rapprochement through soft power and cultural diplomacy receded.

The collapse of U.S.-Cuban tourist relations and the oncoming diplomatic impasse between Washington and Havana can be illuminated further through comparative analysis. Tourism and the everyday life of the empire helped stave off a U.S.-Mexican confrontation during the 1920s and 1930s even though Mexico's land reform more directly impacted North American holdings than did Castro's, and Cárdenas's nationalization of oil posed an even greater challenge to U.S. hegemony than did Cuban agrarian reform. Why couldn't the tourist relationship carry similar weight in Cuba? Both revolutions, after all, centered on issues of identity and political economy.

One striking similarity between the two cases is that the major global confrontations of the day entered the equation rather late in the negotiations over hegemony, identity, and tourism. With the exception of a nervous ambassador here and there, U.S. political leaders initially viewed both revolutions through a regional prism rather than perceiving them as integral components of a larger international danger. Moreover, World War II helped bring Mexico and the United States together, whereas concerns about global communism helped drive Cuba and the United States further apart. Yet to a large extent, tourist-visitor negotiations and their bilateral political consequences arose in the context of U.S. hemispheric hegemony.

The two revolutions nonetheless played out very differently. Castro's revolution gained greater unity of purpose than the Mexican rebellion. Mexico's ethnically diverse population, its myriad of classes and interests, its nascent industrial sector, and its multiple political factions gave its revolution a polyglot character. To hold the community together, revolutionary leaders often espoused rhetoric that proved more radical than their policies, a practice that seemed threatening primarily in the abstract. Cuba's revolution began similarly, but Castro quickly outmaneuvered his competitors, partly through adroit calculation and partly by luck. He rallied the nation with both agrarian and urban reforms and emerged as the singular voice for change. He defied the United States more forcefully than did Plutarco Calles or Alvaro Obregón and gave every indication of remaining at the helm longer than Cárdenas's six years, in turn generating a harsher response.

The most obvious difference between Mexico and Cuba grew out of the history of international tourism itself. In postrevolutionary Mexico, mass tourism carried no real legacy. It arrived contemporaneous to the birth of a new nation, and Mexico's new rulers and their supporters channeled the tourist invasion in directions that served their economic and cultural goals. In contrast, Cuban tourism carried the weight of decades of indignities. Cuban leaders and elements of the travel industry rushed to begin anew—not only to restructure the travel industry but to revise the meaning of becoming

Cuban—but could not produce results quickly enough to salvage a working relationship with Washington officials, the transnational business community, and U.S. tourists.

Both cases demonstrate that tourism has played a vital role in how nations at opposite ends of the power spectrum and occupying very different positions within an empire imagine and behave toward one another and negotiate their respective identities. The passage of time, geographic location, and the unfolding history of empire produced different outcomes.

As Cuba's status as a tropical vacation paradise faded into memory, its position in the everyday life of the empire was eclipsed by others. Even before the revolution, Cuba's Antillean neighbor, Puerto Rico, had begun to position itself as a tourist oasis, a high-end reformist alternative to Cuban decadence. It offered unsurpassed beaches, state-of-the-art hotels, regulated gambling, and an ancient Iberian ambience in Old San Juan. Alongside the Cuba story, an examination of Puerto Rico's rise to tourism eminence offers a study in contrasts.

FIVE

Bootstraps, Beaches, and Cobblestone

Commonwealth Puerto Rico

In May 1958, following his highly publicized confrontation with the hostile crowds of Caracas, Venezuela, Vice President Richard Nixon beat a hasty retreat to more tranquil surroundings in sunny Puerto Rico. The night of his arrival, he spent forty minutes wading through four blocks of historic Old San Juan amid throngs of people who cheered "Arriba Nixon!" Later that evening, in the candlelit dining room of the four-hundred-year-old governor's mansion, La Fortaleza, Governor Luis Muñoz Marín hosted a state dinner. Declared Nixon, "I couldn't think of a better place to be." To which a buoyant Muñoz replied, "Mr. Vice-President, está en su casa" (You are in your house).[1]

Although set apart by his celebrity, Nixon was only one of approximately a quarter of a million U.S. citizens who annually made the trek to welcoming Puerto Rico in the late 1950s.[2] The island had recently acquired a reputation for powdery beaches, crashing surf, luxurious hotels, and tastefully restored colonial streets and alleyways. Equally important, as Fidel Castro cast his shadow across the Caribbean, Puerto Rico stood out as an oasis of political stability. Commonwealth Puerto Rico, the advertisement read, was a post-colonial territory tutored in democratic capitalism by the United States and generously granted autonomy. It had forsworn the turmoil that swept much of the Third World and set out to raise itself by the bootstraps from poverty to prosperity inside of one generation.

Popular constructions of the island were based partly on tourist imaginations and partly on the commonwealth's savvy public relations campaign. In reality, Puerto Rico still struggled to overcome the legacy of a half century of exploitative U.S. colonialism. Acquired by the United States in 1898 as a consequence of the Spanish-American-Cuban-Filipino War, it had been awarded colonial status. Although the colonial government on occasion encouraged vacationers to visit, tourist traffic to Puerto Rico during the first half of the twentieth century remained marginal. The island's main function in the U.S. empire centered on its provision of naval bases at the entrance to the Caribbean Sea, shielding Cuba, the Panama Canal, and other U.S. assets from potential European interlopers.

After a stint as an outspoken *independentista* (an advocate of Puerto Rican independence) in the 1920s and early 1930s, Muñoz Marín negotiated with Washington the passage of Public Law 600, which declared Puerto Rico an *estado libre asociado* (an associated free state). Washington kept control over the island's judiciary and military, but San Juan gained limited autonomy over domestic affairs.[3] Puerto Rican officials in essence swapped political independence for benefits they hoped would prove more advantageous to social and economic progress. Exempted from federal income tax, the new government became free to set its own tax policies, including the power to grant hefty breaks to both U.S. and local investors. At the same time, exports from the island enjoyed tariff-free entry into U.S. markets. Puerto Ricans maintained citizenship rights, first granted by the Jones Act of 1917. And although they did not gain the right to vote in federal U.S. elections, they could emigrate freely and reside legally in the United States.[4]

By comparison to both Mexico and Cuba, Puerto Rico's travel industry got off to a late start. Unlike Cuban officials in the 1920s, Puerto Rican leaders kept a watchful eye on private interests. They welcomed foreign investment but supplemented it with state-owned hotels. Island officials opened the door to legalized gambling but screened organized crime out of their heavily regulated casinos. Determined not to replace agricultural dependence with an addiction to U.S. tourists, planners also determined to limit tourism's contribution to the island's gross domestic product to between 5 and 10 percent, an anomaly in the Caribbean, where some governments depend on tourism for as much as 80 percent of their gross domestic product.[5] In some ways, Puerto Rico's planning more resembled interwar Mexico's, but the tourist trade grew faster, a function of the post–Second World War era, when modern aviation, mass marketing, and consumerism placed the international travel industry on the commercial and cultural equivalent of steroids. The capital city of San Juan mutated overnight from a quiet Caribbean seaport into a beach-lined tropical paradise, complete with high-rise hotels, restaurants, and sunbathers. Even the colonial section of the city, Old San Juan, received a thorough freshening. After the streets had been cleaned and polished, the shiny blue cobblestone gave the district the glow of antiquity so often demanded by modern tourists.

The rapidity of change and the unprecedented presence of tens of thousands of North Americans unnerved many Puerto Ricans. In spite of Muñoz's embrace of commonwealth status, nationalist sentiment continued to pervade Puerto Rican society. The 1951 plebiscite on political status offered a choice only between commonwealth and colonial status, much to the dismay of both independence and statehood advocates. In fact, in the island's first gubernatorial election, held in 1952, the Partido Independentista Puertorriqueño (Puerto Rican Independence Party, PIP), finished a respectable second place, ahead of the Republican Statehood Party.[6] Although the PIP's electoral performance steadily declined over subsequent years, the dream of nationhood resonated across the island and even penetrated the higher circles of the ruling Partido Populare Democratica (Popular Democratic Party, PPD). Despite the government's regulation of the travel industry's growth, outspoken nationalists questioned the wisdom of building five-star hotels when large segments of the population lacked access to education, nutritious diets, and modern housing and worried about the cultural impact of so many visiting northerners.

Independentistas, however, found it difficult to define exactly what "nationalism" meant in Puerto Rico. The term implied the pursuit of independent nationhood, but might partial independence be acceptable? And how might Puerto Rican cultural identity be imagined? Was it chiefly Iberian, an offshoot of an earlier colonialism? What about the island's sizable Afro–Puerto Rican population, the descendants of slaves? What of the indigenous peoples, the Taínos, who had been devastated by Iberian conquest and had long since vanished from the island's census data but whose memory might be infused into postcolonial thinking about nation?[7]

This chapter examines the evolution of Puerto Rico's multifaceted and multipurpose tourist industry from the years immediately preceding the commonwealth era through the late 1950s. It analyzes the planned emergence of the island's cultural contact zones, the debate over tourism that arose within the host society, and the many points of intersection between tourism promotion abroad and identity formation within. It highlights the subtle ways in which tourism provided Puerto Rico with both economic and cultural negotiating space within the framework of empire and analyzes how the history of tourism complicates our understanding of the Cold War.

Colonialism and Tourism

In the early years of the twentieth century, Puerto Rico ranked with Cuba, Haiti, Jamaica, and the Dominican Republic as a tropical attraction for a small, affluent, and adventurous leisure class. By the 1920s, most Americans who traveled to Puerto Rico went by steamship from New York, a four-day voyage that cost about seventy-five dollars. They found few hotels or extravagant tourist amenities. Early guidebooks instead highlighted Puerto Rico's natural beauty—the healing powers of Coamo Springs in the Central Cordillera, the rain forest and waterfalls at the foot of the lofty El Yunque, the wild begonias, orchids, and palm-lined beaches. "Its unbroken mountainous character makes any detailed description of its scenic beauties a waste of time; it could be little more than a series of exclamations of delight," wrote Harry Franck in 1920.[8]

Foreshadowing trends of the 1950s, early travel writers paid homage to Washington's civilizing influence over the island. Philip Marsden's *Sailing South* explained that the United States had acquired Puerto Rico as an afterthought following the crusade to free Cuba but had brought to Puerto Rico modern health care, highways, civil administration, and English-language education. The tourist trade merely extended the rehabilitative value of association with the United States by promising an influx of capital, technology, travel, and conveniences.[9] Despite the sense of mission, the fact was that Puerto Rico lay twelve hundred miles out to sea and in the preaviation age drew only a smattering of wandering northerners. By 1920, when Prohibition went into effect in the United States, San Juan boasted only two tourist hotels and a handful of restaurants. At the same time, Havana, just ninety miles from the mainland, braced for an influx of alcohol-deprived Yankees.

A few Americans who visited during these years developed an appreciation for Puerto Rico's people and culture. In addition to its natural beauty, the island featured three major urban centers (San Juan, Mayaguez, and Ponce) and maintained a relatively extensive system of roads, bridges, and ports.[10] Most travel narratives, however, advanced a derogatory set of perceptions that did not bode well for intercultural understanding. Guidebooks of the early twentieth century disparaged the island's widespread poverty, illiteracy, and health problems and depicted a helpless "mongrel race," a foreign "other" who lived outside the boundaries of the civilized world.[11]

U.S. writers did not ordinarily count the colonial structures imposed on the island as major contributors to poverty. The manly science of dollar diplomacy dictated that the colony be placed on sound fiscal footing. In addition to quelling pockets of armed resistance to U.S. rule and creating an administrative apparatus, North American occupiers and private interests modernized the island's economy. Until 1800, most of the population consisted of subsistence farmers, but growing links to the global economy nourished a slave-plantation sugar boom during the first half of the nineteenth century, followed by a coffee boom that lasted until the U.S. invasion. The passage of the Foraker Act of 1900 granted Puerto Rican exports tariff-free access to U.S. markets after a brief transitional period. Most important, the act's liberal sugar-import quota encouraged U.S. companies to establish absentee sugar plantations, which combined with a U.S. tobacco trust to overwhelm the locally controlled coffee sector and dominate the island's economy. Prosperity for large landowners did not trickle down to day laborers. Wages for cane cutters remained especially low, the concentration of land-ownership left approximately three-quarters of the population landless, and outside of a small needlework industry staffed mainly by underpaid female workers, the colony produced few manufacturing jobs. In 1930, the U.S.-appointed governor, Theodore Roosevelt Jr., estimated that 60 percent of Puerto Rico's workforce was unemployed either part or all of the year.[12]

Some U.S. colonial officials viewed tourism as a means toward economic diversification, but early U.S. tourism in Puerto Rico in fact took on some of the exploitative characteristics that came to define Cuban tourism. Imposed on the island by outsiders and reliant on foreign capital for hotels and infrastructure, tourism was a colonial project, pure and simple. The first coordinated effort to package Puerto Rico for mass tourism came in the late 1930s, when Governor Blanton Winship established the island's first Institute of Tourism. Winship viewed the industry as an antidote to the devastating depression and collapse of the island's sugar trade. Using Florida and Bermuda as models, he launched a road-beautification program and opened a tourism office in New York City that worked to bring conferences and conventions to San Juan.[13]

Winship grasped the centrality of image, advertising, and symbol. He hired a U.S. public relations firm to increase press coverage of the island and to churn out pamphlets and guides trumpeting Puerto Rico's climate, beaches, golf, deep-sea fishing, and legal gambling. The effort portrayed Puerto Rico in condescending terms: a poverty-stricken land whose simple, submissive people awaited the opportunity to pamper their northern benefactors. This effort particularly accented popular constructions of gender, with posters featuring attractive female models in swimsuits posed on San Juan's beaches: "Beautiful señoritas at Canto de Piedras," one caption read.

Another promotional item featured "beautiful girls from Aguadilla at Columbus Park," Christopher Columbus's landing place in Puerto Rico.[14]

Representations of Puerto Rico also depicted a colonial oasis on the cusp of modernity, both an exotic, frontier destination and a safe, familiar part of an expanding American empire. Thus, tourists could relish the sense of masculine adventure and reconnect with U.S. pioneer myths by being abroad in a Spanish-speaking culture while enjoying the convenience of a North American road system and the ease of conducting business in English. As one 1940 guide put it, Puerto Rico was "Spanish in tradition and feeling" yet "North American in purpose and destiny."[15] U.S. tourists, moreover, might imagine themselves as agents of civilization. The tourist, John Jennings noted in *Our American Tropics*, is "the modern goose that lays the golden egg and as such he should be treated with respect."[16]

Governor Winship's campaign failed to take hold, in part because of the depression-plagued 1930s economy and the war that followed but even more because of the rising nationalism that shaped Puerto Rican politics during the decade. The vibrant and often violent nationalist movement was primarily associated with Pedro Albizu Campos, a graduate of Harvard Law School, a former U.S. Army officer, and the leader of the Nationalist Party. In the harsh depression atmosphere, compounded by pummeling hurricanes in 1928 and 1932, Albizu's denunciation of U.S. colonial rule, advocacy of socialist planning, and call to arms found a receptive audience.[17]

At the same time, the "1930s generation" of Puerto Rican intellectuals, led by Antonio S. Pedreira, decried the forced teaching of English in public schools, celebrated the Spanish language and *hispanidad* culture, and denounced Anglo-Saxon society as ruthlessly materialistic and acquisitive. Although the *independentistas* remained a minority, with Albizu and most of his key followers imprisoned by the decade's end, their views and those of the cultural nationalists set the stage for Puerto Rico's quest for a new political status and national identity.[18]

In this context, Puerto Rico first experienced the innovative leadership of Luis Muñoz Marín. The son of Luis Muñoz Rivera, Puerto Rico's resident commissioner in Washington and an advocate of autonomy rather than independence, the younger Muñoz had been educated in the United States, studying law at Georgetown University, and briefly defined himself as a Greenwich Village poet before returning in 1926 to his homeland as an inspired supporter of independence. He stormed at the United States as an "opulent kleptomaniac" that filched "life-giving pennies from the pockets of a pauper."[19] The pragmatist within him, however, led Muñoz ultimately to champion commonwealth status, an ill-defined middle ground between independence and colonialism. As a leader of the Liberal Party in the Puerto Rican Senate, he cleverly denounced the domination of the island's economy by U.S. sugar companies without denouncing capitalism itself. He nonetheless signaled an intention to revamp the economy and endorsed Puerto Rican agronomist Carlos Chardón's plan for land reform and rapid industrialization.[20]

Winship's tourism agenda, particularly his attempt to graft a fun-loving, resort-centered identity onto the island, drew the wrath of both independence and commonwealth advocates. Puerto Rican commentators chafed at Winship's portrayal of the island's inhabitants as humble servants and denounced the travel business as the latest harbinger of dependence. In the columns of *La Democracia*, a liberal party organ, journalist and Muñoz confidante Ruby Black ridiculed the tourism campaign and compared the governor to Sinclair Lewis's fictional Babbitt, a man absorbed by "fishing, golf, and tourism" and too deficient in intellect and energy to attend to the island's substantive needs. "Hunger, rum, death, blood," she wrote, "Babbitt the tourist has us imprisoned in chains of trout, with walls of golf balls."[21]

Muñoz Marín joined the critics. In 1938 he organized the PPD, which melded his moderate commonwealth cause with a populist economic program. The PPD adopted as its symbol an icon of Puerto Rico's rural culture, the straw-hatted *jíbaro* (peasant farmer). The party's leftist slogan, "Pan, tierra, y libertad" (Bread, land, and freedom), promised land redistribution and the creation of new job-producing state-owned industries and generated a powerful coalition of hacendados (local landowners), landless peasants, unemployed workers, and middle-class activists.[22] An immensely talented politician, Muñoz recognized in tourism an issue that carried dividends at the ballot box. In the 1940 legislative elections, he echoed others in his denunciations of Winship's tourism initiatives as an attempt to gloss over the island's social and economic malaise and demonized the unpopular salt tax, which financed tourism promotion.[23] When charges of casino corruption arose, Muñoz even demanded that San Juan's slot machines be tossed into the sea.[24]

Bootstraps

The PPD's smashing 1940 victory at the polls set the stage for Muñoz's domination of Puerto Rican politics for nearly three decades and afforded the island's leaders an opportunity to develop a more locally planned and regulated tourist industry. But tourism counted as only one small element of a larger strategy for modern development. The 1940s constituted a formative moment in the study of what economists have called development. While the U.S. government ladled out funds for postwar reconstruction in Europe, it preached the gospel of private trade and investment to Latin Americans and held up Fulgencio Batista as an exemplary favored client. But as the decade drew to a close, a growing number of social scientists turned their attention to the special requirements for market expansion and economic growth in formerly colonial regions.

Influenced by the British economist John Maynard Keynes, postwar theorists observed the unique challenges faced by "emerging economies" in areas of the world plagued by low educational levels, dependence on one or two export products, obsolete administrative structures, shortages of capital, a lack of infrastructure, rapidly growing populations, and vast discrepancies in wealth. During the late 1940s and early 1950s, Brazilian economist Raul Prebisch conducted painstaking research on Latin America's historic terms of trade and documented how prices for the region's agricultural and mining exports had dropped steadily during previous decades in relation to the price of imported manufactured goods. The implication was that Latin American states could not thrive in a system dominated by private U.S. trading and investment interests and badly needed large infusions of economic aid to spur industrialization and diversification.[25]

The Populares, as the PPD leaders were known, steeped themselves in the emerging literature on development. They resolved that Puerto Rico could escape its reliance on sugar, tortuous rates of unemployment, and soaring population growth—approximately 2.3 million on an island that measured about one hundred miles long and thirty-five miles wide—only via comprehensive industrialization. But the question of how to induce industrialization spawned a range of answers. During the war years, Senator Muñoz worked closely with New Deal governor Rexford Tugwell to launch a number of state-owned manufacturing enterprises. After the war, however, Muñoz vowed that the commonwealth's programs would have "no fixed taboos, no sacred cows in the choice of instrument to achieve a better standard of living."[26] Rather than consistently supporting state ownership or converting to a free-trade approach, the governor combined elements of New Deal capitalism, state ownership, European social democracy, and even a bit of Spanish-style colonial mercantilism.

With his U.S.-educated economic adviser, Teodoro Moscoso, Muñoz established Puerto Rico's Economic Planning Board, or Fomento, and designed policies to exploit the island's access to the U.S. market. The two privatized most of Tugwell's struggling state-owned enterprises and used the government's newly acquired taxing authority to offer eight- to twelve-year exemptions to U.S. and Puerto Rican investors willing to undertake new ventures. Factories bearing U.S. brand names such as Remington Rand, Sylvania, Paper Mate, Union Carbide, Parke-Davis, U.S. Rubber, Textron, Maidenform, and Sunbeam cropped up across the island during the first half of the 1950s.[27]

The Puerto Rican economy appeared on the surface to be a product of North American cloning. But Fomento blended a penchant for U.S. investment with state-financed investments and selective government ownership within key industries. In contrast to Batista's Cuba, Muñoz's Puerto Rico planned for economic distribution as well as growth, launched new social programs for the poor, enforced laws that limited sugar plantations to five hundred acres, and established the Water Resources Authority, reminiscent of the Tennessee Valley Authority. To provide for the island's pool of surplus labor, commonwealth status assured access to federal welfare programs and emigration rights to the United States. Even the program's name, Operation Bootstrap, conveyed multiple meanings. On the one hand, the label might be taken as a tribute to the island's appropriation of the U.S. Protestant work ethic. On the other, it signaled Puerto Rico's readiness to alter without necessarily extinguishing its economic dependence on the United States.[28]

The Muñoz administration simultaneously suppressed the *independentista* movement by prosecuting activists under the island's sweeping "Ley de la Mordaza" (Law of the Muzzle). The loosely worded law made it a crime to attempt, through violence or other means, to overthrow the commonwealth government. San Juan had an ally of sorts in the Federal Bureau of Investigation, which kept files on thousands of Puerto Rican independence activists during the period, including Governor Muñoz, who was erroneously suspected of having had ties to communist movements during the 1930s.[29] Frustrated Puerto Rican nationalists increasingly turned to violence, including the 1950 assassination of San Juan's mayor, the attempted assassination the same year of President Harry S. Truman in Washington, D.C., and a 1954 shooting spree on the floor of the U.S. House of Representatives. Co-opted and repressed, the *independentistas* diminished in strength.

After Muñoz fully assumed power, he delegated to Fomento's Moscoso the task of restructuring the tourist industry. Moscoso and other economic planners never viewed tourism as a saving grace for all of the island's social and economic ills. Indeed, the travel industry to this day has never accounted for more than 10 percent of Puerto Rico's gross national product. Moscoso, moreover, understood the tourist trade to be enormously competitive. While Hawaii, another sugar-dependent U.S. colony with outstanding beachfronts, had established a tourist bureau as early as 1917, Puerto Rico had only limited experience in promotion and advertising. Also unlike the Hawaiian Islands, Puerto Rico faced numerous nearby rivals, including tourism powerhouses such as Cuba, Bermuda, the Bahamas, and the Florida Keys.[30]

Still, a carefully crafted tourism strategy, planned and regulated by a Keynesian-inspired government, might allow Puerto Rico to carve out a market niche that complemented the industrialization effort. Fomento targeted upper- and upper-middle-class northeasterners as the most likely customers. While many visitors would come to the island strictly on business, to look after their investments in industry, others would confine their activities to vacation and leisure. Commonwealth officials did not consider the two groups to be mutually exclusive. Moscoso always stressed how many of the island's foreign investors first discovered Puerto Rico as vacationers. "Scratch a tourist," he was fond of saying, "and you'll find an investor underneath."[31]

In late 1948, Moscoso hired J. Stanton Robbins, an American who had worked on the reconstruction of Virginia's Colonial Williamsburg, to head up Fomento's Office of Tourism. Robbins and his staff immediately began accumulating data and making statistical and financial projections. Tourism brought $151 million to Mexico in 1947 and ranked as that country's leading item of foreign trade. For Hawaii, travel constituted the third-largest industry, a source of $35 million in revenue. A modest initial investment of $1.7 million annually for office staff and industry subsidies, Robbins estimated, would bring one hundred thousand tourists to Puerto Rico by 1952 and generate roughly $15.6 million in revenue. Tourism promised to create at least six thousand new jobs directly related to hospitality, six thousand jobs in ancillary sectors, and approximately $1 million in taxes for badly needed development projects.[32]

Robbins and other tourism promoters pressed the Puerto Rican government to update the island's transportation infrastructure. Commonwealth officials lobbied the federal government to improve San Juan Harbor to allow larger cruise ships to make the city a port of call. Probably even more important were the efforts on behalf of air travel. Pan American Airlines, which first flew to Puerto Rico in the 1920s, inaugurated daily nonstop flights between New York and San Juan in 1946. Three years later, anticipating a postwar travel boom, construction commenced on San Juan's $15 million Isla Verde airport, a facility capable of handling more than five hundred flights per day.[33] At the same time, the Muñoz administration went before the U.S. Civil Aeronautics Board to gain permission for less expensive carriers to service the island.[34] A transportation breakthrough came in 1951 when Fomento received authorization from the U.S. Bureau of Civil Aviation to allow Eastern Airlines to land in San Juan, thus breaking Pan Am's monopoly and spurring lower airfares. Eastern's corporate chief, World War I aviator Eddie Rickenbacker, soon became as important a name as Juan Trippe or Conrad Hilton in Caribbean travel circles. By 1952, the Puerto Rican Tourist Bureau advertised six- to eight-hour flights from New York to the island for $128 round-trip and ten-hour flights from Chicago for $275, using the slogan "a comparatively short distance from the mainland, a million miles from worry and care."[35]

Fomento and the Office of Tourism established a training school for hotel and restaurant employees in 1949.[36] Led by Francesco Betté, a Peruvian with years of experience in the hospitality industry, the school had graduated eleven hundred hoteliers by 1962.[37] Planners also created a system for responding to letters of complaint from demanding North American visitors and set up training courses for taxicab drivers that taught traffic laws, "accident prevention," the basics of the English language, and the finer points of San Juan's history.[38] The government developed surveying methods to gain data on visitors' places of residence, length of stay, choice of hotels, and vacation budgets, useful information for devising advertising campaigns.

The tourist office also conducted studies on the controversial issue of gambling, opposed by many Puerto Ricans for fear of its many unsavory side effects, especially infiltration by organized crime, as had occurred in nearby Cuba. The government cited the nineteen-year-old Nevada experiment to show how regulation could counter organized crime and other undesirable elements.[39] The commonwealth legalized casino gambling in late 1948 and hired a corps of inspectors. Despite protests from the smaller hotels and inns, the government issued licenses only to establishments larger than two hundred rooms, required strict dress codes, placed caps on wagers, prohibited alcoholic beverages on casino premises, and charged operators between five hundred and twenty-eight hundred dollars per month in licensing fees.[40]

To police the industry, the governor's office hired Dr. John Scarne as its gambling consultant. A native of New Jersey, Scarne also served as dean of the Puerto Rican College for Croupiers, Dealers, and Stickmen, known among its students as Dealers' Tech. Rather than importing specialists, the Muñoz administration trained Puerto Ricans in the rudiments of dice, roulette, and blackjack. The college also encouraged research and developed innovative techniques to prevent cheating, including a long stick with a hoop on the end used in craps to retrieve and stir the dice, an alternative to returning them to the dealer's hand.[41] The tactics succeeded. One tourist magazine conducted a

Caribbean-wide survey in 1953 and concluded that Puerto Rico's casinos ranked among the most honestly and scrupulously managed.[42]

Manufacturing Beachfront

Puerto Rico's travel industry hinged on more than economic planning. The bottom line was that the island had been blessed with miles of coastline and magnificent beaches and year-round temperate weather. The beach is a more complex cultural construction than might be commonly assumed. Some nationalities and ethnic groups embrace the oceanfront experience, while others keep a respectful distance from the natural forces of wind and storm that every now and then wreak havoc. Some beaches are public and others private; some discriminate by class, while others exclude by race. Appropriate beach attire often varies by class, ethnicity, gender, and age, ranging from full clothing to skimpy bikinis to the fully natural.[43]

Puerto Rican planners drew heavily on the concept of the tropical beach first popularized in the U.S. colony of Hawaii, especially with the buildup of Honolulu's Waikiki Beach during the early twentieth century. In addition to sun, sand, and surf, the word "Waikiki" evoked images of palm trees, hula girls, romantic lovers, and ukuleles. During the early postwar era, Hawaii, like other tourist destinations, underwent a massive expansion that added high-rise hotels, surfside restaurants, and massive traffic congestion to the picture.[44] By the late 1940s, Mexico's Acapulco and Cuba's Varadero had to some extent mimicked the Hawaiian model, but Puerto Rico's planners saw in Hawaii's golden beaches, shimmering sea, and deluxe hotels a model for their own travel industry. Robbins explained in late 1950, "Hawaii is the 'show piece' of the territories in this important visitor business—she was early to recognize its virtues. Now after thirty years, Hawaii's tourism is its third industry—minor only to sugar and pineapples."[45]

Commonwealth leaders did not envision any ordinary beachfront. U.S. tourists could always find cheaper, closer beaches if they chose. But they could not necessarily find beach blended with tropical exotica. "When all is said and done," one government report observed, "the main thing that the visitor to Puerto Rico can find that he cannot find better or cheaper on the mainland is the combination of sunshine, sand, and salt water." Fomento, therefore, planned tourism promotion and facilities "in such as way as to give the greatest emphasis to upper-income beach resort clientele." In contrast to postwar Cuba, where planners targeted middle-income northerners, San Juan set its sights on the two million or so U.S. families, approximately 4 percent of the country's population, with incomes over ten thousand dollars per year.[46]

The effort first required the creation of modern luxury hotels along San Juan's expansive beachfront. As late as 1940, the capital city claimed only one skyscraper, the ten-story, art deco Banco Popular in Old San Juan.[47] But in 1946, Moscoso and Fomento surveyed the city for suitable building sites, calculating how many rooms each prospective accommodation might contain, the square footage required, investment costs, and profits and jobs generated.[48] They quickly pinned their hopes on the Condado area, located toward the eastern end of the city, along a northern beach-lined coast. Hired consultants advised that the district contained forty-two sites particularly suitable for hotel construction, with a capacity to provide 16,700 rooms. Plans immediately went into effect to have available 2,000 first-class hotel rooms by 1952 and to have 2,000 more onboard by 1960.[49]

No other single event proved as central to the development of Puerto Rican tourism as the planning of the Caribe Hilton Hotel, situated on the western edge of the Condado and immediately to the east of Old San Juan. Puerto Rico's first large hotel venture, the stunning $7.2 million Caribe Hilton was entirely government built and government owned, but its planning and completion demonstrate the multiplicity of postcolonial government agents and private interest groups that made Puerto Rico's travel industry tick. The first step came in 1946 when Moscoso sent out letters to seven U.S. hotel companies proposing a joint venture with the Puerto Rican government that would place management in company hands, reserve ownership for the government, and arrange a sharing of profits. Only the Hilton Corporation, eager to enter the international hotel business, agreed to this public-private partnership. Conrad Hilton thoughtfully responded with a letter in Spanish, and a group of company executives soon found themselves in San Juan.[50]

The small group of Hilton Hotel executives stood alongside Moscoso and peered across the tiny peninsula that jetted out into the shimmering Atlantic. The party had been invited to the island in early 1946 to scope out prospects for the company's first international hotel. After a series of disappointing field trips, Moscoso led them to one last site. At first, no one seemed impressed. To the west sat colonial Old San Juan and its long-neglected collection of ancient cathedrals, chapels, and tenements walled in and protected by centuries-old Spanish fortifications. To the east lay a five-mile-long spit of sand with a dirt road along which a small handful of residences and the solitary Condado Beach Hotel sat. At points, only several hundreds yards separated the choppy ocean from an inland lagoon. Then one of the executives spotted a small plot of land directly below, adjacent to the seventeenth-century San Gerónimo Fort. The windward breezes and crashing waves endowed it with dramatic natural beauty. "This is it," he shouted to Moscoso. "If you can get us this place down there—we have a hotel."[51]

The commonwealth next needed to persuade the U.S. Navy to give up the spectacular windswept strip of peninsula where the proposed hotel would be built. It had been a federal reserve since the 1899 Treaty of Paris that ended the U.S. war with Spain, and in recent times the parcel had been leased to a retired naval officer who owned a home there. The Puerto Rican government rallied allies in the U.S. Department of the Interior, which oversaw territorial affairs, and lobbied the secretary of the navy to negotiate the transfer of the lease to the commonwealth.[52]

When construction was completed in late 1949, the ten-story, three-hundred-room, honeycombed Caribe Hilton stood out boldly on Old San Juan Peninsula. Its dazzling white facade contrasted sharply with the sparkling blue sea, and its modernity juxtaposed the centuries-old San Gerónimo Fort. A testimony to advanced technology, it had a swimming pool carved out of blue coral stone that held saltwater replaced by attendants every four hours. The hotel's open-air entrance took visitors through a manicured tropical garden to the front desk. The interior, air-conditioned throughout, consisted of a tasteful collage of stone, glass, and stainless steel. The building's diagonal positioning guaranteed each guest room a sliding-glass door and balcony that overlooked the ocean.[53]

The hotel beach undoubtedly registered as one of the property's most noteworthy characteristics. Beachfronts are popularly associated with nature, landscapes that take form over millions of years as the result of fierce competition among water, rock, and wind. Yet increasingly in the twentieth century, from Miami to Cannes, the beach has been the product of modern earth-moving machinery, swamp clearance, and the transfer of truckloads of sand over thousands of miles. Richard P. Tucker has chronicled how America's nineteenth- and twentieth-century "insatiable appetite" for tropical, consumer products—sugar, bananas, coffee, and rubber—linked land and vegetation to the web of the global U.S. economic empire and upended long-established ecosystems.[54] The Caribe's beach was similarly a product of human engineering, U.S. capital investment, and consumer privilege, made of powdery coral that would not stick uncomfortably to sunbathers and protected from the Atlantic's harsh surf by a barrier of huge rocks strategically placed fifty yards or so from shore. Indeed, the hotel itself and the surrounding gardens sat atop a filled-in section of what had once been part of the thrashing waterfront.[55]

Five-star luxury hotels in Cuba stood as testimony to the power of multinational capital. Puerto Rico's path to paradise status, however, differed markedly from Cuba's. While Hilton managed the new hotel, it was owned by an elected Puerto Rican government rather than a dictator's favored labor union. The government, moreover, raked in a majority share of the profits. Thus, while Batista's Havana became emblematic of untrammeled private enterprise, San Juan's approach to mass tourism represented only one element of a comprehensive state-guided effort to transform the island's sugar-dependent economy.

The grand opening of the Caribe Hilton constituted nothing less than an extravaganza. Governor Muñoz Marín sent personal invitations to hundreds of prominent Americans, including members of Congress, Vice President Alben Barkley, Eleanor Roosevelt, and publisher Henry Luce.[56] *Life* magazine ran a three-page spread with enlarged photos, and *Time* described the arrival of planeloads of guests, including actresses Alexis Smith and Gloria Swanson, Eddie Rickenbacker, and David Rockefeller. The wealthy guests enjoyed a round of banquets, swimming parties, and tennis matches. On opening night, the casino racked up a one-thousand-dollar net loss for management. "Boy, we gave them a complete party," exclaimed Conrad Hilton.[57]

Within a half dozen years of the Caribe Hilton's opening, a string of new hotels sprang up along the Condado's once sparsely settled sand dunes. Twenty-two-year-old future gonzo journalist Hunter S. Thompson, turned down for a job at the recently established *San Juan Star* in 1959, nonetheless relocated to the island to finish his first novel, *The Rum Diary*. The main character, Paul Kemp, a young semialcoholic newspaper columnist, explained, "Conrad had come in like Jesus and all the fish had followed. Before Hilton there was nothing; now the sky was the limit."[58] The Condado quickly filled with restaurants, souvenir shops, and galleries. Even the Condado Beach Hotel, which dated from the Great War era, received a $1.3 million facelift, including an Olympic-size pool, new dining rooms and lounges, and a redesigned lobby decorated with murals by Spanish artist Hipolito Hidalgo.[59]

The hotel boom spread beyond San Juan. Fomento officers traveled to New York in late 1953 and met with Laurance S. Rockefeller, founder of RockResorts, to discuss a proposed beach and golf club in Dorado, about twenty miles west of San Juan. The $1.6 million project included a first-class, seventy-room hotel, pool, tennis court, and a golf course designed by Robert Trent Jones. After more than a year of haggling, Fomento secured a public-

Prior to the 1950s, San Juan's Condado (shown here ca. 1920) was little more than a narrow strip of road and sand dune between the open Atlantic and the Condado Lagoon. The handful of houses that dotted the seascape included only one hotel, the Condado-Vanderbilt, a onetime Vanderbilt family residence. Proyecto Digitalizació de la Colección de Fotos del Periódico El Mundo, Universidad de Puerto Rico, Recinto, Río Piedras.

private partnership that closely resembled the Hilton deal: the government owned the land and hotel, a Rockefeller company managed the resort, and the two parties agreed split the net profits down the middle.[60]

As with the Caribe Hilton project, the government and its private-sector partners went to considerable lengths to give the property the desired tropical look. Workers literally hacked the palm-laden Dorado layout out of a patch of jungle and an adjoining grapefruit plantation. The golf course similarly emerged from plantation landscape, extensively manicured with carefully cultivated fairways and greens. The government facilitated water and sewer hookups and yielded to Rockefeller's request that the property's two crescent-shaped beaches be awarded private status, a rare privilege in Puerto Rico—the Caribe Hilton and the Condado Beach Hotel claimed the only other hotel-owned beaches. When the resort opened in 1958, it offered private air service from the airport in San Juan and some of the island's most expensive rooms and meals.[61]

By the late 1960s, San Juan's Condado (shown here in 1969) and its main thoroughfare, Ashford Avenue, had been filled in with hotels, apartment buildings, restaurants, and shops. The Caribe Hilton is the elongated white glass structure situated near the top right of the photo, across an inlet that separates it from the rest of the tourist district. Old San Juan lies at the top left, just west of the Condado and the Hilton. Proyecto de Digitalizació de la Colección de Fotos del Periódico El Mundo, Universidad de Puerto Rico, Recinto, Río Piedras.

Manufacturing Image

Fomento and its private-sector partners not only engineered oceanfront settings but also manufactured an overseas image. As had been the case in interwar Mexico and postwar Cuba, infrastructure and attractions alone did not produce Puerto Rico's tourism success. Advertising and image projection helped tourists imagine their vacation experience. As with contemporary Cuban planners, schooling in the English language and North American culture gave Puerto Rican elites an almost innate understanding of the colonizing power's psyche. Puerto Rican tourism promoters also maintained an extensive list of U.S. government, business, and media contacts. But in contrast to Cuba's reputation for gambling, rum, and sex, Puerto Rican planners crafted an image that balanced the island's allure as a tasteful, tropical paradise and as a democratic industrial workshop.

The challenges were many. For more than a half century, U.S. media had portrayed Puerto Ricans according to ethnocentric stereotypes—as childlike people of color whose country had become America's poorhouse. When Tugwell published his memoirs, he chose the title *The Stricken Land* to describe the impoverished island. The unflattering image had been reinforced by the migration of Puerto Ricans—roughly fifty thousand annually by the late 1950s—to the United States. In contrast to the mythical immigrant success stories of the nineteenth century, the new Puerto Rican arrivals congregated in the slums of the urban northeast, took up mainly low-paying, unskilled jobs, and became known as America's unassimilated newcomers. Sociologists who studied New York's Puerto Ricans rushed to conclude that the immigrants lacked community structures, voluntary organizations, and other coping mechanisms. Historian Laura Briggs has explained how the academic work of such notables as Nathan Glazer, Daniel Moynihan, and Oscar Lewis assigned blame for impoverishment not so much to the means of production but to a "culture of poverty," passed down from one generation to the next by promiscuous mothers and broken families. The 1958 Broadway musical *West Side Story* reinforced such images by choreographing its characters as hot-tempered, knife-wielding juvenile delinquents. The popular musical drew an even less flattering image of Puerto Rico itself, a place, according to song, devoid of modern amenities such as washing machines, highways, and Buicks.[62]

The Office of Tourism's initial 1948–49 budget included $250,000 for public relations, a significant portion of which went to hire New York's Hamilton Wright advertising agency, the same firm to which Mexico had turned in the late 1930s. The campaign commenced with a series of news releases that told the story of Operation Bootstrap and the island's industrialization. As the opening date of the Caribe Hilton approached in December 1949, the number of releases, planted editorials, and purchased ads increased and accented "purely tourist material."[63] Robbins tirelessly lobbied Fomento and the governor's office for additional promotional funds. His office issued torrents of memoranda that charted advertising's positive impact on tourism in Florida, Hawaii, Mexico, Cuba, and Bermuda.[64] The tourist bureau began publishing *Qué Pasa in Puerto Rico*, a glossy magazine, still in print today, that featured photographs and articles on leading attractions and listed the island's hotels, inns, and restaurants.[65] That initiative was followed by the monthly *Puerto Rico Travel Newsletter*, a trade publication distributed primarily to U.S.-based travel agents to keep them updated on travel arrangements, accommodations, package deals, and festivals.[66]

Convinced that easy access to travel agents would prove essential to their efforts, the commonwealth government opened a tourist bureau office at Rockefeller Plaza in New York in mid-1950. On hand for the event were politician and civic activist Paul O'Dwyer, Pan Am president Juan Trippe, Nelson Rockefeller, and other dignitaries.[67] The mid-Manhattan location allowed for direct distribution of promotional literature, posters, and sales information to one of the world's heaviest concentrations of travel professionals.[68]

Publications such as *Travel*, *Saturday Review*, and the *New York Times* featured articles, advertisements, and photos that trumpeted the soothing climate, the ease of air travel without passport or visa, and of course the tropical beauty.[69] Ads played on constructions of gender as well, typically picturing female tourists tanning at poolside or shopping in Old San Juan while their masculine counterparts escaped to the golf courses.[70] One ad in the American Society of Travel Agents' *Travel News* included photos of and quotations from happy tourists. Carol Krumm, a government employee from Washington, D.C., raved, "Puerto Rico's a paradise for would-be beachcombers! . . . The water is an incredible blue and the grove of cocoanut palms lining the beach completes a picture every human being seems to have as the ideal place to have cares vanish."[71]

In addition to showcasing Puerto Rico's beaches, the campaign highlighted the island's efforts to lift itself economically. The government organized an industrial open house to celebrate Operation Bootstrap and scheduled it to coincide with the grand opening of the Caribe Hilton.[72] Travelogues, promotional films, and advertisements conveyed an image of Puerto Rico that evoked powerful themes of entrepreneurial self-help. The invented image juxtaposed the island's tropical allure and its modern material progress, its rural simplicity and its advanced consumer offerings, its historic landmarks and its modern architecture, its yearning for change and its stability. "Mañana means tomorrow . . . but it also means future," one Fomento ad announced. "Puerto Rico has shed the mañana complex." A barrage of economic growth statistics followed.[73]

Hamilton Wright regularly treated writers and publishers to free trips to San Juan, tours of the island, and meetings with the governor.[74] Muñoz wrote directly to *New York Times* chief Arthur Hays Sulzberger, "I have been impressed for some time by James Reston's articles. He seems ideally suited to study the political and economic evolution taking place in Puerto Rico and the outcome of the wise U.S. decolonization policy." The governor extended an invitation for Reston to spend a few days in Puerto Rico "as our guest . . . with complete freedom of action."[75] U.S. companies with a stake in Puerto Rico used their pull as well. Eastern Airlines brought along on its inaugural New York–San Juan flight in 1951 a group of "key publishers and editors." The special guests included correspondent Ralph Reichold of the *Pittsburgh Press*, whose subsequent series of articles on Puerto Rico reached some five million readers through the Scripps-Howard distribution service.[76] A full-page Eastern advertisement in *Travel News* announced, "There's profit in Puerto Rico. . . . Profit for you and profit for your clients."[77]

Favorable articles on the commonwealth multiplied. "There are many things of which the Puerto Rican is proud," one author noted in the *Saturday Review*; "he is proud of his first elected governor, Luis Muñoz Marín, son of Puerto Rico's great liberator and one time firebrand Greenwich Village poet." But the deepest pride, the piece continued, "is focused on what Muñoz named Operation Bootstrap."[78] "Island Workshop," *Time* magazine titled one 1956 story on Puerto Rico that announced that for the first time in history, manufacturing had edged ahead of farming as the island's major source of income. Counting four hundred plant openings since the beginning of Bootstrap, the article declared, "Puerto Rico's self-help plan is a smashing success for anyone to see." Per capita income had risen from $122 in 1940 to $434 in 1954, compared to 1954's $201 in the Dominican Republic, $538 in West Germany, and $1,845 in the United States.[79]

High-ranking Puerto Rican officials closely monitored the public relations project. Tourist brochures at times even showed up on the governor's desk for review before being sent to the printer. In August 1949, Gustavo Agrait, an executive assistant to Muñoz, returned a mock-up of a promotional booklet to Robbins's office with several suggestions for revision. A sentence that read, "The road ahead is still steep before [Puerto Rico's] American citizens reach the true American standard of living" caught his eye. "Possibly, it makes one think of a land quite destitute in the niceties of civilization and full of vermin, polluted waters and the like."[80] Later that fall, Agrait ordered the Office of Tourism to cancel publication of a brochure after reviewing its text with the governor, suggesting a new version sans "the old colonial attitude" and "stressing the new-state philosophy."[81] Muñoz's staff was still at it five years later, when an aide forwarded a draft brochure to Muñoz highlighting the need for revision where Puerto Rico had been described as a "colonial possession" and where "patronizing language" had been used.[82]

The media blitz worked. Investment dollars and tourists came to the island in steadily increasing droves throughout the 1950s. The tally of U.S. vacationers in fact exceeded expectations. The newly established Puerto Rican Visitor's Bureau noted in a 1952 study that "while a great number of visitors may still come to the island strictly on business, the advertising has attracted chiefly those who wish to visit the island for pleasure."[83] In 1952, the number of foreign visitors rose to a record high of 97,725, an increase of 15,000 over the previous year. Most arrived from the eastern and central Atlantic United States and confined their stays to the beaches, hotels, and restaurants of San Juan, dropping more than $16.6 million along the way.[84]

Host versus Host in the Contact Zone

The Muñoz administration touted tourism as a contributor to economic development and a source of international prestige. Expecting the surge in annual visitors to jump well above the one hundred thousand mark, the government began to plan in the mid-1950s for a significant expansion in travel infrastructure, especially hotels. In time, the influx of tourists would generate considerable clash between visitors and hosts within Puerto Rico's cultural contact zones, much as tourism promotion had done earlier in Mexico and Cuba. During the first half dozen years of the boom, however, the most profound tension in Puerto Rico arose among the hosts themselves. While the growth in tourist numbers had been impressive, the industry's direct and indirect contribution to the island's net income still amounted to only a little over 1 percent.[85] The trade nonetheless provoked an urgent discussion about how large it should be allowed to become, how fast it should grow, and whether it should be publicly or privately financed. With Puerto Rico unsure of its own identity, the commonwealth's sudden transformation from anonymity to Shangri-la aroused inner turmoil over the direction of the postcolonial future.

In a less developed country, where the legal technicalities of commonwealth status could not completely veil the reality of colonial dependency, the prospect of using tourism to build a self-reliant economy was bound to meet skepticism. Many Puerto Ricans wondered if tourism was a luxury the country could ill afford. The editor of the conservative Spanish-language daily *El Mundo* decried the Caribe Hilton as nothing less than a sellout to foreigners and predicted that the enterprise would surely fail.[86] Even some of Muñoz's loyal supporters questioned the allocation of scarce public funds to the industry. Rafael Picó, head of the government's Planning Commission, argued that the commonwealth would be better served by public investments in education and social welfare.[87] Fomento's skeptical V. R. Esteves advised that public investment in manufacturing would create far more jobs than hotel construction and the hospitality business.[88]

No issue better illustrated the intersection between tourism and the island's class structure than the continuous effort to demolish the infamous slum dwellings of La Perla and remove its nine thousand inhabitants. Perched along the rockbound northern shore of the city adjacent to Old San Juan, the neighborhood was immortalized by sociologist Oscar Lewis's study of Puerto Rican poverty, La Vida. As early as 1949, government tourist planners recommended clearance of the area, but community organizers mobilized, and the resulting political pressure prevented removal.[89] La Perla clung to its slope alongside the busy tourist districts. Soledad, a prostitute profiled in La Vida, related how her work and travels took her back and forth from ghetto to stylish Condado and spoke of "the pain one feels after being in a nice hotel and walking past the Caribe Hilton" only to return home to the nearby slum. "They live in separate worlds, the poor and the rich," she observed.[90]

Economic disparities constituted only one of an array of incongruities. Equally disconcerting for many Puerto Ricans was the prospect of cultural transformation, a concern that generated antitourism discourses parallel to those that arose in late-1950s Cuba. As Puerto Rico geared up for its first year of mass tourism, Raúl Gándara, San Juan's fire chief and a strong Muñoz backer, ridiculed the government's willingness to "degrade itself by buying tourists."[91] The editors of El Mundo warned in a series of 1952 articles that Puerto Rico had already been inundated by an army of "suntarios," rich tourists who cared little about the island and sought only to indulge their love of luxury, sun, and casinos. In search of souvenirs and kitsch, they threatened to degrade Puerto Rico's artistic traditions. In pursuit of illicit sex and drugs, they threatened society's moral well-being. In time, the newspaper predicted, city planners, police, and educators would join artists and prostitutes, jettison their responsibilities toward their native communities, and dutifully genuflect before the tourists.[92]

Some critics even took aim at the foreign styling of the landmark Caribe Hilton. Although Fomento and Hilton officials liked to emphasize that the hotel had been designed by a San Juan firm, Toto and Ferrer, the influence of New York–based consultants Warner Leeds and Associates predominated. "Visitors who search for uniquely native character in this building will not find much of it," Architectural Forum commented; there is "comparatively

Clinging to the rockbound coast directly below Old San Juan, the La Perla shantytown (shown here in 1965) housed approximately nine thousand inhabitants. Residents resisted the commonwealth government's slum-clearance program, and La Perla still stands as a symbol of the inequalities inherent in the globalized tourist world. Proyecto de Digitalizació de la Colección de Fotos del Periódico El Mundo, Universidad de Puerto Rico, Recinto, Río Piedras.

little that is Puerto Rican." Rather, the hotel had "the color, texture, and finish demanded by Americans off to the semi-tropics."[93]

Muñoz and Moscoso fought back. "How do you expect to pay for education and social welfare," Moscoso chided the critics, "if the Commonwealth is barred from earning revenue?"[94] Moreover, the administration cited the favorable terms of the Caribe Hilton transaction as an example of enlightened tourism promotion. While the joint venture handed over day-to-day operation of the hotel to Hilton, it secured ownership for the government. The final contract in fact specified that Hilton would purchase the resort's furnishings and equipment, cover any losses incurred in the first year's operation, and be barred from opening a competing hotel on the island. Finally, the arrangements guaranteed the government 66.67 percent of the hotel's annual gross operating profit.[95]

The Hilton Corporation certainly felt that Fomento had driven a hard bargain. Predicting a spectacular success for the hotel, Caribe manager Frank Wangeman wrote to Conrad Hilton just six months after the opening: "I think we have a gold mine here. Let's buy this hotel before [the Puerto Rican government realizes] how prosperous it is going to be."[96] But Muñoz and Moscoso would hear nothing of it, and by 1953 the enterprise generated one million dollars annually for the government.[97]

In addition, hotel workers occasionally wrung significant concessions from their employers. Modern Puerto Rican labor history traces to the formation of the Federación Libre de Trabajadores (FLT) in 1899 and its subsequent creation of the Partido Socialista. The FLT drew inspiration from Marxist unionists at its inception, especially in the island's sugar fields, but became more moderate during the 1920s, when it affiliated with Puerto Rico's mainstream political parties and the American Federation of Labor. In his radical youth, Luis Muñoz Marín had actively supported both the FLT and the Partido Socialista, and as head of the PPD in the 1930s and 1940s he cultivated the political backing of the more militant Confederación General del Trabajo. During the immediate postwar years, however, Muñoz's PPD, with an assist from the antilabor Taft-Hartley Act, turned against the Confederación, which splintered and eventually disintegrated. Although Muñoz's government hoped that low wages would lure U.S. investment to the island, the governor also stayed on good terms with the AFL-CIO. By 1963, twenty-six AFL-CIO unions had moved into the island's textile and transit industries, dockyards, and hospitality sector.[98]

A labor strike erupted at the Caribe Hilton and another San Juan hotel in January 1955, at the height of the tourist season, when negotiations between Hilton and an AFL-CIO affiliate collapsed as a consequence of disputes over wages, benefits, and overtime. Kitchen workers walked off the job. Women, who have historically played a prominent role in organizing the island's needle, cigar, and hotel industries, comprised a majority of the strikers. Tensions mounted as hotel managers accused picketers of using tacks to deflate tires and sabotage company cars suspected of transporting strikebreakers to work. The Muñoz administration played a direct role in the four-week impasse, finally persuading Hilton to provide a 2 percent pay raise, a 4 percent raise in medical and insurance benefits, and liberalized overtime pay. Governor Muñoz personally intervened with local police to reduce the likelihood of violence. After the dispute had been settled, strikers wrote to express their gratitude, informing Muñoz of their willingness "to die for our governor."[99] In subsequent years, wages in Puerto Rico's increasingly unionized hotel sector steadily rose, and benefits expanded.[100]

The travel industry's rapid growth and the passionate discord it stirred persuaded government planners to reassess their policies during 1954 and 1955. Some expressed concern regarding overbuilding in the Condado.[101] Outside consultants advised that visitors had complained that "San Juan is getting too much like Miami, or other large mainland tropical cities, whereas vacationists like to feel they are in a land with a foreign language, customs, native foods, and dress intact."[102] Picó urged that construction of large, capital-intensive hotels be left to private investors and that modest levels of government support be provided to smaller inns and hostelries, modeled after European bed-and-breakfasts.[103]

By early 1956, Fomento had a new, multifaceted plan. The blueprint, drawing on an extensive report on tourism by economic consultant Sherwood M. Fine, did not envision any slowdown in the Condado's growth. Planners slated a 112-room expansion for the Caribe and the raising of a half dozen new hotels to complement the Hilton anchor. Departing from existing practices that stressed public funding, however, Fomento estimated that two-thirds of the hundred-million-dollar ten-year investment would come from private sources. As Picó had suggested, planners aimed life-giving public subsidies and tax breaks at more modest inns and restaurants, most of which would be locally owned.[104] Fomento also turned its attention beyond the Condado, including Dorado Beach, west of San Juan, and the picturesque public beach at Luquillo, just twenty miles to the east. Within the magical El Yunque rainforest, located amid the lush mountains south of Luquillo, extensive renovations of dated guest cabins and the visitor's restaurant began.[105] In short, the commonwealth government continued carefully to plot the island's travel industry but showed no sign of scaling it back.

Recovering Cobblestone and Manufacturing Identity

The governor's office did not dismiss its critics. The decadelong program included several new components designed to address the island's yearning for social renewal and cultural integrity. Muñoz articulated the new emphasis in a July 1954 speech before San Juan's Rotary Club. Noting that tourism had traditionally been considered little more than a leisure activity, he told the Rotarians that he envisioned modern international travel as a means toward the preservation of "a poetic aura" and the advancement of "social progress." Puerto Ricans, he lectured, had a duty to manage the industry "with delicacy, love, and respect" toward foreign visitors. At the same time, tourism should work as a "manifestation of democracy," serving the interests of the Puerto

Rican people and instilling their children with "love and admiration of the beautiful panoramas of the island." "Tourism must begin at home," he stressed, and must nurture an appreciation for Puerto Rican culture internally as well as internationally.[106] The governor acknowledged that "some distinguished intellectuals" feared that the influx of visitors might disfigure "the culture of our country." The critique carried much merit, he admitted. But his government would use tourism to display to the world "our integrity as a democratic people," to promote peaceful relations among the world's people, to restore and protect the island's parks and national monuments, and to elevate Puerto Rico's place in history and folklore.[107]

The flowery rhetoric might easily be dismissed as boilerplate. Muñoz, after all, loomed as a maestro of political wordsmithing. Yet in the months that followed, the government embarked on an ambitious agenda of historic and cultural preservation. The effort began in Old San Juan.[108] The Iberian walled city had suffered years of neglect, and some streets consisted of row after row of run-down and abandoned structures. Robbins had first proposed refurbishing the area in 1949 through a combination of private funds and public subsidies. He even invited a group of former colleagues from Colonial Williamsburg, led by Kenneth Chorley, to San Juan to examine the prospects for recovering its magnificent architectural heritage. He and his group "are working on various plans to keep the essential character and maintain the area in full usefulness and have it contribute to our tourist development," he explained to the governor.[109]

In 1949, the commonwealth's legislature passed a law designating Old San Juan an "ancient and historic zone," but the restoration project remained dormant until 1955, when the government created the Institute of Puerto Rican Culture, provided it a modest budget, and hired a team of restoration architects.[110] Under the direction of a young Harvard-trained archeologist, Ricardo Alegría, the institute provided guidance to property owners willing to refurbish their homes and offices. Each restoration carried a hefty price tag between $15,000 and $80,000. Fomento spurred the process by granting liberal tax incentives to building owners, and the Government Development Bank provided loans to willing proprietors. Within just a few years, restaurants and gift shops dotted the old neighborhoods, curious tourists milled about the Cathedral de San Juan, and work began on the recovery of a three-hundred-year-old convent and its transformation into the $2.5 million El Convento hotel.[111]

The gradual return of the area's whitewashed arches, garden patios, wrought iron balconies, and blue cobblestone streets did more than create a new tourist attraction. It answered critics who feared that Puerto Rico's lurch toward modernity, including its promotion of tourism, threatened the island's cultural coherence. Initially viewed with skepticism by devout nationalists, the institute soon gained strong popular support, in part because the administration co-opted its harshest critics by filling its administrative positions with large numbers of *independentista* scholars and artists.[112]

Although the institute initially privileged Puerto Rico's European past, it gradually developed archeological projects to recover and promote indigenous Taíno art forms as well. The Taíno population, the pre-Spanish inhabitants of what had once been known as Borínquen (Island of the Brave Lord), had vanished by the mid–eighteenth century. In time, the organization also undertook the study of the island's African cultures, whose presence had long been downplayed or completely denied by Puerto Rican elites. In the township of Loíza Aldea, scholars traced the origins of the popular drum-driven dance rhythms known as *la bomba* to the area's African slave population.[113]

Although the commonwealth's cultural undertakings evidenced Eurocentrism, they nonetheless nurtured a public memory and a sense of identity that sat at odds with traditional colonial narratives. The nationalists of the 1930s had challenged U.S. political and cultural domination by elevating the island's *hispanidad* civilization. The Institute of Puerto Rican Culture complicated that vision and in so doing empowered a people whose political status still registered as colonial.[114] "Although we are very much interested in preserving our cultural heritage," Alegría observed, "we are even more interested in promoting the culture of Puerto Rico today and in the future."[115]

In contrast to Fulgencio Batista's treatment of Old Havana, commonwealth officials did not view Old San Juan's preservation as at variance with commercial tourism. Instead, they made the island's historic ambience a centerpiece of a new ad campaign. In 1954, Fomento allowed its contract with Hamilton Wright to lapse and signed on with New York–based advertising mogul David Ogilvy. As sensitive to the tourist's cultural yearnings as Muñoz was to his constituents' thirst for identity, Ogilvy counseled against overemphasizing Puerto Rico's industrial ambitions and portraying the island as a "New Deal Formosa." The ad agency's public opinion surveys demonstrated that in spite of a half decade of counterspin, most mainlanders still identified Puerto Rico with poverty. When asked how they would rate certain tropical islands for such things as "beautiful beaches," Hawaii ranked first and Puerto Rico last. Puerto Rico similarly placed last for "cleanliness," "modernity," and "general attractiveness." "We must substitute a lovely image of Puerto Rico for the squalid image that now exists," Ogilvy counseled.[116]

Ogilvy set out to advertise the island as if it scored first in the surveys rather than last. Aimed at the upper-income readers of magazines such as the *New Yorker* and *Holiday*, the new public relations campaign painted Puerto Rico as a land of exotic calm yet bustling economic progress. Full-page ads accented the island's exotic beauty with color photos of palm-lined beaches, beautiful mountains, and the pastel architecture of Old San Juan. Others pictured an investors' paradise where successful male executives still found time for a round of golf. Some ads approached artistry. One of the most famous pictured a young Spanish-looking woman elegantly dressed in an evening gown, holding flowers and turned toward an ornate colonial-style patio gate. Presenting the island at once as the embodiment of feminine beauty and masculine economic performance, the text read, "Time stands still in the Puerto Rican patio. . . . You might have stepped back three centuries. . . . Can this really be the Puerto Rico that everyone is talking about? Is this the island American industry is now expanding to, at the rate of three new factories per week? Is this truly the scene of a twentieth century renaissance?"[117]

The island's image gained additional luster in 1956 when Muñoz and Moscoso persuaded Spanish cellist Pablo Casals to move from Franco's Spain to Puerto Rico, his mother's homeland. Casals became the main attraction of the annual Casals Classical Music Festival held each June. The first festival filled San Juan's hotels, restaurants, and shops just prior to the sluggish 1957 summer season. Equally important, it disassociated Puerto Rico from Spanish legends of tyranny, both medieval and modern, and enhanced its reputation for democratic openness and cultural refinement.[118]

The phrase "twentieth century renaissance" undoubtedly exaggerated Puerto Rico's stature. Despite the multiple factory raisings, tourism, and historic restoration, the commonwealth remained desperately poor during the second half of the 1950s. Operation Bootstrap's accomplishments notwithstanding, U.S.-based companies that took advantage of the island's tax-free inducements often pulled up stakes when moratorium periods ended. Despite rapid industrialization, a growing population and the vagaries of the marketplace kept unemployment at 10 to 12 percent, figures that did not take into account the widespread problem of partial employment. And each year, tens of thousands of displaced islanders made the odyssey north to the urban slums of New York, New Jersey, and Connecticut.[119]

Yet the tourist agenda at least attempted to address the island's social inequality, sometimes in a fashion not dissimilar to that of Fidel Castro's early plans for Cuban tourism. In late 1955, the governor's office informed Fomento that it wished to develop a plan for public parks and vacation sites

Girl by a gate
—in old San Juan

TIME STANDS STILL in this Puerto Rican patio. That weathered escutcheon bears the Royal Arms of Spain. You might have stepped back three centuries. In a sense, you have.

You start to wonder. Can this really be the Puerto Rico everybody is talking about? Is this the island where American industry is now expanding at the rate of three new plants a week? Is this truly the scene of a twentieth-century renaissance? Ask any proud Puerto Rican. He will surely answer—yes.

Within minutes from this patio, you will see the signs. Some are spectacular. The new hotels, the four-lane highways, the landscaped apartments. And some are down-to-earth. A tractor in a field, a village clinic, a shop that sells refrigerators. None all these things. But, above all, meet the people.

Renaissance has a way of breeding remarkable men. Men of industry who can also love poetry. Men of courage who can also be tender. Men of vision who can also respect the past. Make a point of talking to these twentieth-century Puerto Ricans.

It won't be long before you appreciate the deeper significance of Puerto Rico's renaissance. You'll begin to understand why men like Pablo Casals and Juan Ramón Jiménez (the Nobel Prize poet) have gone there to live.

© 1958—Commonwealth of Puerto Rico, 666 Fifth Avenue, New York 19, N.Y.

◄ *How to find this patio in old San Juan: Ask for the City Hall. They call it the Ayuntamiento, in Spanish. Walk straight through this 17th Century building and there is your patio. One photograph was taken by Elliott Erwitt.*

Advertising mogul David Ogilvy set out to change Puerto Rico's image as a land of squalor and poverty. This ad, which appeared in several U.S. magazines in 1958, was the result.

"puedan estar al alcance de personas de ingresos modestos" (affordable for people of modest incomes). A subsequent report noted that in light of the influx of rural migrants to the island's urban centers and the migrants' typical inability to purchase or maintain automobiles, the commonwealth should promote a "compact social life" for its working classes and make noncommercial amusements available at the local level. "The situation in Puerto Rico more closely resembles that of Europe than that of the United States and this similarity is strengthened by the tradition, Spanish in origin, of compact social life. This tradition has so many psychological values that it is wisdom to strengthen and encourage it, in distinction to the furthering of commercial entertainment, which is essentially individualistic in texture."[120]

The planners divided the island into a series of urban zones and surveyed each for recreational beach, forest, lake, and river facilities. Each public area would feature campsites, picnic areas, fishing sites, and hiking trails. Popular recreational spaces would calm urban social tensions, officials reasoned, and serve as a means of social control. Idealizing rural life, the report's authors noted that "incontestably, delinquency and neurosis . . . are almost unknown in rural life, at least when it is not infected by a form of urban contempt." But affordable recreation would also relieve discontent aroused by the "general exhibition of luxurious living" and "conspicuous expenditure" associated with foreign tourism.[121] The project for affordable local tourism, like the restoration of Old San Juan, represented a means by which to square the circle—that is, to expand a lucrative international travel industry and transform the island's economy without dissolving long-established cultural arrangements.

Puerto Rican Tourism and Cold War History

In recent years, some academic historians have conceptualized a new field of inquiry, really a subfield of diplomatic history, and labeled it "Cold War history." The release of previously sealed documents in former communist archives and the People's Republic of China, along with the conflict's dramatic and unexpected closure during the late 1980s, no doubt heightened interest in the subject. But the fascination also springs from the presentism of contemporary policymakers and commentators eager to decipher lessons applicable to today's geopolitical setting. Indeed, President George W. Bush has likened the challenge posed by today's religiously inspired terrorism to past ideological threats, including Cold War communism. Some scholars weave from the Cold War's past a celebratory narrative of freedom's triumph over totalitarianism. Others construct a more self-critical account that highlights a new or at least accelerated American internationalism following the Second World War, when Washington abandoned its long-standing traditions of isolationism.[122] Both approaches accent American exceptionalism in world affairs and portray the main currents in history as determined by interstate power rivalries.

Consequently, much of the massive literature on the Cold War has concentrated on its political and military dimensions: the rivalry between two powerful states at the end of the Second World War, the ensuing flashpoints from the Dardanelles in 1946 to Afghanistan in the 1980s, the costly and expensive arms race, and the question of which ideology and which system of political economy should be assigned blame. We know far less about how and why Cold War dynamics varied from region to region of the world and the many ways in which U.S. Cold War policies grew out America's nineteenth- and early-twentieth-century experiences. Most important, we know too little about how the Cold War intersected with longer trends in international relations molded not by nation-states and power rivalries after 1945 but by the steady convergence of interdependent forces, the blurring of national boundaries, the globalization of trade and mass communications, and the slow but continuous movement toward cultural globalism.[123]

Historians have begun only relatively recently to write the social and cultural history of the global Cold War.[124] In *Cold War Orientalism*, a study of postwar Asia in American popular culture, Christine Klein has outlined two distinct but complementary U.S. worldviews in the Cold War. The first, on which most diplomatic historians focus, involved the culture of containment —that is, Washington's determined effort to meet Soviet expansionism with firm and unalterable countermeasures. The other involved a "global imaginary of integration" and a drive to build through cultural as well as political and economic means a U.S.-led capitalist world order. For Klein, the Cold War encompassed more than power politics and ideology. Without the Cold War's integrative imperative, the United States would have done far less to spread modernization, productivity, and technology, and globalization across the noncommunist world would have taken place more slowly.[125]

Similarly expanding the boundaries of Cold War historiography, Gilbert M. Joseph and other scholars of Latin America have noted that the traditional emphasis on the Cold War's political dimensions has obscured the role of ordinary human subjects, especially marginalized groups, racial minorities, and women. The superpowers in fact often projected their Cold War logic onto a complex array of internal, grassroots dynamics—class-driven, ethnic, racial, religious, and ideological. In Latin America, the war and early postwar years marked the mass mobilization of labor, campesinos, and the middle classes inspired by the reformist movements of the 1930s and the democratic impulses of the war against fascism, impulses that harkened back to the liberalism and social activism of the region's nineteenth-century independence movements and the early stages of Mexico's twentieth-century revolution. The international Cold War and its intolerance of leftism in the noncommunist world reinforced Latin America's authoritarian traditions and emboldened U.S.-backed elites to clamp down on the democratizing trends of the early 1940s. Starting with the Central Intelligence Agency–backed overthrow of Jacobo Arbenz Guzmán and Guatemala's social democracy in 1954 and its replacement by a vicious authoritarianism and continuing through the 1970s with U.S.-backed dirty wars in Central America and the southern cone, the Cold War became one of the most deadly epics in modern Latin American history.[126]

The history of U.S. hemispheric tourism further complicates Cold War history. Within a single hemispheric Cold War camp, Batista's Cuba and Muñoz's Puerto Rico imagined and implemented vastly different relationships with U.S. tourists, U.S. corporations, and the U.S. government despite the overarching presence of the Bretton Woods system, the General Agreement on Tariffs and Trade, Cold War military alliances, and the globalizing power of modern cultural corridors and contact zones. To examine these developments through the prism of traditional "Cold War history" is to impose a misleading coherence on a process of empire and integration that both preceded and followed the Cold War.

In light of the Truman and Eisenhower administrations' refusal to address Latin American pleas for assistance, local elites during the early postwar era fell back on their own instincts. For precisely this reason, many socially conservative authoritarian regimes promptly reestablished themselves. Also for this reason, the Puerto Rican commonwealth, America's postcolonial colony, found an opening for reform. While U.S. military bases and federal courtrooms stood as reminders of the colonial presence, San Juan used its limited autonomy and the tourist-visitor relationship to establish a middle ground between the democratic populism of Latin America's war years and the authoritarian excesses endemic to the Cold War.[127] In short, Muñoz and other Puerto Rican officials discovered innovative ways to benefit from Washington's global integrationist goals.

Commonwealth officials, much like Mexico's postrevolutionary leaders, sought not so much a break with the empire but a rearrangement of links and additional breathing space. While U.S. tourists to Havana in the 1950s tended erroneously to ascribe that city's depravity to Cuban national character, American tourists and travel industry specialists often viewed San Juan's modern makeover largely as a consequence of U.S. influence. At the opening of the Caribe Hilton in December 1949, *Time* magazine attributed the raising of the hotel to "Connie" Hilton's financial ingenuity and the power of the Hilton name.[128] Two years later, a writer for *National Geographic* remarked that "if the visitor forgets for a moment the tropical setting," the Condado might be imagined "to be the newer section of a half-dozen cities in continental United States."[129] "I remember San Juan before it got into the bigtime," observed travel writer Horace Sutton in the *Saturday Review* in late 1952, "the buses faded and dented, like old cans on wheels." But now "the buses are new," swank recently built hotels and apartments "cast unfamiliar modern shadows along the lagoon," and "new cabs with two way radios cruise the palm shaded streets." "San Juan is a new Miami with a Spanish accent," Sutton exclaimed.[130]

Contemporary commentators, much like Washington officials and even some Cold War historians, overestimated U.S. influence and exaggerated the significance of the moment. Imperial hubris encouraged a cacophony of U.S. voices to uphold Puerto Rico as a product of a uniquely enlightened colonialism. The fact of the matter was that the commonwealth had grudgingly accepted its continued colonial status as a means of gaining a degree of control over its moribund economy. It similarly used tourism to establish its existence in the minds of both U.S. travelers and Puerto Rican citizens.

The international travel industry does not operate exactly the same way in any two societies. To be sure, the touring impulse speaks to common primordial and modern dreams of adventure and exploration and perhaps did so with renewed vigor in the globalizing context of the mid–twentieth century. Still, the negotiation of identities that lay at the heart of the visitor-host relationship has played out in endless and often unpredictable variety. Such proved to be the case even during the early Cold War, when the call to arms and ideological discipline echoed across the "Free World."

In 1950s Cuba, the underlying forces that generated tourism—capital, technology, and advertising—were allowed to career freely without regulations and in the end unleashed a violent backlash. Puerto Ricans imagined and implemented a very different tourism. The commonwealth faced limited options. Revolution was in the air, but the island's people and leaders demurred from the violence that had swept Mexico and soon enveloped Cuba. Puerto Ricans compromised their sovereignty, but most islanders did not delude themselves that the colonizing power had their interests at heart. They welcomed vacationing Yankees and even labored to pamper them but also organized unions to win fair wages and benefits. Puerto Ricans shared their beaches and cobblestone but simultaneously elevated them as a central element of islanders' postcolonial identity.

Behind the scenes, again in contrast to Batista's Cuba, Puerto Ricans engaged in a relatively open debate over the pros and cons of tourism, the state's role in the economy, and the wisdom of tolerating for one more moment the obscenity of poverty and the humiliation of colonialism. The Muñoz administration repressed the island's most radical nationalist elements and refused directly to challenge U.S. hegemony but more often than not tolerated local critics, organized fair elections, and remained attentive to popular pressures. It is difficult to decipher the inner thoughts and intentions of a politician as talented as Luis Muñoz Marín. But in the end, his policies produced results that contained a consistent—if imperfect—inner logic: a state-guided, diversified economy; a tourist industry whose growth remained capped and contained; and a multicultural identity of which most Puerto Ricans could claim at least partial ownership.

North American officials' and publicists' tendency to take credit for the commonwealth's modernizing achievements was more than delusional or ironic. It ultimately took on tragic characteristics. As the 1950s drew to a close, other Latin American peoples and their governments stepped up their demands for economic development. They turned in growing numbers to the United States to provide the kind of assistance that it had sent to Western Europe a decade earlier. The Cuban Revolution added to the clamor and demonstrated to Washington officials how nationalism and social discontent might combine completely to upend the empire. As Latin American leaders scanned the horizon for a new approach to nation building suitable for the post-Batista era, Puerto Rico's formula—with its bootstraps, beaches, and cobblestone—appeared to fit the bill.

SIX

A Cold War Mirage

Puerto Rico in the 1960s
and 1970s

For one glamorous evening in November 1961, visitor-host roles reversed. It was Puerto Rico Night at the Kennedy White House, and America's handsome first couple played host to Puerto Rican governor Luis Muñoz Marín; his wife, Inés María Mendoza; and Puerto Rico's adopted son, the incomparable Pablo Casals. The president dressed in white tie and tails; the First Lady donned a sleeveless gown. The event featured a state dinner in honor of Muñoz, followed by a concert performed by Casals. The eighty-one-year-old cellist had last performed at the White House in 1904 for President Theodore Roosevelt and guests and had since refused to play at functions sponsored by governments that maintained relations with Francisco Franco, the 1930s dictator who still haunted Casals's native Spain. The cellist made an exception for Kennedy, a gesture of trust in the young president's commitment to democracy. The concert, which featured pieces by Mendelssohn, Schumann, and Couperin, was broadcast live on ABC and NBC radio. Like any savvy host, the president used the visitor's presence to project an idealized national identity. "Art is an integral part of a free society," Kennedy noted. America stood tall as a world power that lauded both artistic creativity and political liberty.[1]

The celebration bespoke the administration's hope-filled beginning and Puerto Rico's special status inside the Kennedy White House. Despite the setback suffered by U.S.-backed Cuban commandos at the Bay of Pigs the previous spring, the administration moved forward with one of the most ambitious inter-American initiatives in history, the Alliance for Progress. The bold exercise of soft power centered on a pledge to pump ten billion dollars into the region's development over the next decade. To guide the new program, the president called on an army of professionally trained social scientists, most of whom adhered to some variation of modernization theory. The

On Puerto Rico Night at the White House, 13 November 1961, U.S. president John F. Kennedy and Puerto Rican governor Luis Muñoz Marín chat with cellist Pablo Casals. Puerto Rico's First Lady, Inés María Mendoza, is to the left, and Jacqueline Kennedy stands to the right of Muñoz. John F. Kennedy Presidential Library, Boston, Massachusetts.

core ideology, not entirely at odds with old-fashioned dollar diplomacy and the postwar Bretton Woods philosophy, prescribed U.S. leadership and public funds to encourage Latin American states to embrace free markets, private investment, and democratization.

Puerto Rico played an important role in the new program. To help formulate and implement the plan, the Kennedy White House drafted two prominent commonwealth officials: Muñoz foreign affairs adviser Arturo Morales Carrión served on the Latin American task force that drafted the initiative, and Fomento director Teodoro Moscoso became the alliance's first administrative coordinator.[2] Puerto Rico served as a frequent point of reference for alliance officials who touted the island as a model for U.S.-backed modernization. The underlying assumptions held that the island had absorbed U.S. capital, trade, technology, and cultural values, especially a faith in hard work, democracy, and liberal capitalism.[3]

Puerto Rico Night at the White House carried special symbolism. The concept of Puerto Rico as a model for reform and development, of course, had derived in no small part from its decadelong buildup as a tourist oasis. Although many North Americans still conceived of the island primarily as an exporter of undesirable immigrants, the visitor-host relationship had also nurtured more flattering cultural constructions. A forward-looking government had pulled an agricultural society up by its bootstraps and in addition to building factories had erected luxury hotels, landscaped the island's sandy beaches, and restored its quaint, aged cobblestone. The tourist gaze juxtaposed the island's tropical allure and its material progress, its Old World ambience and its advanced consumer offerings, its historic landmarks and its modern architecture, its yearning for change and its stability. In short, Puerto Rico shone as a new Cold War paradise, an outpost for capitalist development in a world seemingly tempted by the promises of communism.

In 1969, ten years after the Cuban Revolution and nearing the end of the alliance decade, the number of annual visitors to Puerto Rico topped the one million mark, making it the Caribbean's most heavily visited island. Puerto Rico's surging travel industry, however, complicated its relations with the United States and in retrospect exposed some of the flawed assumptions that underpinned the Alliance for Progress. In addition to becoming meeting places for hemispheric solidarity, the island's cultural contact zones crackled with contentious visitor-host exchanges. Ordinary Puerto Ricans—taxi drivers, waiters, prostitutes, newspaper writers, and others—haggled with Yankees regarding language, race, and constructions of gender and sexuality. The massive influx of affluent U.S. consumers and the accompanying physical transformation of San Juan exacerbated gaps between rich and poor and drew into question Puerto Rico's precarious sense of identity. While modernization narratives asserted that hegemon and colony shared a common Cold War mission, the everyday life of the empire revealed that U.S.–Puerto Rican relations remained firmly grounded in colonial inequality. Equally striking, the island's mixed economy did not in reality embody the North American faith in free-market capitalism and stood in contrast to the prevailing Latin American trend toward military-led privatization and free trade.

Across the rest of Latin America, the alliance faltered. Economies experienced only marginal growth, many of the region's political leaders resisted social reforms, and military coups brought to power a new generation of dictators. Explanations for the disappointing performance abound—bureaucratic caution and inefficiency, the conservatism of Latin American elites, and the Kennedy administration's preference for Cold War stability over social change. An examination of Puerto Rican tourism during the 1960s does not undermine standard accounts but does illuminate the deep cultural divide that separated the United States from even its most politically cooperative colony, expose the erroneous logic that made U.S. leaders imagine that

Puerto Rico's relative success was of their making, and demonstrate the perils of development modeling.

As the alliance floundered, the commonwealth continued to prosper. Tension between visitors and hosts never disappeared, but hosts enjoyed enough agency to smooth the travel industry's sharper edges. Hospitality workers flexed their union muscle, the Institute of Puerto Rican Culture (IPRC) accelerated its identity projects, and Governor Muñoz even distanced himself from some of the Kennedy administration's more hawkish Cold War foreign policies. The governor also threaded an even more difficult needle, positioning his travel policies between the *independentistas'* antitourism agenda and an increasingly popular statehood movement that portrayed tourism as the island's economic savior. Puerto Rico transitioned from one-party dominance to a competitive two-party polity, but the structures of political economy erected during the Muñoz era and the ebb and flow of the empire's everyday, cultural life endured.

During the late 1960s and early 1970s, as the international Cold War lost momentum and the United States and the Soviet Union embraced the spirit of détente, the Cold War in Latin America became more ferociously ideological and violent. Instead of serving as a beacon of Cold War reform, Puerto Rico became a regional anomaly where politics became more pluralistic and markets remained subject to regulation. This chapter explores how the soft power inherent in tourist-host relations intersected and diverged from the soft power of 1960s development aid and nation building. It traces the history of tourism through some of the most dramatic moments of the Cold War and carries it into the era of accelerated globalization.

A Cold War Oasis

The Soviet-American confrontation certainly generated flashpoints that made the world gasp. The Berlin crisis of June 1948, Mao Tse-tung's dispatch of "volunteers" into North Korea in November 1950, the surreal juxtaposition of the Hungarian rebellion and Suez Crisis of October 1956, and of course the Cuban Revolution and its aftermath have all been etched in popular memory as moments of grave danger and moral clarity. Yet their meanings have grown ambiguous over time. Scholars debate their origins and ramifications, the international archival record complicates official accounts, and cinematic remembrances dramatize and obscure each episode's significance.

From the late 1950s through the early 1970s, Puerto Rico experienced its own Cold War glory, chock-full of political passion and commercial opportunity. Muñoz, like many others, initially perceived Cuba's revolutionists to be democratic reformers.[4] *New York Times* correspondent Herbert Matthews urged Fidel Castro to meet with Muñoz and his wife, who might provide the young rebel with wise counsel on state building. "You have two good friends there who wish you and the new Cuba well," Matthews wrote to Castro in early February 1959. "I know I don't have to tell you how sympathetic every Puerto Rican from the Governor and his wife downward were to you and the cause for which you fought, and how anti-Batista they all were." Matthews emphasized that Puerto Rico was "in its most vital respects" an autonomous Latin American nation and that Operation Bootstrap provided an economic model "for all the world."[5]

Castro did not heed the advice. He reluctantly allowed his treasury minister, Rufo López-Fresquet, to visit San Juan, where Muñoz and others conveyed their sympathy for the new government in Havana and discussed options for Cuba's economic planning. But during his long period in exile, Castro had befriended numerous Puerto Rican *independentistas* and shared their disdain for the continuing U.S. colonial presence in Puerto Rico.[6] For his part, Muñoz gradually grew critical of Castro's authoritarianism and the Cuban Revolution's steady drift leftward, although he steadfastly opposed U.S. military intervention.

Thus, instead of forging a reformist partnership with Cuba, the commonwealth government used its well-groomed image to cash in on Cuba's tourism meltdown. An array of publications retold the bootstrap story. Under Muñoz, annual earnings had risen from $125 per capita in 1940 to $514 by 1960, second only to Venezuela in Latin America. In 1958–59 alone, 237 firms had signed contracts with Fomento, including 100 local firms whose control lay in Puerto Rican hands. Formerly a producer of mainly sugar and rum, Puerto Rico now had more than 600 factories churning out manufactured goods and generating thousands of jobs. There was social progress as well: new schools and 86 percent literacy, low-income housing, and even a miniature Tennessee Valley Authority in the town of Caonillas.[7]

The popular and charismatic governor appeared in the U.S. press as the father of modern Puerto Rico. His portrait graced the cover of *Time* magazine in June 1958.[8] The accompanying article trumpeted Operation Bootstrap and provided a personal portrait of the "lusty statesman" who enjoyed drink but worked twelve-hour days, drew an annual salary of ten thousand dollars, and had sixteen years to go on his Federal Housing Administration home mortgage, who enjoyed cruises on yachts offered by wealthy friends but gave his heart to the island's poor. Evenings at La Fortaleza exuded a magical aura.

"You're invited to dinner," the piece quoted Adolf A. Berle, FDR's former assistant secretary of state, as saying, and "presently a couple of people heave in—top government officials, somebody whom you eventually recognize as Pablo Casals, maybe a poet or so."[9] Most of all, in an age of Third World nationalism and revolution, the governor's pragmatism charmed North Americans. "I have some very serious reservations about nationalism in the modern world," he told the *Saturday Review*; "the big need today is to break out of narrow nationalisms and to develop larger human allegiances."[10]

Commonwealth tourism officials did not kid themselves. Ritzy beachfront hotels rather than a headline-grabbing governor remained the island's main selling point. Advances in transportation technology and reduced travel costs made the sale easier. Round-trip fares from New York had fallen from $128 in 1952 to $90 by 1958, "a total of 3200 miles at a cost of 2.8 cents per mile versus 2.9 cents per mile for an average Manhattan subway ride." Daily jet service commenced in late 1959, halving travel time from New York to one and a half hours.[11]

Another spurt in hotel construction and the expansion of San Juan's cultural contact zones followed. By late 1958, government planners had compiled a list of twenty-one new hotel projects with a total of 3,604 rooms. The expansion relied heavily on foreign investors, including Sheraton, the Hotel Corporation of America, and Louis Vaudable, the owner of Maxim's in Paris. But many of these enterprises also received loans from the publicly run Puerto Rican Industrial Development Company, and a few were wholly government owned.[12] Among the spate of new hotels, the publicly owned but privately managed La Concha ranked among the most lavish. Located on Ashford Avenue, the Condado's main thoroughfare, alongside the Condado Beach Hotel, La Concha featured twelve stories and three hundred rooms. When it opened in December 1958, guests marveled at its nightclub, which sat on a block of concrete over the surf's edge and was covered by a dome that looked like a giant inverted clamshell.[13]

Shortly after the La Concha's opening, work began on the 400-room El San Juan, located just east of the Condado in Isla Verde, near the airport. The El San Juan was a public-private venture with the Intercontinental Hotel Group, a subsidiary of Pan American.[14] Then came the El Imperial, a $10-million, five-hundred room extravaganza, Puerto Rico's largest. The Dorado Beach Hotel and Golf Club, which also opened for business in 1958 just west of the capital city, won the distinction of being the island's costliest. The Rockefeller-run project had grown from its inception as a $1.6 million, 70-room hostelry to a 136-room, five-star inn with a price tag of $12 million. The

Robert Trent Jones golf course hired Ed Dudley, of Augusta National fame, as its resident pro.[15]

Cuba's turmoil catapulted Puerto Rico into a leadership position among Caribbean vacation retreats. According to a December 1958 issue of *Time* magazine, Puerto Rico aimed to please the crowd "bored with Miami and scared of going to Havana because of the Cuban revolution."[16] By early 1960, hotels booked for months ahead and the nightclub and restaurant business hummed. *U.S. News and World Report* observed that despite proliferating construction along the Condado, hotel space "was so short that some hotels put up cots in lobbies for new arrivals."[17]

Magnet for tourists, investors, and publicists, Puerto Rico also won praise from leading Cold War politicians. Richard Nixon found refuge there in June 1958. Six months later, Senator John F. Kennedy flew in and made his first major speech on Latin America as a presidential candidate. The following year, yet another presidential hopeful, Democratic senator Hubert Humphrey, visited and lauded the island as a model for democratic development.[18] President Dwight D. Eisenhower, perhaps the nation's most famous vacation enthusiast, made Puerto Rico the first stop on his February 1960 Latin American tour. Ike captured headlines and added further to the island's luster when he took to the fairways of the Dorado Beach Club.[19]

As Fidel Castro gravitated leftward, Washington officials and the press heaped additional praise on Puerto Rico's "peaceful revolution." Unlike other Caribbean countries, the *Saturday Review* editorialized in 1962, Puerto Rico had no revolutionary past. The island was managed pragmatically and in accordance with democratic principles.[20] "Under way here is an American-style revolution that really works," observed *U.S. News and World Report*, offering a "sharp contrast to the violent revolution in nearby Cuba."[21] Guidebooks and travel articles also praised the Puerto Rican "success story" and included descriptions of factory sites, hydroelectric facilities, and other monuments to modernity.[22] *New York Herald Tribune* correspondent Ruth Gruber offered some of the most glowing reviews in her book, *Island of Promise*, published as both a journalistic account and travel guide. More than an investment opportunity or a vacation getaway, she wrote, Puerto Rico sparkled "as a nation with which America shared a spiritual bond," given the island's political system based on constitutional principles and its economic programs based on "self-help." For Gruber, the commonwealth most resembled the state of Israel: both were "new democracies on old soil, pulling themselves up by the bootstraps, with strong and emotional ties to the United States."[23]

A Cold War Program: The Alliance for Progress

As Puerto Rico's tourism industry flourished and the island gained stature as a showcase for self-help and economic development, the international Cold War took a subtle but important new turn. The U.S. confrontation with Cuba continued to escalate following the severing of relations in late 1960 and the implementation of what would become one of history's longest-lasting economic embargos in January 1961. The failed Bay of Pigs adventure in April and the Central Intelligence Agency's ensuing Operation Mongoose, which sought to destabilize Castro's regime and even assassinate the renegade leader, deepened the crisis.

Whereas Washington disowned Cuba, Soviet diplomats arrived on the island bearing trade agreements and military aid, and as geopolitical logic would have it, the competition propelled the superpower rivals headlong toward the Cuban Missile Crisis of October 1962. Calling Soviet leader Nikita Khrushchev's bluff and making several last-minute concessions to soften the blow may have constituted JFK's finest hour, but it chastened cold warriors across North America and the Eurasian landmass. Hard power—nuclear and conventional arsenals, military intervention, and covert operations—remained very much a part of the Cold War. Yet U.S. foreign policymakers rediscovered the importance of soft power, and Washington and Moscow moved tentatively and inconsistently toward détente.

Not since the Marshall Plan had Washington placed so much emphasis on economic aid and cultural diplomacy. Whereas Cold War lines had hardened in Europe by the early 1960s, U.S. leaders directed their energy toward the "developing" world—in Southeast Asia, where decolonization and communism seemed interlocking catastrophes; on the Indian subcontinent, where the Indian-Pakistani rivalry and Soviet diplomatic inroads challenged U.S. influence; and of course in Latin America, where Castro and Che Guevara hoped to export revolution instead of sugar. Historian Stephen G. Rabe has chronicled the Kennedy administration's quixotic quest for Cold War victory in Latin America, driven by the president's designation of the region as "the most dangerous place in the world."[24]

Latin America's Cold War produced the Alliance for Progress.[25] It built on a modest foundation established during Eisenhower's second term, when Ike reversed his earlier opposition and initiated the Inter-American Development Bank and the Social Progress Trust Fund to finance Latin American development and reform. Announced at a celebratory White House ceremony in March 1961 and chartered at an inter-American conference at Punta del Este, Uruguay, in August, the program set an ambitious agenda. Pledging ten billion dollars in U.S. Treasury funds over the coming decade, alliance planners set their sights on achieving regional annual real growth rates of 2.5 percent (that is, 2.5 percent above the region's 3 percent annual population growth), reducing illiteracy, raising life expectancy, and attacking infant mortality. The alliance further promised to bolster democratic regimes, back labor and agrarian reforms, and usher in a new era of human rights and social justice.

The alliance's timing may have been an outgrowth of Cold War events, but its gargantuan objectives reflected the administration's propensity to think big. So did the scale of its failure. Many analysts have reviewed the dismal results. With the exception of Mexico, whose impressive growth had its roots in the 1940s and which received no alliance aid, the region's economies hobbled along at growth rates slightly less than 2 percent annually during the 1960s, failing to keep up with population growth. As for dreams of hemispheric democracy, military forces overthrew six elected governments during the Kennedy years alone, a trend that continued and expanded over the next two decades, making the era of Cold War détente a golden age for state repression in Latin America.[26]

The outcome was clearly not what Kennedy had intended. In her thought-provoking account of the early Peace Corps, a happier Kennedy legacy, historian Elizabeth Cobbs Hoffman has written of "the spirit of the 1960s," which motivated restless and idealistic youths to service in the villages and slums of Africa, Asia, and Latin America.[27] Historians of U.S. foreign relations do not usually look to the spiritual realm to explain foreign policy. Yet the alliance's grandiose failure to advance U.S. interests, much like the Peace Corps's relative success, is difficult to explain in traditional geopolitical terms.

The Peace Corps in fact represented only one symbolic ritual inside of a much larger doctrinal faith that national security adviser and economist Walt Whitman Rostow, the name itself evocative of literary grace, called "modernization." Presumptive and extravagantly ethnocentric, the modernization thesis posited that all societies pass through a handful of universal stages of "development." Using Western Europe and North America as the basis for measurement, Rostow confidently explained the phenomenon in *The Stages of Economic Growth* (1959).[28] Modernization constituted a process whereby societies adapted capital and technology to move from a traditional agrarian foundation into the preconditions for takeoff, forward to industrial takeoff, then to the drive to maturity, and finally to self-sustained growth and high, mass consumption. The theory carried the ring of evolutionary science, and its foreign policy implications—that takeoff undercut the social unrest that led to anti-American revolutions—appealed to hardheaded advocates of real-politik.

Yet the modernization gospel reiterated long-standing cultural understandings of America's destiny in world affairs. In some ways it echoed Manifest Destiny's faith in Anglo-Saxon racial superiority and dollar diplomacy's appeals to manly duty. Shortly after taking office, Rostow sent President Kennedy the good news: "A good many countries in the underdeveloped world will, during the 1960s either complete the take off process or be far advanced in it. . . . When take-off is complete, a nation may be poor but it is normally in a position to draw its external capital from private commercial sources." The implication was that a massive infusion of U.S. foreign aid and other soft powers would uplift living standards throughout the world's former colonial areas, stifle the spread of communism, and legitimize America's global leadership.[29]

The Kennedy team concluded that the time had come to supplement lectures on free enterprise to Latin Americans with U.S. public funds. In his upbeat memo, Rostow estimated that full-bodied U.S. development assistance could propel more than 80 percent of Latin America's population into "self-sustained growth."[30] More than a lending operation, the alliance projected a paternalistic identity that presented the United States as a modernizing agent, willing to assist those who occupied lower levels on the cultural and civilizational scale. In the course of one decade, U.S.-inspired liberal capitalism and representative government would overwhelm the centuries-old remnants of Iberian feudalism. In a telling moment, Rostow told a chamber of commerce meeting in Mexico City that the "development of nations" was "a little like the development of human beings." Societies in the "childhood" of modernization could choose to imitate the world's advanced nations. Just as it was possible to identify and categorize the problems experienced by "an infant of nine months; a child of five; an adolescent of fourteen; a young man of twenty-one," Rostow professed, "the study of economics . . . consists primarily in identifying the sequence of problems to be overcome and the kinds of efforts to solve them which succeeded or failed at different times in different nations."[31]

Alliance planners habitually proclaimed certain societies and nations "models" for democratic modernization. Just as chemists and physicists formulate models to understand molecular behavior, so social scientists identified or constructed examples of progressive societal change. Given Rostow's extracurricular interest in child psychology, the term also appears to have been linked to the concept of "role model," an authority figure or peer whose exemplary behavior warrants emulation. In Latin America, national leaders drawn from the democratic Left tended to win special acclaim. President Romulo Betancourt of Venezuela, a Christian Democrat who opposed both right-wing dictatorship and left-wing radicalism, ranked as a favorite in the Kennedy White House.[32] Others included President Alberto Camargo Lleras, the recently elected moderate reformer in Colombia, and José Pepe Figueres, the father of Costa Rica's 1948 democratic revolution.[33]

Puerto Rico also stood among the most beloved junior partners. Muñoz met with Kennedy in Washington just days before his inauguration, with the two men agreeing "to take measures to make Puerto Rico a meeting place and workshop for the United States and its Latin American neighbors for solving mutual problems and planning great achievements."[34] Berle, who served on the presidential task force that designed the alliance, wrote in the *Saturday Review* of Muñoz's early days as a poet and declared his "greatest poetic achievement" to be the creation of the associated free state as an alternative to either independence or colonial status "when other emerging colonies were following nationalist will-o'-wisps."[35] Historian and presidential aide Arthur Schlesinger Jr. later wrote, "The Puerto Rican experience, indeed, was an important source of ideas behind the Alliance."[36]

The modeling proved defective. Rather than offering a unified and transferable experience for others, each of the showcased states possessed a unique political, economic, and cultural past. Venezuela was an oil-producing state that had only recently rid itself of an oppressive military dictatorship. For a host of historical reasons, Costa Rica boasted a larger middle class than its Central American neighbors and after its 1948 revolution largely dismantled its military, implemented a modern welfare state, and enjoyed decades of electoral stability. Colombia, by contrast, never fully recovered from "la violencia," the decade of political violence that commenced in the same year as Costa Rica's democratic revolution, and the political peace of the early 1960s turned out to be ephemeral. Puerto Rico enjoyed special access to U.S. investment funds and markets as a commonwealth state and had evolved a popularly backed mixed economy.[37]

None of the various models had developed in perfect accord with the principles of Rostovian modernization. Each had doctored and manipulated its capitalist economy, and each had struggled with a degree of social, racial, and economic inequality unknown to either the United States or modern Western Europe. Most important, the various states encountered a common colonial and postcolonial legacy that vastly overshadowed the Cold War as a threat to social and economic well-being. All had suffered the denial of sovereignty for three centuries under Spanish rule and had endured U.S. hegemony in the twentieth century. Each had been left on its own to negotiate the shoals of imperialism.

For Kennedyites, the inherent tyranny of empire constituted the elephant in the Oval Office. Sincere talk of human rights, social justice, and development did not include probing analysis of the history of U.S. empire in Latin America. The two Puerto Rican officials brought aboard the administration's Latin American team, Morales Carrión and Moscoso, reflected Washington's pride of stewardship. According to conventional wisdom, the United States had practiced an exceptional brand of colonialism whose light touch allowed acts of altruism to complement pursuit of self-interest. The Puerto Rican contingent tread lightly on the myth. Morales Carrión occasionally counseled his colleagues that to succeed, the alliance had to "be wedded to Latin American nationalism," but he felt compelled to soft-pedal his commentary.[38] Although Moscoso indulged in the apocalyptic rhetoric of modernization, he acknowledged that the Puerto Rican experience was "not a panacea or literal model for developing areas."[39]

The Alliance for Progress addressed the perceived needs of the Cold War moment but glossed over the history of empire, an omission that doomed the experiment in soft power. Even before Kennedy's one thousand days had begun to fade into a tragic memory, the tried-and-true mechanisms of hard power regained ascendancy. The White House extended diplomatic recognition to governments established by military coup, including Peru in 1962 and the Dominican Republic in 1963, and the flow of U.S. military aid to dictatorships went full steam ahead. Covert intervention unseated popular leftist regimes, as in the case of British Guiana in the mid-1960s.

Tourism hype alone did not lead the American people and their government to misread the hemisphere. But it played an important function as a determinant of cultural discourse. If Cuban tourism had constituted a nightmare, U.S. tourism in Puerto Rico had been sold as a dream come true. Commonwealth officials had orchestrated the merchandising effort, hoping to diversify the island's economy, establish an image and identity, and loosen or at least recast the bonds of dependency. Kennedy officials appropriated much of the advertisement and became its most devout believers.

It is hard to say what kind of tourist the writer Hunter S. Thompson might have been in real life, but the semiautobiographical Paul Kemp, the narrator-journalist of Thompson's *The Rum Diary*, was hardly a model for virtuous tourist behavior and certainly not a poster child for the alliance. Kemp and his associates often subjected Puerto Rican service workers to violent mood swings, cursed local unionists, relished barroom brawls, and of course boozed to the point of fear and loathing. Kemp described the island as awash in U.S. capitalists and hucksters following the money trail but also evidenced an inkling that the oasis was a mirage. Working for an English-language newspaper owned by a burned-out ex-communist named Lotterman, Kemp mused,

> At the time the U.S. State Department was calling Puerto Rico—"*America's advertisement in the Caribbean—living proof that capitalism can work in Latin America*." The people who had come down there to do the proving saw themselves as heroes and missionaries, bringing the holy message of Free Enterprise to the jíbaros. . . . Lotterman simply couldn't cope with it. He went out of his way to attack anything that smelled even faintly of the political left, because he knew he'd be crucified if he didn't. On the other hand, he was a slave to the free-wheeling Commonwealth government whose U.S. subsidies were not only supporting half the new industries on the island, but were paying for most of the *News* advertising. It was a nasty bind—not just for Lotterman, but for a good many others. In order to make money they had to deal with the government, but to deal with the government was to condone "creeping socialism"—which was not exactly compatible with their missionary work.[40]

Trouble in Paradise: Cultural Negotiation and the Everyday Life of Empire

Alliance planners might have gained a fuller understanding of the Puerto Rican model had they studied the visitor-host arrangement and scrutinized the everyday life of the empire. For American tourists and the travel industry's promoters, modernization represented not an abstract sociological theory but a cultural environment in which free enterprise, technology, comfort, and personal security prevailed over natural and social chaos. In the early postwar years, to be "modern" was to be American or at least profoundly influenced by the American way of life. By celebrating Puerto Rico's advance, northern visitors applauded their own national identity, and U.S. political and business leaders added another dimension to Cold War propaganda and public relations.

Most Puerto Ricans aspired to a modern way of life but sought to do so on their terms rather than those imposed by foreign capital and foreign tourists. Despite the commonwealth's Cold War alignment with the United States and its continued political subservience, Puerto Rican resistance to U.S. consumer and cultural power stiffened as the tourist presence grew. In contrast to Puerto Rican discourses on tourism during the early 1950s, which had been dominated by policymakers, intellectuals, and journalists, expressions of discomfort and annoyance toward the tourist hordes sprang up at the grassroots level during the 1960s, pervading San Juan and most of the island.

As the Condado exploded in vacationers and souvenirs, many San Juan residents, much like the citizens of 1950s Havana, complained about overbuilding, congestion, and just plain bad taste. Signs and billboards hanging outside shacks advertised car, boat, and motor scooter rentals, ice-cold beer, and even discounted hairpieces at Sal's Wig Center on Ashford Avenue. In addition to high-rise hotels, condominium buildings made of glass and concrete, usually occupied by local residents, blotted out the ocean views. One government report noted that "specific criticisms have been leveled at the 'Chinese-wall' aspect of hotel developments along the beach and the 'concrete-jungle' appearance of the Condado area in general." Glaring lights, incompatible mixed land use, and a general sense of chaos provoked lament over the shoreline's disappearing beauty.[41]

By the mid-1960s, water pollution had become another problem, a consequence of storm sewers into which houses, apartment buildings, and hotels discharged sewage. Signs prohibiting swimming occasionally appeared on San Juan's beaches and diminished the city's tropical aura. Discarded beverage cans and trash further tarnished appearances.[42] Modern ecotourism and the commodification of environmental protection still lay two decades in the future, but tourism had begun to take a nasty toll on San Juan's natural environment.

Automobile traffic thickened and grew noisier and more dangerous. Letters to local newspapers expressed a general fraying of nerves over traffic jams and automobile exhaust, especially within the restaurant- and hotel-filled Condado. As early as June 1956, the *Island Times* reported a historic marker: the island's one hundredth auto fatality for the year.[43] Urban crime soared, and police raids occasionally yielded large hauls of heroin and marijuana. The *Island Times* observed in late 1963 that "marauding teen-age thugs are degrading many communities with brutal sidewalk muggings and assaults on defenseless and elderly citizens" and that arrests of persons under age fourteen had steadily risen since 1960.[44]

The crime problem extended beyond urban centers, and Puerto Ricans were not the only plaintiffs. Northerners who ventured beyond poolside often felt lost and endangered. One traveler wrote to the editors of the *Times* that on a trip to the countryside, he and his family had stopped in a quaint village only to be greeted by "cold stares" from the local peasants, tugged at by beggars who "could not speak a word of English," and unable to find a suitable restaurant. The family members returned to their car to discover a group of teenage boys breaking into the vehicle.[45] Petty crime might not always have been tied to the tourist invasion, but few visitors seemed to have contemplated the possibility that they were unwitting participants in a protracted contest between colonizer and colonized.

Clashes between tourists and hosts escalated. While policymakers categorized the hospitality industry as a part of the "service sector," hotel and restaurant workers sneered that it might more accurately be labeled the "servility sector." Wages and benefits varied widely in the industry, from well-paid unionized employment to the lowest rung on the shoe-shine ladder, but aggregate data demonstrate that hotel worker wages rose from $3,028 in 1959 to $5,042 in 1967 mainly as a consequence of competition for bragging rights and membership between the thirty-five-hundred-member Hotel and Restaurant Workers Union and the two-thousand-member Teamsters. Union agreements and legislative fiat, moreover, guaranteed a number of benefits, including two weeks' paid vacation, fifteen days of sick leave annually, paid holidays, medical/surgical coverage, and life insurance. Most hospitality jobs nonetheless carried a stigma that equated tourism with colonialism. Some hotel workers even left their jobs for lower-paying positions in manufacturing and commerce.[46] Tourist complaints about slow or inattentive service exacerbated tensions. "It appears that efficiency and service in these eating places," one tourist griped, "are missing words in their vocabulary."[47]

Particularly abrasive to Puerto Rican sensibilities was the tourist's frequent disregard for the Spanish language. Since the earliest days of U.S. colonialism, inhabitants had resented the imposition of English in government and education. Tourism added new layers of complexity to the linguistic divide, and visitor-host negotiations often became lost in translation. "The trouble with you Americans," one correspondent announced in the English-language *Puerto Rico World Journal*, "is that when you come to Puerto Rico you want to be understood in your own language, but don't give a damn to learn our language."[48] In response, an indignant North American wrote that the island's use of U.S. currency accorded him special language rights. Until the commonwealth minted its own coins, he steamed, you "better damn well learn the language of the country that feeds you."[49]

The language issue percolated all the way up to La Fortaleza. Governor Muñoz was moved on one occasion to write to the Hilton management about a recent trip to the Castellano Hilton in Spain, where he noticed menus printed in Spanish as well as English. Could a similar practice be implemented in San Juan? The bilingual menu, he observed, not only would be convenient in a bilingual society but would also be appreciated by tourists as a point of interest.[50] Hilton menus nevertheless remained solely in English.

Of all the cultural affronts that accompanied tourism, few touched as sensitive a chord as racism. Like Mexico and Cuba, Puerto Rican society had never been free of racial prejudice. From the days of slavery, upper- and middle-class circles had shunned interracial marriages. In the twentieth century, political leaders and academics downplayed to the point of extinction the island's African heritage. Yet Puerto Rico had no history of rigid, racial separation. The tourist business threatened to extend Jim Crow, introduced by military units after the U.S. takeover of the island at the turn of the twentieth century, to other areas of Puerto Rican life. In late 1949, rumors swirled that the Caribe Hilton would implement the color bar. The *Puerto Rico Weekly Libre*, a Marxist *independentista* organ, greeted the hotel's opening with a front-page illustration of the impressive new building, in the likeness of a battleship, flying a large flag that read "Jim Crow."[51]

The Caribe did not adopt racial segregation, but reports periodically surfaced throughout the 1950s and early 1960s that other hotels and inns had done so or had attempted to do so. American expatriate journalist Earl Parker Hanson reported in 1955 that while most of San Juan's hotels accepted African American customers for accommodations and meals, a number of hotel beaches prohibited black sunbathers and swimmers. African Americans might "rent rooms, eat in the dining room, drink in the bars, play in the casinos, tip the bellboys," but they might not "sun themselves on the hotel's beaches or swim in the hotel's ocean."[52]

Mandated racial separation represented only one manifestation of racism. North American dissatisfaction with service in hotels and restaurants at times gave way to sweeping generalizations about national character. After attending the grand opening of the Caribe Hilton in late 1949, Carl Hilton penned a scathing letter to his brother, Conrad, complaining that the native workers seemed to have a warped view of service, exhibiting little sense of timing and discipline. The hired "peons" were "child-like or even dog-like; it is not what you say when directing their efforts it is your tone of voice that counts." At the same time, Hilton theorized that Puerto Ricans suffered an "inferiority complex" that made them extremely sensitive to criticism and prone to "quit and sulk." "It may be better to pay them weekly rather than twice a month," he advised, "because two weeks pay is a hell of a lot of dough for one of those 'pelaos' to hold in his hands; it may cause him to think he won't have to work again for a long time."[53]

Culture clash often occurred on an individual basis and received only limited press. Although much of the tourist district remained outside the daily lives of most Puerto Ricans, it did bring Yankees and locals together in the uniquely intimate setting provided by the beach. In a country alive with populism, proposals to privatize the coastline always constituted, as one government official put it, "a very delicate matter." By the early 1960s, the Caribe Hilton and the Condado Beach Hotel in San Juan and the Rockefeller-owned Dorado Beach complex just west of the city still ranked as the island's only accommodations with private beach rights.[54] Consequently, at the public seaside, Anglos and Puerto Ricans of different classes, races, and gender and in various stages of undress came into unusually intimate contact.[55]

Since their opening to both sexes in the late nineteenth century, public beaches, summer resorts, and swimming pools in the United States had produced dual effects. The new public spaces eroded boundaries between women and men, freeing women of restrictive, Victorian standards of decorum that associated mixed-sex recreation with promiscuity. But public beaches and the like also led to increasing incidents of harassment that required the negotiation of new rules of etiquette.[56] Puerto Rico's 1960s beachfront at times became a negotiating site. Although popular tourist literature historically depicted Puerto Rico as an alluring and welcoming female, U.S. visitors, particularly women, frequently complained of sexual harassment on San Juan's beaches. Most common were complaints of catcalls and stares, but charges of assault and rape arose as well. The Condado beachfront, one writer to an island newspaper complained, had become a meeting ground for "degenerates" who "are exposing themselves, masturbating, saying ugly, filthy things to women, beating up women, stealing, and making a general nuisance of themselves."[57]

Although many Puerto Ricans, women and men, welcomed the loosening restraints and adjusted willingly, some struck a defensive tone. In a letter to the *Island Times*, one local woman expressed disgust at the habits of American women who walked the beaches alone in "tight bathing suits" and then complained about being harassed: "Do Puerto Rican gentlemen let their women walk on the beaches alone?," she asked. The answer no implied that blame should be assigned to the victim of harassment. The correspondent added a discourse on multiculturalism: "Remember, you are a guest and a foreigner in this country and therefore abide with the customs and culture."[58]

During the late 1950s, while tourists and hosts confronted the human body and contested cultural constructions of sexuality at surfside, U.S. pharmaceutical companies and the Food and Drug Administration tested hormonal contraception (the birth control pill) on unknowing Puerto Rican women in commonwealth health clinics. Although feminists in both the United States and Puerto Rico had long advocated birth control, colonial race and gender relations also shaped the testing methods. U.S. colonial officials had tended to view working-class Puerto Rican women as submissive wives, mothers, lovers, and prostitutes of mixed race, unwilling or unable to forgo procreation. In the early commonwealth era, U.S. and Puerto Rican planners viewed these "dangerous mothers," or Madonna/whores, as an impediment to efforts to stem population growth and spur economic growth.[59] Thus, when a group of U.S. scientists led by Harvard University's Gregory Pincus, seeking to elude religious and cultural criticisms on the mainland proposed large-scale human experiments of contraceptives in 1955, Puerto Rican officials welcomed the researchers to paradise.

The tests went forward at more than sixty low-income health clinics, where, contrary to myth, working-class women embraced the chance to regulate births and improve their lives. Providers in clinical cultural contact zones, however, did not inform the women that they were participants in a human experiment. Eager to achieve an effectiveness rate of 100 percent, Pincus turned to the G. D. Searle pharmaceutical company to provide pills that included high dosages of estrogen, produced under the brand name Enovid, shown in laboratory tests to sustain high levels of effectiveness in preventing pregnancy. Among the Puerto Rican subjects, Enovid also inflicted severe side effects, including nausea, dizziness, headaches, and evidence of reproductive cancer. Although some scientists and clinicians expressed concern, the trials continued.[60]

Back in the tourist districts, another aspect of the empire's sexual life proceeded apace. Puerto Rico never achieved the fame accorded to Cuba as a free zone for sexual license. Studies showed that the majority of visitors to the island were upper-income married men, a sizable portion of whom traveled with their spouses or other family members.[61] Locals nonetheless frequently observed North American men, tourists and sailors, in the company of prostitutes. A male staff writer for El Mundo decried how few U.S. tourists understood the accepted place of the prostitute in Puerto Rican male culture, which tolerated within limits discreet relationships between married men and women hired for sex. Americans, he complained, either self-righteously condemned the practice or, having been removed from the constraints of U.S. society, openly and randomly sought "women of the streets."[62]

The Condado in particular became a favored haunt for streetwalking prostitutes, predominantly Puerto Rican but also migrant workers from other
areas of Latin America. When San Juan municipal authorities officials cracked
down on the street traffic in June 1968 with an ordinance mandating stricter
fines for solicitation, the business divided and dispersed: working-class elements of the trade relocated to designated city bars and the dock area of Old
San Juan, while elite practitioners, including some from the United States and
Europe, moved indoors to the city's hotel casinos to service a high-income
clientele. Outspoken Puerto Rican opponents of gambling claimed that eliminating the casinos posed the only answer to the prostitution problem. Business interests and the commonwealth government resisted that solution. A
prohibition of gambling might divert up to seventy thousand visitors annually
to other Caribbean-Atlantic destinations.[63]

Sexuality and cultural identity intersected at multiple levels. Some contributors to the editorial pages set their sights on the presence of homosexuals in
the Condado. Beginning in Old San Juan in the 1950s, Puerto Rico had
developed one of the few gay scenes in the Caribbean. As tourism flourished,
it contributed to the creation of a small homosexual subculture of hotels,
restaurants, and clubs that catered mainly to North Americans. Although
most Puerto Ricans seemed willing to tolerate the subculture, it at times
conflicted with the island's Catholic patriarchal value system. One concerned
citizen who identified himself as a descendant of an old Spanish family
lamented the turning of the capital into a "slum, a haven for all kinds of
undesirable characters," including "the tight pant wiggle-walking homosexuals and their counterpart, the lesbians, with their 'I don't give a damn'
behavior."[64]

The harshest and certainly among the most clever denunciations of tourism appeared in the Spanish-language proindependence newspaper *Claridad*, more often than not in the form of political cartoons. The nationalist
organ regularly published drawings of Yankee tourists decked out in comical
tourist attire (Bermuda shorts, flowered dresses, straw hats, and cameras),
always ostentatious and demanding.[65] One particularly caustic representation featured a tourist-filled hand-pulled rickshaw driven by a dark-skinned
Puerto Rican servant. As the driver struggled up and down San Juan's hilly
avenues and streets, the tourists passed "McKinley Street," "Pikes Peak
Street," and "Gannet Peak Street." The caricatured tourists exclaimed, "Estos
Nombres Siendo Muy Perecios a los Que Tenieimos en U.S.A." (These names
sound so similar to those we have in the U.S.A.) and "Esta Gente No Tie-
niendo Nada De Imagination" (These people have no imagination). The

cartoon insultingly inferred that Puerto Rico had no identity other than that bequeathed to it by the colonial power.

Tourism, Identity, and Postcolonialism

Antitourism sentiment ran broad and deep across the island throughout the 1960s and into the 1970s but was inconsistently layered. In the end, it did not produce the type of cataclysm that subsumed Cuba in the late 1950s. While everyday discourse on tourism continued to stoke strong opinions, one of the more ironic features of the island's political life during the tumultuous 1960s was that conservative advocates of statehood, who championed rapid tourism growth and alignment with the mainland's Republican Party, replaced the left-leaning *independentistas* as the most serious competitor to the Partido Populare Democratica (PPD). The pro-statehood Partido Nuevo Progresista de Puerto Rico (New Progressive Party, PNP), known prior to 1960 as the Republican Statehood Party, steadily gained ground in legislative elections and in a 1967 plebiscite on political status rallied nearly 40 percent of voters to the statehood cause. The independence option, in contrast, won the support of less than 1 percent of the electorate.[66]

The rightward shift made Muñoz's PPD, the creators of the island's travel structures, the commonwealth's main guardian against unbridled Cuban-style tourism. In January 1960, as San Juan hotels turned down customers for lack of space, statehood leader Luis Ferré savaged the PPD-led government for "dragging its heels" on tourism development and failing to take full advantage of Cuba's tourism collapse. When Muñoz defended his policy of planned growth as the prudent way to wean Puerto Rico from dependence on sugar, Ferré shot back, "Tourism will solve Puerto Rico's problems" and urged the government to move "full steam ahead."[67]

The agile Muñoz administration continued to encourage hotel and condominium construction along the Condado and eastward to Isla Verde. The Hotel Corporation of America opened the Miramar Charter house in 1960; Holiday Inn, Shoreham, and Sheraton quickly followed; and Fomento predicted—accurately, as it turned out—that the island would host more than one million tourists and rake in $175 million in gross receipts annually by 1970. In almost the same breath, Muñoz officials insisted that theirs was a deliberate approach, aimed to ease San Juan's blight and overcrowding. Tourist numbers had risen more than 40 percent in the last two years, and one government spokesperson observed, "We can't handle another 40% and frankly we don't want it."[68]

During the hotly contested 1968 gubernatorial election, which brought the first statehood government to power, Moscoso even adopted the language of the industry's staunchest critics. In "Shangri-La or Hamburger Heaven?," the economist admitted that San Juan had suffered overdevelopment. Condado, previously "one of most beautiful and pleasant" spots in all of Puerto Rico, had become "an almost continuous clifflike mass of cement on both sides," where "garish hamburger stands and other tawdry small shops" dominated. Yet the ever-optimistic Moscoso concluded that if government—presumably led by the PPD—conscientiously regulated the industry, travel would still prove itself an asset to Puerto Rico's economic and cultural well-being.[69]

To maintain its populist image, the Muñoz government also expanded free public recreational spaces. Even in the fast-developing and real-estate-rich Isla Verde beach area, the administration forged ahead, opening a $350,000 public bathing area in the summer of 1960.[70] The following year, commonwealth legislators approved a new 5 percent recreational tax on all tourist hotel bills, with the revenue raised dedicated to the building and maintenance of public parks and beaches.[71]

Muñoz and Fomento also perfected their blending of tourism and identity politics. By the mid-1960s, the rehabilitation of Old San Juan had reached an advanced stage, with some 120 restored historic structures complementing the Condado's concrete jungle.[72] Relieving some of the pressure on beachfront Condado, the historic 115-room El Convento hotel, a former colonial-era Carmelite convent, opened in January 1962, offering "authentic architecture of Old Spain in the New World," the *Island Times* editorialized. "Probably one of the monumental restorations in the Western Hemisphere," declared the *New York Times.*[73]

With an enlarged budget of $1.2 million by 1968, the IPRC extended more generous subsidies to local artists to resurrect and commodify the island's folk art. Wood carvings of *los tres reyes* (the New Testament's three kings), *santos* (likenesses of the saints), hand-sewn needlework, and African-inspired carnival masks gained prominent display in Old San Juan's souvenir and gift shops, whence bargain-hungry mainlanders could cart them home. Art galleries and bookstores filled in the district's colonial storefronts, as did popular restaurants, bakeries, and bars. Festivals commemorating the feast of San Juan de Bautista, the city's patron saint, and the annual celebration of the African *bomba* in Loiza de Aldea, located just east of San Juan, catered to foreign tourists and Puerto Ricans alike.[74]

PNP leaders and other statehood advocates lambasted the various identity projects as manifestations of a chauvinistic "incipient nationalism." The critics ridiculed the palming off of peasant handicrafts as art and belittled the promotion of an "invented" multicultural past.[75] "Culture is not static," Ferré hammered, "but rather progresses, and Puerto Rican culture today is a culture that came with roots in Spain and has already grown roots in the Anglo-Saxon culture."[76] The vitriol filled newspaper editorials and stirred university classroom discussions. Professor Rafael Rivera Garcia of the University of Puerto Rico's fine arts department applauded the reconstruction of Spanish Old San Juan but questioned the government's glorification of the *bomba* and the presence of African patterns on the IPRC's official seal.[77]

A handful of North Americans joined in, usually voicing agreement with the statehood activists. Expat commentator Earl Hanson joined statehood enthusiasts in criticizing the government's "cultural nationalism." A culture is not just language, art, and history, the transplanted Yankee preached, but "a way of looking at things, a way of living and working together."[78] Historian Daniel Boorstin, an outspoken critic of modern mass tourism, weighed in as well. Writing in the *Yale Review*, Boorstin castigated Puerto Rican officials for their invention of an artificial past and their "obsession with status." Calling the island's "lack of history" a blessing, he advised the Muñoz government to work instead on solving the island's social problems. Giving Rostow's theory of economic stages a cultural spin, Boorstin wrote, "In Puerto Rico, there is a growing communal self-consciousness, an impulse to self-discover. It sometimes seems a kind of adolescent *Weltanschauung*."[79]

The IPRC's critics correctly assessed the fluid nature of culture and the obvious presence of Iberian and Yankee influences in Puerto Rican society. Moreover, they grasped the many ways in which the state had appropriated indigenous and African symbols to advance Muñoz's political agenda. But they underestimated the power of a popular memory that centered on collective resentment toward colonialism in all of its manifestations. The canonization of indigenous and African history and myth and its fusion with Puerto Rican anticolonialism helped crystallize cultural constructions that countered the cultural and consumer power of tourists and the ongoing U.S. presence as a whole.[80]

The attacks probably facilitated Munoz's political tightrope walk. Despite its electoral decline, *independentista* sentiment remained alive and strong on the island. Polls showed that the public remained emotionally attached to the idea of nationhood and often sympathized with militant nationalist groups even while disapproving of their tactics.[81] And in light of the rise of a popular statehood movement, advocates of nationhood more often than not joined forces with the PPD. The Spanish-language *Claridad*, for example, turned its satirical pens on the PNP's market-oriented policies and its love affair with tourists. One editorial invoked the widespread notion that tourism bred colonial subservience: "They would have us serve the community merely as laundresses, dishwashers, elevator operators, garbage collectors, and shoe shiners for the comfort of the Americans who come to the little island."[82] Another article printed shortly after Hawaii's absorption into the Union charged that under Ferré's leadership, Puerto Rico would suffer the "Hawaiian syndrome whereby the native population would be assigned bit parts as museum exhibits.[83] "Anuncio!!," read one mock classified advertisement, "Se Vende una Isla con 2,400,000 Habitantes" (Will Sell an Island with 2.4 million Inhabitants).[84]

Most U.S. tourists continued to seem to soak up Puerto Rico's foreign ambience. In addition to beachcombing, cultural sightseeing flourished. Old San Juan's sixteenth-century fortress, El Morro, visited by nearly 70 percent of all vacationers who arrived on the island by airline, registered as a "must see." Closely resembling its cousin in Havana, El Morro sat high above the blue Atlantic at the western edge of the old city, guarding the entrance to San Juan Harbor. From the ancient fort, visitors could easily traipse to La Fortaleza and then a few blocks south into the heart of Old San Juan.[85] Allene Agor Deiver's letter to the *Island Times* spoke for many tourists: "When I travel I try to get to know the language, culture, and society."[86]

The Muñoz administration occasionally buttressed its nationalist credentials by placing itself mildly in opposition to Washington's increasingly confrontational Cold War policies. Following the Bay of Pigs fiasco in April 1961 and the U.S.-assisted assassination of the right-wing Dominican dictator Rafael Trujillo in June, the governor met with President Kennedy and counseled against additional U.S. militarism, suggesting instead a policy of sending nonmilitary assistance to prodemocracy anti-Castro and anti-Trujillo groups.[87] When the Dominican military grabbed power in a fall 1963 coup, Muñoz cabled Kennedy, "I unreservedly favor taking a hard line toward the usurping government of Santo Domingo. No recognition. No economic aid." But contrary to alliance principles, the administration granted recognition in a bid to extinguish the island's unrest. The strategy failed, and two years later the U.S. Marines landed on the shores of Santo Domingo to forestall a civil war.[88]

Governor Muñoz vigorously opposed U.S. Defense Department plans to expropriate the Puerto Rican island of Vieques, located just seven miles east of the larger, main island. The U.S. Navy had begun munitions tests and military practice at Vieques in 1938 and in 1941 initiated the expropriation of large swaths of territory. Following Cuba's revolution, U.S. military leaders went so far as to recommend that the entire island be seized as a military base and training area. At that point, Muñoz intervened and pleaded with Kennedy that the land seizure would uproot eight thousand inhabitants, violate the Puerto Rican constitution, and inspire anti-U.S. activism in Puerto Rico and across the Caribbean. "Puerto Rico has only recently emerged from colonial status," he argued, and the United States "is still charged by some people with colonial rule over Puerto Rico, a charge which is unjustified but can be made effective if given a dramatic symbol."[89] Muñoz's personal appeal helped stymie the proposal, but nearly two-thirds of the island remained under the domain of the U.S. military and a sore point in U.S.-Puerto Rican relations.

Given the widespread presence of nationalist sensitivities across the still-colonized island, it is not surprising that the PPD's economic and cultural policies, including its tourism agenda, maintained popular support. Thus, when Ferré and the PNP finally took the governor's mansion in 1968, they chose not to dismantle the IPRC and even reappointed its outspoken director, Ricardo Alegría. And in 1969, the IPRC expanded its multicultural mission when it launched what became the popular annual National Indigenous Festival.[90]

Nor did Governor Ferré gain an opportunity vastly to expand the tourism sector. By 1968, the commonwealth's travel sector, with its nearly ten thousand first-class hotel rooms and one million travelers annually, had produced ten thousand jobs and generated roughly two hundred million dollars annually.[91] But the industry suddenly slumped in 1969 and 1970, when the tally of arriving guests declined. Panicked analysts at the time attributed the slowdown to the Condado's unsightly overdevelopment, the high price of Puerto Rico's hotels and restaurants relative to newer, less regulated Caribbean resorts, competition with cut-rate airfares to Europe, and a firebombing incident in San Juan that accompanied the seating of the statehood government. In retrospect, the setback appears to have been a normal feature of the cyclical global economy, somewhat more severe in the recession-prone travel industry.[92] "Tourism can be a fickle industry," the San Juan Star commented in August 1971.[93]

The scare encouraged the prostatehood government to expand funding for advertising, improve the Isla Verde airport, clean up Condado's beaches, and improve Old San Juan's dock facilities to accommodate large cruise ships. "We recognize and unequivocally adopt the basic principles that tourism is ideally suited to Puerto Rico as a permanent part of our economy," the Tourism Development Company declared in its 1971 annual report.[94] The industry nonetheless struggled through the recession-plagued 1970s and 1980s before finally recovering the following decade. By fiscal year 2001–2, the annual number of overnight nonresident visitors had grown modestly to a little more than 1.2 million, only slightly above the levels reached in the late 1960s. Cruise passenger movement, nonresident and resident combined, landed another 1.276 million land lovers at various island ports, typically for stays of a few hours.[95]

Whether ruled by the PPD or the PNP, Puerto Rico managed to avoid some of the typical shortcomings that plagued tourism promotion in many other developing countries. Although the island remained one of the three- or four-busiest tourist attractions in the Caribbean, Puerto Rican planners stayed true to their word and kept tourism income below 5 percent of the commonwealth's total gross national product.[96] Planners also assured that large numbers of the jobs in the hospitality industry did what most analysts doubted was possible: pay decent wages and benefits. While some jobs measured up to the industry's stereotypical low-wage servility, minimum-wage laws and government support for independent trade unions helped make the commonwealth's hotel workers the most highly compensated in the region, with the highest average earnings per occupied hotel room. Labor costs in Puerto Rico's hotel industry ran more than triple those in Jamaica in the late 1960s and early 1970s and four times larger than such costs in Barbados. Concomitantly, hotels operating in Puerto Rico took in the lowest rates of profit in the area—bad news for investors but a badly needed shot in the arm for Puerto Rican workers.[97]

International Tourism, Détente, and Globalization

As Puerto Rico's travel industry reacted to the vagaries of the late-twentieth century world economy, the Soviet-U.S. Cold War followed an inconsistent trajectory. The lowering of tensions that followed the Cuban Missile Crisis blossomed into an era of détente during the 1970s, followed by a reintensification of the nuclear arms race and Third World military interventions during the 1980s. All the while, the migration of capital and labor and the intensified pace of global investment and trade undermined the Cold War's ideological coherence and superpower authority. Vietnam and Cuba defied Washington's military and economic power; Afghanistan and Poland stood up to Moscow's iron hand.

By 1967, thirteen million persons worldwide spent fourteen billion dollars on travel outside of their countries of residence. U.S. tourists accounted for the lion's share of the global boom, their numbers having grown at an annual rate of 10.3 percent since 1951.[98] Alarmed by the nation's growing balance-of-payments deficit and convinced that foreign travel had become a drag on the U.S. economy, President Lyndon B. Johnson reversed the U.S. government's encouragement of world travel and launched his "See America First" campaign. In addition to a mass advertising blitz complete with images of purple mountains majesty, LBJ's program included a proposed one-hundred-dollar tax on foreign air travel. Seasoned legislator that he was, Johnson should have known better. The measure met a hostile reception on Capitol Hill, where airlines, travel agencies, and other transnational interests pulled out all the stops and killed the measure. The ASTA *Travel News* denounced the tax as a violation of the "inalienable rights of Americans to travel freely around the world" and organized a letter-writing campaign to Congress that declared the proposal "as evil as the Berlin Wall." As the age of détente approached, U.S. travelers paid little heed to the Texan's plea to stay home on the range. Consumerism easily trumped Cold War patriotism.[99]

In Latin America, the Alliance for Progress receded into popular memory. Scholars and commentators have frequently noted Camelot's eternal flame in South and Central America. John F. Kennedy became an icon in both U.S. and Latin American collective memory. As such, the thirty-fifth president's significance became as malleable as any element in popular culture and subject to a multiplicity of meanings and legacies. Photos of JFK often hang alongside those of the Pope and national heroes in Latin American homes. Perhaps because of his youth, his Catholicism, his stated commitment to social justice, his sad death, or some combination of all those factors, Kennedy and the Alliance for Progress maintained their popularity despite the enormity of the program's failure.[100]

As Kennedy and his successors lost faith in the efficacy of soft power, they increasingly tolerated or embraced military dictators and right-wing death squads to help manage the increasingly volatile empire. In 1973, with help from the Nixon-Kissinger White House, Augusto Pinochet overthrew Chile's democratically elected government and imposed his homicidal rule. Argentina's generals took power in 1976 and conducted seven years of secret war during which more than fifteen thousand coup opponents mysteriously disappeared. Right-wing death squads roamed the city streets and country roads of Central America during the 1980s bearing Washington's approval and often U.S.-issued weapons.[101]

The Bretton Woods system also veered right. As the U.S. economy shifted from a manufacturing to a service base and U.S. consumers became dependent on foreign manufacturers for their creature comforts, Keynesian modernization theory gave way to supply-side dogma. Pinochet's Chile served as a testing ground for the infamous "Chicago Boys," the South Side university economic advisers who distributed Milton Friedman's instructional booklet on tax cuts and deregulation to the dictator's financial team.[102] During the 1980s, U.S. president Ronald Reagan and British prime minister Margaret Thatcher struck what Joseph Stiglitz has called the "Washington consensus," a regimen of International Monetary Fund and World Bank policies that tied financial aid to the recipient's fiscal constraint, elimination of barriers to free trade, and privatization of public enterprises.[103]

In this bloodcurdling and socially regressive context, tourism remained a potent manifestation of U.S. soft power across the hemisphere. U.S. and increasingly other international tourists continued to wield their consumer and cultural muscle in arbitrary and offensive ways, imposing their languages and demands for service. The renewed popularity of cruise vacations in the 1970s and 1980s, with San Juan a major port of call, proved well suited to the ideological orientation of the Reagan years. International crews, often recruited from the developing world, sailed outside the reach of national labor legislation and steered clear of minimum wages and mandated benefits. For travelers, the Americanized environment of luxury ship served as the destination itself, often obviating the cultural power of Puerto Rico and other host societies.[104] The emergence of the Internet in the 1980s and 1990s enhanced the traveler's ability to investigate and plan vacation options, from airfares to hotel offerings to escort services and child prostitution rings.

Yet the tourist system still provided mechanisms, albeit imperfect, for hosts to assert themselves. In Puerto Rico, the cultural displays and festivals initiated by the PPD remained fixtures of the tourist circuit. With the Populares return to power in the mid-1980s, the commonwealth reaffirmed its government-regulated industry standards and implemented innovative state policies. For example, hotels that enacted energy conservation programs received an 11 percent reduction in their electricity bills from the government-owned utility. Even the statehood government, elected in 1994, extended government investment guarantees to stoke financing for tourism. Government was not the only agent of host power. Colleges and universities on the island launched business programs to train students for higher-level management positions in the hospitality industry. Labor unions and local entrepreneurs continued to rely on tourism growth to advance their interests.[105]

In short, the little island that had once been erroneously thought a model for enlightened colonialism and Cold War modernization had actually assembled a political economy and an identity-producing machine that anticipated late-century globalization. Rather than being utterly swallowed by U.S. and transnational power, Puerto Rico had negotiated a modicum of economic and cultural independence despite its commonwealth political status. Puerto Rico had become synonymous not only with beachfront luxury, architectural glitter, and Old World patina but also with its once ignored Taíno past and the African diaspora. Puerto Rico's concocted identity embodied many contradictions, but Moscoso grasped the essential secret of the island's success. As he explained at a tourism conference in April 1961, "In the jargon of the advertising trade, an image has been created; we have emerged from anonymity. That, for a tiny island half way across the Atlantic, is no mean accomplishment."[106]

The shifting tides of the Cold War undoubtedly helped shape postwar Puerto Rico's political economy and travel industry. The repression of radical nationalists, the war preparedness imposed on Vieques, and perhaps most of all the commonwealth's savvy public relations strategies represented important manifestations of the Cold War's influence. Puerto Rico's rise as the Caribbean's premier vacation spot, moreover, was directly tied to Cuba's collapse as a Cold War playground. Yet when viewed through the prism of international tourism, the history of the Cold War in Latin America often emerges as a series of fleeting events, some hopeful, many more horrific. Despite the prospect of Armageddon, the optimism of the Alliance for Progress, and Washington's unblushing support for some of the world's most ruthless military juntas, the most enduring contours in hemispheric relations still sprang from Latin America's colonial past, the U.S. drive for empire, and the modern era's integration of markets and identities.

The commonwealth of Puerto Rico's achievements lay not only in eclectic economic planning but in fashioning an everyday life of empire that preserved agency for visitors and hosts alike. Cold War Americans found in Puerto Rico's hotels, beaches, and swimming pools confirmation that global uplift could be achieved through consumerism rather than communism. San Juan's modern skyline, along with the advertisements that lured visitors there, conveyed an image of a Puerto Rico at one with America's faith in capital, markets, and technology. At the same time, Puerto Ricans invented a sense of self rooted in a glorified multicultural past. In contrast to Cuba's sad experience, tourism provided Puerto Rico a degree of negotiating space that enabled it to manipulate U.S. hegemony, assert its power, and communicate its existence both at home and abroad.

Puerto Rico's tourism success can be overstated. Tourism, after all, represented a newly installed element of empire that rapidly infiltrated the daily lives of growing numbers of local inhabitants. The Condado's overtaxed infrastructure, discarded litter bobbing in the surf, and the vacationer's wealth and self-centeredness could make empire more of an intimate, cultural affront than when it had consisted primarily of military bases and sugar plantations. Tourism nonetheless constituted a softer power that Puerto Rico's activist state, local elites, organized labor, and even local beachgoers challenged and contained. Visitors and hosts negotiated services and prices, beach privileges, language and idioms, and cultural norms. Tourism on the island thus simultaneously reinforced and undermined identities, blurred the line between the inside and the outside of the empire, and contributed to the globalization of culture in a mobile world. By the end of the twentieth century, the outcome could be simultaneously applauded and lamented by hosts and guests alike.

The Puerto Rican people and even their government have not yet sorted out their ambivalence toward tourism and tourists. Rather, a mutually offsetting appreciation and disdain for U.S. visitors seems to have become a permanent fixture of Puerto Rican culture. The tourist industry built over two decades has granted enough latitude to accommodate both sentiments, and Muñoz became adept at juggling all sentiments. Praised abroad for abandoning narrow nationalisms and raising Puerto Rico by its bootstraps, the governor also used tourism to construct and popularize an idealized national identity within the confines of a colonial, commonwealth existence—no small feat.

Conclusion

The U.S. hemispheric empire has been shaped by many hands and by many imaginations. Throughout the twentieth century, the empire's life has played out every day in some of its most crowded public spaces: parks, beaches, museums, cathedrals, airports and railroad stations, and hotel lobbies and restaurants. In these arenas, travelers and hosts have encountered, observed, insulted, admired, and reimagined one another. Together, they have enriched the empire's increasingly complex everyday life and helped to construct the transnational cultural context in which political economy and diplomacy took place.

Comparative analysis brings into focus the various ways in which the process has worked. U.S. visitors and their southern hosts first met one another on a mass scale in postrevolutionary Mexico. Bartenders and would-be cowboys, prostitutes and clients, casino owners and local labor unions, Lone Eagles and poets, border officials and railroad managers, archeologists and history buffs, collectively wielding a veritable arsenal of soft powers, entered into two decades of skirmishing and negotiation. They did not calculate national debt payments, transfer arms, or delineate geographic borders. They left such matters to government aides. Instead, their summit meetings established patterns of production and consumption; leisure and employment; race, class, and gender relations; and national identities.

International scholars are accustomed to probing identities during times of war and political crisis, when patriotism and fear often lead combatant societies to exaggerate their uniqueness and idealize their national character. An examination of peoples immersed in the rituals of modern leisure yields a more complex and arguably more well-rounded understanding of modern imagined communities. Let loose in cultural contact zones, tourists often experience pangs of insecurity and fits of chauvinism. At the same time, many unwind, peel off layers of stress, pursue educational opportunities and self-improvement, and relax traditional social and cultural taboos. In so doing, they often discover and attempt to interpret at least the most salient elements of the host's way of life. Hosts often approach more powerful visitors with caution, simultaneously ingratiate and assert themselves, educate the foreign intruder, but also open their own minds to newly imported cultural attitudes and values. U.S. tourists have indeed helped to Americanize the rest of the world, but they and those who have hosted them have also internationalized America.

In interwar Mexico, visitors and hosts alike evidenced growing awareness of the international moment. The emerging aviation revolution, railroad and automobile links, global depression, and world war certainly brought the distant neighbors into closer alignment, as did domestic enthusiasms for reform and social engineering. Tourist relations allowed Mexican hosts to negotiate a subtle redistribution of power without disrupting the essential structures of empire. When the casinos, saloons, and brothels along the border shut down, U.S. tourists did not lose interest in things Mexican but instead delved further south, reaching to Mexico City and points beyond to indulge in less unilateral and more equitable encounters of empire. Governments in Mexico City and Washington soon sanctioned and replicated the rapprochement through the diplomacy of the Good Neighbor.

Tourist power, however, has not always played out benevolently. An army of individuals and interest groups grounded U.S.-Cuban tourist relations fully in the system of inequality and tyranny that had already emerged out of the Platt Amendment, the U.S. naval presence, and North American domination of the island's sugar industry. North American office workers and churchgoers, employees of the U.S. Navy, airline companies, hotel chains, and mobsters built a tourist environment that catered to pleasure seekers. More authoritarian than Mexico's one-party electoral system, the Batista regime denied agency to exactly those Cubans who might have contained tourist excesses. There was no substantive Good Neighbor policy toward Cuba. Instead, the traditional bonds of empire tightened, hegemonic habits dictated that the people of Cuba be denied their civil rights so that northern visitors might enjoy unfettered freedom. The monstrous disconnect between Cuban aspirations for sovereign identity and the reality of oppression ultimately fired the revolution that brought Fidel Castro to power, led to the U.S.-Cuban diplomatic standoff, and subverted the Castro government's efforts to reconfigure the visitor-host arrangement.

Hosts at times asserted themselves through confrontation, as in postrevolutionary Mexico and revolutionary Cuba. In other cases, an amalgam of finesse, deception, and theatrics empowered the host society. Puerto Rico's commonwealth status can be best understood as a mythical decolonization that fell far short of sovereignty. Commonwealth officials understood the fiction but used their limited autonomy to diversify the island's economy and fiction but used their limited autonomy to diversify the island's economy and establish a carefully planned and contained tourism industry. Tourism represented much more than a source of income; it offered a stage on which to proclaim Puerto Rico's identity, independent of what had been imposed by Spanish and U.S. overlords. The performance proved convincing enough to make U.S. leaders and the press showcase the island's development as an accomplishment to be replicated across the empire. At the same time, along Puerto Rico's beaches, in charming Old San Juan, and in hotels and restaurants, visitors and hosts entered a more honest process of culture clash and negotiation. Local hotel workers, union organizers, beachgoers, waiters, journalists, and others asserted themselves in countless ways and kept up the pressure on government officials to do likewise.

Skeptics might question the reality of both tourist and host agency. Once put into place, the travel industry and the transnational interests that feed it certainly develop their own perpetual motion. Like the world economy itself, the tourist system is propelled forward by technology, capital, and consumerism. Like the fashion industry, it feeds on mass culture, advertising, and fads. The three studies presented here show that if allowed to operate freely, these forces may career recklessly, disrupt cultures, and dehumanize societies. However, the Mexican and Puerto Rican examples demonstrate that when supervised by a community-based or at least community-responsive authority, these forces can promote economic betterment, national confidence, and even a modicum of international understanding.

Skeptics might also consider the confluence of tourism, identity, and foreign policy to have been coincidental rather than determinative. Analysts of culture, after all, cannot demonstrate cause-and-effect relationships with scientific rigor. To demonstrate tourism's significance, I have documented the repetitive overlap of tourist and policymaker language deployed to represent self and other; illuminated the simultaneous timing of major trends and changes in transportation and communications technology, tourism, and international politics; exposed the presence of state officials amid the traveling public; analyzed visitor and host government efforts to both promote and contain the travel industry; examined the host's manipulation of cultural symbols during periods of revolutionary change; and plotted the many ways in which subsequent travel discourses cross-fertilized with domestic culture to contextualize U.S. foreign relations. If the linkages between the political and cultural lives of the empire—the empire's political and economic structures and its everyday life—appeared in only one or even two of three cases, the evidence might be less compelling. But in all three case studies, visitor-host relations contributed to, echoed, or illuminated signature features of inter-American political and economic relations. Whether the subject is world war, Cold War, decolonization, revolution, nation building, development, terms of trade, property disputes, military assistance, military bases, or any other number of topics identified with the history of U.S. foreign relations, tourism injects itself into the discussion.

Some diplomatic historians have expressed dissatisfaction with the recent "cultural turn" in the field on the grounds that it deemphasizes the central importance of power.[1] This critique, however, is based on a narrow conception of power as a coercive force wielded primarily by governments. Power hierarchies in fact lie at the center of cultural analysis. Studies of discourse explore the power that U.S. society has bestowed on men over women, whites over people of color, adults over children, Hollywood stars over moviegoers, travel writers over tourists, presidential spokespersons over the press, and tourists over hosts. They deconstruct relationships that are all too often taken for granted in everyday life, both at home in the United States and across the empire, and submit them to rigorous intellectual analysis to explain their origins and lay bare the power inequalities that underpin them.

The cultural approach particularly lends itself to an analysis of soft power, a subject that political scientists have mined to great benefit but historians have only recently begun to ponder. Soft power is manifested in numerous ways and carries multiple ramifications. While state-sponsored economic aid and cultural diplomacy are the varieties of soft power most familiar to international-relations scholars, soft power seeps into nearly all aspects of everyday life in a rapidly globalizing world. U.S. consumerism hardly made the hemispheric empire irresistible for Latin Americans but could make it survivable. By extension, the empire stood a better chance of enduring the weight of the oppression it often produced. In a political and economic context that featured death squads, dictatorships, U.S. military intervention, demeaning labor conditions, human rights nightmares, and Central Intelligence Agency–backed coups, the tourist-host relationship allowed for at least marginal economic betterment, expressions of nationalism and cultural pride, and exposure to a U.S. presence other than that associated with militarism and corporate domination.

Tourism never represented a panacea. In interwar Mexico and Cold War Puerto Rico, where it contributed to improved inter-American relations, the travel industry remained subject to regulation and containment. In Batista's Cuba, where hosting officials lauded tourism's redemptive qualities, the everyday life of empire proved as corrosive of development and self-determination as some of the harshest manifestations of hard power. In short, tourist soft power provided Latin American hosts with negotiating space that might be exploited or squandered.

The history of tourism provides scholars of international relations an opportunity to place international political history in a larger context. The everyday life of empire is less susceptible to fits and starts than its diplomatic and military life. As globalization shrinks geographic distances and the pace of modern life compresses time, it is tempting to view each dramatic geopolitical moment as the opening of a new chapter in history. It has become fashionable in recent years to reference the terrorist attacks of 11 September 2001 as such a turning point. But the post–9/11 world, in which the word "empire" seems to have come back into vogue among U.S. neoconservatives, remains firmly linked to the history that produced the modern Middle East and the United States rise to global leadership. In twentieth-century inter-American relations, FDR's proclamation of the Good Neighbor, Cuba's drift to the left under Fidel Castro, and President John F. Kennedy's Alliance for Progress all came under the glare of the media spotlight and certainly merit the scholarly analysis they have generated. But they also merit a place in the larger scheme of imperial history.

An examination of twentieth-century U.S. tourism in Latin America illuminates the underlying contours of empire—not only the ongoing systems of political and economic domination but also the ways in which cultural constructions of the Latin American "other" persisted from the age of Manifest Destiny to the era of dollar diplomacy and on through the development decade. At the same time, subtle shifts in power and perception become more visible. While U.S. domination began in the early and mid–nineteenth century predominantly as a military and territorial presence, the late 1800s introduced U.S. productive power to the mix, mainly in the form of an extractive industrial presence in mining, agriculture, rail, and shipping. The twentieth century added U.S. consumer power to the blend, including the ever-growing tourist presence. As the everyday life of the empire extended beyond military bases and corporate enclaves, inter-American cultural discourse added layers of complexity. Old stereotypes based on popular constructions of class, race, and gender by no means disappeared, and encounters within the contact zones did not always end on friendly terms, but hosts often gained the ability to manipulate and direct the visitor's gaze, to dispute tourist preconceptions, to appropriate and exploit tourist expectations, and even to invent identities.

The negotiating process continued as the twentieth century came to a close. In fact, the size of the traveling public grew exponentially after 1970, and tourist-host diplomacy increasingly became a multilateral phenomenon, in some cases placing new constraints on U.S. tourist power. North Americans on holiday at Latin American beaches, hotels, historic sites, and elsewhere discovered that the region's allure drew a growing influx of vacationers from Britain, Canada, France, Germany, Italy, Japan, the Netherlands, and the Nordic countries as well as a huge inundation of local South and Central American travelers. The hospitality industry spawned an array of European-, Canadian-, and South American–based firms that competed with U.S. companies. Tourism ranked with media, popular entertainment, sports, the women's rights movement, the peace movement, human rights advocacy, Doctors without Borders, migratory labor, and multinational business as a major force for the meeting of peoples and pocketbooks, the blurring of borders, and the collision and hybridization of cultural practices.

By the mid-1990s, the $3.4 trillion international travel industry had spun multiple innovations. Global environmental movements of the 1970s helped inspire ecotourism that meshed travel and environmental protection. The creation of national parks and land reserves lured adventurers to the wilds of the Amazon, the rainforests of Costa Rica, and the savannahs of Africa. Travelers of course expended thousands of gallons of jet fuel to reach their green destinations, small property owners often bore the brunt of their government's well-intentioned land grabs, and the commodification of nature at times placed unsustainable pressure on the land. The trend nonetheless promised revenue and at least some containment power to many host communities.[2] The variations in consumer demand and marketing schemes were endless: cooking classes in France or Italy and weight-reduction programs aboard cruise ships, hedonism resorts in Jamaica and Bible study in the Holy Land, youth hostels and elder hostels, snow skiing in Calgary and surfing in Australia, and the list goes on.[3]

Latin America experienced a number of industry breakthroughs. Beginning in the 1970s, the cruise vacation came roaring back into vogue, not only along the docks of Old San Juan but across much of the world. From a mere half million passengers a year in 1970, this segment of the travel industry grew to more than five million consumers by 1995. Offering ease of luggage transport, onboard entertainment, expanded menus and bar service, and swimming pools, modern cruise lines made the ship a destination in and of itself. If ecotourism arose from some of the same impulses that inspired the invention of Earth Day in 1970, the green consciousness inherent to the purchase of a cruise vacation might be compared to the purchase of a 1970 Cadillac. The Carnival fleet introduced enlarged cabins, and ship tonnage gradually grew throughout the 1980s and 1990s, featuring not only spacious accommodations but more storage space for food and drink, recreational facilities, exercise rooms, and by the 1990s even movie complexes. Freedom of the seas also allowed internationally owned cruise ships large and small, with their multinational crews, to evade many governmental attempts to regulate wages, hours, and working conditions.[4]

Vacation aboard an ocean liner promised a nostalgic return to the leisurely travel cultures of the early twentieth century, updated with the modern amenities for the age of globalized markets. Meanwhile, Mexico's Yucatán Peninsula, home of the ancient Mayans, offered what was rumored to be the region's first computer-generated tourist resort at Cancún. In fact, tourist studies specialist Evan R. Ward has explained that Cancún first arose in the imagination of bankers at the Banco de Mexico who began scouting the country's extensive coasts in the 1960s in search of the perfect tourism cash cow. They settled on Cancún, a beautiful Caribbean island within easy reach by air from numerous major U.S. cities. Computer-assisted design software helped developers imagine the filling-in of uninviting mangrove swamps and brush on the western portion of the island. Like Miami Beach in the 1920s, bulldozers uprooted the mangrove, and architects and construction workers extended the area's sandy beaches and built a pyramid-dotted skyline of five-star hotels, complete with resort amenities and restaurants. Officials at the Mexican government's Consejo Nacional de Turismo envisioned Cancún as a point of entry for a tourist corridor that would extend south to another planned resort at Playa del Carmen, continue on to the ancient seaside ruin of Tulum, and penetrate inland to the already heavily visited site of Chichén Itzá and the colonial city of Mérida, an arc of surf and antiquity that would become known as the Mayan Riviera.[5]

By the turn of the twenty-first century, Cancún had become Mexico's most heavily visited tourist destination, attracting more than three million visitors annually.[6] The megaresort did not imbibe the neoliberal market strategy of the era. Due to a dearth of risk takers, the Mexican government built and owned the first several resort hotels, with assistance from an Inter-American Development Bank loan. Private capital followed, but Mexican and foreign investment approximated a fifty-fifty split, with European-owned establishments outnumbering North American. A large U.S. expatriate population, along with tourists from a wide array of North American, South American, European, Asian, and Mexican locations, turned Cancún into a truly transnational community in spite of the presence of U.S. retail outlets such as Wal-Mart and Starbucks. The labor force, however, was solidly Mexican and filled in adjoining areas, especially mainland Cancún City, whose population swelled from 117 in 1970 to 40,000 by 1979. Workers migrated from across the country to take up manual positions in hotels and restaurants, join construction crews, land public service jobs, and fill administrative positions in the travel industry.[7]

At first blush, Cancún culture seems to revolve around little more than indulgence in sun, surf, and lime-twisted Coronas. Yet as government planners envisioned at the project's onset, hundreds of thousands who visit the glitzy resort each year take time out to drive about an hour south to Tulum and indulge in at least a brief ancient history lesson. And three hours inland by car or bus lies Chichén Itzá. Designated in the 1980s a World Heritage Site and administered by the government's Instituto Nacional de Antropología, the complex evokes as much awe today as it did in Carnegie archeologist Sylvanus G. Morley's day and draws approximately 1.7 million visitors annually.[8]

Contemporary Tijuana is another story. Tijuana regained its former glory as a party town during the Second World War with an influx of U.S. sailors as well as casual day traffic from southern California. By 2005, the city attracted approximately 4.5 million visitors annually. Some of the traffic stayed loyal to the city's tourism heritage and sought out strip joints, cheap lap dances, illicit drugs, and underage drinking dens. But the city's travel industry had diversified, and the central business district also showcased upscale venues for the sale of Taxco silver, art, and Cuban cigars, along with a number of high-end restaurants. Much has changed recently as the Mexican government has tried to clamp down on organized crime and authorities have engaged in pitched battles with modern-day gangsters. The crime syndicates, often armed with U.S.-purchased weapons that flow easily across the border, engage in numerous rackets, including drug trafficking, migrant smuggling, prostitution, and kidnapping. Although the violence has not been aimed at tourists, its impact has spilled over into the travel world. In March 2008, the fashionable restaurant Hacienda Cien Años, which once drew tourists, was identified by U.S. authorities as a money-laundering front. Military troops presently patrol the city's streets, circumventing the narco-infiltrated local police force.

The fear of violence and stricter post-9/11 requirements for reentering the United States nonetheless inspired a 50 percent drop in tourism in 2007 and the likelihood of further decline in 2008.[9]

The violence, in fact, spread across most of the Mexico-U.S. border during 2008 and 2009 as Mexico's drug cartels countered the government's war on drugs with a terror campaign. Booming consumer demand for narcotics in both Mexico and the United States provided the backdrop. Highly publicized and grisly murders, carried out in some cases by hit men formerly employed in U.S.-trained antidrug squads, became a part of everyday life for border residents. At the end of 2008, Mexican authorities attributed an estimated thirty-five hundred murders to the drug wars, and evidence mounted that state and federal government offices had been thoroughly infiltrated by the cartels and their political allies. In October 2008, the government of Felipe Calderón softened its military-minded approach by proposing the legalization of possession of small amounts of marijuana, cocaine, and methamphetamines. The initiative, however, drew scorn from the George W. Bush administration in Washington, D.C., which had provided funding for the crackdown in Mexico and elsewhere in Latin America.[10]

With more than six hundred murders in 2008, Tijuana suffers one of the country's highest murder rates. Numerous tourist towns have recovered from past crime waves. Miami Beach was awash in cocaine and guns in the 1980s, only to bounce back to art deco chic by the end of the 1990s. Tijuana may face similar prospects. A number of citizens' groups, including the city's artists, have begun to deploy their own soft power and mobilize rallies for peace. Although soft power alone may not be enough to reduce the bloodshed, the Calderón administration's proposed decriminalization indicates that Mexico City is considering innovative new policies. Elected in 2008, President Barack Obama made his first official visit to Mexico in April 2009 when he publicly acknowledged that the United States shared responsibility for the crisis. To contribute to a serious solution, Washington will need to reconsider its policies on drugs and sentencing, mental health care, drug rehabilitation, and gun control.[11]

In the small city of Jalpa, in Zacatecas, northwest of Mexico City, another manifestation of the ever-changing borderlands tourist system is emerging. Local officials and businesses in Jalpa have successfully targeted former residents, transplants to U.S. cities such as Los Angeles and Chicago, as prime tourism customers. Each December, the children and grandchildren of emigrants from the city return for the holidays and a fourteen-day-long festival that features prayer, rodeo, wrestling matches, and the crowning of a festival queen. City leaders welcome the influx not only to rake in holiday revenues but more importantly because the prodigal children remit thousands of dollars each year to the local economy. Emigrant remittances have helped to build roads, extend the electrical grid, and establish schools and scholarship programs. A local branch of the Zacatecas Autonomous University recently opened, for example, after local, state, and the federal governments combined to match remitted dollar contributions to fund its construction. Evoking the gringo wanderlust of the 1920s, many of the returning Jalpanese savor the rural pace of life: the sweet guava fruit, the coconut milk spiked with gin, and the picturesque central plaza. But more than visiting a premodern oasis, Mexican Americans also reaffirm their sense of national identity. During their two-week sojourn, young tourists are likely to visit extended family members, listen to old-timers reminisce about the time the town played host to Pancho Villa and his revolutionary army, or strike up romances with locals.[12] The U.S. labor force may be globalized, but with the border nearby and the always thickening knot of modern communications, individual workers maintain strong ancestral cultural bonds. Their thirst for attachment to Mexico further complicates the everyday life of the empire and illustrates once again the blurring of boundaries that is central to the tourist system of interaction.

To the east, there are signs that the lure of travel may eventually outlive revolutionary passion in Cuba. Much to the chagrin of the current U.S. government, Havana grabbed the tourist spotlight in the 1990s with a potent blend of state controls and private investment. In the mid-1980s, even before the end of the Cold War and the evaporation of the Soviet dole, Fidel Castro eyed tourism as a potential source of scarce foreign exchange. The Castro regime accordingly implemented economic reforms that permitted government joint enterprises with private foreign investors, subject to a tax rate of 30 percent on earnings. In 1995, further liberalization permitted direct foreign investment minus government partnership, and Canadian, European, and South American capital almost immediately poured into a revitalized Cuban travel industry. The ongoing U.S. economic embargo, beefed up in 1996 by the Helms-Burton Act, which opened channels for U.S. investors to take legal action against foreign companies that utilized confiscated American property in Cuba, failed to curb the growth. By the late 1990s, one million Canadians, Spaniards, French, Italians, British, and South Americans visited Washington's hemispheric nemesis annually. In addition, thousands of U.S. citizens evaded Washington's travel restrictions each year, typically flying from Canada or Cancún to Havana, where welcoming Cuban officials make it their business not to stamp U.S. passports.[13]

As tourist revenues approached one billion dollars annually, tourism replaced sugar as the island's largest source of foreign exchange. Many of the premier establishments of the 1950s, including the Hotel Nacional, Meyer Lansky's Riviera, and the Hotel Habana Libre (formerly the Havana Hilton), wound up on the auction block and underwent renovation to accommodate the global clientele. New hotels arose as well, most notably Havana's sumptuous 462-room Melía Cohiba in 1998, declared by Frommer's guide the capital's most modern hostelry, complete with pool, Jacuzzis, and cigar-tasting bar.[14] Varadero Beach sprang back to life and became by the turn of the twenty-first century the largest resort in the Caribbean, outfitted with its own international airport.[15]

Cuban officials have not considered the boom an unqualified success. Fidel Castro likes capital more than he likes capitalism. A string of government corporations, mostly under the thumb of the Cuban military, still own the majority of the island's hotels and maintain considerable holdings in restaurants, car rental agencies, marinas, and bus companies. The influx of dollar-rich tourists has led to a spike in purse snatching and other petty crimes, and to the government's lament, tourist-related prostitution appears to be flourishing, albeit not on the scale of the Batista era. Speculation regarding Cuba's future has become a cottage industry in recent years, especially following Fidel Castro's surgery in 2006 at the age of seventy-nine and the abrupt transfer of power to his brother Raúl. Although the new regime did not radically alter state policies, the incoming Obama administration extended a hand to Cuba in early 2009 when it lifted restrictions on Cuban-American family travel and dollar remittances to the island. Raúl Castro in turn signaled a willingness to engage Washington on a range of issues. Many Latin American leaders sensed a historic shift when Obama announced at a hemispheric gathering at Port of Spain, Trinidad and Tobago, in April 2009 that the United States sought "a new beginning with Cuba." U.S.-Cuban relations remain deeply unsettled, but should these tentative steps expand into a full-fledged dialogue, tourism is likely to prove a powerful facilitator. The tourist-host relationship was among the last elements of the intimate U.S.-Cuban relationship to reach closure in the 1960s. In the early twenty-first century, it may stand among the first linkages to become fully reestablished.[16]

The end of the Cold War also produced ripple effects in Puerto Rico's tourist industry. From 1970 to the dawn of the new century, the island's annual tourist count ticked upward only modestly, from 1 million to 1.2

million, not counting short-term visits by cruise passengers. Other Caribbean powerhouses, most notably Cancún and low-wage Jamaica and the Dominican Republic, experienced the most robust growth. The combination of slow growth and planning kept tourism's share of Puerto Rico's gross national product at 5.5 percent.[17] The Condado experienced a decrease in congestion as the tourist district spread east toward San Juan's airport in Isla Verde. Old San Juan featured locally owned condominiums and bars and restaurants that catered to natives as much as tourists. Adjacent San Juan Harbor and the opening of factory outlet stores and trinket shops, along with the nearby Bacardi rum distillery, made the old walled city one of the most popular ports of call on the cruise line circuit.[18]

Off Puerto Rico's east coast, the empire made a U-turn. Although the Muñoz administration fended off the U.S. military's plan to expropriate Vieques and relocate its population in the early 1960s, the U.S. Navy considered most of the tropical island its dominion. Annual military exercises, with live ammunition and ordnance, continued until 1999, when a civilian security guard was accidentally killed during bombing tests. Both procommonwealth and prostatehood governments pressed Washington to desist from war games, and civilian protests rankled U.S.-commonwealth relations until 2001, when the U.S. government finally yielded and abandoned the site. The last military practices took place on 1 May 2003, but more than sixty years of military use had left behind a legacy of unemployment, environmental damage, and high rates of cancer among the island's inhabitants.[19]

When the U.S. Navy dismantled its Vieques base, Puerto Rico inherited a relatively undeveloped tourist oasis most remarkable for its wild horses, two bioluminescent bays, lush tropical forests, and pristine beaches. Community activists viewed tourism as a means by which to provide jobs for the impoverished ten thousand or so local inhabitants but hoped to prevent an inundation of U.S. and multinational megaresorts.[20] Development thus far has been modest, with most of the new tourist accommodations consisting of modestly sized inns and guesthouses. The island's two small towns, Isabel Segunda and Esperanza, have witnessed a proliferation of guesthouses, T-shirt shops, and restaurants, but Best Western, Hilton, Marriott, Nikko, Novotel, Oberoi, Sheraton, Sofitel, and other big brands have stayed away.[21]

Tourism is in many ways theater, a dramatic and comedic play in which hosts and guests display their self-importance. Tourism has both reinforced and undermined identities over the past century or so. It helped globalize culture, blurred the lines between the empire's center and its dependencies, and demonstrated the fragility of national identity in a mobile world. Given the elaborate playacting, it is not surprising that some social commentators have misread tourism's impact. At one level, host societies have often appeared blindly to accept North American prescriptions for political status, economic development, and tourism promotion. Uncle Sam's traveling public perceived Mexico's bars and dance halls, Cuba's casinos and brothels, and Puerto Rico's five-star elegance as suggesting subservience. Yet on close examination, the terms of dominance often become murky. Host policies toward foreign investment, workers' wages, urban planning, environmental protection, heritage preservation, and grassroots negotiations regarding constructions of class, race, gender, manners, language, and national identity more often than not produced a prolonged tug-of-war between visitors and hosts.

Tourism studies in one sense confirm the cliché that we live in a small world. International leisure travel became possible on a mass scale only in the late nineteenth and early twentieth centuries with the advent of modern transportation systems, the extension of global communications, and the integration of the world capitalist system. All of these developments shrank the planet, linked humanity together as never before, and unhinged familiar societal patterns around the globe. Globalization at times seems to promise to make the world one bland place. Yet the world remains large and expansive, and cultural and national differences survive and are even reinvented as they collide, clash, and mesh. At bottom, ordinary men and women, visitors and hosts alike, join with governments, businesses, and labor in extending hegemony, blurring national boundaries, initiating new international connections and deepening those that already exist, and most of all negotiating identities.

Events at the beginning of the twenty-first century have shown that the outcome of those negotiations carries enormous consequences. Although some commentators propose that a stark line exists between the globalizing trends of the present and future and nationalisms frozen in the past, the two trends—localism and globalism—evolved symbiotically throughout the twentieth century. The Second World War, the Cold War, and the ethnic conflicts of the post–Cold War era arose from an array of geopolitical and economic issues, but the associated deaths and atrocities also demonstrated the power of identity politics. Indeed, today's proliferation of local, regional, and global terrorist networks—in Sri Lanka, Afghanistan, and Palestine, to name just a few—arose from the anguish of the powerless, whose lives have been rubbed raw by the erosion of cultural identities. Sovereignty and power in the modern world imply the ability to define and characterize oneself as well as to enjoy political self-determination and economic justice.

On 11 September 2001, agents of al-Qaeda set out to rectify what they viewed as eighty years of imperialism, an imposition of power that not only transferred Ottoman colonies to the British and French, sent Arab oil west, and established Israel in the heart of Palestine but also undermined centuries of culture based on the teachings of Muhammad and a hierarchy of tribes and clans. In the Middle East, international tourism has not been the main culprit, but the diminution of identity that helped motivate al-Qaeda's aggression in many ways resembled the cultural angst that shook heavily touristed Cuba in the late 1950s. Cubans had been thought to be permanently wed to the cultural norms of North America, but as the insults and inequalities inherent in empire took their toll, many Cubans set off with Fidel Castro to rediscover their Cubanness. In our time, the world was thought to have been inexorably marching in the direction of free-market institutions and a homogenous secular materialism—what Benjamin Barber has labeled "McWorld"—when the terrorists not only reaffirmed their affiliation to tribe and religion but carried their hatred and bloodthirstiness to the citadel of world capitalism.[22]

Historian Greg Grandin has argued that the George W. Bush administration's recent embrace of empire is hardly a novelty but rather is the latest chapter in a long history of U.S. unilateralism, military preemption, and economic expansionism practiced on Latin America for nearly two centuries. In that sense, the lower Western Hemisphere has provided a workshop or laboratory for the current militarization of the clash between McWorld and jihad.[23] Grandin's approach yields great insight for understanding today's global violence. This study, however, illustrates that Latin America has also provided the United States with a testing ground for soft power, serving as a stage on which modern U.S. consumer and cultural power engaged a cultural and racial "other." Tourism and other manifestations of soft power did not make empire either instantly humane or irresistible for Latin Americans. It did not eliminate inequalities, human suffering, or cultural antagonisms. But more than military confrontation, tourism provided modest choices. U.S. citizens might behave as cultural unilateralists hell-bent on possessing and dominating the Latin other or as cultural multilateralists, willing to respect, negotiate, and exchange cultural differences. Latin Americans, elite and commoners, might indiscriminately accept North American norms and bow to North American demands. Or they might resist, negotiate, and contain U.S. influences while simultaneously forging and expressing their own cultural identities.

Tourism is not the only or even the most important determinant of cultural integrity or degradation. It is only one component of a complex and constantly mutating process that bequeaths physical makeup and personality to each and every imagined community around the world, including the larger imagined global community. Although globalization is a fact of modern life, the history of international tourism teaches that globalization can be imagined in more than one way. It has most certainly been conceptualized as a means by which the wealthy impose demands on the poor and conditions that livelihoods and nations be organized in accordance with free-market ideology and military muscle. It has also been associated with a cultural process that pressures local communities to surrender their independent identities, spins stereotypes, and assigns civilizational sophistication to favored groups at others' expense. But it can also be imagined as a means to both global and local self-realization, a system of dense interconnectedness and collapsing geographical distances that still encourages cultural diversity and hybridization and community-based social and economic planning. It can be a world torn apart by the demands of McWorldists and jihadists alike or a world that is open to us all.

Notes

Abbreviations

AGN   Archivo General de la Nación, Mexico City, Mexico

AGPR   Archivo General de Puerto Rico, San Juan, Puerto Rico

CHC   Cuban Heritage Collection, Otto Richter Library, University of Miami,
       Coral Gables, Florida

DGL   DeGolyer Library, Southern Methodist University, Dallas, Texas

DMP   Dwight Morrow Papers, Archives and Special Collections, Amherst College,
       Amherst, Massachusetts

DSCF   U.S. Department of State Central File, Cuba

HHCR   Hilton Hotel Corporation Records, Conrad N. Hilton College Library and
       Archives, University of Houston, Houston, Texas

HIR   Hilton International Records, Conrad N. Hilton College Library and Archives,
       University of Houston, Houston, Texas

HMP   Herbert Matthews Papers, Manuscripts Division, Columbia University
       Library, New York, New York

JDP   Josephus Daniels Papers, Manuscript Division, Library of Congress,
       Washington, D.C.

JFKL   John F. Kennedy Presidential Library, Boston, Massachusetts

LMML   Luis Muñoz Marín Library, Trujillo Alto, Puerto Rico

OG   Records of the Office of the Governor, Archivo General de Puerto Rico, San
       Juan, Puerto Rico

PAA   Pan American Airlines Archive, Coral Gables, Florida

Introduction

1 Joseph, LeGrand, and Salvatore, *Close Encounters*, esp. Gilbert M. Joseph's introductory essay, "Toward a New Cultural History of U.S.-Latin American Relations," 3–46.
2 For a helpful summary of poststructural theory and the history of U.S. foreign relations, see Emily S. Rosenberg, "Turning to Culture," in *Close Encounters*, ed. Joseph, LeGrand, and Salvatore, 497–99, 506–7.
3 Feifer, *Tourism in History*; Lenèek and Bosker, *Beach*, 29–38. On science, travel, and empire, see Pratt, Imperial Eyes, esp. 15–68, 111–43.
4 Especially helpful to understanding the rise of mass tourism in the United States is Aronson, *Working at Play*.
5 Hoganson, *Consumer's Imperium*, 153–208.
6 *Compendium of Tourism Statistics*; Löfgren, *On Holiday*, 5, 7. On the 1920s, see Pells, *Not Like Us*, 10–11. On the 1960s, see U.S. Department of Commerce, Office of Business Economics, *Survey of Current Business*, 27; *Travel News*, June 1963, 4.
7 On tourism and economics, see, for example, Britton, "Political Economy"; Bryden, *Tourism and Development*; Conway, *Tourism and Caribbean Development*; Duvall, *Tourism*; Goldstone, *To Make the World*; Kadt, *Tourism*; Lea, *Tourism and Development*; Lundberg and Lundberg, *International Travel*; Pattullo, *Last Resorts*; Potter et al., *Contemporary Caribbean*; Scranton and Davidson, *Business of Tourism*; Wahab, *Tourism, Development, and Growth*.
8 On tourist theory and culture, see Baranowski and Furlough, *Being Elsewhere*; Crouch, *Visual Culture*; Desmond, *Staging Tourism*; Judd and Fainstein, *Tourist City*; Kirshenblatt-Gimblett, *Destination Culture*; Kaur and Hutnyk, *Travel Worlds*; Lanfant, Allcock, and Bruner, *International Tourism*; MacCannell, *Tourist*; Picard and Woods, *Tourism, Ethnicity, and the State*; Valene L. Smith, *Hosts and Guests*; Krista A. Thompson, *Eye for the Tropics*; Urry, *Tourist Gaze*.
9 My work has benefited from that of three predecessors whose studies illuminate the structural foundations of the travel industry in the Spanish Caribbean and Mexico. See Berger, *Development*; Rosalie Schwartz, *Pleasure Island*; Evan R. Ward, *Packaged Vacations*. Pathbreaking works on the history of tourism include Susan C. Anderson and Tabb, *Water, Leisure, and Culture*; Feifer, *Tourism in History*; Foss, *On Tour*; Fussell, *Abroad*; Koshar, *German Travel Cultures*; Leed, *Mind*; Swinglehurst, *Cook's Tours*; Turner, *British Travel Writers*.

The history of U.S. tourism includes Bacchilega, *Legendary Hawai'i*; Belasco, *Americans on the Road*; Brown, *Inventing New England*; Cocks, *Doing the Town*; Dubinsky, *Second Greatest Disappointment*; Dulles, *Americans Abroad*; David Farber and Bailey, "Fighting Man"; Findlay, *Magic Lands*; Frankel, *Observing America*; Krahulic, *Provincetown*; Kropp, *California Vieja*; Levenstein, *Seductive Journey*; Levenstein, *We'll Always Have Paris*; Judy Mattivi Morley, *Historic Preservation*; Rothman, *Devil's Bargain*; Sears, *Sacred Places*; Sellars, *Preserving Nature*; Shaffer, *See America First*; Souther, *New Orleans*; Stanonis, *Creating*; Stowe, *Going Abroad*; Sutton, *Travelers*.
10 Ruiz, *On the Rim*, 42–60; Taylor, "Wild Frontier."

11 The most helpful interpretations of the revolution include Cockroft, *Intellectual Precursors*; Hart, *Revolutionary Mexico*; Katz, *Life and Times*; Knight, *Mexican Revolution*; Krauze, Meyer, and Reyes, *Historia*; Moreno, *Yankee Don't Go Home*; Ruiz, *Great Rebellion*. The introductory literature on Mexican culture is voluminous, but for a good start, see Joseph and Henderson, *Mexico Reader*; Knight, *Mexico*; Krauze, *Mexico*.

12 Ricardo D. Salvatore, "The Enterprise of Knowledge: Representational Machines of Informal Empire," in *Close Encounters*, ed. Joseph, LeGrand, and Salvatore, 69–106. On Mexico, see Berger, *Development*, esp. 2, 93–115; Vaughn and Lewis, *Eagle and the Virgin*. On Puerto Rico, see Dávila, *Sponsored Identities*; Haslip-Viera, *Taíno Revival*; Morris, *Puerto Rico*.

13 Rosalie Schwartz, *Pleasure Island*; Pérez, *On Becoming Cuban*, esp. 165–98. On sex tourism, see Enloe, *Bananas, Bases, and Beaches*; Suzy Kruhse–Mount Burton, "Sex Tourism and Traditional Australian Male Identity," in *International Tourism*, ed. Lanfant, Allcock, and Bruner, 192–204.

14 On Havana's urban development, see Scarpaci, Segre, and Coyula, *Havana*, 76–86.

15 Elaine Tyler May, *Homeward Bound*.

16 On multicultural Cuba, see Pérez, *Cuba: Between Reform and Revolution*, 3–48; Scarpaci, Segre, and Coyula, *Havana*, 1–50; Fuente, *Nation for All*; Eric Williams, *From Columbus to Castro*.

17 For an introduction to Puerto Rico, see Ayala and Bernabe, *Puerto Rico*; Cabán, *Constructing*; Dávila, *Sponsored Identities*; Flores, *Bomba to Hip Hop*; Flores, *Divided Borders*; Haslip-Viera, *Taíno Revival*; Morales Carrión, *Puerto Rico*; Lopez, *Puerto Ricans*; Picó, *Historia*; Quany, *Puerto Rican Identity*; Ramos de Santiago, *Gobierno*; Scarano, *Puerto Rico*.

18 Urry, *Tourist Gaze*, 1–7.

19 Maier, *Among Empires*, 24–25.

20 On dollar diplomacy, the authoritative book is Rosenberg, *Financial Missionaries*, 32–34, 36. On race, gender, and empire, see also Horsman, *Race*; Hunt, *Ideology*; Kramer, *Blood*; Krenn, *Color*; Love, *Race*; Stephanson, *Manifest Destiny*.

21 Works on the history of U.S. foreign relations that have probed tourist relations include Costigliola, *Awkward Dominion*; Endy, *Cold War Holidays*; Engerman, "Research Agenda"; Hoganson, *Consumer's Imperium*, 153–208; Iriye, *Cultural Internationalism*; Kuisel, *Seducing*; Paterson, *Contesting Castro*; Pells, *Not Like Us*; Pérez, *On Becoming Cuban*; Skwiot, "Itineraries." An innovative early work on tourism and international relations is Enloe, *Bananas, Bases, and Beaches*.

22 In many ways, Perkins offered the first realist interpretation of inter-American relations in *Hands Off*, with Bemis, *Latin American Policy*, following closely behind. For more recent works, see, for example, Collin, *Theodore Roosevelt's Caribbean*; Healy, *Drive*; Zakaria, *Wealth*.

23 The literature on development is extensive. Rostow's *Stages* is the classic diffusionist text. For a good analysis of modernization and diffusionist thought and U.S. foreign policy, see Latham, *Modernization*. See also Cullather, "Development?"; Engerman et

al., *Staging Growth*; Escobar, *Encountering Development*; Staples, *Birth*; Carlota Mc-Allister, "Rural Markets, Revolutionary Souls, and Rebellious Women in Guatemala," in *In from the Cold*, ed. Joseph and Spenser, 350–77. For a critique of neoliberalism and the International Monetary Fund, see Stiglitz, *Globalization*.

24 On the rise of revisionism and inter-American relations, see Rosenberg, "Turning to Culture," 501–3. Among the best-known statements of the revisionist thesis are Kolko, *Confronting*; LaFeber, *New Empire*; Paterson, *Contesting Castro*; Robert Freeman Smith, *United States and Revolutionary Mexico*; William Appleman Williams, *Tragedy*. For an overview of dependency theory, see Louis A. Pérez Jr., "Dependency," in *Explaining*, ed. Hogan and Paterson, 162–65; Frank and Gills, *World System*. For a cogent deconstruction of both modernization and dependency theories, see Escobar, *Encountering Development*.

25 Geertz, *Interpretation*, 5, 10–17, 44–46, 196, 207.

26 Kennan, *American Diplomacy*.

27 William Appleman Williams, *Empire*, 12, 194.

28 For a spirited critique of the cultural turn, see Buzzanco, "What Happened." For a more recent critique, see Thomas Alan Schwartz, "Explaining the Cultural Turn."

29 Benedict Anderson, *Imagined Communities*, esp. 5–7.

30 Iriye (*Cultural Internationalism*, 13–51) has applied the concept of imagined community to explain the rise of modern transnational groups and a global consciousness that he terms "cultural internationalism."

31 On public memory, see, for example, Blight, *Beyond the Battlefield*; Kammen, *Mystic Chords*; Kropp, *California Vieja*; Rosenberg, *Date*.

32 Rosenberg, "Turning to Culture," 497–99.

33 William Roseberry, "Hegemony and the Language of Contention," in *Everyday Forms*, ed. Joseph and Nugent, 360.

34 The cultural scholarship is too massive to list here, but for excellent summaries, see Emily S. Rosenberg, "Considering Borders," in *Explaining*, ed. Hogan and Paterson, 176–93; Emily S. Rosenberg, "Turning to Culture," 497–514. Hixson, *Myth*, deploys a cultural approach and delivers a strikingly innovative synthesis of the history of U.S. foreign relations.

35 Endy, *Cold War Holidays*, esp. 1–7, 125–49.

36 Levenstein, *We'll Always Have Paris*, ix–xiii.

37 Said, *Orientalism*, 7, 75, 99.

38 Quoted in Jayes, " 'Strangers,'" 304.

39 Jennings, *Our American Tropics*, 188.

40 Klein, *Cold War Orientalism*, 14–17, 58, 100–142. Said's work has stimulated a diverse literature that has at times challenged and expanded his original ideas. For examples in the history of inter-American relations, see Kaplan, *Anarchy*; Kaplan and Pease, *Cultures*; Renda, *Taking Haiti*. See also Said, *Culture and Imperialism*. On missionaries, philanthropy, and consumerism, see Hoganson, *Consumer's Imperium*; Hunter, *Gospel*; Anna Johnson, *Missionary Writings*.

41 De Grazia, *Irresistible Empire*, esp. 474, 555–56. On soft power, see also Nye, *Bound to*

Lead; Maier, *Among Empires*, 65. On U.S.-European cultural relations, see also Jessica Gienow-Hecht, "Cultural Transmission," in *Encyclopedia of U.S. Diplomatic History*, ed. DeConde et al., 403–4; Kroes, *If You've Seen One*; Kuisel, *Seducing*; Pells, *Not Like Us*; Wagnleitner, *Coca-Colonization*.

42 De Grazia, *Irresistible Empire*, 474, 555.

43 In addition to Nye, *Bound to Lead*, see Nye, *Paradox*, esp. 8–12; Nye, *Soft Power*, 5–18.

44 On empire, consumerism, and U.S. households, see Hoganson, *Consumer's Imperium*, esp. 13–56.

45 Rosenberg, "Considering Borders," 176–93.

46 My approach to culture (the approach that has driven recent literature) contrasts with that which portrays culture as a static phenomenon easily imposed by the powerful on the weak. For a more static view of cultural imperialism, see the classic Dorfman and Mattelart, *How to Read*; Dorfman, *Empire's Old Clothes*. For a critique of the very concept of cultural imperialism, see Tomlinson, *Cultural Imperialism*, esp. 1–33, 173–79. On cultural transfer, see Gienow-Hecht, "Cultural Transmission." For an excellent overview of the traditional scholarship on empire and an introduction to the new cultural approach, see Gilbert M. Joseph, "Toward a New Cultural History," in *Close Encounters*, ed. Joseph, LeGrand, and Salvatore, 3–46; Steve J. Stern, "The Decentered Center and the Expansionist Periphery: The Paradoxes of the Foreign-Local Encounter," in *Close Encounters*, ed. Joseph, LeGrand, and Salvatore, 47–68.

47 Quoted in *New York Times*, 27 May 2007.

48 Boorstin, *Image*, 77–117.

49 Koshar, *German Travel Cultures*, 8; Boorstin, *Image*, 90–99.

50 MacCannell, *Tourist*, esp. 8, 156. To further explore the concept of cultural modernity, see Berman, *All That Is Solid*; Giddens, *Modernity*; Tomlinson, *Cultural Imperialism*, esp. 146–47.

51 Rosenberg, "Turning to Culture," 508–9.

52 Franck, *Trailing Cortez*, 323.

53 Lizabeth Cohen, *Consumer's Republic*, 62–109.

54 Hard-hitting critiques of tourism include Barry, Wood, and Preusch, *Other Side*; Patullo, *Last Resorts*. On the commodification of culture, see esp. Lanfant, Allcock, and Bruner, *International Tourism*, 4–9. On world's fairs, see Rydell, *All the World's a Fair*; Rydell, *World*.

55 On Cuba, see Pérez, *On Becoming Cuban*. In recently acquired Hawaii at the turn of the century, non-Hawaiian scholars and writers translated and altered indigenous folk legends to produce the popular Anglo-American image of Hawaii, at once primitive and exotic. See Bacchilega, *Legendary Hawai'i*.

56 On Mexico, see Gruening, *Mexico*, 519–21. On Puerto Rico, see Dávila, *Sponsored Identities*.

57 Lanfant, Allcock, and Bruner, *International Tourism*, 4–9.

58 Scott, *Domination*; Scott, *Weapons*; Kelly, *Race Rebels*.

59 "Boyd AAA 'Motor Scout,'" *Asheville Sunday Citizen*, 14 February 1926, *Los Angeles Times*, 15 August 1926, *Florida Times Union*, n.d., all in Ag1994.0957, Box 2, DGL.

60 Quoted in Squier, *Gringa*, 153.

61 Quoted in Pérez, *On Becoming Cuban*, 469.

62 Mexican Tourist Association, *Mexico: The Faraway Land Nearby*, 1937, in Villalba, *Mexican Calendar Girls*, 70. For analysis of femininity and national identity in Mexico, see Villalba, *Mexican Calendar Girls*, 22–27; Berger, *Development*, 93–99.

63 Tomlinson, *Globalization*, 3.

64 Ibid., 3–10.

65 Pratt, *Imperial Eyes*, 6–7. For an overview and a discussion of the recent boom in borderlands literature and its usefulness to the study of international relations, see Nathan J. Citino, "The Global Frontier: Comparative History and the Frontier-Borderlands Approach," in *Explaining*, ed. Hogan and Paterson, 194–211.

66 Catherine C. LeGrand, "Living in Macondo: Economy and Culture in a United Fruit Company Banana Enclave," in *Close Encounters*, ed. Joseph, LeGrand, and Salvatore, 333–68.

67 Roger T. Daniels, *Guarding*; Duany, *Puerto Rican Nation*; García, "I Am the Other"; Gabaccia and Ruiz, *American Dreaming*; Ngai, *Impossible Subjects*; Takaki, *A Different Mirror*.

68 Wharton, *Building*.

69 Gilbert M. Joseph makes this point in regard to Cold War scholarship in "What We Now Know and Should Know: Bringing Latin America More Meaningfully into Cold War Studies," in *In from the Cold*, ed. Joseph and Spenser, 17.

70 William Appleman Williams, *Empire*, 4.

71 For two generations, most history undergraduates have been exposed to Braudel, *Mediterranean*, esp. 704–5, 757, 770–71, 773–76, 1238–44.

72 Theodore Roosevelt quoted in Ninkovich, *Modernity and Power*, 4.

73 Franklin Roosevelt quoted in ibid., 114. On the Cold War, see, for example, Leffler, "American Conception"; Leffler, *Preponderance*.

74 On common stereotypes, see, for example, Levenstein, *We'll Always Have Paris*, ix–x, 277–80; Pérez, *On Becoming Cuban*, 165–98.

75 McAlister, *Epic Encounters*, 5–6.

76 Dean, *Imperial Brotherhood*, 3.

77 *New York Times*, 29, 30 October 2000.

78 Franklin Roosevelt to Josephus Daniels, 15 March 1938, Reel 60, JDP.

79 Frank Ragano and Selwyn Raab, "Havana 1958: Out on the Town with the Mob," in *Reader's Companion*, ed. Ryan, 164; Paterson, *Contesting Castro*, 52.

80 H. McIntyre, Secretary to the President, "Informal, Extemporaneous Remarks of the President, Fargo, North Dakota, 4 October 1937," Reel 60, JDP.

81 Quoted in Endy, *Cold War Holidays*, 185.

82 Ibid., 33–37; Rosenberg, *Spreading*, 105–6.

83 Friedman, *Nazis and Good Neighbors*; Haines, "Under the Eagle's Wing"; Rosalie Schwartz, *Pleasure Island*, 107–8.

84 Endy, *Cold War Holidays*, 5, 31.

85 Ibid., 103–23, 43–54, 81–99.

86 Quoted in Paterson, *Contesting Castro*, 56.

87 Roorda, *Dictator Next Door*.

88 Hart, *Empire and Revolution*, 394, 396–99. For interpretations of the Good Neighbor policy that stress strategic considerations, see Dallek, *Franklin D. Roosevelt*, 38–39, 62–66, 86–87, 122–24, 175–76; Gellman, *Good Neighbor Diplomacy*; Schuler, *Mexico*; Wood, *Making*; Woods, *Roosevelt Foreign Policy Establishment*. For a favorable assessment of the Good Neighbor policy that includes a cultural perspective, see Pike, *FDR's Good Neighbor Policy*. For interpretations that stress U.S. economic motives, see Gardner, *Economic Aspects*, 47–63; Green, *Containment*; LaFeber, *Inevitable Revolutions*, esp. 80–85; Pérez, *Cuba: Between Reform and Revolution*, 260–81; Spenser, *Impossible Triangle*, 133–51.

89 Standard accounts of the U.S. policy and the Castro revolution include Benjamin, *United States*; Domínguez, *Cuba*; Domínguez, *To Make a World*; Dallek, *Unfinished Life*, 534–39; Samuel Farber, *Origins*; Ernest R. May and Zelikow, *Kennedy Tapes*; Morris H. Morley, *Imperial State*; Paterson, *Contesting Castro*; Arthur M. Schlesinger Jr., *Thousand Days*, 215–24; Sweig, *Inside*; Thomas, *Cuba*.

90 An exception is Pérez, *Cuba in the American Imagination*.

91 Leonard H. Price (Commercial Attaché, U.S. Embassy Havana) to Department of State, 7 October 1959, 937.724/10-759, DSCF.

92 In February and March 1959, the U.S. embassy in Havana reported on Castro's relaxation of antigambling laws. See E. A. Gilmore Jr. (Embassy Counselor for Economic Affairs) to Department of State, 20 February 1959, 837.12/2-2059, DSCF; Gilmore to Department of State, 19 March 1959, 837.12/3-1959, DSCF; Gilmore to Department of Commerce, 24 March 1959, 837.12/3-2459, DSCF; Gilmore to Department of Commerce, 26 March 1959, 837.12/3-2659, DSCF. In the summer of 1959, the Castro regime reorganized the Cuban Tourism Commission (Leonard H. Price to Department of State, 29 June 1959, 837.181/6-2959, DSCF; Price to Department of State, 12 August 1959, 837.181/18-1259, DSCF).

93 Latham, *Modernization*, 69–108. Additional works on the alliance include Baily, *United States*, 82–131; LaFeber, *Inevitable Revolutions*, 150–61; Levinson and de Onís, *Alliance*; Rabe, *Most Dangerous Area*, 148–72; Taffet, *Foreign Aid*; Joseph S. Tulchin, "The Promise of Progress: U.S. Relations with Latin America during the Administration of Lyndon B. Johnson," in *Lyndon Johnson*, ed. Warren I. Cohen and Tucker, 211–43; William O. Walker III, "Mixing the Sweet with the Sour: Kennedy, Johnson, and Latin America," in *Diplomacy*, ed. Kunz, 42–79.

94 Koshar, *German Travel Cultures*, 11.

95 Maier, "Consigning."

96 Tomlinson, *Globalization*, 29.

97 Barber, *Jihad*, esp. xi–xxxii.

98 Sheller, *Consuming the Caribbean*, 2.

Chapter 1

1. *New York Times*, 16, 18 December 1927; Berg, *Lindbergh*, 172–73; Lindbergh, *Autobiography of Values*, 87–88; Ross, *Last Hero*, 165.
2. Quoted in Nicholson, *Dwight Morrow*, 313. See also McBride, *Story*, 135–37.
3. Davison (a New York-based Business Associate) to Dwight Morrow, 14 November 1927, Eric H. Palmer (*Brooklyn Daily Times*) to Morrow, 5 December 1927, both in Series X, Box 3, Folder 19, DMP.
4. Speech by Alfonso F. Ramirez, "Discursos Pronuncados en la Sesion Solemne Efectuada por al Camara de Siputados en Honor del Aviador Norteamericano. Coronel Charles A. Lindbergh, Published 1928, Mexico City," 15 December 1927, Series X, Box 3, Folder 19, DMP.
5. Berger, *Development*, 14.
6. Koshar, *German Travel Cultures*, 75.
7. For a recent rendition of this argument, see Rhodes, *United States Foreign Policy*.
8. Costigliola, *Awkward Dominion*; Warren I. Cohen, *Empire*; De Grazia, *Irresistible Empire*; Iriye, *Cultural Internationalism*; Leffler, *Elusive Quest*; Rosenberg, *Spreading*; Rupp, *Worlds*; Wilson, *American Business*.
9. Toor, *Guide*, vii.
10. Hart, *Empire and Revolution*, 260. On the U.S. economic presence, see also Pletcher, *Rails*; Ruiz, *People*.
11. Hart, *Empire and Revolution*, 148, 153, 163–83.
12. For an excellent overview of the historiography of the Mexican Revolution, see Joseph and Nugent, *Everyday Forms*, 3–23.
13. Katz, *Secret War*; Joseph, *Revolution from Without*; Meyer, *Mexican Revolution*; Quirk, *Affair*; Robert Freeman Smith, *United States and Revolutionary Mexico*.
14. Hart, *Empire and Revolution*, 344–45.
15. Spenser, *Impossible Triangle*, 1–5, 18–31.
16. Ibid., 75–87.
17. For an understanding of the everyday life of the Mexican Revolution, see Joseph and Nugent, *Everyday Forms*, esp. the introductory essay, 3–23. On Mexican pragmatism during these years, see Hart, *Empire and Revolution*, esp. 340, 346, 361–63; Spenser, *Impossible Triangle*, esp. 62–70, 120–29. On Calles, see Buchenau, *Plutarco Elías Calles*; Krauze, *Plutarco E. Calles*. On General Electric and International Telephone and Telegraph, see Thomas F. O'Brien, *Making*, 108.
18. On Vasconcelos, see Folgarait, *Mural Painting*; McPherson, *Yankee No!*, 15. On linkages between popular culture and state formation, see Vaughn and Lewis, *Eagle and the Virgin*; Joseph and Nugent, *Everyday Forms*, esp. introduction, 6–9; Desmond Rochfort, "The Sickle, the Serpent, and the Soil: History, Revolution, Nationhood, and Modernity in the Murals of Diego Rivera, José Clemente Orozco, and David Alfaro Siquieros," 43–56; Stephen E. Lewis, "Education and the 'Indian Problem,'" 176–95.
19. Hunt, *Ideology*; Horsman, *Race*; Hoganson, *Fighting*; Stephanson, *Manifest Destiny*; Kaplan and Pease, *Cultures*; Kramer, *Blood*; Love, *Race*.

20 Hart, *Empire and Revolution*, 367.
21 H. L. Mencken in *New York World*, clipping, Series X, Box 5, Folder 114, DMP.
22 Roger T. Daniels, *Guarding*; Gabaccia and Ruiz, *American Dreaming*.
23 Hart, *Empire and Revolution*, 272.
24 Quoted in Jayes, "Strangers," 302–4.
25 Quoted in Hart, *Empire and Revolution*, 41.
26 U.S. Embassy in Mexico City, Press Release, "'American Tourist Traffic to Mexico on the Increase,' says Daniels, Ambassador to Mexico," 1934, Box 660, JDP.
27 Ruiz, *On the Rim*, 49.
28 Terry, *Terry's Guide to Mexico* (1927), 97g.
29 Ruiz, *On the Rim*, 43–45.
30 Ibid., 43, 49–50.
31 Quoted in Taylor, "Wild Frontier."
32 D. Midland to E. Phillipe, Michigan, n.d., "Gene" to "Andy Orr Eugene Oregon," n.d., both in Ag2000.1370.2, DGL.
33 Hart, *Empire and Revolution*, 255; Taylor, "Wild Frontier."
34 Hart, *Empire and Revolution*, 367; Ruiz, *On the Rim*, 51. For an excellent discussion of Johnson's Mexican experience, see Horne, *Black and Brown*, 25–38. See also Jack Johnson, *Autobiography*, 111–22; Geoffrey C. Ward, *Unforgivable Blackness*, 400–402.
35 Spenser, *Impossible Triangle*, 1–5.
36 Taylor, "Wild Frontier."
37 Hart, *Empire and Revolution*, 366.
38 Kropp, *California Vieja*, 19, 103–56.
39 Babcock and Weigle, *Great Southwest*.
40 Seymour, *Across the Gulf*, 10–12.
41 Banning, *In Mexican Waters*, 3.
42 Cudahy, *Mañanaland*, 20–21.
43 Ibid., 24–25. See also Greenberg, *Manifest Manhood*, 1–17, 47–53, 78–87.
44 Cudahy, *Mañanaland*, 35.
45 Carr, *Old Mother Mexico*, 7.
46 Foster, *Gringo*, 81.
47 Ibid., 83.
48 Niblo, *War*, 15.
49 Foster, *Gringo*, 124.
50 Graham, *In Quest*, 281.
51 Ibid., 291.
52 Ibid., 313.
53 Ibid., 265.
54 Hoganson, *Consumer's Imperium*, esp. 200–208.
55 Sheridan, *My American Diary*, 151.
56 See, for example, Cole, *Roosevelt*.
57 Slocum, *Where Tex Meets Mex*, 73.
58 Ibid., 26.

59 Ibid., 61–62.

60 Delpar, *Enormous Vogue*, 15–62. See also Gilbert M. Joseph, "Toward a New Cultural History," in *Close Encounters*, ed. Joseph, LeGrand, and Salvatore, 20; Hart, *Empire and Revolution*, 367–68.

61 Givner, *Katherine Anne Porter: Conversations*, 86.

62 Ibid., 121–22.

63 Givner, *Katherine Anne Porter: A Life*, 238–39.

64 Givner, *Katherine Anne Porter: Conversations*, 125.

65 Ibid., 127.

66 Ibid., 125–26.

67 Quoted in Delpar, *Enormous Vogue*, 27.

68 Gruening, *Mexico*.

69 Gosse, *Where the Boys Are*, 15, 30.

70 The National University seminars produced two books: Herring and Terrill, *Genius of Mexico*; Herring and Weinstock, *Renascent Mexico*.

71 Delpar, *Enormous Vogue*, 137.

72 "Vendedores Chucharas, MEX, 2100," n.d., A92000.1370.1, DGL.

73 "Vendedore de Petates, 117," n.d., A92000.1370.1, DGL.

74 "Xochimilco, Mexico, 618," n.d., A92000.1370.1, DGL.

75 "Piasajes de Mexico, 34.N," n.d., Untitled, Young Female in Colorful Dress and Lace, n.d., "Un Tipo de Mestiza, Merida, Yucatán, 141," n.d., all in A92000.1370.1, DGL.

76 Photo of Colima Mercado, April 1925, AG2000.1370.6, DGL.

77 "Vendedor de Loza, 2720," n.d., A92000.1370.1, DGL.

78 "Coscomatepec, VER, Pico de Orizaba, Mexico, 2446," n.d., A92000.1370.1, DGL.

79 R. I. Falon to Mrs. S. H. Wigg, Mill Valley, Calif., "Guadalajara, Uruapan, Patzcuaro, and Morelia Acueducto, Morelia, Mich. 702," n.d., AG2000.1370.4 DGL.

80 "Guadalajara, Uruapan, Patzcuaro, and Morelia, 1920s," AG2000.1370.4, DGL; Rosalind A. Hughes, Mexico Travels, Annotated Album, 1924–25, AG1999.1258sx, DGL.

81 Missouri Pacific Iron Mountain, *Mexico, a Foreign Land a Step Away* (brochure), Folder 1908, DGL.

82 National Railways of Mexico and Operated Lines, *Twenty Days in Mexico: The Egypt of the Americas*, 1923, Folder National Railways of Mexico Pamphlet, DGL.

83 Ibid.

84 Terry, *Terry's Guide to Mexico* (1927), xxxvi–xxxvii.

85 Ibid., addendum.

86 Ibid.

87 *Mexican Railway: The Standard Gauge and Short Line from Mexico City to Veracruz*, ca. 1923–24, Folder National Railways of Mexico Pamphlet, DGL.

88 Hart, *Empire and Revolution*, 127–28.

89 Dwight Morrow to Frank Kellogg, 8 November 1927, with Memorandum of Conversation between Calles and Morrow at Santa Barbara Ranch, Series X, Box 5, Folder 114, DMP; Terry, *Terry's Guide to Mexico* (1935), ccxivia.

90 *Mexican Railway: The Standard Gauge and Short Line from Mexico City to Veracruz*, ca. 1923–24, 112, Folder National Railways of Mexico Pamphlet, DGL.

91 *Tour of Mexico: American Association of Traveling Passenger Agents*, Forty-ninth Annual Convention, October 1924, Folder, A 1435, DGL.

92 Ibid.

93 Terry, *Terry's Guide to Mexico* (1927), xxxiv–xxxv, addendum. On the Yucatán, see Seymour, *Across the Gulf*.

94 Construction of the Pan-American Highway extended as far south as Monterrey by the mid-1920s (Terry, *Terry's Guide to Mexico* [1927], xxxvii–xxxix).

95 "Boyd AAA 'Motor Scout,'" *Asheville Sunday Citizen*, 14 February 1926, *Los Angeles Times*, 15 August 1926, *Florida Times Union*, n.d., all in Ag1994.0957, Box 2, DGL

96 *Survey Magazine*, 1 July 1932, 298–300.

97 Delpar, *Enormous Vogue*, 99.

98 Lears, *No Place*, 184–85.

99 MacCannell, *Tourist*, 8.

100 Terry, *Terry's Guide to Mexico* (1927), 426. For a sampling of travel writing on Teotihuacán, see *Review of Reviews*, 2 August 1935, 70–72; *St. Nicholas*, 2 August 1935, 20–22.

101 Gruening, *Mexico*, 519–21.

102 Ibid.; *Mexican Railway: The Standard Gauge and Short Line from Mexico City to Veracruz*, ca. 1923–24, Folder National Railways of Mexico Pamphlet, DGL.

103 Gruening, *Mexico*, 521.

104 Zapata Alonzo, *Overview*, 181–85.

105 Sylvanus Griswold Morley, *Introduction*, esp. introduction by J. Eric S. Thompson, ix; Evan R. Ward, *Packaged Vacations*, 107.

106 Berger, *Development*, 15–26, 35–36, 40–41.

107 Proyecto Presentado al Primer Congreso Nacional de Turismo by de León, 22 April 1930, File 144/6236, AGN; Berger, *Development*, 31.

108 Delpar, *Enormous Vogue*, 57.

109 Berger, *Development*, 14, appendix A, 121.

110 Hart, *Empire and Revolution*, 343–61.

111 Spenser, *Impossible Triangle*, 92–94, 103–7, 129–51.

112 Remarks of President Coolidge to President Calles, 27 September 1927, Series 10, Box 1, Folder 84, DMP.

113 Dwight Morrow to Frank Kellogg, 8 November 1927, with Memorandum of Conversation between President Calles and Ambassador Morrow at Santa Barbara Ranch, Series X, Box 5, Folder 114, DMP.

114 Hart, *Empire and Revolution*, 363.

115 Dwight Morrow to Frank Kellogg, 3 August 1928, Series X, Box 2, Folder 171, DMP; Thomas Lamont to Dwight Morrow, 17 January, 24 July 1930, both in Series X, Box 3, Folder 4, DMP.

116 Speech at Meeting of the Royal Institute of International Affairs, London, 3 March

1930, Series II, Box 1 Folder 135a, DMP. For another example of Morrow's promotional activities, see Morrow's Commencement Speech at Harvard University, 21 June 1928, Series II, Box 2, Folder 125, DMP.

117 *Saturday Evening Post*, 12 May 1928, 3–4, 19 May 1928, 10–11; McBride, *Story*, 134.

118 William Spratling to Dwight Morrow, 1 August 1930, Series X, Box 4, Folder 130, DMP; Joseph C. Satterwaite to Arthur Springer c/o Dwight Morrow in Englewood, New Jersey, 11 June 1929, including a one-hundred-dollar check for Spratling, Series 10, Box 4, Folder 129, DMP. See also Morrow, *Casa Mañana*.

119 Ambrosio Puente (Governor of Morelos) to Heschul Johnson (Interim Chargé d'Affairs, U.S. Embassy), Series X, Box 2, Folder 18, DMP.

120 Spratling, *File*, 36–38; Wolfe, *Fabulous Life*, 271–73.

121 Brenner, *Your Mexican Holiday*, 147; Wolfe, *Fabulous Life*, 271–75.

122 Chase, *Mexico*, 129.

123 Ibid., 270.

124 Ibid., 187.

Chapter 2

1 Josephus Daniels to Franklin D. Roosevelt, 1 March 1934, Reel 59, JDP.

2 Ibid.

3 Ibid.

4 Berger, *Development*, appendix A, 121; *New York Times*, 3 January 1937; *Mexican Art and Life*, March 1937.

5 *New York Times*, 24, 29 July 1935.

6 Howard Vincent O'Brien, *Notes*, 11.

7 Hart, *Empire and Revolution*, 371–72; Krauze, *Lázaro Cárdenas*, 95–96, 108–45. For a sample critique of the Cárdenas reforms, see Arturo Anguiano, "Cárdenas and the Masses," in *Mexico Reader*, ed. Joseph and Henderson, 456–60.

8 Dallek, *Franklin D. Roosevelt*, 38–39, 62–66, 122–24, 175–76; Gardner, *Economic Aspects*, 47–63; Gellman, *Good Neighbor Diplomacy*; Pike, *FDR's Good Neighbor Policy*; Schuler, *Mexico*; Wood, *Making*; Woods, *Roosevelt Foreign Policy Establishment*.

9 Proyecto Presentado al Primer Congreso Nacional de Turismo by de León, 22 April 1930, File 144/6236, AGN; Berger, *Development*, 31.

10 Niceford Guerro Jr. (Secretary to President Rubio) to José J. Razo (Department of Tourism), enclosing report by Guillermo Durante de Carbaga, 28 October 1931, File 144/6351, AGN.

11 *Pan American Union*, August 1936, 651.

12 Berger, *Development*, 24–25.

13 Scully and Scully, *Motorists' Guide*, v–vi.

14 Ibid., 2.

15 Ibid., 2, 7, 19–20.

16 Berger, *Development*, 39–43.

17 Rosalie Schwartz, *Pleasure Island*, 62–67.

18 Scully and Scully, *Motorists' Guide*, 26–27.

19 *Monterrey Mexico: The City of Mountains and Sunshine, Angel Cueva, Manager*, ca. late 1930s, Folder Grand Hotel Ancira Pamphlet, DGL.

20 Spratling, *File*, 38.

21 Ibid., 78. On Spratling, see also Littleton, *Color*; Mark, *Silver Gringo*; Morrill, *William Spratling*.

22 Spratling, *File*, 60.

23 Ibid., 98–99.

24 Josephus Daniels, *Shirtsleeve Diplomat*, 435–36.

25 "Address of Josephus Daniels, American Ambassador, to Members of the Tenth Seminar, 13 July 1935," Box 718, JDP. See also nearly identical language in "Draft Press Release on Ambassador's Trip to Southern States," 1935, Box 666, JDP.

26 Josephus Daniels, *Shirtsleeve Diplomat*, 483.

27 Josephus Daniels to Franklin Roosevelt, 26 September 1935, Reel 59, JDP.

28 Franklin Roosevelt to Josephus Daniels, 19 July 1936, Reel 60, JDP.

29 *Mexican Railway: The Standard Gauge and Short Line from Mexico City to Veracruz*, ca. 1923–24, Folder National Railways of Mexico Pamphlet, DGL.

30 Squier, *Gringa*, 233.

31 Hoganson, *Consumer's Imperium*, 166–67, 171, 177.

32 Terry, *Terry's Guide to Mexico* (1927), xxviii.

33 Ibid.

34 Delpar, *Enormous Vogue*, 40–41.

35 Brenner, *Your Mexican Holiday*, 97.

36 Ibid, xi–x.

37 Mackie and Dick, *Mexican Journey*, 3.

38 Ibid., xi.

39 Creed Tourist and Information Bureau at Sanborn, *The Keys to Mexico City*, ca. 1923–27, Miscellaneous Mexico Box, DGL.

40 Boorstin, *Image*, 89–90.

41 Terry, *Terry's Guide to Mexico* (1927), 238.

42 *Hotel Geneve, Mexico City* (pamphlet), 1932, Folder, Hotel Geneve, Mexico City, DGL; Sydney Newnes Hillyard to Dwight Morrow, 26 July 1929, Series X, Box 2, Folder 152, DMP. According to Terry the hotel's rates began at five dollars daily (*Terry's Guide to Mexico* [1927], 238–39, 533).

43 Hotel Regis, *Old Mexico*, 1928, Miscellaneous Mexico Box, DGL; *Mexican Railway: The Standard Gauge and Short Line from Mexico City to Veracruz*, ca. 1923–24, Folder National Railways of Mexico Pamphlet, DGL.

44 Howard Vincent O'Brien, *Notes*, 100.

45 Ibid., 39–40.

46 Terry, *Terry's Guide to Mexico* (1935), 96b.

47 Ibid., 240–43.

48 Ibid., 242.

49 *Mexican Railway: The Standard Gauge and Short Line from Mexico City to Veracruz*, ca. 1923–24, Folder National Railways of Mexico Pamphlet, DGL.

50 Fuentes, *Death*, 17–18.

51 Merritt-Hawkes, *High Up*, 46

52 Kropp, *California Vieja*, 207–60.

53 Howard Vincent O'Brien, *Notes*, 18–19, 27.

54 Wells, *Panmexico*, 261.

55 Howard Vincent O'Brien, *Notes*, 123.

56 Spenser, *Impossible Triangle*, 103–5, 143–44.

57 Ibid., 55, 121; Hart, *Empire and Revolution*, 361; Townsend, *Lazaro Cardenas*, 112; Krauze, *Lázaro Cárdenas*, 95–96, 138–45.

58 Barretto, *Bright Mexico*, 219–20. Complaints about taxi strikes also appear in Franck, *Trailing*, 321.

59 Franck, *Trailing*, 359, 365.

60 Miller, *Mexico around Me*, x.

61 Haas, *Letters*, 31.

62 Greene, *Lawless Roads*, 255.

63 Ibid., 32.

64 *New Yorker*, 17 June 1939, 91.

65 *Nation*, 2 September 1939, 250.

66 Haas, *Letters*, 18–19.

67 Ibid., 17.

68 Barretto, *Bright Mexico*, 153.

69 Virtue, *South*, 25–28, 37, 62–63.

70 W. E. B. Du Bois to Frank Tannenbaum, 13 February 1937, 548.1/1, Cárdenas Papers, AGN. On African Americans and the Mexican Revolution, see Horne, *Black and Brown*.

71 Merritt-Hawkes, *High Up*, 2, 45.

72 Squier, *Gringa*, 58.

73 Ibid., 141.

74 Riley, *Daylight*, 22.

75 Henry Albert Phillips, *New Designs*, 221.

76 Howard Vincent O'Brien, *Notes*, 11, 18–19.

77 Quoted in Niblo, *Mexico*, 5–6.

78 Howard Vincent O'Brien, *Notes*, 147.

79 Squier, *Gringa*, 156.

80 Spenser, *Impossible Triangle*, 143–44; Barretto, *Bright Mexico*, 220.

81 Riley, *Daylight*, 145–46.

82 Spratling, *File*, 77–78.

83 Wolfe, *Fabulous Life*, 350.

84 Border Problems Memo, Nuevo Laredo Consulate, 26 July 1934, Box 665, JDP.

85 Squier, *Gringa*, 153.

86 Ibid., 56.

87 Townsend, *Lazaro Cardenas*, 100–101; Krauze, *Lázaro Cárdenas*, 106; Herring, "Cardenas Triumphs."

88 *New York Times*, 2 August 1936, 23 February, 23 July 1937; "Reporting Ambassador Daniels' Trip to El Paso, Chihuahua, and Torreon," 29 March 1934, Box 665, JDP.

89 Cavetano Blanco Vigil and F. Coudrier to Pascual Ortiz Rubio, 23 January 1932, File 144/765b, AGN; Ricardo Mimeranza Castillo to Raul Castellanos, 8 October 1937, Folder, 548.2/19, AGN. On the CTNT's formation, see Berger, *Development*, 56–57.

90 Ramón Beteta (Undersecretary of the Foreign Office), "Greetings to the Hotel-Men of the United States" (speech), *Mexican Art and Life*, October 1938, DGL; Hart, *Empire and Revolution*, 398.

91 Berger, *Development*, 50.

92 Pascual Ortiz Rubio to Lázaro Cárdenas, 15 November 1940, 9 December 1938, 18 July 1936, Folder 548.2/6, AGN.

93 Carlos F. Osuna to Pascual Ortiz Rubio, 19 October 1936, Folder 548.2/6, AGN.

94 Manuel del Valle to Lázaro Cárdenas, 24 July 1940, Folder 548.2/6, AGN.

95 See, for example, Ruth St. Albans for Edward Bernays Inc. to Lázaro Cárdenas, 15 February 1935, Folder 548.2/7, AGN; Clarence S. Rose to Cárdenas, 1 September 1937, Hamilton Wright to Cárdenas, 14 January 1938, Godofredo Beltrán to Cárdenas re: A. J. Welch (M. H. Hackett Inc.), 3 November 1938, all in Folder 548.2/1, AGN. On the New York City travel office, see *New York Times*, 30 May 1934.

96 Godofredo Beltrán, "Extracto" of C. A. Tozier (Aetna Life and Casualty) to Lázaro Cárdenas, 24 May 1938, Folder 548.2/1, AGN; George E. Leach (Mayor of Minneapolis) to Cárdenas, 5 January 1938, Folder 548.2/25, AGN; William Green (President, American Federation of Labor) to Cárdenas, 27 January 1940, Folder 548.3/3, AGN; Howard Jones (President, Youngstown College) to Cárdenas, 21 July 1937, Folder 548.2/23, AGN; Joseph E. Elliot (director of Alvin Tours International) to Cárdenas, 9 July 1937, Folder 548.2/24, AGN.

97 Hart, *Empire and Revolution*, 395–97; Krauze, *Lázaro Cárdenas*, 148–58.

98 *New York Times*, 9 August 1938; Berger, *Development*, 66–67.

99 *New York Times*, 23 May 1938.

100 Berger, *Development*, 67.

101 Ibid., 75–76.

102 *Miami Herald*, 27 May 1938; Memo, Departamento Consular, Seccion Commercial # 6502, 10 January 1938, Folder 548.2/1, AGN.

103 Berger, *Development*, appendix A, 121.

104 See, for example, Pemex Travel Club Bulletin 142-A, June 1943, Miscellaneous Mexico Box, DGL.

105 Berger, *Development*, 77–82.

106 Mexican Tourist Association, *Mexico: The Faraway Land Nearby*, 1939, DGL. See Villalba, *Mexican Calendar Girls*, 20–24; Berger, *Development*, 93–99.

107 *New York Times*, 26 May, 29 July 1935.

108 *Harper's Monthly*, June 1937, 46–56.

109 *Review of Reviews*, 12 November 1936, 12.

110 James L. Calaway to Lázaro Cárdenas, 13 August 1939, Folder 548.3/3, AGN.

111 M. F. Sessions to Lázaro Cárdenas, 1 February 1938, Folder 548.3/3, AGN.

112 See, for example, Oliver Babcock to Lázaro Cárdenas, 19 June 1939, Folder 548.3/3, AGN.

113 Scully and Scully, *Motorists' Guide*, 117.

114 Dallek, *Franklin D. Roosevelt*, 39.

115 Niblo, *Mexico*, 75–141. See also Dwyer, "Diplomatic Weapons."

116 Dwyer, "Diplomatic Weapons," 393.

117 Rosalie Schwartz, *Pleasure Island*, 105–7; Hart, *Empire and Revolution*, 397; Freire-Medeiros, "Hollywood Musicals."

118 Rosalie Schwartz, *Pleasure Island*, 107–8.

119 Franklin Roosevelt to Josephus Daniels, 15 March 1938, Reel 60, JDP.

120 "Trip to Yucatán," March 1936, Box 666, JDP.

121 H. McIntyre (Secretary to the President), "Informal, Extemporaneous Remarks of the President, Fargo, North Dakota, 4 October 1937," Reel 60, JDP.

122 *New York Times*, 21 April 1943.

123 *Guide of Mexico*, July 1940, Miscellaneous Mexico Box, DGL.

124 Berger, *Development*, appendix A, 121.

125 Bloom, *Adventures*, 2, 3, 7; Rebecca M. Schreiber, "Resort to Exile: Willard Motley's Writings on Postwar U.S. Tourism to Mexico," in *Adventures*, ed. Bloom, 45.

Chapter 3

1 *Time*, 20 January 1958, 32.

2 *Saturday Evening Post*, March 1953, 32–33.

3 *Time*, 20 January 1957, 32; *New York Times*, 29, 31 March 1953.

4 Edward J. Bash (Assistant Commercial Attaché) to Department of State, 14 August 1958, 837.45/8–2758 Havana Embassy HBS, DSCF; *Time*, 20 January 1957, 32.

5 Lizabeth Cohen, *Consumer's Republic*, esp. 18–135.

6 Pérez, *Cuba in the American Imagination*.

7 The prevailing conservatism of the early postwar years and its constraining impact on sexual relations and family structure are emphasized in Elaine Tyler May, *Homeward Bound*, esp. 114–61. An important corrective that highlights greater diversity in culture constructions of gender and sexuality can be found in Meyerowitz, *Not June Cleaver*.

8 Gould, *Spanish-American War*; Hoganson, *Fighting*; LaFeber, *New Empire*, 326–406; Offner, *Unwanted War*; Pérez, *War of 1898*.

9 Skwiot, "Itineraries," 44–60; Rosalie Schwartz, *Pleasure Island*, 20–30.

10 Rosalie Schwartz, *Pleasure Island*, 33.

11 Skwiot, "Itineraries," 89–90.

12 Pérez, *On Becoming Cuban*, 167; on prostitutes, see 193–94.

13 Scarpaci, Segre, and Coyula, *Havana*, 112.

14 Terry, *Terry's Guide to Cuba*, 1.

15 Ibid., 2, 155.

16 Ibid., 5.

17 Skwiot, "Itineraries," 91–93.

18 Rosalie Schwartz, *Pleasure Island*, 22, 45.

19 *Havana Post*, 29–31 January 1927; *New York Times*, 29–31 January 1927.

20 Argote-Freyre, *Fulgencio Batista*, 36; Scarpaci, Segre, and Coyula, *Havana*, 63.

21 Tucker, *Insatiable Appetite*, 14–22; Scarpaci, Segre, and Coyula, *Havana*, 63.

22 Ibid., 64, 122.

23 Terry, *Terry's Guide to Cuba*, 342–45.

24 Ibid., 312.

25 Ibid., 35.

26 Argote-Freyre, *Fulgencio Batista*, 127–35; Pérez, *Cuba under the Platt Amendment*, 321–32.

27 Benjamin, *United States*, 119–32; Domínguez, *Cuba*, 110–33; Thomas, *Cuba*, 737–58.

28 Skwiot, "Itineraries," 181.

29 Pérez, *Cuba under the Platt Amendment*, 284–95.

30 Quoted in Evan R. Ward, *Packaged Vacations*, 96. See also Skwiot, "Itineraries," 175–91.

31 *Doctrina*, 31, CHC.

32 Ibid., 9.

33 Maribona, *Turismo*, 86.

34 *Doctrina*, 9, CHC. On the Cuban love affair with Florida, see *Doctrina*, 20, CHC; Pérez, *On Becoming Cuban*, 432–44.

35 Batista, *Growth and Decline*, 193–94.

36 Skwiot, "Itineraries," 237.

37 C. A. Boonstra (Counselor for Economic Affairs) to Department of State, "Report on Airport Improvements at Rancho Boyeros International Airport (José Martí) since Compania de Aeropuertos Intercionales S.A. (CAISA) Assumed Control in December 1952," 5 September 1956, 937.724/9–556, DSCF.

38 *Doctrina*, 15–16, CHC.

39 Ibid., 45–59.

40 See, for example, *New York Times*, 27 January 1940, 19 August 1947, 19 September 1951.

41 On the confederation's response to the Batista coup, *New York Times* journalist Herbert Matthews noted that the U.S. labor attaché to the embassy in Havana said that labor had been caught "flat footed" by the coup but had made peace with the new regime (Notes, 9 April 1952, Folder—Cuban Reports 1952–1960, Box 2, HMP; see also *New York Times*, 3 April 1952).

42 *Doctrina*, 45–59, CHC.

43 Graebner, *Age of Doubt*, 24–25, 62–63.

44 Leffler, "American Conception"; Leffler, *Preponderance*.

45 Zeiler, *Free Trade*; Zeiler and Eckes, *Globalization*.

46 Hogan, *Marshall Plan*; Merrill, *Bread*; Merrill, "Shaping"; Pach, *Arming*.

47 Quoted in McPherson, *Yankee No!*, 9, 10–37. See also Rabe, *Eisenhower*, 3–4, 97.

48 Latham, *Modernization*, 72–75; Escobar, *Encountering Development*, 29.

49 Endy, *Cold War Holidays*, 48; see also 33–54.

50 Earl D. Johnson to John Foster Dulles, 26 May 1954, Record Group 59, Box 20, Department of State Records, National Archives of the United States, College Park, Maryland.

51 Quoted in Evan R. Ward, *Packaged Vacations*, 17; for background on the Rockefellers, see 7–20.

52 Endy, *Cold War Holidays*, 37. On Pan Am's rise, see Bender and Altschul, *Chosen Instrument*.

53 *Jet Age*, 1958, CHC.

54 Rosalie Schwartz, *Pleasure Island*, 108.

55 Kathleen Baird, Report for the Conrad N. Hilton Foundation, 1997, updated 2001, HHCR; *Time*, 12 December 1949.

56 Strand, Oral History, 16.

57 Kathleen Baird, Report for the Conrad N. Hilton Foundation, 1997, updated 2001, HHCR. For more on Hilton, see Evan R. Ward, *Packaged Vacations*, 21–42.

58 Hilton, *Be My Guest*, 267, 265, 262.

59 Wharton, *Building*, 8–11.

60 Boorstin, *Image*, 89–90.

61 Endy, *Cold War Holidays*, 35, 115.

62 Klein, *Cold War Orientalism*, 67–99; Endy, *Cold War Holidays*, 38.

63 McAlister, an American studies scholar, has used the concept of "moral geographies" to analyze how popular media have assisted U.S. viewers in navigating the shoals of Middle East politics since 1945 (*Epic Encounters*, 4–12).

64 Endy, *Cold War Holidays*, 145.

65 Klein, *Cold War Orientalism*, 110.

66 Paterson, *Contesting Castro*, 35, 40–41.

67 Ibid., 35–36; Morris H. Morley, *Imperial State*, 46–55; Domínguez, *Cuba*, 54–109; Thomas, *Cuba*, 311–409.

68 Quoted in Paterson, *Contesting Castro*, 25–26.

69 Quoted in Pérez, *On Becoming Cuban*, 431; see also 399–434.

70 C. A. Boonstra (Counselor of Embassy for Economic Affairs) to Department of State, "Report on Airport Improvements at Rancho Boyeros International Airport (José Martí) since Compania de Aeropuertos Intercionales S.A. (CAISA) Assumed Control in December 1952," 5 September 1956, 937.724/9–556, DSCF.

71 Cuban Tourism Institute, *Welcome to Havana 1955*, CHC; Ford, *Fiesta Lands*; Martin and Martin, *Standard Guide*, 374.

72 C. A. Boonstra (Counselor of Embassy for Economic Affairs) to Department of State, 21 July 1955, 837.181/7–2155, DSCF.

73 Scarpaci, Segre, and Coyula, *Havana*, 78, 82, 123; Batista, *Growth and Decline*, 196.

74 Scarpaci, Segre, and Coyula, *Havana*, 82–84.

75 Tommy Lasorda, "Havana, 1950–1959: Baseball, Batista, and the Bearded Ones," in *Reader's Companion*, ed. Ryan, 189.

76 Pérez, *On Becoming Cuban*, 270; see also 255–78; Paterson, *Contesting Castro*, 49–51.

77 Langston Hughes, "Havana Nights and Cuban Color Lines, 1930," in *Reader's Companion to Cuba*, ed. Ryan, 91.

78 Allyn C. Donaldson (Director, Office of Special Consular Services) to Senator Stuart Symington, 8 August 1957, with Enclosure from Alphonse J. Lynch (Attorney), 837.411/8–157, DSCF.

79 Scarpaci, Segre, and Coyula, *Havana*, 121–22.

80 Martin and Martin, *Standard Guide*, 376; Rosalie Schwartz, *Pleasure Island*, 177.

81 Some scholars have also theorized that Trafficante worked as a double agent for Castro. See Arthur M. Schlesinger Jr., *Robert Kennedy*, 504. Also see "CIA Family Jewels," 27 June 2007, at National Security Archive Web site at <www.gwu.edu/nsarchiv> (accessed 14 July 2007).

82 Montague, *Meyer Lansky*, 130–31.

83 *Times of Havana*, 16 January 1958.

84 Conrad N. Hilton to Carl Hilton, 24 April 1950, Carl H. Hilton Papers, Box 3, HHCR.

85 Curt Strand, "The Hilton Development Program," Hotel Management, n.d., RG 1, Box 10, HHCR; "Hilton Hotel Organization," February 1959, Box 4, HIR.

86 *Havana Post*, 22 March 1958.

87 John W. Houser (Vice President and General Manager, Hilton Hotels International) to Conrad N. Hilton, 3 June 1954, Box 4, HIR.

88 Leonard H. Price (Commercial Attaché) to Department of State, 5 May 1958, 837.181/5–558, DSCF.

89 Ibid. On Luciano, see Montague, *Meyer Lansky*, 111–12, 119–20, 129.

90 Batista, *Growth and Decline*, 197–98; *Cuba: Ideal Vacation Land, 1949–1950*, CHC; Ford, *Fiesta Lands*, 165.

91 Martin and Martin, *Standard Guide*, 377–78; Ford, *Fiesta Lands*, 165.

92 On the African American civil rights movement and the Cold War, see Carol Anderson, *Eyes off the Prize*; Borstelmann, *Cold War*; Dudziak, *Cold War*; Plummer, *Window*; Von Eschen, *Race*.

93 Elaine Tyler May, *Homeward Bound*, esp. 114–61, 183–207; Meyerowitz, *Not June Cleaver*, esp. 1–16.

94 Cuban Tourism Institute, *Welcome to Havana 1955*, CHC.

95 *Holiday*, December 1957, 66–77.

96 Cuban Tourist Commission, *Cuba: The Inviting Island Next Door*, n.d.; Cuba Mail Line, *Take a Trip to Cuba: The Year-Round Paradise*, n.d., CHC; Cuban Tourism Institute, *Welcome to Havana 1955*, CHC; *In Gay Havana*, CHC; Roberts, *Havana*, 221–23.

97 For a sampling, see Clark, *All the Best*, 83–100; Lanks, *Highway*, 3–4; Martin and Martin, *Standard Guide*, 381; Roberts, *Havana*, 220–23; *Travel*, December 1956, 18–22.

98 Gjelten, *Bacardi*, 169.

99 Lanks, *Highway*, 26.

100 Ibid., 198–218.

101 Ibid., 26.

102 Pérez, *On Becoming Cuban*, 469–70.

103 Terry, *Terry's Guide to Cuba*, 200–201.

104 Macaulay, *Rebel*, 25–26.

105 Graham Greene, "Havana and Santiago de Cuba, 1957," in *Reader's Companion*, ed. Ryan, 151.

106 Frank Ragano and Selwyn Raab, "Havana 1958: Out on the Town with the Mob," in *Reader's Companion*, ed. Ryan, 163–64.

107 Ibid., 170.

108 Pérez, *On Becoming Cuban*, 192–93.

109 Quoted in McClay, *I Love Lucy*, 17.

110 Pérez, *On Becoming Cuban*, 181, 191, 205; Rosalie Schwartz, *Pleasure Island*, 120–21.

111 Rosalie Schwartz, *Pleasure Island*, 100, 139; Montague, *Meyer Lansky*, 130.

112 The two best books on the mob's heyday in Cuba are English, *Havana Nocturne*; Sáenz Rovner, *Cuban Connection*.

113 *Time*, 20 January 1957, 32; Edward J. Bash (Assistant Commercial Attaché) to Department of State, 14 August 1958, 837.45/8–2758 Havana Embassy HBS, DSCF.

114 Ragano and Raab, "Havana, 1958," 165; Gjelten, *Bacardi*, 170.

115 Leonard H. Price (Commercial Attaché) to Department of State, 11 September 1957, 837.12/9–1157, DSCF; Edward J. Bash (Assistant Commercial Attaché) to Department of State, 14 August 1958, 837.45/8–2758 Havana Embassy HBS, DSCF.

116 *New York Times*, 5 January 1958.

117 Cuban Tourist Commission, *Cuba*, n.d., CHC.

118 Roberts, *Havana*, 200.

119 Martin and Martin, *Standard Guide*, 386.

120 Standard accounts of the Cuban Revolution include Bonachea and San Martín, *Cuban Insurrection*; Draper, *Castroism*; Samuel Farber, *Origins*; Halperin, *Rise*; Matthews, *Cuban Story*; Matthews, *Fidel Castro*; Ruiz, *Making*; Szulc, *Fidel*.

121 Sweig, *Inside*, 1–16, 25–26.

122 Gjelten, *Bacardi*, 194–95.

123 Paterson, *Contesting Castro*, 35–36; Domínguez., *Cuba*, 54–109; Thomas, *Cuban Revolution*, 311–409.

124 Quoted in Pérez, *On Becoming Cuban*, 469–70.

125 Quoted in ibid., 469.

126 Quoted in ibid., 469–70, 472; McClay, *I Love Lucy*, 12. On anti-Americanism, see also McPherson, *Yankee No!*, 38–76.

127 Scarpaci, Segre, and Coyula, *Havana*, 96.

128 Morris H. Morley, *Imperial State*, 52, 54, 76, 99, 112; Thomas, *Cuban Revolution*, 381–85.

129 Scarpaci, Segre, and Coyula, *Havana*, 78.

130 Pérez, *On Becoming Cuban*, 198–218.

131 *Time*, 4 March 1957, 40; *Editor and Publisher*, 2 March 1957; Paterson, *Contesting Castro*, 74–78.

132 *New York Times*, 24 February 1957.

133 Allyn C. Donaldson (Director of the Office of Special Consular Services) to Senator Everett Dirksen, 10 April 1957, 737.00/3–1957, DSCF; *New York Times*, 14 March 1957; Sweig, *Inside*, 18–19.

134 Clark, *Cuban Tapestry*, 3–4.

135 *Holiday*, December 1957, 66–77.

136 English, *Havana Nocturne*, 210–11; Ragano and Rabb, "Havana, 1958," 164.

137 Quoted in Paterson, *Contesting Castro*, 92.

138 McPherson, *Yankee No!*, 48.

139 Ibid., 107–8.

140 John Foster Dulles to U.S. Embassy, Mexico City, 12 April 1958, 837.181/4–1858, DSCF.

Chapter 4

1 *Havana Post*, 23 March 1958.

2 Ibid., 22 March 1958.

3 *Hotel Monthly*, March 1958, 19–20.

4 *Havana Post*, 23 March 1958.

5 Robert J. Caverly to Kathleen Baird, 2 July 1990, RG 1, Box 10, HHCR; Rosalie Schwartz, *Pleasure Island*, 191.

6 Sweig, *Inside*, 105.

7 Castro, *Historia*.

8 Sweig, *Inside*, 104.

9 Notes, 21 March 1958, Box 2, Folder: Cuban Reports 1952–1960, HMP.

10 Endy, *Cold War Holidays*, 137.

11 Frances Knight (Director of the U.S. Passport Office), "Don't Be an Ugly American," *Parade*, June 1960, 4; Klein, *Cold War Orientalism*, 85–89.

12 Casparius, Oral History.

13 C. Allan Stewart (Deputy Director Office of Middle American Affairs) to Edward Cohn of Lynchburg, Virginia, 8 July 1958, FW837.181/6-2858, DSCF. On the urban underground, see Sweig, *Inside*, 104–13.

14 The best account of the general strike is Sweig, *Inside*, 114–47.

15 *New York Times*, 10 April 1958.

16 Casparius, Oral History.

17 Paterson, *Contesting Castro*, 160–72.

18 *New York Times*, n.d., Box 3, Folder: Clippings, Notes, Letters, HMP.

19 Ibid.

20 Frank Ragano and Selwyn Raab, "Havana, 1958: Out on the Town with the Mob," in *Reader's Companion*, ed. Ryan, 163, 166, 168. English covers the story in *Havana Nocturne*, 224–34.

21 *New York Times*, 1958, Box 3, Folder: Clippings, Notes, and Letters, HMP.

22 Leonard H. Price (Commercial Attaché) to Department of State, 12 December 1958, 837.181/12-1258, DSCF.

23 *Wall Street Journal*, 12 November 1958.

24 Gosse, *Where the Boys Are*, 1–5.

25 Ibid., 99.

26 Macaulay, *Rebel*.

27 Leonard H. Price (Commercial Attaché) to Department of State, 5 May 1958, 837.181/5-558; Price to Department of State, 9 May 1958, 837.181/5-958, DSCF.

28 *Havana Post*, 2 October 1958.

29 Ibid., 1 October 1958.

30 Ibid., 23 October 1958.

31 *Holiday*, December 1957, 66–77.

32 Ragano and Raab, "Havana, 1958," 174.

33 Paterson, *Contesting Castro*, 195–215.

34 *Times Talk*, February 1959, Box 3, Folder: Clippings, HMP; López-Fresquet, *My Fourteen Months*, 67; Ruby Hart Phillips, *Cuba*, 395.

35 Casparius, Oral History; Rodolfo Casparius to Arthur E. Elmiger, 19 January 1959, RG 1, Box 10, HHCR; López-Fresquet, *My Fourteen Months*, 12–13.

36 *New York Times*, 2 January 1959.

37 Rodolfo Casparius to Arthur E. Elmiger, 19 January 1959, RG 1, Box 10, HHCR; Casparius, Oral History.

38 Rodolfo Casparius to Arthur E. Elmiger, 19 January 1959, RG 1, Box 10, HHCR; Casparius, Oral History.

39 Rodolfo Casparius to Arthur E. Elmiger, 19 January 1959, RG 1, Box 10, HHCR; Ruby Hart Phillips, *Cuba*, 402.

40 Wayne S. Smith, *Closest of Enemies*, 38–41; Earl E. T. Smith, *Fourth Floor*, 190–93; Ruby Hart Phillips, *Island*, 399–402; Casparius, Oral History.

41 Rodolfo Casparius to Arthur E. Elmiger, 19 January 1959, RG 1, Box 10, HHCR.

42 Wayne S. Smith, *Closest of Enemies*, 40–41.

43 Rodolfo Casparius to Arthur E. Elmiger, 19 January 1959, RG 1, Box 10, HHCR.

44 Paterson, *Contesting Castro*, 234–35.

45 Casparius, Oral History.

46 Herbert Matthews, First Lecture at CCNY, 15 March 1961, Box 2, Folder: Cuban Revolution—CCNY Lectures, March 1961, HMP.

47 Paterson, *Contesting Castro*, 232; Rosalie Schwartz, *Pleasure Island*, 196–97.

48 Herbert Matthews to Dryfoos, Merz, Catledge, Marel, Freedman, 15 March 1960, Box 2, Folder: Cuba—Memoranda, HMP.

49 Ibid.

50 Leonard H. Price (Commercial Attaché, U.S. Embassy Havana) to Department of State, 4 February 1959, 837.181/2-459DSCF.

51 Robert J. Caverly to Kathleen Baird, 2 July 1990, RG 1, Box 10, HHCR.

52 Ibid.

53 Quoted in Hilton Hotels International Press Release, 13 January 1959, RG 1, Box 10, HHCR. On Castro's economic planners, see *Business Week*, 1 August 1959, 70–72. On the moderate nature of the newly appointed ministry, see López-Fresquet, *My Fourteen Months*, 71–75.

54 "Land of Opportunity, Playland of the Americas," *Cuba Magazine*, 1959, CHC.

55 E. A. Gilmore Jr. (Counselor for Economic Affairs) to Department of State, 13 February 1959, 837.45/2-1259, DSCF; Leonard H. Price (Commercial Attaché) to Department of State, 4 February 1959, 837.181/2-459, DSCF.

56 E. A. Gilmore Jr. (Counselor for Economic Affairs) to Department of State, 13 February 1959, 837.45/2-1259, DSCF.

57 Ibid.; E. A. Gilmore Jr. (Counselor for Economic Affairs) to Department of State, 19 March 1959, Transmitting Text of Law 86, 19 February 1959, 837.12/3-1959, DSCF.

58 E. A. Gilmore Jr. (Counselor for Economic Affairs) to Department of State, 20 February 1959, 837.12/2-2059, DSCF; Gilmore to Department of State, 24 March 1959, 837.12/3-2459, DSCF.

59 E. A. Gilmore Jr. (Counselor for Economic Affairs) to Department of State, 20 February 1959, 837.12/2-2059, DSCF.

60 *Newsweek*, 2 March 1959, 47.

61 E. A. Gilmore Jr. (Counselor for Economic Affairs) to Department of State, 24 March 1959, 837.12/3-2459, DSCF.

62 Sidney H. Willner to Conrad N. Hilton, 9 June 1959, RG 1, Box 10, HHCR.

63 Daniel M. Braddock (Minister-Counselor) to Department of State, 19 March 1959, 837.53/3-1959, DSCF.

64 Fidel Castro, Interview, 15–19 February 1959, Rancho Alto, Sierra de Cojímar, Box 2, Folder Cuba Reports 1952–1960, HMP.

65 Fidel Castro, Interview by Ruby Phillips, 13 July 1959, Box 2, Folder: Cuba Reports 1952–1960, HMP.

66 Ibid.

67 Robert J. Caverly to Conrad N. Hilton, 1 February 1959, RG 1, Box 10, HHCR.

68 Ibid., 11 February 1959.

69 Ibid.

70 *Revolución*, 10 February 1959.

71 Leonard H. Price (Commercial Attaché) to Department of State, 29 June 1959, 837.181/6-2959, DSCF; Price to Department of State, 12 August 1959, 837.181/18-1259, DSCF; Rosalie Schwartz, *Pleasure Island*, 200.

72 Leonard H. Price (Commercial Attaché) to Department of State, 19 October 1959, 837.181/10-1959, DSCF.

73 Ibid., 7 October 1959, 937.724/10-759, DSCF.

74 *Time*, 20 April 1959, 42.

75 *Havana Post*, 24 January 1959.

76 Robert J. Caverly to Conrad N. Hilton, 5 October 1959, RG 1, Box 10, HHCR.

77 Scarpaci, Segre, and Coyula, *Havana*, 134–35; Wayne S. Smith, *Closest of Enemies*, 49–50.

78 Paterson, *Contesting Castro*, 241–54.

79 McPherson, *Yankee No!*, 38–76.

80 Pérez, *Cuba in the American Imagination*, 240.

81 Ibid., 238–56.

82 Ambassador Philip Bonsal to Gerald W. Russell, Transportation and Communication, American Republics REA, Department of State, 8 May 1959, 911.72327/5-859, DSCF.

83 Godofreda Torres Neda to Conrad N. Hilton, 19 October 1959, RG 1, Box 10, HHCR.

84 Quoted in Pérez, *On Becoming Cuban*, 496.

85 Gregory R. Dillon (Hilton, Beverly Hills) to Robert J. Caverly, 7 February 1959, RG 1, Box 10, HHCR.

86 Conrad N. Hilton to Sidney H. Willner, 11 June 1959, RG 1, Box 10, HHCR.

87 Robert J. Caverly to Conrad N. Hilton, 1 February 1959, RG 1, Box 10, HHCR.

88 Ibid., 27 January 1959.

89 Gregory R. Dillon to Sam Young (President, El Paso National Bank), 23 May 1959, RG 1, Box 10, HHCR.

90 Robert J. Caverly to Herbert C. Blunk, Thomas F. Troy, and Donald M. Mumford, 8 April 1959, RG 1, Box 10, HHCR; López-Fresquet, *My Fourteen Months*, 105–12.

91 Morris H. Morley, *Imperial State*, 81.

92 Sidney H. Willner to Conrad N. Hilton, 9 June 1959, RG 1, Box 10, HHCR.

93 Ibid.

94 Gregory R. Dillon to Sam Young, 19 May 1959, RG 1, Box 10, HHCR; Conrad N. Hilton to Sidney Willner, 11 June 1959, RG 1, Box 10, HHCR.

95 Cárdenas quoted in Eric Solov, "Cuba Sí, Yanquis No! The Sacking of the Instituto Cultural México-Norteamericano in Morelia, Michoacán," in *In from the Cold*, ed. Joseph and Spenser, 216.

96 Arthur E. Elmiger to Conrad N. Hilton, 27 July 1959, RG 1, Box 10, HHCR.

97 *Jack Parr Show* transcript, NBC, 12 October 1959, RG 1, Box 10, HHCR.

98 *New York Times*, 29 April 1959.

99 Quoted in Pérez, *On Becoming Cuban*, 490.

100 Quoted in ibid.

101 Quoted in Paterson, *Contesting Castro*, 257.

102 Quoted in Pérez, *On Becoming Cuban*, 490.

103 *Business Week*, 1 August 1959, 70–72.

104 Notes, July 1959, Folder Cuba Reports 1952–1960, Box 2, HMP.

105 *Fortune*, September 1959, 110–13.

106 *New York Herald Tribune*, 4 August 1959.

107 Quoted in Rosalie Schwartz, *Pleasure Island*, 201.

108 *Time*, 2 November 1959, 24.

109 Ibid.

110 Quoted in McPherson, *Yankee No!*, 62.

111 McPherson views the flyover as the last straw that permitted Castro to justify a staunch anti-American posture and in turn led the Eisenhower administration to abandon all hope of normal diplomatic relations (ibid., 59–64).

112 *Time*, 2 November 1959, 24.

113 McPherson, *Yankee No!*, 67; Rabe, *Eisenhower*, 127.

114 *New York Times*, 23 November 1959.

115 Arthur E. Elmiger to Conrad N. Hilton, 23 November 1959, RG 1, Box 10, HHCR.

116 *Havana Post*, 19 April 1960.

117 Ibid., 18 May 1960.

118 Quoted in Paterson, *Contesting Castro*, 257.

119 Quoted in Higgins, *Perfect Failure*, 48.

120 Ambrose, *Eisenhower*, 557, 584; Rabe, *Eisenhower*, 129–33, 170–73.

121 Quoted in Pérez, *On Becoming Cuban*, 482–83.

122 Sidney H. Willner to Fabian A. Kwiatek (Office of the Assistant Legal Adviser for International Claims, Department of State), 17 July 1960, RG 1, Box 10, HHCR; Earle Palmer Brown to Robert J. Caverly, 6 June 1961, RG 1, Box 10, HHCR.

123 *Havana Post*, 12, 17 June 1960.

124 1960 Annual Report, Box 1, HIR. On the Carte Blanche, see Robert J. Caverly to Kathleen Baird, 2 July 1990, Robert J. Caverly, "Habana Hilton," 15 June 1960, both in RG 1, Box 10, HHCR.

125 Quoted in *Havana Post*, 4 May 1960; McClay, *I Love Lucy*, 10.

126 *New York Times*, 22 January 1961.

127 Ibid., 4 May 1965; Right to Travel to Cuba Campaign, available at <www.righttotraveltocuba.org/history/index (accessed 19 January 2009).

128 Right to Travel to Cuba Campaign, available at <www.righttotraveltocuba.org/history/index (accessed 19 January 2009).

Chapter 5

1 *Time*, 23 June 1958, 30.

2 Ibid., 8 January 1965, 24.

3 The most recent and most thorough account of Puerto Rico's postwar political evolution appears in Ayala and Bernabe, *Puerto Rico*, 95–116, 136–73.

4 Ibid.

5 *Development of Tourism*, 2:12.

6 Fernandez, *Disenchanted Island*, 182–83, 212–14.

7 Blatt, *Study*; Brameld, *Remaking*; Dávila, *Sponsored Identities*; Flores, *Divided Borders*; Haslip-Viera, *Taíno Revival*; Lopez, *Puerto Ricans*; Morales Carrión, *Puerto Rico*; Morris, *Puerto Rico*; Ramos de Santiago, *Gobierno*.

8 Franck, *Roaming*, 256.

9 Marsden, *Sailing South*, 123–212.

10 Blythe, *American Bride*, is the memoir of an American schoolteacher stationed in rural Puerto Rico and within certain limits depicts Puerto Rico in positive terms.

11 For a thoughtful analysis of early U.S. cultural constructions of Puerto Rico, see García, "I Am the Other." A partial list of early travel commentary includes Dinwiddie, *Puerto Rico*; Hamm, *Porto Rico*; Rector, *Story*; Robinson, *Porto Rico*; Seaburg, *Porto Rico*; Verrill, *Puerto Rico*.

12 Cabán, *Constructing*, 107–13, 247–48, 251; Ayala and Bernabe, *Puerto Rico*, 14–26; Mintz, *Workers*. For an introduction to Puerto Rico's colonial economies, see

Scarano, *Sugar and Slavery*; Picó, *Libertad y Servidumbre*; Figueroa, *Sugar*. On violent resistance to the introduction of U.S. rule, see Picó, *Guerra*.

13 Institute of Tourism, Annual Report, 15–17, 34–52, 30 January 1938, OG, Box 702, AGPR.

14 Ibid.

15 Colby, *Puerto Rico*, 9.

16 Jennings, *Our American Tropics*, 188.

17 Cabán, *Constructing*, 228–29; Knight, *Caribbean*, 268–69.

18 Morales Carrión, *Puerto Rico*, 334–35.

19 *Time*, 23 June 1958, 30–32.

20 Morales Carrión, *Puerto Rico*, 232–34; Fernandez, *Disenchanted Island*; Maldonado, *Teodoro Moscoso*, 12–36.

21 Ruby Black, dispatch to *La Democracia*, 15 September 1937, Folder 11, Document 196, Centro de Investigaciones Historíca, University of Puerto Rico, Rio Piedras, Puerto Rico.

22 Dávila, *Sponsored Identities*, 30.

23 Tom Ferris to William D. Leahy, 13 March 1940, OG Box 2003, AGPR.

24 Maldonado, *Teodoro Moscoso*, 119–20; Alegría, Oral History.

25 Latham, *Modernization*, 42–43.

26 *Time*, 23 June 1958, 32.

27 Ibid., 14 May 1956, 43–44.

28 Aitken, *Poet*; Ayala and Bernabe, *Puerto Rico*, 179–200; Dietz, *Economic History*; Gruber, *Puerto Rico*; Hancock, *Puerto Rico*; Earl Parker Hanson, *Transformation*; Maldonado, *Teodoro Moscoso*; Morales Carrión, *Puerto Rico*; *Time*, 23 June 1958; Weisskoff, *Factories*.

29 *New York Times*, 2 August 2000.

30 H. C. Barton Jr. to Teodoro Moscoso, with attached report, "Toward the Development of a Policy for Tourism," 15 February 1955, Jane Nicole Mariana (Director, Puerto Rico Visitors Bureau), "Report on Trip to Hawaii 1953," Teodoro Moscoso to Jose R. Noguera (Director, Bureau of the Budget), 4 December 1951, all in OG, Box 2036, AGPR.

31 Quoted in Harold Underhill, " 'Mr. Bootstrap' Becomes 'Mr. Ambassador,'" *The Diplomat*, 15 June 1961, Teodoro Moscoso Papers, Box 9, JFKL; Moscoso to Marco A. Rigau (Executive Assistant to the Governor) 25 February 1955, OG, Box 2036, AGPR.

32 Frank T. Martocci (Consultant) to Robert Sanchez Vilella (Executive Secretary), 23 February 1949, with enclosure, J. Stanton Robbins, "Part I: Tourism and What It Is," OG, Box 2036, AGPR; Office of Tourism, "Summary of 1949–1950 Budget," n.d., OG, Box 2037, AGPR.

33 *Pan American Clipper*, 10 July 1946, Box 20, PAA; *Fiftieth Annual Report of the Governor of Puerto Rico, Fiscal Year 1949–1950*, 96–97, OG, Box 2037, AGPR.

34 J. Stanton Robbins to Luis Muñoz Marín, 8 July 1949, OG, Box 2036, AGPR.

35 *Saturday Review*, 18 October 1952, 47. On rates, see also Pan American Press Release, 11 May 1950, Box 342, PAA; "Synopsis: Pan American's Operations to Puerto Rico," 2 June 1953, Box 64, PAA.

36 Miguel Angel Barasorda (Office of Tourism) to Luis Laboy (Secretary to the Governor), August 1949, OG, Box 2039, AGPR.

37 Carpenter, "Puerto Rico's Planned Development," 150.

38 *Puerto Rico Travel Newsletter*, December 1956, OG, Box 2037, AGPR.

39 "Report on Nevada Legalized Gambling," 14 May 1950, OG, Box 2038, AGPR.

40 Earl Parker Hanson, *Transformation*, 203. On the concerns of smaller hoteliers, see *El Imparcial*, 15 August 1949; Carpenter, "Puerto Rico's Planned Development," 219–21.

41 *Newsweek*, 16 November 1953, 66.

42 Carpenter, "Puerto Rico's Planned Development," 145–48.

43 Lenèek and Bosker, *Beach*; Löfgren, *On Holiday*.

44 Löfgren, *On Holiday*, 216–20.

45 "Speech to Be Delivered by J. Stanton Robbins on 14 November 1950 at Biloxi, Mississippi, before the National Association of Travel Officials," OG, Box 2037, AGPR.

46 Fomento, "Towards the Development of a Policy for Tourism," ca. 1954–55, OG, Box 2036, AGPR.

47 Colby, *Puerto Rico*, 9.

48 William Ludlow to Rafael Picó, 9 January 1947, OG, Box 2003, AGPR.

49 *Fiftieth Annual Report of the Governor of Puerto Rico, Fiscal Year 1949–1950*, 90, OG, Box 2037, AGPR; "Speech to be Delivered by J. Stanton Robbins on 14 November 1950 at Biloxi, Mississippi, before the National Association of Travel Officials," OG, Box 2037, AGPR.

50 Teodoro Moscoso to Board of Directors, Compania de Fomento Industrial de Puerto Rico, 16 October 1946, OG, Box 2003, AGPR; *Caribe News*, 9 December 1949, Box 17, HHCR. See also Maldonado, *Teodoro Moscoso*, 121–22.

51 Maldonado, *Teodoro Moscoso*, 122.

52 Teodoro Moscoso to Jesús T. Piñero, 20 November 1947, Teodoro Moscoso to Board of Directors, Compañia de Fomento, 16 October 1946, both in OG, Box 2003, AGPR; Guillermo Rodríguez Benítez (Fomento) to Cruz Ortiz Stella, 17 February 1950, OG, Box 2039, AGPR; "Puerto Rico: Showcase for Development," Teodoro Moscoso Papers, Box 9, JFKL.

53 *Hotel Monthly*, February 1950, 27–40; *Time*, 12 December 1949, 87–95; *Life*, 26 December 1949, 72–74; *Caribe News*, 9 December 1949, Box 17, HHCR.

54 Tucker, *Insatiable Appetite*. On beaches worldwide, see Löfgren, *On Holiday*, 221.

55 Guillermo Rodríguez Benítez (Fomento) to Cruz Ortiz Stella, 17 February 1950, OG, Box 2039, AGPR.

56 Luis Muñoz Marín to Alben Barkley, 28 October 1949, OG, Box 2039, AGPR.

57 *Life*, 26 December 1949, 72–74.

58 Thompson, *Rum Diary*, 13.

59 *National Geographic*, April 1951, 423.

60 Carlos M. Passalacqua (Economic Development Administration) to Laurance S. Rockefeller, 29 December 1953, OG, Box 2039, AGPR; *Time*, 23 June 1958; Carlos M. Passalacqua (Economic Development Administration) to Marco A. Rigau (Executive

Assistant to the Governor), 24 August 1954, OG, Box 2039, AGPR; Evan R. Ward, *Packaged Vacations*, 55–70.

61 *Saturday Review*, 6 December 1958, 38–39.

62 Tugwell, *Stricken Land*; Briggs, *Reproducing Empire*, 172–88; Sanchéz Korrol, *From Colonia to Community*, 3–4, 132.

63 Leonard Bourne (Hamilton Wright) to Stanton Robbins, 28 January 1949, Esteban A. Bird (Tourism Advisory Board) to Luis Muñoz Marín, 17 January 1949, both in OG, Box 2037, AGPR; Teodoro Moscoso to Gustavo Agrait (Public Relations Official), 1 March 1949, Leonard Bourne to Teodoro Moscoso, 25 February 1949, both in OG, Box 1435, AGPR.

64 J. Stanton Robbins to Tourist Advisory Board, 16 September 1949, OG, Box 2037, AGPR.

65 William H. Stead, "Fomento: The Economic Development of Puerto Rico," National Planning Association, March 1958, Teodoro Moscoso Papers, Box 7, JFKL.

66 *Puerto Rico Travel Newsletter*, December 1956, OG, Box 2037, AGPR.

67 Stanton Robbins to Luis Muñoz Marín, 18 April 1950, OG, Box 2037, AGPR.

68 "Suggested Reorganization of Office of Tourism," n.d., Ian Gileadi to Stanton Robbins, 25 August 1949, both in OG, Box 2037, AGPR.

69 Hamilton Wright Jr. to Teodoro Moscoso, 6 December 1948, Wright to Jesús T. Piñero, 17 May 1948, both in OG, Box 1436, AGPR; Wright to Arthur Hays Sulzburger, 30 November 1950, OG, Box 1435, AGPR.

70 These representations of gender and tourism had become standard fare of the travel section of the *New York Times* by the late 1950s and early 1960s. See, for example, *New York Times*, 2 February, 13 April 1958, 10 April 1960.

71 *Travel News*, October 1951, 171.

72 Hamilton Wright Jr. to Teodoro Moscoso, 29 September 1949, OG, Box 1435, AGPR.

73 *Saturday Review*, 18 October 1952, 49.

74 See, for example, Leonard Bourne to Anne O'Hare McCormick (*New York Times*), 25 September 1952, OG, Box 1435, AGPR.

75 Luis Muñoz Marín to Arthur Hays Sulzberger, 24 February 1953, OG, Box 1429, AGPR.

76 William Van Dusen (Vice President, Eastern Airlines) to Luis Muñoz Marín, 7 August 1951, OG, Box 1429, AGPR.

77 *Travel News*, November 1951, 33.

78 *Saturday Review*, 18 October 1952, 48.

79 *Time*, 14 May 1956, 43–44.

80 Gustavo Agrait to Beverly E. Miller (Office of Tourism), 16 August 1949, OG, Box 2037, AGPR.

81 Gustavo Agrait to Donald O'Connor (Acting Director, Office of Tourism), 18 October 1949, OG, Box 2037, AGPR.

82 T. Vidal to Luis Muñoz Marín, 23 November 1954, OG, Box 2036, AGPR.

83 Puerto Rico Visitor's Bureau, "A Report on Travel Advertising," OG, Box 2038, AGPR.

84 Marco A. Rigau (Executive Assistant to the Governor) to Belén C. Brown (Fomento),

10 February 1953, Belén Brown, "Visitantes en Puerto Rico durante el Año Fiscal 1951–1952," n.d., both in OG, Box 2037, AGPR.

85 Fomento, "Towards the Development of a Policy for Tourism," ca. 1954–55, OG, Box 2036, AGPR.

86 Wangeman, Oral History, 222.

87 Maldonado, *Teodoro Moscoso*, 128–32.

88 V. R. Esteves to Roberto Sanchez Vilella (Executive Secretary, Governor's Staff), 25 February 1949, OG, Box 2036, AGPR; Frank T. Martocci to Carlos M. Passalacqua (President, Puerto Rico Industrial Development Company), 22 July 1954, OG, Box 2038, AGPR.

89 J. Stanton Robbins to Luis Muñoz Marín, 8 July 1949, OG, Box 2036, AGPR; *New York Times*, 3 December 1961.

90 Lewis, *Vida*, 183–88, 244; *Island Times*, 22 January 1960.

91 Quoted in Maldonado, *Teodoro Moscoso*, 121.

92 *El Mundo*, 8, 9, 16, 17 October 1952.

93 *Architectural Forum*, March 1950, 97.

94 Quoted in Maldonado, *Teodoro Moscoso*, 123–24.

95 José Raul Cancio (Legal Counsel) to Gustavo Agrait (Executive Assistant to the Governor), 9 January 1950, OG, Box 2039, AGPR.

96 Wangeman, Oral History, 27; Conrad Hilton to Frank Wangeman, 7 May 1951, Conrad Hilton to Guillermo Rodriguez (Puerto Rico Industrial Development Company) 16 March 1951, both in Box 4, HHCR.

97 Enrique Bird to Teodoro Moscoso, 19 February 1954, OG, Box 2039, AGPR.

98 Ayala and Bernabe, *Puerto Rico*, 62, 98–99, 141–42, 145–46, 154, 232–33.

99 Memorandum to Luis Muñoz Marín, 26 January 1955, Teodoro Moscoso to Muñoz Marín, 28 January 1955, both in OG, Box 2039, AGPR. The strike was reported extensively in San Juan's newspapers, including *El Mundo*, 22, 24, 26, 29 January 1955; *El Imparcial*, 25, 28, 29 January 1955. On women and the labor movement, see Altagracia Ortiz, "Puerto Rican Women Workers in the Twentieth Century: A Historical Appraisal of the Literature," in *Puerto Rican Women's History*, ed. Matos Rodríguez and Delgado, 41–44.

100 For example, between 1961 and 1967, weekly earnings for hotel workers rose from an average of $37.81 to $59.47, a 57 percent increase that easily outpaced inflation. Union agreements reached in 1968 allowed for significant monthly pay increases, vacation and sick leave up to twenty-two days each, additional holidays, pensions, and other benefits. See *Development of Tourism*, 2:19, 6:106–27.

101 H. C. Barton to Teodoro Moscoso and attached report, 15 February 1955, OG, Box 2036, AGPR.

102 Fred L. Nino (Horwath and Horwath) to Teodoro Moscoso, 20 May 1954, OG, Box 2036, AGPR.

103 Carlos M. Passalacqua (President and General Administrator) to Rafael Picó, 13 November 1953, OG, Box 2036, AGPR.

104 Frank T. Martocci to Carlos M. Passalacqua, 22 July 1954, OG, Box 2038, AGPR; H. C.

Barton to Teodoro Moscoso and attached report, 15 February 1955, OG, Box 2036, AGPR; *Puerto Rico Travel Newsletter*, May 1956, OG, Box 2037, AGPR; Carpenter, "Puerto Rico's Planned Development," 105, 117–28.

105 *Puerto Rico Travel Newsletter*, May, August, October 1956, OG, Box 2037, AGPR.

106 Jane Nicole de Mariani (Director, Department of Tourism) to Marco A. Rigau (Executive Assistant to Governor), 23 July 1954, and Enclosed Speech, 21 July 1954, OG, Box 2037, AGPR.

107 Ibid.

108 J. Stanton Robbins to Roberto Sanchez Vilella, 26 April 1949, OG, Box 2036, AGPR

109 Ibid.

110 Earl Parker Hanson, *Transformation*, 206.

111 *Island Times*, 1, 15, 29 January, 26 February, 3 March 1960; *New York Times*, 3 December 1961; *Saturday Review*, 14 September 1968, 50; *Travel*, April 1969, 30; Gruber, *Puerto Rico*, 145–60.

112 Dávila, *Sponsored Identities*, 142.

113 "Los Primeros Dieciocho Meses del Instituto de Cultura Puertorriqueño," 1957, 173, 5, LMML; *Island Times*, 16 February, 30 March 1962; *San Juan Star*, 15 April 1996; Alegría, Oral History.

114 Arlene Dávila, "Local/Diasporic Taínos: Towards a Cultural Politics of Memory, Reality, and History," in *Taíno Revival*, ed. Haslip-Viera, 33–53.

115 Quoted in Gruber, *Puerto Rico*, 167; Morales Carrión, *Puerto Rico*, 338–43.

116 Ogilvy, *Confessions*, 79–80; Glatzer, *New Advertising*, 116; H. C. Barton Jr. (Fomento Office of Economic Research) to Teodoro Moscoso, 15 February 1955, OG, Box 2036, AGPR; Carpenter, "Puerto Rico's Planned Development," 157–58.

117 *New Yorker*, 15 March 1958, 28–29; Ogilvy, *Ogilvy on Advertising*, 133; Glatzer, *New Advertising*, 116.

118 *Puerto Rico Travel Newsletter*, September 1956, OG, Box 2037, AGPR.

119 Dietz, *Economic History*, 340–410.

120 "Plans for Affordable Tourism," n.d., File 137, #3, LMML.

121 Ibid.

122 Major academic journals devoted to the subject include the *Cold War History Bulletin* and *Cold War History*. The literature on the Cold War is indeed massive and growing, but to sample the terms of the traditional debate, see Gaddis, *Cold War*, which assigns the bulk of the blame for the Cold War's onset to Joseph Stalin's relentless quest to expand the Soviet communist system. Lafeber's *America, Russia, and the Cold War* acknowledges Stalin's ruthless dictatorship and Soviet expansionism but also highlights how America's appetite for economic and military expansion, along with a tendency to exaggerate the Soviet threat, helped provoke the conflict.

123 On the era's globalizing trends, see Iriye, *Cultural Internationalism*, 11, 131–85.

124 A few works that mine the Cold War's rich international social and cultural history include Bradley, *Imagining Vietnam*; De Grazia, *Irresistible Empire*; Endy, *Cold War Holidays*; Gienow-Hecht, *Transmission Impossible*; Gleijeses, *Conflicting Missions*; Hogan, *Marshall Plan*; Latham, *Modernization*; Maier, *Among Empires*, Pérez, *On*

Becoming Cuban; Rotter, *Comrades*; Staples, *Birth*; Suri, *Power and Protest*; Westad, *Global Cold War*.

125 Klein, *Cold War Orientalism*, 22–28.

126 Joseph and Spenser, *In from the Cold*, 3–29. On the Guatemala intervention, see Cullather, *Secret History*; Gleijeses, *Shattered Hope*; Grandin, *Last Colonial Massacre*; Immerman, *CIA*; Stephen C. Schlesinger and Kinzer, *Bitter Fruit*; Streeter, *Managing*.

127 Ayala and Bernabe (*Puerto Rico*, 151–52) have contrasted Puerto Rico's moderately reformist modernization to the populist governments of Perón in Argentina, Vargas and Goulart in Brazil, and Arbenz in Guatemala and implied that continued dependency on the United States inhibited more assertive policies. I see the same contrasts in political orientation but conclude that Puerto Rico's ability to maneuver within the context of empire helps explain the island's avoidance of the types of militarism and authoritarianism that emerged so prominently in Argentina, Brazil, Guatemala, and elsewhere.

128 *Time*, 12 December 1949, 87–90.

129 *National Geographic*, April 1951, 423.

130 *Saturday Review*, 18 October 1952, 48.

Chapter 6

1 *New York Times*, 14 November 1961; Muñoz Marín, Oral History, 15.

2 Report of the Task Force on Immediate Latin American Problems, Teodoro Moscoso Papers, Box 9, JFKL; Morales Carrión, *Puerto Rico*, 299; Arthur M. Schlesinger Jr., *Thousand Days*, 764–65, 790–91; Levinson and de Onís, *Alliance*, 54; Rabe, *Most Dangerous Area*, 166, 28.

3 Report of the Task Force on Immediate Latin American Problems, Teodoro Moscoso Papers, Box 9, JFKL.

4 *New York Times*, 20 January 1959.

5 Herbert Matthews to Fidel Castro, 2 February 1959, Box 3, Folder "Notes, Clippings, Letters for Chapter 4," HMP.

6 López-Fresquet, *My Fourteen Months*, 100–103.

7 See, for example, Gruber, *Puerto Rico*, 58–85.

8 *Time*, 23 June 1958, 30–37.

9 Ibid., 31.

10 *Saturday Review*, 5 December 1959, 26.

11 *Time*, 1 December 1958, 31; *New York Times*, 6 December 1959.

12 Carpenter, "Puerto Rico's Planned Development," 176–78.

13 *Puerto Rico Travel Newsletter*, May 1956, OG, Box 2037, AGPR; *Time*, 23 June 1958; *Saturday Review*, 6 December 1958, 10.

14 *Puerto Rico Travel Newsletter*, August 1956, OG, Box 2037, AGPR; *Puerto Rico World Journal*, 17 July, 1 August 1956.

15 *Saturday Review*, 6 December 1958, 10.

16 *Time*, 1 December 1958, 31.

17 *U.S. News and World Report*, 28 March 1960, 56.

18 *New York Times*, 3 December 1959.

19 Ibid., 3 March 1960; *Island Times*, 3 March 1960.

20 *Saturday Review*, 17 October 1964, 40–41.

21 *U.S. News and World Report*, 28 March 1960, 55; *Time*, 23 June 1958, 34.

22 Aitken, *Poet*; *Saturday Review*, 17 October 1964, 40–41; Hancock, *Puerto Rico*; *Travel*, April 1961, 22–25; Earl Parker Hanson, *Transformation*.

23 Gruber, *Puerto Rico*, 205–14.

24 Rabe, *Most Dangerous Area*, 151.

25 Important works on the Alliance for Progress include Baily, *United States*, 82–131; Simon G. Hanson, *Dollar Diplomacy*; LaFeber, *Inevitable Revolutions*, 150–96; Latham, *Modernization*, 69–108; Levinson and de Onís, *Alliance*; Rabe, *Most Dangerous Area*, 148–72; Scheman, *Alliance*; Taffet, *Foreign Aid*; Joseph S. Tulchin, "The Promise of Progress: U.S. Relations with Latin America during the Administration of Lyndon B. Johnson," in *Lyndon Johnson*, ed. Warren I. Cohen and Tucker, 211–43; William O. Walker III, "Mixing the Sweet with the Sour: Kennedy, Johnson, and Latin America," in *Diplomacy*, ed. Kunz, 42–79.

26 Rabe, *Most Dangerous Area*, 141, 151. On dictatorship and the 1970s, see Alexander, *Tragedy*; Feitlowitz, *Lexicon*; Hitchens, *Trial*; Klare and Arnson, *Supplying Repression*; Kornbluh, *Pinochet File*; LaFeber, *Inevitable Revolutions*, 197–270; Tulchin, *Argentina*.

27 Hoffman, *All You Need*; Fisher, *Making Them*; Gary May, "Passing the Torch and Lighting Fires: The Peace Corps," in Paterson, *Kennedy's Quest*; Rice, *Bold Experiment*.

28 Rostow, *Stages*. See also Rostow, *Eisenhower, Kennedy, and Foreign Aid*.

29 Quoted in Latham, *Modernization*, 69; also quoted in Merrill, *Bread*, 172.

30 Latham, *Modernization*, 69.

31 Ibid., 92.

32 Rabe, *Most Dangerous Area*, 99–101.

33 Latham, *Modernization*, 115; Teodoro Moscoso, Oral History; *Saturday Review*, 17 October 1964, 40.

34 *New York Times*, 19 January 1961.

35 *Saturday Review*, 17 October 1964, 40.

36 Arthur M. Schlesinger Jr., *Thousand Days*, 764–65.

37 On Costa Rica, see Booth, *Costa Rica*; LaFeber, *Inevitable Revolutions*, 11–12, 100–111, 186–89; Longley, *Sparrow*. On U.S.-Colombian relations, see Randall, *Colombia*. On Venezuela, see Alexander, *Romulo Betancourt*; Rabe, *Eisenhower*; Rabe, *Road*; Rivas, *Missionary Capitalist*.

38 Rabe, *Most Dangerous Area*, 180.

39 Teodoro Moscoso, "Industrial Development in Puerto Rico," Paper Prepared for the Organization for European Economic Co-Operation, Second Study Conference on Economic Development Problems, 10–15 April 1961, Teodoro Moscoso Papers, Box 9, JFKL.

40 Thompson, *Rum Diary*, 69–70.

41 *Saturday Review*, 6 January 1968, 53–54, 87–88; *Development of Tourism*, 3:60.

42 "The Interagency Study of the Puerto Rican Economy: Part 10. Tourism Sector Study," 30 June 1978, Box 143, PAA.

43 *Island Times*, 21 June 1956.

44 Ibid., 9 November 1963, 7 July 1956.

45 Ibid., 5 February 1960. See also *Puerto Rico World Journal*, 12, 16 May 1956.

46 *Development of Tourism*, 2:136, 3:59, 6:107–9.

47 *Island Times*, 8 April 1960.

48 *Puerto Rico World Journal*, 12 May 1956.

49 Ibid., 16 May 1956.

50 Carlos M. Passalacqua (General Manager, Fomento) to William Land (General Manager, Caribe Hilton), 6 October 1955, OG, Box 2039, AGPR.

51 *Puerto Rico Libre*, 31 January 1950.

52 Earl Parker Hanson, *Transformation*, 293.

53 Carl Hilton to Conrad Hilton, 16 January 1950, Box 3, HHCR.

54 Carlos M. Passalacqua (Fomento) to Laurance Rockefeller, 4 March 1954, OG, Box 2039, AGPR.

55 Löfgren, *On Holiday*, 224–29.

56 Ibid.; Aronson, *Working at Play*, 73–100; Wiltse, *Contested Waters*, 13–22, 76–89.

57 *Island Times*, 26 February, 8 July 1960.

58 Ibid., 20 May 1960.

59 Carmen Teresa Whalen, "Labor Migrants or Submissive Wives: Competing Narratives of Puerto Rican Women in the Post–World War II Era," in *Puerto Rican Women's History*, ed. Matos Rodríguez and Delgado, 206–26.

60 Briggs, *Reproducing Empire*, 129–46.

61 *Development of Tourism*, 2:30.

62 *El Mundo*, 9 October 1952.

63 *Development of Tourism*, 6:108–10, 7:49.

64 *Island Times*, 11 March 1960. For background on San Juan's gay subculture, see the tourist guidebook *Access: Gay U.S.A.* On the challenges facing San Juan's contemporary gay community, see *San Juan Star*, 13, 20 February, 5, 6 June 1995.

65 See, for example, *Claridad*, January 1959, January, March 1960.

66 Fernandez, *Disenchanted Island*, 182–83, 212–14; John Henry Baker, "Relationship."

67 *New York Times*, 24 January 1960.

68 Ibid., 6 November 1960.

69 *Saturday Review*, 6 January 1968, 53–54, 87–88.

70 *Island Times*, 12 May 1960.

71 Carpenter, "Puerto Rico's Planned Development," 217.

72 *Saturday Review*, 14 September 1968, 50, 93–95.

73 *Island Times*, 26 January 1962; *New York Times*, 3 December 1961.

74 *Travel*, April 1961, 22–25; Chiesa de Pérez, *Enjoy*, 125–26, 175; *Saturday Review*, 14 September 1968, 98–99.

75 *Puerto Rico World Journal*, 12 July 1956; *San Juan Star*, 15 April 1996; Alegría, Oral History.

76 Quoted in Dávila, *Sponsored Identities*, 41; *Puerto Rico World Journal*, 21 June 1956; Alegría, Oral History.

77 *Island Times*, 1 June 1962. For responses, see *Island Times*, 8, 15 June 1962.

78 Ibid., 18 May 1962.

79 Boorstin, "Self-Discovery," 245.

80 See Arlene Dávila, "Local/Diasporic Taínos: Towards a Cultural Politics of Memory, Reality, and Imagery," in *Taíno Revival*, ed. Haslip-Viera, 33–54; Jorge Duany, "Making Indians Out of Blacks: The Revitalization of Taíno Identity in Contemporary Puerto Rico," in *Taíno Revival*, ed. Haslip-Viera, 55–82.

81 *Free Puerto Rico* (Newsletter of the Free Puerto Rico Committee), Winter 1988, 3; Duany, "Making Indians." As late as 1986, an opinion poll published in the statehood organ *El Nuevo Dia* revealed that 44 percent of those questioned sympathized with the patriotic aims of the Macheteros, an armed clandestine proindependence movement.

82 *Claridad*, 2 April 1960.

83 Ibid., 1 June 1959

84 Ibid., 29 August 1959.

85 *Development of Tourism*, 2:62–64.

86 *Island Times*, 27 July 1962.

87 "Memorandum de la Conversacion con Kennedy," 18 January 1961, Folder 4, Document 1, LMML; "Memorandum para el Record: Entrevista con el President Kennedy," 27 June 1961, Folder 3, Document 25, LMML.

88 Luis Muñoz Marín to John F. Kennedy, 30 September 1963, Folder 1, Document 1, LMML.

89 Ibid., 28 December 1961, Folder 3, Document 1, LMML.

90 Dávila, *Sponsored Identities*, 220–32.

91 *Puerto Rico, U.S.A.*, 25–26. In addition to the creation of ten thousand jobs directly related to tourism, analysts estimated up to three times that number indirectly related to tourism in spin-off enterprises.

92 *San Juan Star*, 12 May, 9 August 1971; Diago, Oral History. On the firebombings, see John Henry Baker, "Relationship," 16.

93 *San Juan Star*, 9 August 1971.

94 Ibid., 10 June 1971.

95 Puerto Rico Tourism Company, "Tourism Activity in Fiscal Years," 2005, available at <www.gotopuertorico.com/pressRoom/mediaResources/tourist—economic—indicators.htm> (accessed 17 January 2009); Diago, Oral History.

96 Diago, Oral History; *Development of Tourism*, 2:12.

97 *Development of Tourism*, 2:102.

98 Endy, *Cold War Holidays*, 192.

99 Ibid., 184–91.

100 See, for example, Rabe, *Most Dangerous Area*, 1–2. On popular memory as cultural icon, see Rosenberg, *Date*, 3–4.

101 On 1970s U.S.-backed dictatorships, see, for example Grandin, *Empire's Workshop*, esp. 49, 59–63, 71–72, 77–90, 95–104, 163–72; Gustafson, *Hostile Intent*; Lafeber,

Inevitable Revolutions, 197–264; Sheinin, *Argentina*, 160–63; Stern, *Remembering*, 22, 161; Wright, *State Terrorism*.

102 Grandin, *Empire's Workshop*, 163–72; Kline, *Shock Doctrine*, 73–131.

103 Stiglitz, *Globalization*, 16–22.

104 Dickinson and Vladimir, *Selling*, 65–69; Diago, Oral History.

105 Diago, Oral History.

106 Teodoro Moscoso, "Industrial Development in Puerto Rico," Paper Prepared for the Organization for European Economic Co-Operation, Second Study Conference on Economic Development Problems, 10–15 April 1961, Teodoro Moscoso Papers, Box 9, JFKL.

Conclusion

1 For the historiographical skirmish over culture, see Hogan and Paterson, *Explaining*.

2 Honey, *Ecotourism*; *New York Times*, 17 December 2006.

3 On culinary tourism, see, for example, *New York Times*, 28 January 1990. On Jamaica's hedonism tourism for singles, see, for example, *New York Times*, 19 October 2003.

4 Dickinson and Vladimir, *Selling*, esp. 37, 41–45, 49, 54–62.

5 Evan R. Ward, *Packaged Vacations*, 105–34. See also Siegel, *Cancún's User Guide*, 71, 84; Rebecca Torres and Janet Henshell Momsen, "Gringolandia: Cancún and the American Tourist," in *Adventures*, ed. Bloom, 58–76.

6 Evan R. Ward, *Packaged Vacations*, 105–34.

7 Ibid., 118, 124, 134.

8 *Excelsior*, 7 July 2008.

9 *Los Angeles Times*, 17 February 2008; Catherine Elsworth, "Tijuana Tourism Halved by Kidnapping Scares," 7 March 2008, <www.telegraph.co.uk> (accessed 27 June 2008); *New York Times*, 23, 31 August 2008.

10 Silja J. A. Talvi, "As the Violence Soars," 14 October 2008, <www.alternet.org> (accessed 15 January 2009); *Los Angeles Times*, 11 October 2008.

11 "Mexico Drug Violence Kills 11," <http://bbc.co.uk> (accessed 15 January 2009).

12 *Los Angeles Times*, 23 December 2007; *New York Times*, 17 April 2009.

13 Evan R. Ward, *Packaged Vacations*, 137–54, 185–86.

14 <www.frommers.com/destinations/havana> (accessed 30 June 2008).

15 Evan R. Ward, *Packaged Vacations*, 185; Stanley, *Cuba*, 230.

16 Christopher P. Baker, *Cuba Handbook*, 86–88, 439; *New York Times*, 18 April 2009.

17 Puerto Rico Tourism Company, "Tourism Activity in Fiscal Years," 2005, available at <www.gotopuertorico.com/pressRoom/mediaResources/tourist—economic—indicators.htm> (accessed 17 January 2009); Diago, Oral History.

18 Dickinson and Vladimir, *Selling*, 38.

19 Rabin, Oral History; <www.viequeslibre.addr.com>.

20 Rabin, Oral History.

21 Laursen and Truesdell, *Let's Go*, 173–88.

22 Barber, *Jihad*.

23 Grandin, *Empire's Workshop*.

Bibliography

Archives

Amherst College, Archives and Special Collections, Amherst, Massachusetts
    Dwight W. Morrow Papers
Archivo General de la Nación, Mexico City, Mexico
    Lázaro Cárdenas Papers
    Pascual Ortíz Rubio Papers
    Emilio Portes Gil Papers
Archivo General de Puerto Rico, San Juan, Puerto Rico
    Economic Development Administration Records
    Records of the Office of the Governor
Center for Puerto Rican Studies, Hunter College, New York, New York
Centro de Investigaciones Historícas, University of Puerto Rico, Río Piedras, Puerto Rico
    Ruby Black Papers
Columbia University Library, Manuscripts Division, New York, New York
    Herbert Matthews Papers
    Frank Tannenbaum Papers
Conrad N. Hilton College Library and Archives, University of Houston, Houston, Texas
    Hilton Hotel Corporation Records
    Hilton International Records
Cuban Heritage Collection, Otto Richter Library, University of Miami, Coral Gables, Florida
DeGolyer Library, Southern Methodist University, Dallas, Texas
John F. Kennedy Presidential Library, Boston, Massachusetts
    Teodoro Moscoso Papers
Library of Congress, Manuscript Division, Washington, D.C.
    Josephus Daniels Papers
Luis Muñoz Marín Library, Trujillo Alto, Puerto Rico
    Teodoro Moscoso Papers
    Luis Muñoz Marín Papers

National Archives of the United States, College Park, Maryland
    Department of State Records
Pan American Airlines Archive, Coral Gables, Florida
U.S. Department of State Central File, Cuba. Frederick, Md.: University Publications of
    America, 1987.

Periodicals

American Historical Review
American Studies International
Annals of Tourism Research
Architectural Forum
Bohemia
Business Week
Cinema Journal
Claridad
Cuba Magazine
The Diplomat
Diplomatic History
Editor and Publisher
Excelsior
Harper's Monthly
Havana Post
Holiday
Hotel Monthly
El Imparcial
Island Times
Jet Age (Pan Am)
Journal of American–East Asian Relations
Journal of American History
Journal of San Diego History
Life
Los Angeles Times
Miami Herald
Mexican Art and Life
El Mundo
Nation
National Geographic
Newsweek
New York Herald Tribune
New York Times
New Yorker
El Nueva Dia

Pacific American Historical Review
Parade
Pan American Clipper
Pan American Union
Pemex Travel Club Bulletin
La Prensa
Puerto Rico Libre
Puerto Rico World Journal
Qué Pasa en Puerto Rico
Revolución
Review of Reviews
San Juan Star
Saturday Evening Post
Saturday Review
Survey Magazine
Time
Times of Havana
Times Talk
Travel
Travel News (American Society of Travel Agents)
U.S. News and World Report
Wall Street Journal
Yale Review

Web Sites

http://bbc.co.uk
www.alternet.org
www.frommers.com/destinations/havana
www.gotopuertorico.com
www.gwu.edu/nsarchiv
www.marketresearch.com
www.onecaribbean.org/information
www.righttotraveltocuba.org
www.telegraph.co.uk
www.viequeslibre.addr.com

Oral Histories

Ricardo Alegría (former director of the Institute of Puerto Rican Culture), by the author,
   San Juan, Puerto Rico, 6 June 1999.
Rudolfo Casparius (former manager of the Havana Hilton), by the author, Houston,
   Texas, 27 March 2001, recording housed at the Conrad N. Hilton College Library and
   Archives, Houston, Texas.

Carlos Diago (former Puerto Rican Tourism Bureau official and professor of business at
Sacred Heart University, Santurce), by the author, San Juan, Puerto Rico, 10 June 1999.

Luis Muñoz Marín, John F. Kennedy Presidential Library, Boston, Massachusetts.

Teodoro Moscoso, Luis Muñoz Marín Library, Trujillo Alto, Puerto Rico.

Katherine Anne Porter, in Joan Givner, ed., *Katherine Anne Porter: Conversations*
(Jackson: University Press of Mississippi, 1987).

Robert Rabin (director of the Vieques Museum), by the author, Isabel Segunda, Vieques,
Puerto Rico, 5 June 1997.

Robert Strand, n.d., Conrad N. Hilton College Library and Archives, Houston, Texas.

Frank G. Wangeman, by Cathleen D. Baird, Houston, Texas, 28 October 1993, 27–28 April
1996, Hilton Hotel Corporation Records, Conrad N. Hilton College Library and
Archives, Houston, Texas.

Fiction, Memoirs, Travelogues, and Government Documents

Access: Gay U.S.A. New York: Access, 1998.

Aitken, Thomas, Jr. *Poet in the Fortress: The Story of Luis Muñoz Marín.* New York: New
American Library, 1964.

Baker, Christopher P. *Cuba Handbook.* Chico, Calif.: Moon, 1997.

Banning, George Hugh. *In Mexican Waters.* Boston: Lauriat, 1925.

Barretto, Larry. *Bright Mexico.* New York: Farrar and Rinehart, 1935.

Batista, Fulgencio. *The Growth and Decline of the Cuban Republic.* New York: Devin-
Adair, 1964.

Blythe, Marion. *An American Bride in Porto Rico.* New York: Revell, 1911.

Boorstin, Daniel J. *The Image: A Guide to Pseudo-Events in America.* 25th anniv. ed. New
York: Vintage, 1992.

———. "Self-Discovery in Puerto Rico." *Yale Review* 45 (Winter 1955): 229–45.

Brenner, Anita. *Your Mexican Holiday: A Modern Guide.* New York: Putnam's, 1932.

Carr, Harry. *Old Mother Mexico.* Boston: Houghton Mifflin, 1931.

Castro, Fidel. *La Historia Me Absolverá.* Havana: Editora Política, 1964.

Chase, Stuart. *Mexico: A Study of Two Americas.* New York: Macmillan, 1932.

Chiesa de Pérez, Carmen. *Enjoy Puerto Rico: Intimate Views and Tours.* New York:
Vantage, 1961.

Clark, Sydney. *All the Best in Cuba.* New York: Dodd, Mead, 1946.

———. *Cuban Tapestry.* New York: McBride, 1948.

Colby, Merle. *Puerto Rico: A Profile in Pictures.* New York: Duell, Sloan, and Pearce, 1940.

Compendium of Tourism Statistics. Madrid: World Tourism Organization, 1996.

Cudahy, John. *Mañanaland: Adventuring with Camera and Rifle through California in
Mexico.* New York: Duffield, 1928.

Daniels, Josephus. *Shirtsleeve Diplomat.* Chapel Hill: University of North Carolina Press,
1947.

Development of Tourism in the Commonwealth of Puerto Rico. 7 vols. South Pasadena,
Calif.: Stanford University Research Institute for the Puerto Rican Economic
Development Administration, 1968.

Dinwiddie, William. *Puerto Rico: Its Conditions and Possibilities.* New York: Harper, 1899.

Doctrina, Proyectos y Actividades del Instituto Cuban del Turismo, 20 Febrero 1953–20 Febrero 1954. Havana: Republic of Cuba, Instituto del Turismo, 1954.

Ford, Norman D. *Fiesta Lands: Through Cuba, Mexico, Guatemala and Other Countries along the Pan American Highway on a Shoestring.* Greenlawn, N.Y.: Harian, 1954.

Foster, Harry L. *Gringo in Mañanaland.* London: Lane, 1924.

Franck, Harry A. *Roaming through the West Indies.* New York: Blue Ribbon, 1920.

———. *Trailing Cortez through Mexico.* New York: Stokes, 1935.

Fuentes, Carlos. *The Death of Artemio Cruz.* New York: Farrar, Straus, and Giroux, 1964.

Graham, Stephen. *In Quest of El Dorado.* New York: Appleton, 1923.

Greene, Graham. *The Lawless Roads.* London: Windmill, 1939.

Gruber, Ruth. *Puerto Rico: Island of Promise.* New York: Hill and Wang, 1960.

Gruening, Ernest. *Mexico and Its Heritage.* New York: Century, 1928.

Haas, Elise S. *Letters from Mexico.* San Francisco: Gravehorn, 1937.

Hamm, Margherita Arlina. *Porto Rico and the West Indies.* London: Neely, 1899.

Hancock, Ralph. *Puerto Rico: A Success Story.* Princeton: Van Nostrand, 1960.

Hanson, Earl Parker. *Transformation: The Story of Modern Puerto Rico.* New York: Simon and Schuster, 1955.

Herring, Hubert. "Cardenas Triumphs in Mexico." *Current History*, 25 September 1935, 636–38.

Herring, Hubert, and Katherine Terrill, eds. *The Genius of Mexico.* New York: Committee on Cultural Cooperation with Latin America, 1931.

Herring, Hubert, and Herbert Weinstock, eds. *Renascent Mexico.* New York: Committee on Cultural Cooperation with Latin America, 1935.

Hilton, Conrad. *Be My Guest.* New York: Simon and Schuster, 1957.

In Gay Havana. Havana: Cuban Tourist Commission, n.d.

The Inviting Island Next Door. Havana: Cuban Tourist Commission, n.d.

Jennings, John E. *Our American Tropics.* New York: Crowell, 1938.

Johnson, Jack. *The Autobiography of Jack Johnson in and out of the Ring.* New York: Citadel, 1992.

"Land of Opportunity, Playland of the Americas." *Cuba Magazine*, 1959.

Lanks, Herbert C. *Highway across the West Indies.* New York: Appleton-Century-Crofts, 1948.

Laursen, Lucas, and Lauren Truesdell. *Let's Go Puerto Rico.* New York: St. Martin's, 2006.

Lewis, Oscar. *La Vida: A Puerto Rican Family in the Culture of Poverty—San Juan and New York.* New York: Random House, 1965.

Lindbergh, Charles A. *Autobiography of Values.* New York: Harcourt, Brace, Jovanovich, 1976.

López-Fresquet, Rufo. *My Fourteen Months with Castro.* Cleveland: World, 1966.

Macaulay, Neill. *A Rebel in Cuba.* 1970; Micanopy, Fla.: Wacahoota, 1999.

Mackie, Edith, and Sheldon Dick. *Mexican Journey: An Intimate Guide to Mexico.* New York: Dodge, 1935.

Maribona, Armando. *Turismo in Cuba.* Havana: Editorial Lex, 1959.

Marsden, Phillip S. *Sailing South*. Boston: Houghton Mifflin, 1921.

Martin, Lawrence, and Sylvia Martin. *The Standard Guide to Mexico and the Caribbean*. New York: Funk and Wagnalls, 1958.

McBride, Mary Margaret. *The Story of Dwight W. Morrow*. New York: Farrar and Rinehart, 1930.

Merritt-Hawkes, O. A. *High Up in Mexico*. London: Nicholson, 1936.

Miller, Max. *Mexico around Me*. New York: Reynall and Hitchcock, 1937.

Morley, Sylvanus G. *An Introduction to the Study of Mayan Hieroglyphs*. 1915; New York: Dover, 1975.

Morrow, Elizabeth Cutter. *Casa Mañana*. Croton Falls, N.Y.: Spiral, 1932.

O'Brien, Howard Vincent. *Notes for a Book about Mexico*. Chicago: Willett, Clark, 1937.

Ogilvy, David. *Confessions of an Advertising Man*. London: Southbank, 2008.

——. *Ogilvy on Advertising*. New York: Vintage, 1985.

Phillips, Henry Albert. *New Designs for Old Mexico*. New York: National Travel Club, 1939.

Phillips, Ruby Hart. *Cuba: Island of Paradox*. New York: McDowell, Obolensky, 1961.

Puerto Rico, U.S.A. Washington, D.C.: Office of the Commonwealth of Puerto Rico, 1969.

Rector, Charles H. *The Story of Beautiful Porto Rico: A Graphic Description of the Garden Spot of the World by Pen and Camera*. Chicago: Laird and Lee, 1898.

Riley, Marcene. *Daylight through Mexico*. Boston: Humphries, 1939.

Roberts, W. Adolphe. *Havana: The Portrait of a City*. New York: Coward-McCann, 1953.

Robinson, Albert G. *The Porto Rico of To-Day: Pen Pictures of the People and the Country*. New York: Scribner's, 1899.

Rostow, W. W. *The Stages of Economic Development: A Non-Communist Manifesto*. Cambridge: Cambridge University Press, 1960.

Scully, Michael, and Virginia Scully. *Motorists' Guide to Mexico*. Dallas: Southwest, 1933.

Seaburg, Joseph B. *Porto Rico: The Land of the Rich Port*. Vol. 12 of *The World and Its People*. New York: Silver, Burdett, 1903.

Selected Statistics of the Tourism Industry in Puerto Rico, 2002–2004. San Juan: Puerto Rico Tourism Company, Office of Research and Statistics, 2005.

Seymour, Ralph Fletcher. *Across the Gulf: A Narration of a Short Journey through Parts of Yucatán*. Chicago: Alderbrink, 1928.

Sheridan, Clare. *My American Diary*. New York: Boni and Liveright, 1922.

Siegel, Jules. *Cancún's User Guide*. 6th ed. Cancun: Communication Company, 2006.

Slocum, George Mertz. *Where Tex Meets Mex: A Report of Recent Ramblings on Both Sides of the Rio Grande*. Mt. Clemens, Mich.: Rural, 1927.

Smith, Earl E. T. *The Fourth Floor: An Account of the Castro Communist Revolution*. New York: Random House, 1962.

Smith, Wayne S. *The Closest of Enemies: A Personal and Diplomatic Account of U.S.-Cuban Relations since 1957*. New York: Norton, 1987.

Spratling, William. *File on Spratling: An Autobiography*. Boston: Little, Brown, 1967.

Squier, Emma Lindsay. *Gringa: An American Girl in Mexico*. Boston: Houghton Mifflin, 1934.

Stanley, David. *Cuba: A Lonely Planet Survival Kit*. Melbourne, Australia: Lonely Planet, 1997.

Terry, Philip T. *Terry's Guide to Cuba*. Boston: Houghton Mifflin, 1926.

———. *Terry's Guide to Mexico*. Boston: Houghton Mifflin, 1927, 1935.

Thompson, Hunter S. *The Rum Diary*. New York: Simon and Schuster, 1998.

Townsend, William Clayton. *Lazaro Cardenas: Mexican Democrat*. Ann Arbor, Mich.: Wahr, 1952.

Toor, Frances. *Guide to Mexico*. New York: McBride, 1936.

Tugwell, Rexford G. *The Stricken Land*. Garden City, N.Y.: Doubleday, 1947.

U.S. Department of Commerce, Office of Business Economics. *The Survey of Current Business*. Washington, D.C.: U.S. Government Printing Office, 1963.

Verrill, A. Hyatt. *Puerto Rico: Past and Present*. New York: Dodd and Mead, 1914.

Wells, Carveth. *Panmexico*. New York: McBride, 1937.

Secondary Sources

Alexander, Robert J. *Romulo Betancourt and the Transformation of Venezuela*. Piscataway, N.J.: Transaction, 1982.

———. *The Tragedy of Chile*. Westport, Conn.: Greenwood, 1978.

Ambrose, Stephen E. *Eisenhower*. Vol. 2, *The President*. New York: Simon and Schuster, 1984.

Anderson, Benedict. *Imagined Communities: Reflections on the Origin and Spread of Nationalism*. London: Verso, 1983.

Anderson, Carol. *Eyes off the Prize: The United Nations and the African American Struggle for Human Rights*. New York: Cambridge University Press, 2003.

Anderson, Susan C., and Bruce H. Tabb, eds. *Water, Leisure, and Culture: European Historical Perspectives*. Oxford: Berg, 2002.

Argote-Freyre, Frank. *Fulgencio Batista: From Revolutionary to Strongman*. New Brunswick, N.J.: Rutgers University Press, 2006.

Aronson, Cynthia. *Working at Play: A History of Vacations in the United States*. New York: Oxford University Press, 1999.

Ayala, César J., and Rafael Bernabe. *Puerto Rico in the American Century: A History since 1898*. Chapel Hill: University of North Carolina Press, 2007.

Babcock, Barbara A., and Marta Weigle, eds. *The Great Southwest of the Fred Harvey Company and the Santa Fe Railroad*. Phoenix: Heard Museum with the University of Arizona Press, 1996.

Bacchilega, Christina. *Lengendary Hawai'i and the Politics of Place: Tradition, Translation, and Tourism*. Philadelphia: University of Pennsylvania Press, 2007.

Baily, Samuel L. *The United States and the Development of South America, 1945–1975*. New York: New Viewpoints, 1976.

Baker, John Henry. "The Relationship of Student Activism at the University of Puerto Rico to the Struggle for Political Independence in Puerto Rico, 1923–1971." Ph.D., diss., Boston College, 1973.

Baranowski, Shelley, and Ellen Furlough, eds. *Being Elsewhere: Tourism, Consumer Culture, and Identity in Modern Europe and North America*. Ann Arbor: University of Michigan Press, 2001.

Barber, Benjamin R. *Jihad vs. McWorld: Terrorism's Challenge to Democracy*. New York: Ballantine, 1996.

Barry, Tom, Beth Wood, and Deb Preusch. *The Other Side of Paradise: Foreign Control in the Caribbean*. New York: Grove, 1984.

Belasco, Warren. *Americans on the Road: From Autocamp to Motel, 1910–1945*. Cambridge: MIT Press, 1979.

Bemis, Samuel Flagg. *The Latin American Policy of the United States*. New York: Harcourt, Brace, 1943.

Bender, Marylin, and Selig Altschul. *The Chosen Instrument: Pan Am, Juan Trippe, the Rise and Fall of an American Entrepreneur*. New York: Simon and Schuster, 1982.

Benjamin, Jules R. *The United States and the Origins of the Cuban Revolution: An Empire for Liberty in an Age of National Liberation*. Princeton: Princeton University Press, 1990.

Berg, Scott A. *Lindbergh*. Berkeley: Berkeley Trade, 1999.

Berger, Dina. *The Development of Mexico's Tourist Industry: Pyramids by Day, Martinis by Night*. New York: Palgrave Macmillan, 2006.

Berger, Dina, and Andrew Wood, eds. *Holiday in Mexico: Essays on Tourism and Tourist Encounters*. Durham, N.C.: Duke University Press, forthcoming.

Berman, Marshall. *All That Is Solid Melts into Air: The Experience of Modernity*. New York: Penguin, 1988.

Blatt, Irwin B. *A Study of Culture Change in Modern Puerto Rico*. Palo Alto, Calif.: R & E Research Associates, 1979.

Blight, David. *Beyond the Battlefield: Race, Memory, and the Civil War*. Amherst: University of Massachusetts Press, 2002.

Bloom, Nicholas, ed. *Adventures into Mexico: American Tourism beyond the Border*. Lanham, Md.: Rowman and Littlefield, 2006.

Bonachea, Ramón L., and Marta San Martín. *The Cuban Insurrection, 1952–1959*. New Brunswick, N.J.: Transaction, 1974.

Booth, John A. *Costa Rica: Quest for Democracy*. Boulder, Colo.: Westview, 1999.

Borstelmann, Thomas. *The Cold War and the Color Line: American Race Relations in the Global Arena*. Cambridge: Harvard University Press, 2003.

Bradley, Mark Philip. *Imagining Vietnam and America: The Making of Postcolonial Vietnam, 1919–1950*. Chapel Hill: University of North Carolina Press, 2000.

Brameld, Theodore. *The Remaking of a Culture: Life and Education in Puerto Rico*. New York: Harper, 1959.

Braudel, Fernand. *The Mediterranean and the Mediterranean World in the Age of Phillip II*. Berkeley: University of California Press, 1995.

Briggs, Laura. *Reproducing Empire: Race, Sex, Science, and U.S. Imperialism in Puerto Rico*. Berkeley: University of California Press, 2002.

Britton, Stephen G. "The Political Economy of Tourism in the Third World." *Annals of Tourism Research* 9, no. 3 (1982): 331–58.

Brown, Dona. *Inventing New England: Regional Tourism in the Nineteenth Century.* Washington, D.C.: Smithsonian Institution Press, 1995.

Bryden, John M. *Tourism and Development: A Case Study of the Commonwealth Caribbean.* Cambridge: Cambridge University Press, 1973.

Buchenau, Jürgen. *Plutarco Elías Calles and the Mexican Revolution.* Lanham, Md.: Rowman and Littlefield, 2006.

Buzzanco, Robert. "What Happened to the New Left: Toward a Radical Reading of American Foreign Relations." *Diplomatic History* 23 (Fall 1999): 575–607.

Cabán, Pedro A. *Constructing a Colonial People: Puerto Rico and the United States, 1898–1932.* Boulder, Colo.: Westview, 1999.

Carpenter, Bruce Rogers. "Puerto Rico's Planned Development of Tourism." Ph.D. diss., American University, 1964.

Cockroft, James D. *Intellectual Precursors of the Mexican Revolution, 1900–1913.* Austin: University of Texas Press for the Institute of Latin American Studies, 1968.

Cocks, Catherine. *Doing the Town: The Rise of Urban Tourism in the United States.* Berkeley: University of California Press, 2001.

Cohen, Lizabeth. *A Consumer's Republic: The Politics of Mass Consumption in Postwar America.* New York: Knopf, 2003.

Cohen, Warren I. *Empire without Tears: America's Foreign Relations, 1921–1933.* New York: Knopf, 1987.

Cohen, Warren I., and Nancy Bernkopf Tucker, eds. *Lyndon Johnson Confronts the World: American Foreign Policy, 1963–1968.* New York: Cambridge University Press, 1994.

Cole, Wayne S. *Roosevelt and the Isolationists, 1932–1945.* Lincoln: University of Nebraska Press, 1983.

Collin, Richard H. *Theodore Roosevelt's Caribbean: The Panama Canal, the Monroe Doctrine, and the Latin American Context.* Baton Rouge: Louisiana State University Press, 1990.

Conway, Dennis. *Tourism and Caribbean Development.* Hanover, N.H.: University Field Staff International, 1983.

Costigliola, Frank. *Awkward Dominion: American Political, Economic, and Cultural Relations with Europe, 1919–1933.* Ithaca: Cornell University Press, 1983.

Cronon, David E. *Josephus Daniels in Mexico.* Chapel Hill: University of North Carolina Press, 1960.

Crouch, David, ed. *Visual Culture and Tourism.* Oxford: Berg, 2002.

Cullather, Nick. "Development? It's History." *Diplomatic History* 24 (Fall 2000): 641–53.

——. *Secret History: The CIA's Classified Account of Its Operations in Guatemala, 1952–1954.* Stanford: Stanford University Press, 1999.

Dallek, Robert. *Franklin D. Roosevelt and American Foreign Policy, 1933–1945.* New York: Oxford University Press, 1979.

——. *An Unfinished Life: John F. Kennedy, 1917–1963.* New York: Penguin, 2004.

Daniels, Roger T. *Guarding the Golden Door: American Immigration Policy and Immigrants since 1882.* New York: Hill and Wang, 2004.

Dávila, Arlene M. *Sponsored Identities: Cultural Politics in Puerto Rico.* Philadelphia: Temple University Press, 1997.

Dean, Richard D. *Imperial Brotherhood: Gender and the Making of Cold War Foreign Policy*. Amherst: University of Massachusetts Press, 2001.

DeConde, Alexander, Richard Dean Burns, and Fredrik Logevall, eds. *Encyclopedia of American Foreign Policy*. 2nd ed. New York: Scribner, 2002.

De Grazia, Victoria. *Irresistible Empire: America's Advance through Twentieth-Century Europe*. Cambridge: Belknap Press of Harvard University Press, 2005.

Delpar, Helen. *The Enormous Vogue of Things Mexican: Cultural Relations between the United States and Mexico, 1920–1935*. Tuscaloosa: University of Alabama Press, 1992.

Desmond, Jane. *Staging Tourism: Bodies on Display from Waikiki to Sea World*. Chicago: University of Chicago Press, 1999.

Dickinson, Bob, and Andy Vladimir. *Selling the Sea: An Inside Look at the Cruise Industry*. New York: Wiley, 1997.

Dietz, James L. *Economic History of Puerto Rico: Institutional Change and Capitalistic Development*. Princeton: Princeton University Press, 1986.

Domínguez, Jorge I. *Cuba: Order and Revolution*. Cambridge: Harvard University Press, 1978.

———. *To Make a World Safe for Revolution: Cuba's Foreign Policy*. Cambridge: Harvard University Press, 1989.

Dorfman, Ariel. *The Empire's Old Clothes: What the Lone Ranger, Babar, and Other Innocent Heroes Do to Our Minds*. New York: Pantheon, 1983.

Dorfman, Ariel, and Armand Mattelart. *How to Read Donald Duck: Imperialist Ideology in the Disney Comic*. 2nd ed. New York: International General, 1984.

Draper, Theodore. *Castroism, Theory and Practice*. New York: Praeger, 1965.

Duany, Jorge. *Puerto Rican Nation on the Move: Identities on the Island and in the United States*. Chapel Hill: University of North Carolina Press, 2002.

Dubinsky, Karen. *The Second Greatest Disappointment: Honeymooning and Tourism at Niagara Falls*. New Brunswick, N.J.: Rutgers University Press, 1999.

Dudziak, Mary L. *Cold War and Civil Rights: Race and the Image of Democracy*. Princeton: Princeton University Press, 2002.

Dulles, Foster Rhea. *Americans Abroad: Two Centuries of European Travel*. Ann Arbor: University of Michigan Press, 1964.

Duvall, David. *Tourism in the Caribbean: Trends, Development, Prospects*. London: Routledge, 2004.

Dwyer, John J. "Diplomatic Weapons of the Weak: Mexican Policymaking during the U.S.-Mexican Agrarian Dispute, 1934–1941." *Diplomatic History* 26 (Summer 2002): 375–95.

Endy, Christopher. *Cold War Holidays: American Tourism in France*. Chapel Hill: University of North Carolina Press, 2004.

Engerman, David. "Research Agenda for the History of Tourism: Towards an International Social History." *American Studies International* 32 (October 1994): 3–31.

Engerman, David, Nils Gilman, Mark Haefele, and Michael E. Latham, ed. *Staging Growth: Modernization, Development, and the Cold War*. Amherst: University of Massachusetts Press, 2003.

English, T. J. *Havana Nocturne: How the Mob Owned Cuba—and Then Lost It to the Revolution*. New York: HarperCollins, 2008.

Enloe, Cynthia. *Bananas, Bases, and Beaches: Making Feminist Sense of International Relations*. Berkeley: University of California Press, 1990.

Escobar, Arturo. *Encountering Development: The Making and Unmaking of the Third World*. Princeton: Princeton University Press, 1995.

Farber, David, and Beth Bailey. "The Fighting Man as Tourist: The Politics of Tourist Culture in Hawai'i during World War II." *Pacific American Historical Review* 65 (November 1996): 641–60.

Farber, Samuel. *Origins of the Cuban Revolution Reconsidered*. Chapel Hill: University of North Carolina Press, 2006.

Feifer, Maxine. *Tourism in History: From Imperial Rome to the Present*. New York: Stein and Day, 1985.

Feitlowitz, Marguerite. *A Lexicon of Terror: Argentina and the Legacies of Torture*. New York: Oxford University Press, 1999.

Fernandez, Ronald. *The Disenchanted Island: Puerto Rico and the United States in the Twentieth Century*. Westport, Conn.: Praeger, 1996.

Figueroa, Luis. *Sugar, Slavery, and Freedom in Nineteenth-Century Puerto Rico*. Chapel Hill: University of North Carolina Press, 2005.

Findlay, John. *Magic Lands: Western Cityscapes and American Culture after 1940*. Berkeley: University of California Press, 1992.

Fisher, Fritz. *Making Them Like Us: Peace Corps Volunteers in the 1960s*. Washington, D.C.: Smithsonian Institution Press, 1998.

Flores, Juan. *Divided Borders: Essays on Puerto Rican Identity*. Houston: Arte Publico, 1993.

———. *From Bomba to Hip Hop: Puerto Rican Identity and Latino Identity*. New York: Columbia University Press, 2000.

Folgarait, Leonard. *Mural Painting and Social Revolution in Mexico, 1910–1940: Art and the New Order*. Cambridge: Cambridge University Press, 1998.

Foss, Michael, ed. *On Tour: The British Traveler in Europe*. London: O'Mara, 1989.

Frank, Andre Gunder, and Barry Gills. *The World System*. London: Routledge, 1997.

Frankel, Robert. *Observing America: The Commentary of British Visitors to the United States, 1890–1950*. Madison: University of Wisconsin Press, 2007.

Freire-Medeiros, Bianca. "Hollywood Musicals and the Invention of Rio de Janeiro." *Cinema Journal* 41 (Summer 2002): 52–67.

Friedman, Max Paul. *Nazis and Good Neighbors: The United States Campaign against the Germans in Latin America in World War II*. Cambridge: Cambridge University Press, 2003.

Fuente, Alejandro de la. *A Nation for All: Race, Inequality, and Politics in Twentieth-Century Cuba*. Chapel Hill: University of North Carolina Press, 2001.

Fussell, Paul. *Abroad: British Literary Traveling between the Wars*. New York: Oxford University Press, 1980.

Gabaccia, Donna, and Vicki L. Ruiz. *American Dreaming, Global Realities: Rethinking U.S. Immigration History*. Urbana: University of Illinois Press, 2006.

Gaddis, John Lewis. *The Cold War: A New History*. New York: Penguin, 2006.

García, Gervasio Luis. "I Am the Other: Puerto Rico in the Eyes of North Americans." *Journal of American History* 87 (June 2000): 39–64.

Gardner, Lloyd C. *Economic Aspects of New Deal Diplomacy*. Madison: University of Wisconsin Press, 1964.

Geertz, Clifford. *The Interpretation of Cultures*. New York: Basic Books, 1973.

Gellman, Irwin. *Good Neighbor Diplomacy*. Baltimore: Johns Hopkins University Press, 1979.

Giddens, Anthony. *Modernity and Self-Identity*. Cambridge: Polity, 1991.

Gienow-Hecht, Jessica. *Transmission Impossible: American Journalism as Cultural Diplomacy in Postwar Germany, 1945–1955*. Baton Rouge: Louisiana State University Press, 1999.

Givner, Joan, ed. *Katherine Anne Porter: Conversations*. Jackson: University Press of Mississippi, 1987.

———. *Katherine Anne Porter: A Life*. New York: Simon and Schuster, 1982.

Gjelten, Tom. *Bacardi and the Long Fight for Cuba: The Biography of a Cause*. New York: Viking, 2008.

Glatzer, Robert. *The New Advertising: The Great Campaigns from Avis to Volkswagen*. New York: Citadel, 1970.

Gleijeses, Piero. *Conflicting Missions: Havana, Washington, and Africa, 1959–1976*. Chapel Hill: University of North Carolina Press, 2002.

———. *Shattered Hope: The Guatemalan Revolution and the United States, 1944–1954*. Princeton: Princeton University Press, 1991.

Goldstone, Patricia. *To Make the World Safe for Tourism*. New Haven: Yale University Press, 2001.

Gosse, Van. *Where the Boys Are: Cuba, Cold War America, and the Making of a New Left*. London: Verso, 1993.

Gould, Louis L. *The Spanish-American War and President McKinley*. Lawrence: University Press of Kansas, 1983.

Graebner, William. *Age of Doubt: American Thought and Culture in the 1940s*. Prospect Heights, Ill.: Waveland, 1998.

Grandin, Greg. *Empire's Workshop: Latin America, the United States, and the Rise of the New Imperialism*. New York: Holt, 2007.

———. *The Last Colonial Massacre: Guatemala in the Cold War*. Chicago: University of Chicago Press, 2004.

Green, David. *The Containment of Latin America: A History of the Myths and Realities of the Good Neighbor Policy*. New York: Quadrangle, 1971.

Greenberg, Amy S. *Manifest Manhood and Antebellum Empire*. Cambridge: Cambridge University Press, 2005.

Gustafson, Kristian. *Hostile Intent: U.S. Covert Operations in Chile, 1964–1974*. Dulles, Va.: Potomac, 2007.

Haines, Gerald. "Under the Eagle's Wing: The Franklin Roosevelt Administration Forges an American Hemisphere." *Diplomatic History* 1 (October 1977): 373–88.

Halperin, Maurice. *The Rise and Decline of Fidel Castro: An Essay in Contemporary History*. Berkeley: University of California Press, 1972.

Hanson, Simon G. *Dollar Diplomacy: Modern Style: Chapters in the Failure of the Alliance for Progress*. Washington, D.C.: Inter-American Affairs, 1970.

Hart, John Mason. *Empire and Revolution: The Americans in Mexico since the Civil War*. Berkeley: University of California Press, 2002.

———. *Revolutionary Mexico: The Coming and Progress of the Mexican Revolution*. Berkeley: University of California Press, 1987.

Haslip-Viera, Gabriel, ed. *Taíno Revival: Critical Perspectives on Puerto Rican Identity and Cultural Politics*. Princeton: Wiener, 2001.

Healy, David. *Drive toward Hegemony: The United States in the Caribbean, 1898–1917*. Madison: University of Wisconsin Press, 1988.

Higgins, Trumbull. *The Perfect Failure: Kennedy, Eisenhower, and the CIA at the Bay of Pigs*. New York: Norton, 1987.

Hitchens, Christopher. *The Trial of Henry Kissinger*. London: Verso, 2001.

Hixson, Walter. *The Myth of American Diplomacy*. New Haven: Yale University Press, 2008.

Hoffman, Elizabeth Cobbs. *All You Need Is Love: The Peace Corps and the Spirit of the 1960s*. Cambridge: Harvard University Press, 1998.

Hogan, Michael J. *The Marshall Plan: America, Britain, and the Reconstruction of Western Europe, 1947–1952*. Cambridge: Cambridge University Press, 1987.

Hogan, Michael J., and Thomas G. Paterson, eds. *Explaining the History of American Foreign Relations*. Cambridge: Cambridge University Press, 2004.

Hoganson, Kristin L. *Consumer's Imperium: The Global Production of American Domesticity, 1865–1920*. Chapel Hill: University of North Carolina Press, 2007.

———. *Fighting for American Manhood: How Gender Politics Provoked the Spanish-American and Philippine-American Wars*. New Haven: Yale University Press, 1998.

Honey, Martha. *Ecotourism and Sustainable Development: Who Owns Paradise?* Washington D.C.: Island, 1999.

Horne, Gerald. *Black and Brown: African Americans and the Mexican Revolution*. New York: New York University Press, 2005.

Horsman, Reginald. *Race and Manifest Destiny: The Origins of American Racial Anglo-Saxonism*. Cambridge: Harvard University Press, 1981.

Hunt, Michael H. *Ideology and U.S. Foreign Policy*. New Haven: Yale University Press, 1987.

Hunter, Jane. *The Gospel of Gentility: American Women Missionaries in Turn-of-the-Century China*. New Haven: Yale University Press, 1984.

Immerman, Richard H. *The CIA in Guatemala: The Foreign Policy of Intervention*. Austin: University of Texas Press, 1982.

Iriye, Akira. *Cultural Internationalism and World Order*. Baltimore: Johns Hopkins University Press, 1997.

Jayes, Janice Lee. " 'Strangers to Each Other': The American Encounter with Mexico, 1877–1910." Ph.D. diss, American University, 1999.

Johnson, Anna. *Missionary Writings and Empire, 1800–1860.* Cambridge: Cambridge University Press, 2003.

Joseph, Gilbert M. *Revolution from Without: Yucatán, Mexico, and the United States, 1880–1924.* Durham, N.C.: Duke University Press, 1988.

Joseph, Gilbert M., and Timothy J. Henderson, eds. *The Mexico Reader: History, Culture, Politics.* Durham, N.C.: Duke University Press, 2002.

Joseph, Gilbert M., Catherine C. LeGrand, and Ricardo D. Salvatore, eds. *Close Encounters of Empire: Writing the Cultural History of U.S.–Latin American Relations.* Durham, N.C.: Duke University Press, 1998.

Joseph, Gilbert M., and Daniel Nugent, eds. *Everyday Forms of State Formation: Revolution and the Negotiation of Rule in Modern Mexico.* Durham, N.C.: Duke University Press, 1994.

Joseph, Gilbert M., and Daniela Spenser, eds. *In from the Cold: Latin America's New Encounter with the Cold War.* Durham, N.C.: Duke University Press, 2008.

Judd, Dennis R., and Susan S. Fainstein, eds. *The Tourist City.* New Haven: Yale University Press, 1999.

Kadt, E., ed. *Tourism: Passport to Development.* Oxford: Oxford University Press, 1979.

Kammen, Michael. *Mystic Chords of Memory: The Transformation of Tradition in American Culture.* New York: Vintage, 1993.

Kaplan, Amy. *The Anarchy of Empire in the Making of U.S. Culture.* Cambridge: Harvard University Press, 2002.

Kaplan, Amy, and Donald Pease, eds. *Cultures of United States Imperialism.* Durham, N.C.: Duke University Press, 1993.

Katz, Friedrich. *The Life and Times of Pancho Villa.* Stanford: Stanford University Press, 1998.

———. *The Secret War in Mexico: Europe, the United States, and the Mexican Revolution.* Chicago: University of Chicago Press, 1981.

Kaur, Raminder, and John Hutnyk, eds. *Travel Worlds: Journeys in Contemporary Cultural Politics.* London: Zed, 1998.

Kelly, Robin D. G. *Race Rebels: Culture, Politics, and the Black Working Class.* New York: Free Press, 1994.

Kennan, George. *American Diplomacy, 1900–1950.* Chicago: University of Chicago Press, 1951.

Kirshenblatt-Gimblett, Barbara. *Destination Culture: Tourism, Museums, and Heritage.* Berkeley: University of California Press, 1998.

Klare, Michael T., and Cynthia Arnson. *Supplying Repression: U.S. Support for Authoritarian Regimes Abroad.* Rev. ed. Washington, D.C.: Institute for Policy Studies, 1981.

Klein, Christina. *Cold War Orientalism: Asia in the Middlebrow Imagination, 1945–1961.* Berkeley: University of California Press, 2003.

Kline, Naomi. *The Shock Doctrine: The Rise of Disaster Capitalism.* New York: Metropolitan, 2007.

Knight, Alan. *The Caribbean: Genesis of a Fragmented Nationalism.* New York: Oxford University Press, 1990.

———. *The Mexican Revolution.* 2 vols. Cambridge: Cambridge University Press, 1986.

———. *Mexico: The Colonial Era.* Cambridge: Cambridge University Press, 2002.

Kolko, Gabriel. *Confronting the Third World: United States Foreign Policy, 1945–1980.* New York: Pantheon, 1988.

Kornbluh, Peter. *The Pinochet File: A Declassified Dossier on Atrocity and Accountability.* Washington, D.C.: National Security Archive, 2003.

Koshar, Rudy. *German Travel Cultures.* New York: Oxford University Press, 2000.

Krahulic, Karen Christel. *Provincetown: From Pilgrim Landing to Gay Resort.* New York: New York University Press, 2007.

Kramer, Paul A. *The Blood of Government: Race, Empire, the United States, and the Philippines.* Chapel Hill: University of North Carolina Press, 2006.

Krauze, Enrique. *Lázaro Cárdenas.* Mexico City: Fondo de Cultura Económica, 1995.

———. *Mexico: Biography of Power: A History of Modern Mexico, 1810–1996.* New York: HarperCollins, 1997.

———. *Plutarco E. Calles: Reformar Desde el Origin.* Mexico City: Fondo de Cultura Económica, 1987.

Krauze, Enrique, Jean Meyer, and Cayetano Reyes. *Historia de la Revolución Mexicana, 1924–1928: La Reconstucción Económica.* Mexico City: Colegio de México, 1981.

Krenn, Michael L. *The Color of Empire: Race and American Foreign Relations.* Lanham, Md.: Potomac, 2006.

Kroes, Rob. *If You've Seen One, You've Seen the Mall: Europeans and American Mass Culture.* Urbana: University of Illinois Press, 1996.

Kropp, Phoebe S. *California Vieja: Culture and Memory in a Modern American Place.* Berkeley: University of California Press, 2006.

Kuisel, Richard. *Seducing the French: The Dilemma of Americanization.* Berkeley: University of California Press, 1993.

Kunz, Diane B., ed. *The Diplomacy of the Crucial Decade: American Foreign Relations during the 1960s.* New York: Columbia University Press, 1994.

LaFeber, Walter. *America, Russia, and the Cold War, 1945–2006.* 10th ed. Boston: McGraw-Hill, 2008.

———. *Inevitable Revolutions: The United States and Central America.* 2nd ed. New York: Norton, 1993.

———. *The New Empire: An Interpretation of American Expansionism, 1860–1898.* Ithaca: Cornell University Press, 1963.

Lanfant, Marie-Françoise, John B. Allcock, and Edward M. Bruner, eds. *International Tourism: Identity and Change.* London: Sage, 1995.

Latham, Michael E. *Modernization as Ideology: American Social Science and "Nation Building" in the Kennedy Era.* Chapel Hill: University of North Carolina Press, 2000.

Lea, John. *Tourism and Development in the Third World.* London: Routledge, 1988.

Lears, T. Jackson. *No Place of Grace: Antimodernism and the Transformation of American Culture, 1880–1920.* New York: Pantheon, 1981.

Leed, Eric J. *The Mind of the Traveler: From Gilgamesh to Global Tourism.* New York: Basic Books, 1991.

Leffler, Melvyn P. "The American Conception of National Security and the Beginnings of the Cold War, 1945–1948." *American Historical Review* 89 (April 1984): 346–81.

——. *The Elusive Quest: America's Pursuit of European Stability and French Security, 1919–1933*. Chapel Hill: University of North Carolina Press, 1979.

——. *A Preponderance of Power: National Security, the Truman Administration, and the Cold War*. Stanford: Stanford University Press, 1992.Lenèek, Lena, and Gideon Bosker. *The Beach: The History of Paradise on Earth*. New York: Viking, 1998.

Levenstein, Harvey. *Seductive Journey: American Tourists in France from Jefferson to the Jazz Age*. Chicago: University of Chicago Press, 1998.

——. *We'll Always Have Paris: American Tourists in France since 1930*. Chicago: University of Chicago Press, 2004.

Levinson, Jerome, and Juan de Onís. *The Alliance That Lost Its Way: A Critical Report on the Alliance for Progress*. Chicago: Quadrangle, 1970.

Littleton, Taylor D. *The Color of Silver: William Spratling, His Life and Art*. Baton Rouge: Louisiana State University Press, 2000.

Löfgren, Orvar. *On Holiday: A History of Vacationing*. Berkeley: University of California Press, 1999.

Longley, Kyle. *The Sparrow and the Hawk: The United States and Costa Rica during the Rise of José Figueres*. Tuscaloosa: University of Alabama Press, 1997.

Lopez, Adalberto, ed. *The Puerto Ricans: Their History, Culture, and Society*. Cambridge: Harvard University Press, 1980.

Love, Eric T. L. *Race over Empire: Racism and United States Imperialism, 1865–1900*. Chapel Hill: University of North Carolina Press, 2004.

Lundberg, Donald E., and Carolyn B. Lundberg. *International Travel and Tourism*. New York: Wiley, 1993.

MacCannell, Dean. *The Tourist: A New Theory of the Leisure Class*. Berkeley: University of California Press, 1999.

Maier, Charles S. *Among Empires: American Ascendancy and Its Predecessors*. Cambridge: Harvard University Press, 2006.

——. "Consigning the Twentieth Century to History." *American Historical Review* 105 (June 2000): 807–31.

Maldonado, A. W. *Teodoro Moscoso and Puerto Rico's Operation Bootstrap*. Gainesville: University of Florida Press, 1997.

Mares, Roberto. *Lázaro Cárdenas*. Mexico City: Grupo Editorial Tomo de C.V., 2004

Mark, Joan T. *The Silver Gringo: William Spratling and Taxco*. Albuquerque: University of New Mexico Press, 2000.

Mart, Michelle. *Eye on Israel: How America Came to View Israel as an Ally*. Albany: State University of New York Press, 2006.

Matos Rodríguez, Félix V., and Linda C. Delgado, eds. *Puerto Rican Women's History: New Perspectives*. Armonk, N.Y.: Sharpe, 1998.

Matthews, Herbert. *Cuban Story*. New York: Braziller, 1961.

——. *Fidel Castro*. New York: Simon and Schuster, 1969.

May, Elaine Tyler. *Homeward Bound: American Families in the Cold War Era*. New York: Basic Books, 1988.

May, Ernest R., and Philip D. Zelikow. *The Kennedy Tapes: Inside the White House during the Cuban Missile Crisis*. Cambridge: Harvard University Press, 1993.

McAlister, Melani. *Epic Encounters: Culture, Media, and U.S. Interests in the Middle East, 1945–2000*. Berkeley: University of California Press, 2001.

McClay, Michael. *I Love Lucy: The Complete Picture History of the Most Popular Television Show Ever*. New York: Warner, 1995.

McCullough, David. *Truman*. New York: Simon and Schuster, 1992.

McPherson, Alan. *Yankee No! Anti-Americanism in U.S.-Latin American Relations*. Cambridge: Harvard University Press, 2003.

Merrill, Dennis. *Bread and the Ballot: The United States and India's Economic Development*. Chapel Hill: University of North Carolina Press, 1990.

———. "Shaping Third World Development: U.S. Foreign Aid and Supervision in the Philippines, 1948–1953." *Journal of American–East Asian Relations* 2 (Summer 1993): 137–59.

Meyer, Lorenzo. *Historia de la Revolución Mexicana, 1928–1934*. Vol. 13, *El Conflicto Social y los Gobiernos Maximoto*. Mexico City: El Colegio de México, 1978.

———. *The Mexican Revolution and the Anglo-American Powers: The End of Confrontation and the Beginning of Negotiation*. La Jolla, Calif.: Center for U.S.-Mexican Studies, University of California, San Diego, 1985.

Meyerowitz, Joanne, ed. *Not June Cleaver: Women and Gender in Postwar America, 1945–1960*. Philadelphia: Temple University Press, 1994.

Mintz, Sidney W. *Workers in the Cane: A Puerto Rico Life History*. New Haven: Yale University Press, 1960.

Montague, Art. *Meyer Lansky: The Shadowy Exploits of New York's Master Manipulator*. Alberta: Altitude, 2005.

Morales Carrión, Arturo. *Puerto Rico: A Political and Cultural History*. New York: Norton, 1983.

Moreno, Julio. *Yankee Don't Go Home: Mexican Nationalism, American Business Culture, and the Shaping of Modern Mexico, 1920–1950*. Chapel Hill: University of North Carolina Press, 2003.

Morley, Judy Mattivi. *Historic Preservation and the Imagined West: Albuquerque, Denver, and Seattle*. Lawrence: University Press of Kansas, 2006.

Morley, Morris H. *Imperial State and Revolution: The United States and Cuba, 1952–1986*. Cambridge: Cambridge University Press, 1987.

Morley, Sylvanus Griswold. *An Introduction to the Study of the Maya Hieroglyphs*. 1915; New York: Dover, 1975.

Morrill, Penny Chitton. *William Spratling and the Mexican Silver Renaissance*. New York: Abrams, 2002.

Morris, Nancy. *Puerto Rico: Culture, Politics, and Identity*. Westport, Conn.: Praeger, 1995.

Ngai, Mai. *Impossible Subjects: Illegal Aliens and the Making of Modern America*. Princeton: Princeton University Press, 2005.

Niblo, Stephen R. *Mexico in the 1940s: Modernity, Politics, and Corruption*. Wilmington, Del.: Scholarly Resources, 1999.

——. *War, Diplomacy, and Development: The United States and Mexico, 1938–1954.* Wilmington, Del.: Scholarly Resources, 1995.

Nicholson, Harold. *Dwight Morrow.* New York: Harcourt, Brace, 1935.

Ninkovich, Frank. *Modernity and Power: A History of the Domino Theory in the Twentieth Century.* Chicago: University of Chicago Press, 1994.

Nye, Joseph S., Jr. *Bound to Lead: The Changing Nature of American Foreign Policy.* New York: Free Press, 1990.

——. *The Paradox of American Power.* New York: Oxford University Press, 2002.

——. *Soft Power: The Means to Success in World Politics.* New York: Public Affairs, 2004.

O'Brien, Thomas F. *Making the Americas: The United States and Latin America from the Age of Revolutions to the Era of Globalization.* Albuquerque: University of New Mexico Press, 2007.

Offner, John L. *An Unwanted War: The Diplomacy of the United States and Spain over Cuba, 1895–1898.* Chapel Hill: University of North Carolina Press, 1992.

Pach, Chester J., Jr. *Arming the Free World: The Origins of the United States Military Assistance Program, 1945–1950.* Chapel Hill: University of North Carolina Press, 1991.

Paterson, Thomas G. *Contesting Castro: The United States and the Triumph of the Cuban Revolution.* New York: Oxford University Press, 1999.

——, ed. *Kennedy's Quest for Victory: American Foreign Policy, 1961–1963.* New York: Oxford University Press, 1989.

Pattullo, Polly. *Last Resorts: The Cost of Tourism in the Caribbean.* New York: Monthly Review Press, 1999.

Pells, Richard. *Not Like Us: How Europeans Have Loved, Hated, and Transformed American Culture since World War II.* New York: Basic Books, 1997.

Pérez, Louis A., Jr. *Cuba: Between Reform and Revolution.* New York: Oxford University Press, 1989.

——. *Cuba in the American Imagination: Metaphor and the Imperial Ethos.* Chapel Hill: University of North Carolina Press, 2008.

——. *Cuba under the Platt Amendment.* Pittsburgh: University of Pittsburgh Press, 1986.

——. *On Becoming Cuban: Identity, Nationality, and Culture.* Chapel Hill: University of North Carolina Press, 1999.

——. *The War of 1898: Cuba and the United States in History and Historiography.* Chapel Hill: University of North Carolina Press, 1998.

Perkins, Dexter. *Hands Off: A History of the Monroe Doctrine.* Boston: Little, Brown, 1941.

Picard, Michel, and Robert E. Woods, eds. *Tourism, Ethnicity, and the State in Asian and Pacific Societies.* Honolulu: University of Hawai'i Press, 1997.

Picó, Fernando. *La Guerra después de la Guerra.* Río Piedras, P.R.: Huracán, 1987.

——. *Historia General de Puerto Rico.* Río Piedras, P.R.: Huracán, 1988.

——. *Libertad y Servidumbre en el Puerto Rico del Siglo XIX: Los Jornaleros Utuadeños en Vísperas del Auge del Café.* Río Piedras, P.R.: Huracán, 1979.

Pike, Frederick P. *FDR's Good Neighbor Policy: Sixty Years of Generally Gentle Chaos.* Austin: University of Texas Press, 1995.

Pletcher, David. *Rails, Mines, and Progress: Seven American Promoters in Mexico, 1867–1911.* Ithaca: Cornell University Press, 1958.

Plummer, Brenda Gayle, ed. *Window on Freedom: Race, Civil Rights, and American Foreign Relations, 1945–1988*. Chapel Hill: University of North Carolina Press, 2007.

Potter, Robert, David Barker, Dennis Conway, and Thomas Klak. *The Contemporary Caribbean*. New York: Prentice Hall, 2004.

Pratt, Mary Louise. *Imperial Eyes: Travel Writing and Transculturalization*. London: Routledge, 1992.

Quany, Jorge. *Puerto Rican Identity on the Island and in the United States*. Chapel Hill: University of North Carolina Press, 2002.

Quirk, Robert E. *An Affair of Honor*. Lexington: University of Kentucky Press for the Mississippi Valley Historical Association, 1962.

Rabe, Stephen G. *Eisenhower and Latin America: The Foreign Policy of Anti-Communism*. Chapel Hill: University of North Carolina Press, 1989.

———. *The Most Dangerous Area of the World: John F. Kennedy and Communist Revolution in Latin America*. Chapel Hill: University of North Carolina Press, 1999.

———. *The Road to OPEC: United States Relations with Venezuela, 1919–1976*. Austin: University of Texas Press, 1982.

Ramos de Santiago, Carmen. *El Gobierno de Puerto Rico*. San Juan: Editorial Universitaria, Universidad de Puerto Rico, 1970.

Randall, Stephen J. *Colombia and the United States: Hegemony and Interdependence*. Athens: University of Georgia Press, 1992.

Renda, Mary A. *Taking Haiti: Military Occupation and the Culture of U.S. Imperialism*. Chapel Hill: University of North Carolina Press, 2001.

Rhodes, Benjamin D. *United States Foreign Policy during the Interwar Period, 1918–1941: The Golden Age of American Diplomatic and Military Complacency*. Westport, Conn.: Praeger, 2001.

Rice, Gerard T. *The Bold Experiment: JFK's Peace Corps*. South Bend, Ind.: Notre Dame University Press, 1985.

Rivas, Darlene. *Missionary Capitalist: Nelson Rockefeller in Venezuela*. Chapel Hill: University of North Carolina Press, 2001.

Roorda, Eric Paul. *The Dictator Next Door: The Good Neighbor Policy and the Trujillo Regime in the Dominican Republic, 1930–1945*. Durham, N.C.: Duke University Press, 1998.

Rosenberg, Emily S. *A Date Which Will Live: Pearl Harbor in American Memory*. Durham, N.C.: Duke University Press, 2005.

———. *Financial Missionaries to the World: The Politics and Culture of Dollar Diplomacy, 1900–1930*. Durham, N.C.: Duke University Press, 2003.

———. *Spreading the American Dream: American Economic and Cultural Expansion, 1890–1945*. New York: Hill and Wang, 1982.

Ross, Walter S. *The Last Hero: Charles A. Lindbergh*. New York: Harper and Row, 1964.

Rostow, W. W. *Eisenhower, Kennedy, and Foreign Aid*. Austin: University of Texas Press, 1985.

Rothman, Hal. *The Devil's Bargain: Tourism in the Twentieth Century American West*. Lawrence: University Press of Kansas, 1998.

Rotter, Andrew J. *Comrades at Odds: The United States and India, 1947–1964.* Ithaca: Cornell University Press, 2000.

Ruiz, Ramón Eduardo. *Cuba: The Making of a Revolution.* Amherst: University of Massachusetts Press, 1968.

———. *The Great Rebellion: Mexico, 1910–1924.* New York: Norton, 1980.

———. *On the Rim of Mexico: Encounters of the Rich and Poor.* Boulder, Colo.: Westview, 1998.

———. *The People of Sonora and the Yankee Capitalists.* Tucson: University of Arizona Press, 1988.

Rupp, Leila J. *Worlds of Women: The Making of an International Women's Movement.* Princeton: Princeton University Press, 1997.

Ryan, Alan, ed. *The Reader's Companion to Cuba.* New York: Harcourt Brace, 1997.

Rydell, Robert. *All the World's a Fair.* Chicago: University of Chicago Press, 1984.

———. *World of Fairs: A Century of Progress Expositions.* Chicago: University of Chicago Press, 1993.

Sáenz Rovner, Eduardo. *The Cuban Connection: Drug Trafficking, Smuggling, and Gambling in Cuba from the 1920s to the Revolution.* Translated by Russ Davidson. Chapel Hill: University of North Carolina Press, 2008.

Said, Edward. *Culture and Imperialism.* New York: Knopf, 1993.

———. *Orientalism.* New York: Vintage, 1979.

Sanchéz Korrol, Virginia E. *From Colonia to Community: The History of Puerto Ricans in New York City, 1917–1948.* Westport, Conn.: Greenwood, 1983.

Scarano, Francisco. *Puerto Rico: Cinco Siglos de Historia.* San Juan: McGraw-Hill, 1993.

———. *Sugar and Slavery in Puerto Rico, 1800–1850.* Madison: University of Wisconsin Press, 1984.

Scarpaci, Joseph, Roberto Segre, and Mario Coyula. *Havana: Two Faces of the Antillean Metropolis.* Chapel Hill: University of North Carolina Press, 2002.

Scheman, L. Ronald, ed. *The Alliance for Progress: A Retrospective.* Westport, Conn.: Praeger, 1988.

Schlesinger, Arthur M., Jr. *Robert Kennedy and His Times.* Boston: Houghton Mifflin, 1978.

———. *A Thousand Days: John F. Kennedy in the White House.* Boston: Houghton Mifflin, 1965.

Schlesinger, Stephen C., and Stephen Kinzer. *Bitter Fruit: The Untold Story of the American Coup in Guatemala.* Garden City, N.Y.: Doubleday, 1982.

Schuler, Friedrich E. *Mexico between Hitler and Roosevelt: Mexican Foreign Relations in the Age of Lázaro Cárdenas.* Albuquerque: University of New Mexico Press, 1999.

Schwartz, Rosalie. *Pleasure Island: Tourism and Temptation in Cuba.* Lincoln: University of Nebraska Press, 1997.

Schwartz, Thomas Alan. "Explaining the Cultural Turn—Or Detour?" *Diplomatic History* 31 (January 2007): 143–48.

Scott, James C. *Domination and the Arts of Resistance: Hidden Transcripts.* New Haven: Yale University Press, 1990.

——. *Weapons of the Weak: Everyday Forms of Peasant Resistance*. New Haven: Yale University Press, 1985.

Scranton, Philip, and Janet F. Davidson, eds. *The Business of Tourism: Place, Faith, and History*. Philadelphia: University of Pennsylvania Press, 2007.

Sears, John F. *Sacred Places: American Tourist Attractions in the Nineteenth Century*. New York: Oxford University Press, 1989.

Sellars, Richard West. *Preserving Nature in the National Parks: A History*. New Haven: Yale University Press, 1997.

Shaffer, Margarite S. *See America First: Tourism and National Identity, 1880–1940*. Washington D.C.: Smithsonian Institution Press, 2001.

Sheinin, David M. K. *Argentina and the United States: An Alliance Contained*. Athens: University of Georgia Press, 2006.

Sheller, Mimi. *Consuming the Caribbean: From Arawaks to Zombies*. London: Routledge, 2003.

Skwiot, Christine M. "Itineraries of Empire: The Uses of U.S. Tourism in Cuba and Hawai'i, 1898–1959." Ph.D. diss., Rutgers University, 2002.

Smith, Robert Freeman. *The United States and Revolutionary Mexico, 1916–1932*. Chicago: University of Chicago Press, 1972.

Smith, Valene L., ed. *Hosts and Guests: The Anthropology of Tourism*. Philadelphia: University of Pennsylvania Press, 1989.

Souther, J. Mark. *New Orleans on Parade: Tourism and the Transformation of the Crescent City*. Baton Rouge: Louisiana State University Press, 2006.

Spenser, Daniela. *The Impossible Triangle: Mexico, Soviet Russia, and the United States in the 1920s*. Durham, N.C.: Duke University Press, 1999.

Stanonis, Anthony J. *Creating the Big Easy: New Orleans and the Emergence of Modern Tourism, 1918–1945*. Athens: University of Georgia Press, 2006.

Staples, Amy L. S. *The Birth of Development: How the World Bank, Food and Agricultural Organization, and World Health Organization Have Changed the World, 1945–1965*. Kent, Ohio: Kent State University Press, 2006.

Stephanson, Anders. *Manifest Destiny: American Expansionism and the Empire of Right*. New York: Hill and Wang, 1995.

Stern, Steve. *Remembering Pinochet's Chile: On the Eve of London, 1998*. Durham, N.C.: Duke University Press, 2006.

Stiglitz, Joseph E. *Globalization and Its Discontents*. New York: Norton, 2003.

Stowe, William W. *Going Abroad: European Travel in Nineteenth-Century American Culture*. Princeton: Princeton University Press, 1994.

Streeter, Stephen M. *Managing the Counter-Revolution: The United States and Guatemala, 1954–1961*. Athens: Ohio University Press, 2001.

Suri, Jeremi. *Power and Protest: Global Revolution and the Rise of Détente*. Cambridge: Harvard University Press, 2005.

Sutton, Horace. *Travelers: The American Tourist from Stagecoach to Space Shuttle*. New York: Morrow, 1980.

Sweig, Julia E. *Inside the Cuban Revolution: Fidel Castro and the Urban Underground*. Cambridge: Harvard University Press, 2002.

Swinglehurst, Edmund. *Cook's Tours: The Story of Popular Travel*. Poole, Dorset: Blandford, 1982.

Szulc, Tad. *Fidel: A Critical Portrait*. New York: Morrow, 1986.

Tabb, Bruce. *Water, Leisure, and Culture: European Historical Perspectives*. Oxford: Berg, 2002.

Taffet, Jeffrey S. *Foreign Aid as Foreign Policy: The Alliance for Progress in Latin America*. New York: Routledge, 2007.

Takaki, Ronald. *A Different Mirror: A History of Multicultural America*. Boston: Backbay, 1994.

Taylor, Lawrence D. "The Wild Frontier Moves South: U.S. Entrepreneurs and the Growth of Tijuana's Vice Industry, 1908–1938" *Journal of San Diego History* 48 (Summer 2002), available online at <http://www.sandiegohistory.org/journal/2002-3/fron tier.htm>. Accessed 19 December 2008.

Thomas, Hugh. *Cuba: The Pursuit of Freedom*. New York: Harper and Row, 1971.

Thompson, Krista A. *An Eye for the Tropics: Tourism, Photography, and Framing the Caribbean Picturesque*. Durham, N.C.: Duke University Press, 2006.

Tomlinson, John. *Cultural Imperialism: A Critical Introduction*. Baltimore: Johns Hopkins University Press, 1991.

———. *Globalization and Culture*. Chicago: University of Chicago Press, 1999.

Tucker, Richard P. *Insatiable Appetite: The United States and the Ecological Degradation of the Tropical World*. Lanham, Md.: Rowman and Littlefield, 2007.

Tulchin, Joseph S. *Argentina and the United States: A Conflicted Relationship*. Boston: Twayne, 1990.

Turner, Katherine. *British Travel Writers in Europe, 1750–1800*. London: Ashgate, 2000.

Urry, John. *The Tourist Gaze: Leisure and Travel in the Contemporary World*. London: Sage, 1990.

Vaughn, Mary Kay, and Stephen E. Lewis, eds. *The Eagle and the Virgin: Nation and Cultural Revolution in Mexico, 1920–1940*. Durham, N.C.: Duke University Press, 2006.

Villalba, Angela. *Mexican Calendar Girls: Chicas de Calendarios Mexicanos*. San Francisco: Chronicle, 2006.

Virtue, John. *South of the Color Barrier: How Jorge Pasquel and the Mexican League Pushed Baseball toward Racial Integration*. Jefferson, N.C.: McFarland, 2008.

Von Eschen, Penny M. *Race against Empire: Black Americans and Anti-Colonialism, 1937–1953*. Ithaca: Cornell University Press, 1997.

Wagnleitner, Reinhold. *Coca-Colonization and the Cold War: The Cultural Mission of the United States in Austria after the Second World War*. Chapel Hill: University of North Carolina Press, 1994.

Wahab, Salah. *Tourism, Development, and Growth: The Challenge of Sustainability*. London: Routledge, 1997.

Ward, Evan R. *Packaged Vacations: Tourism Development in the Spanish Caribbean*. Gainesville: University Press of Florida, 2008.

Ward, Geoffrey C. *Unforgivable Blackness: The Rise and Fall of Jack Johnson*. New York: Knopf, 2004.

Weisskoff, Richard. *Factories and Food Stamps: The Puerto Rico Model of Development.* Baltimore: Johns Hopkins University Press, 1985.

Westad, Odd Arne. *The Global Cold War: Third World Interventions and the Making of Our Times.* Cambridge: Cambridge University Press, 2005.

Wharton, Annabel Jane. *Building the Cold War: Hilton International Hotels and Modern Architecture.* Chicago: University of Chicago Press, 2001.

Williams, Eric. *From Columbus to Castro: The History of the Caribbean, 1492–1969.* New York: Vintage, 1984.

Williams, William Appleman. *Empire as a Way of Life.* 1980; Brooklyn: IG, 2007.

———. *The Tragedy of American Diplomacy.* Cleveland: World, 1959.

Wilson, Joan Hoff. *American Business and Foreign Policy, 1920–1933.* Boston: Beacon, 1971.

Wiltse, Jeff. *Contested Waters: A Social History of Swimming Pools in America.* Chapel Hill: University of North Carolina Press, 2007.

Wolfe, Bertram D. *The Fabulous Life of Diego Rivera.* New York: Cooper Square, 2000.

Wood, Bryce. *The Making of the Good Neighbor Policy.* New York: Columbia University Press, 1961.

Woods, Randall H. *The Roosevelt Foreign Policy Establishment and the Good Neighbor: The United States and Argentina.* Lawrence: University Press of Kansas, 1979.

Wright, Thomas C. *State Terrorism in Latin America: Chile, Argentina, and International Human Rights.* Lanham, Md.: Rowman and Littlefield, 2007.

Zakaria, Fareed. *Wealth to Power: The Unusual Origins of America's World Role.* Princeton: Princeton University Press, 1998.

Zapata Alonzo, Gualberto. *An Overview of the Mayan World: With Synthesis of the Olmec, Totonac Zapotec, Mixtec, Teotihuacan, Toltec, and Aztec Civilizations.* 7th ed. Mérida, Mexico: Dante, 1988.

Zeiler, Thomas W. *Free Trade, Free World: The Advent of GATT.* Chapel Hill: University of North Carolina Press, 2002.

Zeiler, Thomas W., and Alfred Eckes. *Globalization and the American Century.* New York: Oxford University Press, 2005.

Index

Playa del Carmen, 247; Puerto Rico, 4, 14, 188, 201, 226–27; Varadero Beach (and Playa Azul), 109, 112, 126–27, 131, 188, 251; Waikiki Beach, 188. *See also* San Juan: Caribe Hilton

Bennett, Tony, 128

Berle, Adolph, 216, 221

Bermuda, 186

Betencourt, Romulo, 221

Bicardi Corporation, 134, 252

Black, Ruby, 183

Bonsal, Philip, 169, 170

Boorstin, Daniel, 13, 232

Bow, Clara, 38

Bowman, John McE., 107

Bowman, Wirt G., 37

Boyd, F. Morrison, 17, 53–54

Brando, Marlon, 132

Braniff Airlines, 117

Braudel, Fernand, 20

Brenner, Anita, 75–76

Bretton Woods system, 114–15, 208, 212, 236–37

British Guiana, 222

Bucareli Accords, 33, 59

Burton, Richard, 119

Bush, George H. W., 21

Bush, George W., 21, 206, 254

Byner, Wittner, 46

Calderón, Felipe, 249

California, 35, 41, 80; Los Angeles, 35, 47, 51, 249; San Diego, 37

Calles, Plutarco Elías, 29, 45, 46, 47, 54, 59–62, 68, 81, 90, 91, 175

Calloway, Cab, 128

Camacho, Manuel Ávila, 96; meeting with President Roosevelt, 99–100

Camargo Lleras, Alberto, 221

Canada, 69, 70, 95, 111, 246, 251

Cancún, 58, 101, 247–48, 251

Cárdenas, Lázaro, 67, 68, 81, 89–93, 95, 100, 165, 175

Carnegie Foundation, 31, 57, 98

Carnival cruise line, 247

Carol, Cindy, 119

Carr, Henry, 42–43

Carrillo, Julián, 48

Carter, Jimmy, 21, 174

Casals, Pablo, 204, 211–12, 216

Casparius, Rodolfo, 150, 151, 152

Castro, Fidel, 6, 23, 103, 119, 123, 124, 138, 177, 215, 217, 218, 233, 242, 245; and agrarian reform, 165, 166, 167, 168, 175; compared to Luis Muñoz Marín, 217; daily habits of, 153, 158, 166; early image of in U.S., 148, 166–70; arrival in Havana, 150, 153; illness and future of regime, 251; interview with Herbert Matthews, 134, 136; and mobsters, 149, 157–58; nationalization policies, 161, 170, 171; revitalization of tourism (1990s), 250–51; and social reform, 161, 171; trip to U.S. (1959), 164, 167; views on gambling, 23, 142, 154, 155, 156–57; views on tourism, 23, 142, 144, 153–61, 168, 171; views on U.S. government, 144, 162, 169. *See also* Cold War: and Cuba; Cuba; Revolution

Castro, Raúl, 155, 165, 251

Catherwood, Frederick, 57

Caverly, Robert J., 155, 159, 164. *See also* Hilton Hotel Corporation

Cedillo, General Saturno, 91

Céspedes, Carlos Manuel de, 107, 108

Chapultepec, 65, 77

Chapultepec Conference (1945), 115

Chardón, Carlos, 183

Chase, Stuart, 46, 63–64

Chichén Itzá, 41, 53, 55, 57–58, 81, 90, 98–99, 248

Chile, 235–36

Choley, Kenneth, 202

Cinema, 38, 61, 72, 119, 131–32, 139, 191

Ciudad Juárez, 36, 37–38

Clark, Sydney A., 137

Clinton, Bill, 12, 21

107, 132–33, 135–36, 139; female tourists in, 131; Gran Casino Nacional, 107, 108, 109, 132; housing stock in, 136; illegal narcotics in, 4, 130, 132, 157; Jockey Club, 103; José Martí International Airport, 122, 160, 163; Malecón, 106, 109; Marianao, 107, 108, 111, 122, 136; Miramar, 122; Montmartre, 129, 132; Old Havana, 14, 108, 109, 110, 128, 136; San Souci, 103, 129, 132; Shanghai Theater, 130; Tropicana nightclub, 103, 128, 129, 141, 171; Vedado, 109, 122, 124, 136

—Hotels: Capri, 124, 132, 149, 152; Colina, 124; Commodore, 132, 138; Deauville, 132; El Presidente, 109; Flamingo, 124; Habana Libre, 171, 251; Hilton, 118, 124, 125–26, 141–42, 145, 146, 148, 150–53, 155, 157, 158, 159, 163, 165, 172; Melía Cohiba, 251; Nacional, 103, 109, 132, 152, 171, 251; Palace, 109; Plaza, 151; Riviera, 124–25, 132, 150, 152, 170, 251; Rosita de Hornedo, 171; Sevilla-Biltmore, 108, 109, 132, 151; St. Johns, 124, 171

Havemeyer, Horace, 108
Hawaii, 126, 186
Hemingway, Ernest, 106
Herman, Woody, 128
Herring, Hubert C., 47–48, 95
Hershey, Milton, 109
Herter, Christian, 167, 169
Hilton, Conrad N., 117–18, 125–26, 141–42, 163–64, 170, 187, 189, 191, 200, 208
Hilton Hotel Corporation, 117–18, 144, 163–66, 170, 171. *See also* Caverly, Robert J.; Havana: Hilton Hotel; San Juan: Caribe Hilton; Wangeman, Frank; Willner, Sydney
Hispanidad, 182, 203
Hoover, Herbert, 21
Hope, Bob, 72
Hopper, Hedda, 141
Hotel Greeters of Mexico, 92
Houston, John, 119

Huerta, Victoriano, 33
Hughes, Langston, 124
Hull, Cordell, 47
Humphrey, Hubert, 217

Immigration to U.S.: Mexican, 18, 35, 63, 249–50; Puerto Rican, 194, 204
Independentistas. See Puerto Rico: independentistas
Inman, Samuel Guy, 47
International Commission of Bankers on Mexico, 60
International Monetary Fund, 6, 24, 26, 114, 237
Isle of Pines, 126
Isolationism, 22, 23, 31, 206

Jalpa, 249–50
Jamaica, 111, 180, 235, 246, 251
Jennings, John, 10, 182
Johnson, Jack, 39, 83
Johnson, Lyndon, 21, 47, 236
Jolson, Al, 38
Jones Act, 178
July 26th Movement. *See* Revolution: Cuban (1959)

Keaton, Buster, 38
Kefauver, Estes, 104, 132, 147
Kennan, George F., 7, 22
Kennedy, Jaqueline Bouvier, 211–12
Kennedy, John F., 21, 24, 211–12, 217, 219, 221, 222, 233–34, 236, 245; vacation in Havana (1957), 138

La bomba, 16, 231
Labor, 5; AFL-CIO, 200; in Cancún, 248; Confederación General de Trabajadores de Mexico, 81; Confederación General del Trabajo de Puerto Rico, 200; Confederación Regional de Obreros Mexicanos, 81; Confederation of Cuban Workers, 113; Confederation of Railway

93, 94; Ministry of Foreign Affairs, 70; Mixed Pro-Tourism Commission, 58, 68; National Commission on Tourism, 68; National Department of Colonial Buildings, 72; National Railway of Mexico, 51, 68, 90; National Tourism Committee (Comité Nacional de Turismo, CTNT), 90; National Revolutionary Party (Partido Nacional Revolucionario, PNR), 68, 90; oil industry in, 67, 91–92; Pemex, 92; political party system in, 68; prostitution in, 30, 38–39, 42, 85; rail travel to, 35, 51–53; religion in, 33, 42, 54, 59, 77, 82; road system in, 53, 54, 70; subsidies for travel industry in, 67, 90–91; telephone system in, 59–60; tourism revenue in, 66, 95; tourism subsidies in, 3, 90–91; tourist tally in, 30, 38, 66; and U.S. border, 37, 88, 100–101, 105; U.S. private investment in, 32, 34. *See also* Cárdenas, Lázaro; Mexico City

Mexico City, 17, 44, 52, 53, 54, 65, 66, 71, 76–79, 98, 100–101; Balbuena airfield, 29; Bottoms Up restaurant, 101; Chapultepec, 65, 77; Club Venus, 100; Cocoanut Grove restaurant, 100; Guadelupe Hidalgo, 54; Lady Baltimore restaurant, 78; National Congress on Tourism (1930), 69; nightlife in, 85; petty crime in, 80; Raffles nightclub, 101; San Angel Inn, 78; Sanborn's restaurant, 78–79; taxis in, 81, 86–87; Xochimilco, 54; Zahler's restaurant, 78; *zócalo*, 78, 101
—Hotels: Geneve, 77, 79; Iturbide, 44; Mancera, 77; Reforma, 77–78, 79, 88, 92; Regis, 65, 77; Ritz, 77; Waldorf, 100

Miami, 121, 164, 201
Michoacán, 31, 67; Lake Pátzcuaro, 49; Morelia (capital city), 49
Miller, Max, 81
Miranda, Carmen, 97
Missouri Pacific Railroad, 51, 52, 90
Mixed Pro-Tourism Commission, 58, 68

Modernization theory, 4, 6, 19, 211, 212, 219–23. *See also* Alliance for Progress; Puerto Rico; Rostow, W. W.
Montmartre, 129, 132
Monte Albán, 55
Monterrey, 51, 52, 70; Camacho-Roosevelt meeting (1943), 99–100; Gran Hotel Ancira, 70
Morales Carrión, Arturo, 212, 222
Morelia, 49
Morley, Sylvanus G., 57, 99, 248
Morones, Luis, 81
Morrow, Dwight W., 29, 32, 59–62, 67, 71, 72
Morrow, Elizabeth Cutler, 29, 61
Moscoso, Teodoro, 184, 185, 189, 190, 212, 222, 231
Moynihan, Daniel Patrick, 194
Muñoz Marín, Luis, 177, 178, 182–83, 184, 191, 196, 199, 200, 201–2, 207, 209, 215–16, 231, 232, 233, 239; compared to Fidel Castro, 217
Muñoz Rivera, Luis, 182

Nassau, 111
National Railway of Mexico, 51, 68, 90
National University Summer Seminar (Mexico City), 47–48, 95
Neibuhr, Reinhold, 114
New Mexico, 41, 55
New York and Cuba Mail Steamship Company (Ward Line), 53, 107
Niven, David, 119
Nixon, Richard M., 120, 164, 167, 217, 236; trip to Caracas, Venezuela (1958), 115, 177; trip to San Juan, Puerto Rico (1958), 177, 217
North American Free Trade Agreement (1994), 101
Nuevo Loredo, 51, 88

Oaxaca, 90, 101; Monte Albán, 54, 90
Obama, Barack, 249, 251

Obregón, Alvaro, 33, 45, 47, 68, 175

O'Brien, Howard Vincent, 66, 80, 86–87

O'Dwyer, Paul, 195

Ogilvy, David, 203–4

Operation Bootstrap, 183–85, 204, 215. *See also* Moscoso, Teodoro; Puerto Rico

Organization of American States, 161

Orientalism, 10–11, 36, 55

Oriente Province (Cuba), 134, 140, 142, 146

Orizaba Peak, 49–50

Orozco, José, 34

Osuna, Carlos F., 91

Paige, Satchel, 83–84

Pais, Frank, 134

Panama, 5, 6, 41, 83, 178

Pan American Airlines, 17, 90, 117, 122, 138, 154, 186; Intercontinental Hotel Corporation, 117, 148. *See also* Trippe, Juan T.

Pan-American Highway, 17, 54, 64, 69–70, 72, 74, 90

Pani, Alberto J., 45, 77, 88

Parr, Jack, 160, 166

Pazos, Felipe, 155

Peace Corps, 219

Pedreira, Antonio S., 182

Peninsular and Occidental Steamship, 107

Pershing Expedition, 33

Peru, 222

Phillips, Henry Albert, 85

Pico, Rafael, 197, 201

Pinochet, Augusto, 9, 236, 237

Platt Amendment, 105, 110, 242

Playa del Carmen, 247

Porfiriato. *See* Diaz, Porfirio

Porter, Katherine Anne, 46–47, 48, 72

Portes Gil, Emilio, 58, 68

Postcards, 48–50

Power, Tyrone, 72

Prebisch, Raul, 184

Prió Socarrás, Carlos, 110–11

Progreso, 41, 53, 81

Prohibition, 3, 4, 30, 37, 107

Public Law 600, 178

Puerta Vallarta, 119

Puerto Rico, 4–5, 14, 24, 112, 176, 243; African Puerto Ricans, 5, 178, 203, 232, 238; air travel to, 186–87, 216; anti-subversion laws in, 185; birth control trials in, 228; cap on tourism as percentage of GDP in, 178, 185, 252; coffee industry in, 180; commonwealth status of, 4, 178, 209, 243; crime in, 224–25; cruise ships to, 234–35, 237, 246–47; domestic tourism in, 204–5; economic planning in, 4, 178, 184; gambling in, 4, 178, 183, 187, 229; *independentistas* in, 178, 179, 182, 185, 203, 214, 215, 229–30, 232–33; Institute of Puerto Rican Culture, 202–3, 231–32, 234; National Indigenous Festival, 234; needlework industry in, 180, 200; New Progressive Party (Partido Progresista Nuevo, PNP), 230, 231, 232–33, 234–35, 237; per capita income in, 196, 215; Popular Democratic Party (Partido Populare Democratica, PPD), 179, 183, 184, 230, 231, 235, 237; Public Law 600, 178; Puerto Rican Economic Development Administration (Fomento), 184, 186, 187, 189, 198, 201, 231; Puerto Rican Independence Party (Partido Independentista Puertorriqueño), 179; Puerto Rican Industrial Development Corporation, 216; Puerto Rican Tourist Bureau, 187; Socialist Party (Partido Socialista), 200; statehood movement in, 179; Taínos in, 5, 178, 203, 232, 234, 238; tax incentives for investment in, 4, 178, 185; tourism advertising campaigns in, 181, 193–97, 203–5; tourism and economic planning in, 4, 178, 183, 185–93, 201, 204–6, 230–31, 237; tourism and energy conservation in, 237; tourism and jobs in, 234; tourism in compared to Cuba and Mexico, 4, 178, 191, 193–94, 203, 207, 208, 222,

238, 243; tourism revenue in, 197, 230; tourist tally in, 4, 197, 213, 230, 234–35; unemployment in, 181, 204; U.S. colonial rule in, 5, 177–78, 180–83, 225; U.S. military bases in, 178; U.S. private investment in, 4, 185, 204, 215. *See also* Beaches: Puerto Rico; Hilton, Conrad N.; Hilton Hotel Corporation; Muñoz Marín, Luis; Operation Bootstrap; San Juan; Vieques Island

Puig, José Manuel, 57

Quevado, José, 90

Reagan, Ronald, 237

Revolution, 8, 115, 209, 244; Cuban (1933); 110; Cuban (1959), 6, 19, 20, 23, 24, 133–39, 142–47, 150–53, 209, 210, 214, 217, 218, 220; Cuban revolution compared to Mexican revolution, 19, 102, 121, 175–76; Mexican, 3, 19, 20, 33–35, 36, 39, 43, 62, 209; and Puerto Rico, 209, 215, 216, 217; Student Revolutionary Directorate (Cuba), 134, 137. *See also* Castro, Fidel; Cuba; Mexico

Ricardo, Ricky. *See* Arnez, Desi

Rickenbacker, Eddie, 187, 191

Rickey, Branch, 123

Riley, Marcene, 85

Rio de Janeiro, 97

Rio Pact, 115

Rivera, Diego, 34, 47, 48, 61–62, 67, 71, 72, 88

Robbins, J. Stanley, 186, 188, 196, 202

Roberts, W. Adolphe, 133

Robinson, Jackie, 123

Rockefeller, David, 191

Rockefeller, Laurence S., 116, 191–92

Rockefeller, Nelson, 97, 116, 195

Rodríguez, Abelardo L., 37, 40, 68, 89

Rogers, Ginger, 125

Rogers, Will, 61

Roosevelt, Eleanor, 99, 191

Roosevelt, Franklin, 20–21, 22, 66, 72, 73; and Cuba, 106; fishing at Magdalena Bay, 72–74, 98; global settlement with Mexico, 96–97; Good Neighbor Policy, 23, 63, 95–98, 110, 171, 245; interest in leisure travel in Mexico, 98; state visit to Mexico (1943), 99–100

Roosevelt, Theodore, 5–6, 20, 26

Roosevelt, Theodore, Jr., 181

Rostow, W. W., 219–21. *See also* Alliance for Progress; Modernization theory; Puerto Rico

Rubio, Ortiz Pascual, 68, 69, 91

Rubottom, R. Roy, 138

Rumba, 15, 109, 129

Sandino, Augusto, 34, 116

San Juan, 126; Ashford Avenue, 193, 216, 224; assassination of mayor (1950), 185; Condado, 189, 191, 193, 201, 216, 224, 227, 229, 239, 252; hotel construction in, 189–91, 216; Hotel Corporation of America, 216; Isla Verde airport, 186, 234, 252; La Perla, 198, 199; Old San Juan, 176, 178, 189, 193, 229, 233, 234, 252; Old San Juan restoration, 202–3, 231; prostitution in, 198, 228–29; traffic congestion in, 224; water pollution in, 224

—Hotels: Caribe Hilton, 118, 125, 189–91, 198–200, 201, 208, 226–27; Condado Beach, 189, 201, 216; El Convento, 231; El San Juan, 216; El Imperial, 216; Holiday Inn, 230; La Concha, 216; Miramar House, 230; Sheraton, 216, 230

San Luis Potosí, 91

San Miguel de Allende, 53, 85, 90, 101

Schlesinger, Arthur M., Jr., 221

Scully, Michael and Virginia, 70, 95

September 11, 2001, 245, 253–54

Sert, José Luis, 123

Seymour, Ralph Fletcher, 42

Sheffield, James R., 34, 46, 50, 51, 59, 78

Sheridan, Clare, 44–45

United Nations, 114, 161; World Tourism Organization, 2

United States: and border with Mexico, 37, 88, 100–101; Central Intelligence Agency, 116, 124, 167, 170, 218; Department of Commerce, 69; Department of the Interior, 190; Department of State, 22, 120, 140, 142, 144, 146, 163, 169, 173; Department of Treasury, 97, 174; Federal Bureau of Investigation, 147, 185; and foreign aid, 115, 218; gender arrangements in, 3, 4, 8, 37, 106, 127–28, 131–32; Helms-Burton Act (1996), 250; House of Representatives and Puerto Rican nationalists shooting incident (1954), 185; incomes in (1950s), 106, 188–89; industrial revolution in, 36–37; Marshall Plan, 60, 115, 116, 117, 218; Mexican immigration to, 18, 35, 63, 249–50; military intervention in Mexico, 62; National Security Council, 115, 162, 167; Peace Corps, 219; Puerto Rican immigration to, 194, 204; racism and race relations in, 3–5, 8, 35–36, 123–24, 127–28, 220; Social Progress Trust Fund, 218; and tourist expenditures abroad, 2, 69; and tourists abroad, 2, 66; trade embargo on Cuba, 173, 218; travel restrictions to Cuba, 173–74, 251

Urrutia, Manuel, 153, 154

Uxmal, 53

Valles, Manuel del, 90

Vasconcelos, José, 34–35, 47, 58, 68

Vaughn, Sarah, 128

Venezuela, 115, 116, 177, 215, 221–22

Veracruz, 53, 54, 74

Vieques Island, 233–34, 252

Villa, Francisco (Pancho), 33, 250

Volstead Act (1919). *See* Prohibition

Wangeman, Frank, 200. *See also* Hilton Hotel Corporation

Ward Line. *See* New York and Cuba Mail Steamship Company

Wells, Carveth, 80

Wells Fargo, 76, 90

West Side Story, 194

Williams, Tennessee, 119

Williams, William Appleman, 7, 19

Williamsburg, Virginia, 186, 202

Willner, Sydney, 157, 163. *See also* Hilton Hotel Corporation

Wilson, Henry Lane, 33

Wilson, Woodrow, 31, 33, 41, 62

Winship, Blanton, 181, 182

World War I, 19, 23, 31, 33, 41, 46, 62, 100

World War II, 19, 21, 22, 23, 66, 96, 99–100, 105, 114, 206, 248, 253

Wright, Hamilton, 93, 203

Yucatán, 30, 101; Cancún, 58, 101, 247–48, 250, 251; Chichén Itzá, 41, 53, 55, 57–58, 81, 90, 98–99, 248; Mayaland Tours, 81; Mayan Riviera (Riviera Maya), 101, 247; Mérida, 53, 247; Playa del Carmen, 247; Progreso, 41, 53, 81; Tulum, 247; Uxmal, 53

Zapata, Emilio, 35, 61–62, 82